INDIANA

WILDLIFE ENCYCLOPEDIA

— AN ILLUSTRATED GUIDE TO —

BIRDS, FISH, MAMMALS, REPTILES, AND AMPHIBIANS

SCOTT SHUPE

Skyhorse Publishing

Skyhorse Publishing books may be purchased in bulk at special discounts for sales promotion, corporate gifts, fund-raising, or educational purposes. Special editions can also be created to specifications. For details, contact the Special Sales Department, Skyhorse Publishing, 307 West 36th Street, 11th Floor, New York, NY 10018 or info@skyhorsepublishing.com.

Skyhorse® and Skyhorse Publishing® are registered trademarks of Skyhorse Publishing, Inc.®, a Delaware corporation.

Visit our website at www.skyhorsepublishing.com.

10 9 8 7 6 5 4 3 2 1

Library of Congress Cataloging-in-Publication Data is available on file.

Cover design by David Ter-Avanesyan
Cover photos by Scott Shupe

Print ISBN: 978-1-5107-7721-7
Ebook ISBN: 978-1-5107-7722-4

Printed in China

ACKNOWLEDGMENTS

The author gratefully acknowledges the following individuals who contributed to the completion of this book. In no particular order those individuals are:

Rob Mottice, Senior Aquarist at the Tennessee Aquarium in Chattanooga, for help in identifying fresh water fish species photographed at that facility.

David Wilkins, Curator at the South Carolina Aquarium in Charleston, for his help in identifying fresh water fish species photographed at his facility.

Larry Warner, North Carolina Aquarium on Roanoke Island, for his help in identifying fresh water fish species photographed at his facility.

The staff of the North Carolina Aquarium at Pine Knoll Shores, for help in identifying fresh water fish species photographed at that facility.

John R. MacGregor for providing a number of amphibian and mammal photographs used in this book and for providing technical information and scientific advice regarding reptiles and amphibians.

Matthew R. Thomas for help in identifying several species of darters and minnows photographed by the author for this book as well as for his technical advice and icthyological expertise; and for providing a large number of fish photographs used in the book.

Amy Berry, Clay Hill Memorial Forest and Nature Center, for providing fish & amphibian specimens for photography.

Dr. Gordon Weddle, Campbellsville University, for providing fish & amphibian specimens for photography.

Dr. Richard Kessler, Campbellsville University, for help collecting fish specimens for photography.

Jim Harrison and Kristin Wiley of the Kentucky Reptile Zoo for allowing the author to trap on their property mammal and fish specimens for photography and for allowing me to photograph snakes at their facility.

Clinton Cunningham for assistance in acquiring and photographing herpetology specimens.

Kathleen Mount for assistance in acquiring and photographing herpetology specimens.

Judy Tipton for alerting me to the presence of and allowing me to photograph nesting birds in her yard.

Tim Johnson for helping secure lizard specimens for photography.

Matt Wagner and John Hardy from the Mississippi Museum of Natural History for helping to ID fishes photographed in aquariums at that facility.

Brainard Palmer-Ball of the Kentucky Ornithological Society for help identifying fall warblers photographed by the author for this book.

Barbara Graham for taking the author spelunking in the sandstone caves of eastern Kentucky searching for bats to photograph.

Candy McNamee for guiding the author on a search for migratory birds along the Texas coast.

Karen Finch for guiding the author in a search for migratory birds.

Dr. Tim Spier, Murray State University, for his help in collecting fish specimens for photography.

Jennifer Rader of the Kansas Department of Wildlife, Parks and Tourism for allowing me to photograph fresh water stream fishes at the Southeast Kansas Nature Center.

John Hewlett who accompanied the author in the field and helped locate and collect fish & reptile specimens for photography.

James Kiser for providing several photographs.

Matthew Broadway of the Indiana Department of Natural Resources for providing information on the Red Squirrel in Indiana.

Don Martin of Don Martin Bird Photography for contributing several of the more excellent bird photos in the book.

T. Travis Brown for several photo contributions.

David Speiser, www.lilibirds.com, for several professional quality bird photo contributions.

Phil Myers, University of Michigan for contribution of small mammal photos.

Konrad Schmidt of North America Native Fish Association for contributions of several excellent fish photos.

Dave Neely for photo contributions.

Sterling Daniels, TWRA Wildlife Biologist for his photo contribution.

Michael Jeffords of the Illinois Natural History Survey for his photo contribution.

Tom Murray for his photo contribution.

Roger Tabor USFWS for his photo contribution.

Wayne T. Helfrich for his photo contribution.

Margaret Novak for her photo contribution.

Brant Fisher, Indiana Department of Natural Resources. for providing a photo of the rare Hoosier Cavefish.

Brian Zimmerman for providing several excellent fish photos.

The North American Native Fish Association whose website featuring member photo galleries was a valuable resource in providing hard-to-find fish photos.

Last but certainly not least I would like to thank my editor, Jason Katzman of Skyhorse Publishing.

In our negotiations Jason has not only shown patience and a willingness to compromise, but also great faith in this author. He has also exhibited extraordinary entrepreneurial courage in taking on a huge project of which this book is but a single step.

Finally, this book is dedicated to the author's three sons. Haydn, Ken, and Kyle Shupe. Though now adults, as youngsters their keen eyes, youthful enthusiasm and unflinching companionship were responsible for the author getting many of the photographs in this book. More importantly, their presence in this world has consistently provided this author with the motivation to repeatedly bite off more than I can chew.

PHOTOGRAPHERS

Most of the over 600 plus wildlife photographs that appear in this book were taken by the author. However, many of the really good photographs were contributed by several other wildlife photographers from across the USA. Those individuals were critical to the completion of this book and their remarkable photographs add much to its content. The names of those additional photographers and the number of photos each contributed appear below.

Konrad Schmidt—21
Matthew R. Thomas—20
John R. MacGregor—14
David Speiser, www.lilibirds.com—7
Don Martin Bird Photography—4
Brian Zimmerman—4
James Kiser—3
T. Travis Brown—3
Phil Myers—2
Dave Neely—2
Tom Murray—1
Michael Jeffords—1
Margaret Novak—1
Wayne T. Helfrich—1
Nathan Peterson—1
Brant Fisher, Indiana Department of Natural Resources—1

Thanks also to many other photographers who offered their help but whose photographs I was not able to use due to redundancy or timing constraints. A complete list of photo credits appears in the back of this book.

Figure 1.
Counties of Indiana

TABLE OF CONTENTS

viii INDIANA WILDLIFE ENCYCLOPEDIA

INDIANA

WILDLIFE ENCYCLOPEDIA

INTRODUCTION

From the earliest European exploration and settlement of Indiana, the state's wildlife has played an important role. Native Americans living in the region sustained themselves largely by harvesting mammals, birds, and fish for sustenance, as well as fashioning clothing from fur and hides. Bone and antler were fashioned into tools, and sinew provided string and bindings. The first Europeans in the state were mostly hunters, trappers and traders who came in search of Beaver fur and buckskins.

Beginning almost with the first European Settlement of Indiana and continuing well into the early 1900s, untold millions of birds and mammals were hunted, killed and shipped to large cities like Chicago, Detroit, or New York to provide inexpensive table fare for their burgeoning human populations. The period throughout the 1800s is often referred to by todays conservationists as the days of "Market Hunting." During this time period Indiana's large herbivores such as the Bison and the Eastern Elk were hunted to extinction and the White-tailed Deer and Wild Turkey were also all but extirpated. Accounts exist of shipments of waterfowl and shorebird carcasses numbering in the thousands being shipped by rail to large cities.

While the state's wildlife is still an important resource for trappers, hunters, and fishermen, wildlife is also increasingly important for its capacity to enhance the lives of those who value nature. Though the age-old practice of hunting and fishing is the most obvious example of how wildlife can enrich our lives, for many the opportunity to simply observe wildlife and experience nature also serves to enhance our existence.

In more recent history the pursuit of wildlife has evolved to encompass more benign activities such as bird watching, wildlife photography, etc. In fact, the numbers of Americans who enjoy these non-consumptive forms of wildlife-related recreation today exceed the numbers of those who hunt and fish. These interests and activities have broadened so considerably that the US Fish & Wildlife Service, in its most recent assessment of the economic impact of wildlife in America, lists a broad category labeled "Wildlife Watching." The economic impact of wildlife watching in America today far exceeds the impact that hunters and fishermen have on the economy.

With interest in wildlife and nature continuing to grow throughout Indiana, the need for a single, simple reference to the state's wildlife has become evident. There are available a number of excellent books that deal specifically with the state's birds, reptiles, mammals, fishes, etc. But there are none that combine all the state's wildlife into a comprehensive, encyclopedic reference. This volume is intended to fill that niche. It is hoped that this book will find favor with school librarians, life science teachers, students of field biology classes, and professional naturalists as well as with the general populace.

As might be expected with such a broad-spectrum publication, intimate details about the natural history of individual species is omitted in favor of a format that provides more basic information.

In this sense this volume is not intended for use as a professional reference, but instead as a usable layman's guide to the state's wildlife. For those who wish to explore the information regarding the state's wildlife more deeply, a list of references for each chapter appears in the back of the book and includes both printed and reliable Internet references.

Embracing the old adage that a picture is worth a thousand words, color photographs are used to depict and identify each species. Below each photograph is a table that provides basic information about the biology of each animal. This table includes a state map with shaded area showing the species' presumed range in the state, as well as general information such as size, habitat, abundance, etc. The taxonomic classification of each species is also provided, with the animal's Class, Order, and Family appearing as a heading at the top of the page.

The range maps shown in this book are not intended to be regarded as a strictly accurate representation of the range of any given species. Indeed, the phrase "Presumed range in Indiana," which accompanies each species range map, should be literally interpreted as a presumption only. The ranges of many species in the state are often not well documented. The range maps for some species in this book may be regarded at best as an "educated guess."

Furthermore, many wide-ranging species are restricted to regions of suitable habitat. Thus an aquatic species like the Beaver, while found statewide, would not be expected to occur in the middle of an upland field. In rare instances some species may have recently expanded their historical range into the state. The Nine-banded Armadillo, for instance, is an example of an animal that has only recently begun to appear in Indiana. Due to the fact that it is presently continuing to expand its range, available data regarding its distribution may lag behind its actual area of occurrence. Conversely, other species that may have once been found throughout a large geographic area may now have disappeared from much of their former range. A number of fish species, for example, are rare or extirpated in the state due to water quality degradation of many of Indiana's rivers and streams.

Further complicating the issue of species distribution is the fact that animals like birds and bats, possessed with the ability of flight, are capable of traveling great distances. Many species of both birds and bats are migratory and regularly travel hundreds or even thousands of miles annually. It is not uncommon for these migratory species to sometimes appear in areas where they are not typically found. The mechanisms of migration and dispersal of many animals is still a bit of a mystery and the exact reason why a bird from another portion of the country (or even from another continent) should suddenly

appear where it doesn't belong is often speculation. Sometimes these appearances may represent individuals that are simply wandering. Other times it can be a single bird or an entire flock that has been blown off course by a powerful storm or become otherwise lost and disoriented. Whatever the cause, there are many bird species that have been recorded in the state that are not really a part of Indiana's regularly occurring native fauna, and their occasional sightings are regarded as "accidental." On the other hand, some bird species may appear somewhere in the state once every few years dependent upon weather conditions or availability of prey in their normal habitat. Although these types of "casual species" could be regarded as belonging among Indiana's native bird fauna, their occurrence in the state is so sporadic and unpredictable that deciding which species should be included becomes very subjective. The point is that the reader should be advised that while all the bird species depicted in this volume can be considered to be members of the state's indigenous fauna, not every bird species that has ever been seen or recorded in the state is depicted in this book.

For readers who wish to delve into more professional and detailed information about the vertebrate zoology of Indiana, the list of references shown for each chapter should adequately provide that opportunity.

The pages that follow are intended to introduce Indianans to the remarkable diversity, wondrous beauty and miraculous lives of the state's wildlife species. It is hoped that this introduction will lead to a greater awareness, concern and appreciation for Indiana's natural heritage. It is further hoped that acquiring that awareness and appreciation will lead to a better stewardship of the living things with which we share this planet. And more importantly, the natural ecosystems upon which both they and we ultimately depend.

CHAPTER 1

THE FACE OF THE LAND

— NATURAL REGIONS OF INDIANA —

Defining and understanding the natural regions of Indiana is the first step in understanding the natural history of the state. Man-made political boundaries such as county lines and state borders are meaningless to wildlife, whereas natural features like rivers, uplands, or plains can be important elements in influencing the distribution of the state's wildlife.

The major considerations used in determining and delineating natural regions are factors such as elevation, relief (topography), drainages (rivers & streams), geology, and climate. All these are important elements that can determine the limits of distribution for living organisms. It follows then that some knowledge of these factors is essential when involved in the study of the state's natural history. The study of natural regions is known as Physiography, which means "physical geography" or literally "the face of the land." While the terms geography and physiography are closely related and sometimes used interchangeably, geography is a broader term which includes such things as human culture, resource use, and humanity's impact on the land, while physiography deals only with elements of geography created by nature.

The term most often used to define a major natural region is "Physiographic Division." There are ten of these physiographic divisions across the United States and Canada. Each of these 10 major divisions can be subdivided into smaller units called "Physiographic Provinces," and each province can be further divided into even smaller units known as "Physiographic Sections." Among the ten Physiographic Divisions of the US and Canada, there is only one that impacts the state of Indiana. The entire state of Indiana is contained within the *Interior Plains Division* (see Figure 2 on page 4).

Shown in purple on the map in Figure 2, the Interior Plains Division includes not only all of the state of Indiana but also most of the great plains states and the American Midwest. This large division extends from the Appalachian Highlands in the east all the way to the Rocky Mountains in the west.

This huge region is characterized mainly by gently rolling plains and an absence of the significant uplifts that form mountain ranges. Historically the dominant plant communities in this division were grasslands and deciduous forests.

Each Physiographic Division of North America can be subdivided into smaller units known as Physiographic Provinces. The map on page 9 (Figure 7) shows how the major divisions of the eastern US are divided into provinces. The provinces of the Interior Plains Division are the Great Plains Province, the Interior Low Plateau Province, and the Interior Lowland Province. Two of these, the Interior Low Plateau Province and the Interior Lowland Province, occur in Indiana.

The largest of these two provinces is the *Interior Lowland Province*. In Indiana this province encompasses approximately the northern three-fourths of the state. For the most part, this province is a relatively flat plain. The generally flat topography in this province is the result of several periods of glacial invasion extending from north to south. In popular terms these glacial episodes are known as "Ice Ages," and the last of these ended only quite recently in geological terms (approximately 15,000 years ago).

The vast sheets of ice that covered most of Indiana during these ice ages bulldozed and flattened much of the landscape to create the flat to gently rolling plains that are common in the area today. During periods of warmer climates, these glaciers receded and left behind masses of rocks and sediment known as Moraine. Melting ice from retreating glaciers formed new waterways which

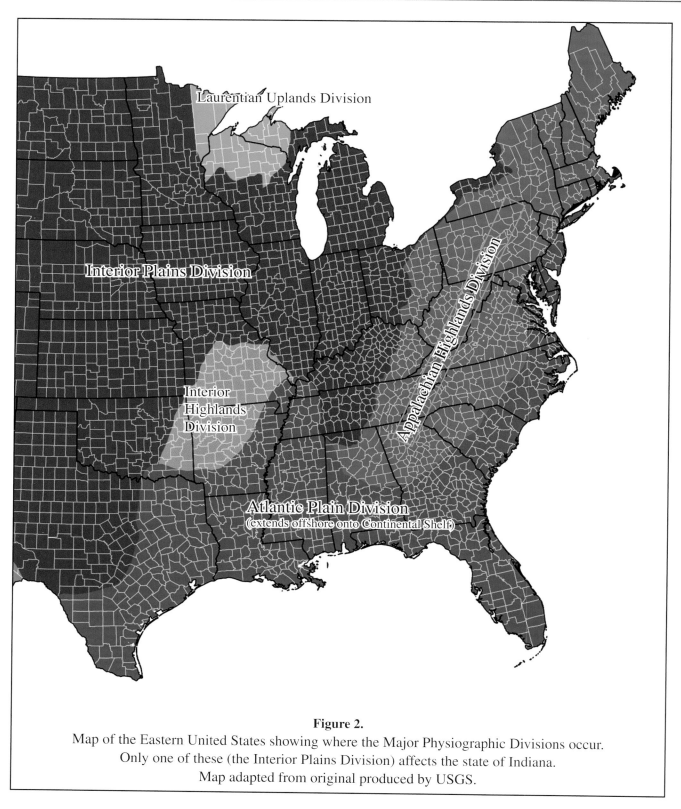

Figure 2.
Map of the Eastern United States showing where the Major Physiographic Divisions occur.
Only one of these (the Interior Plains Division) affects the state of Indiana.
Map adapted from original produced by USGS.

eroded these moraine deposits. Many of the topographical features seen in the Interior Lowland Province today were created by both the movement of glaciers and the erosional impact of the state's waterways. Among the other significant topographical features in this province are the low hills and valleys in the east-central portion of the state. This is where the highest elevation in Indiana occurs, at 1,257 feet (Hoosier Hill in Wayne County).

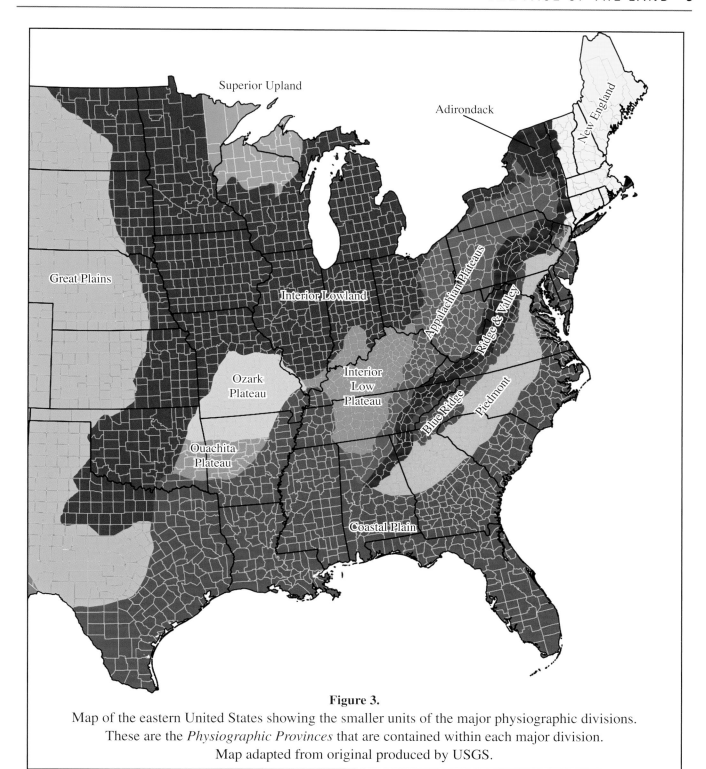

Figure 3.
Map of the eastern United States showing the smaller units of the major physiographic divisions.
These are the *Physiographic Provinces* that are contained within each major division.
Map adapted from original produced by USGS.

In the southern tip of Indiana more irregular landscapes of rolling hills, valleys and uplands make up the state's other province, the *Interior Low Plateau Province.* This province escaped the impact of glaciation and in fact the boundary between the two provinces marks the southernmost extension of the state's glacial events. Despite the fact that much of this region is lower in elevation than the Interior Lowland Province, the landscape here can be fairly rugged in places, having ridges and hills interlaced with stream bottomlands and valleys.

Figure 4.
The Natural Regions of Indiana.
Map adapted from original produced by Indiana Geological Survey.

Wide, flat valleys occur along the Ohio and Wabash River floodplains and the lowest elevation in the state (320 feet) can be found at the confluence of the state's two largest rivers (the Ohio and the Wabash).

The map of Indiana shown above (Figure 4) is derived from maps created by the Indiana Geological Survey. It shows how that agency defines the four main *natural regions* of Indiana. Meanwhile Figure 5 on page 7 shows how that agency designates an even more refined map of

the state's natural regions. This map provides a much more in-depth vision of the physiography of Indiana.

Referencing these maps can be useful in helping to understand the distribution of Indiana's vertebrate wildlife species. Some species may occur in the state only in a particular region. And when reading the species accounts that appear throughout this book there are sometimes references to how a species' range relates to the state's physiographic partitions. For example, in a

Figure 5.
On this map of Indiana the orange line shows the southernmost extent of glaciation events in Indiana.
The red line shows the southernmost extent of the *most recen*t glacial episode in Indiana, known as the Wisconsin
Glaciation Event. That glacial episode ended only about 15,000 years ago.

discussion of a species' distribution the phrase "found in Indiana only in the Northern Moraine and Lake Region" may be used. Another example might be "endemic to the Northern Moraine and Lake Region."

Glaciation in Indiana

As is the case in much of North America, the physiography of Indiana has been significantly impacted by the advancement and retreat of huge glacial ice sheets.

On the map above (Figure 5) the red and orange lines denote the boundaries of two significant glacial events

which helped shape the topography of Indiana. The orange line represents the southernmost extension of glaciers in the state and it is also the border between the two physiographic provinces of Indiana, the Interior Low Plateau Province and the Interior Lowland Province (shown in Figure 3, page 5).

The red line on the map above marks the point reached by state's most recent glacial event (known as the Wisconsin Glaciation) and it also serves to delineate the division between the Central Till Plain Region and the Southern Hills and Lowlands Region (shown in Figure 4 on page 6).

CHAPTER 2

ECOREGIONS & WILDLIFE HABITATS OF INDIANA

— PART 1—ECOREGIONS —

First, it should be noted that in ecology, as in the study of most scientific disciplines, different opinions exist among experts as to the definition of a particular habitat or ecoregion (such as types of forests). Man's understanding of the earth's ecology continues to evolve and not every ecologist adopts the same model or criteria in describing habitats and ecosystems. Moreover, different models may be used by different researchers based on the needs of their research. The ecological model adopted here is derived from the ecoregions used by the Environmental Protection Agency (www.epa.gov/wed/ecoregions).

The Environmental Protection Agency recognizes a total of 14 "Level I Ecoregions" in the US and Canada. Each of these Level I Ecoregions consists of several progressively smaller divisions, known respectively as Level II Ecoregions, Level III Ecoregions, and Level IV Ecoregions. The maps that follow in this chapter are derived from the US Environmental Protection Agency's ecoregion framework.

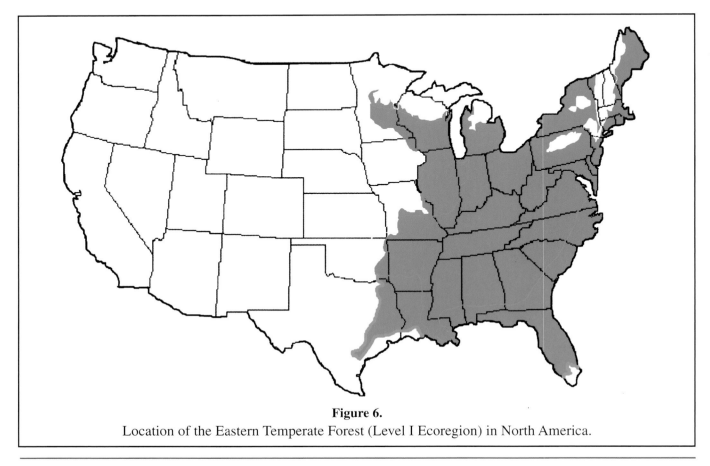

Figure 6.
Location of the Eastern Temperate Forest (Level I Ecoregion) in North America.

Level I Ecoregions

The entire state of Indiana falls within one of the larger of North America's 14 Level I ecoregions known as *Eastern Temperate Forest* (see Figure 6 on the previous page). The designation of Indiana as a forest habitat is based on the state's naturally occurring ecoregions, i.e., the historical natural conditions found in the state prior to the changes wrought by European settlers. Obviously, today much of Indiana is not forested. In fact, even prior to European settlement the natural habitats of the state included large expanses of Tallgrass Prairies. Significant amounts of wetlands in the form of swamps and marshes were also distributed throughout the state, especially along the floodplains of major rivers and in glaciated regions. Thus, although the level I habitat type is designated as forest,

Indiana has always contained a variety of other habitats that were embedded within the boundaries of the Eastern Temperate Forest Level I Ecoregion.

Level II Ecoregions

The Eastern Temperate Forest (Level I Ecoregion) consists of 5 Level II Ecoregions. Those level II ecoregions are the *Ozark-Ouachita-Appalachian Forest,* the *Southeast US Plains,* the *Mississippi Alluvial and Southeast Coastal Plains*, the *Mixed Wood Plains*, and the *Central US Plains*. Three of these five level II ecoregions occur in Indiana. The level II ecoregions that affect Indiana are the Mixed Woods Plains (extreme northern Indiana), the Central USA Plains (mostly in central Indiana), and the Southeast USA Plains in the southwestern portion of the state.

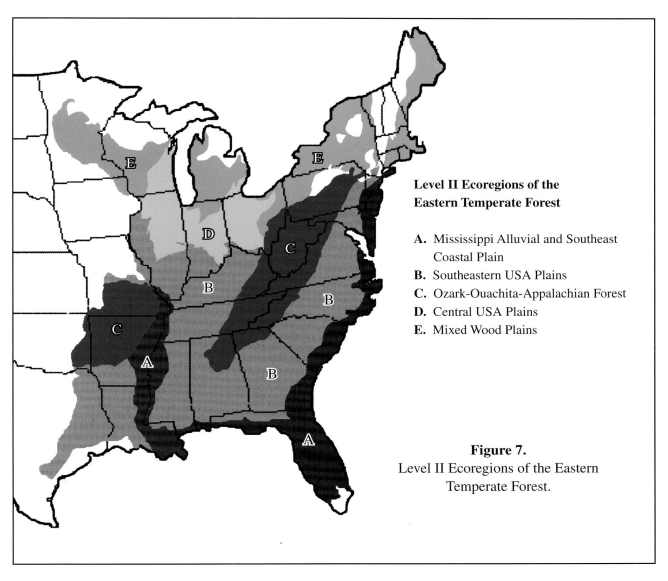

**Level II Ecoregions of the
Eastern Temperate Forest**

A. Mississippi Alluvial and Southeast
   Coastal Plain
B. Southeastern USA Plains
C. Ozark-Ouachita-Appalachian Forest
D. Central USA Plains
E. Mixed Wood Plains

Figure 7.
Level II Ecoregions of the Eastern
Temperate Forest.

Figure 7 on the previous page shows how the Eastern Temperate Forest Level I Ecoregion is depicted at Level II.

A written description of the three Level II ecoregions affecting Indiana is as follows.

Central USA Plains

In Indiana this ecoregion roughly corresponds to the physiographic province known as the Interior Lowlands (see Figure 3). Originally this region was primarily hardwood forest with oak, hickory, maple, elm, ash, and beech as the dominant tree species. Significant areas of tall grass prairies also occurred here, along with marshes, especially in the northwestern part of the state. The rich soils and relatively level terrain makes this an attractive region for growing crops, and today the region is dominated by agriculture.

Southeastern USA Plains

Hardwoods are dominant in this ecoregion with more drought tolerant species such as oaks and hickories being more common. Pines also occur in some areas. Wetland swamps and marshes were once common in river valleys and lowlands.

This ecoregion supports the highest number of herbaceous plants and shrubs in North American (over 2,500 species). Modern agriculture has drastically altered the natural habitats in this region and in fact pristine examples of the original habitat are virtually non-existent today, with nearly all of this forest type being regenerative growth.

Mixed Wood Plains

This ecoregion extends well northward and includes parts of Ontario and Quebec in Canada as well as much of the New England states. The term "Mixed Woods Plains" is appropriately descriptive as the endemic tree species are a mix of deciduous and coniferous evergreens. Historically the area was much more heavily forested. Today the area contains some agricultural lands but less than is seen in the more southerly areas of the state. There is a mosaic of surviving areas of forest. Wetlands and some glacial lakes also occur in this region.

Level III Ecoregions

Each level II ecoregion is divided into smaller Level III Ecoregions.

The **Central USA Plains** Level II Ecoregion consists of four level III ecoregions. Three of these cover parts of Indiana. The *Central Corn Belt Plains* and the *Eastern Corn Belt Plains* are dominant in northeastern, central, and southeastern Indiana, while the *Huron/Lake Erie Plains* barely enters the state in the eastern half of Allen County.

The **Southeastern USA Plains** level II ecoregion contains a total of 8 smaller ecoregions at level III, but only two of them are found in Indiana. They are the *Interior Plateau* and the *Interior River Valleys and Hills*.

Finally, the **Mixed Wood Plains** at level II is divided into 7 smaller level III ecoregions, only one of which (the *Southern Michigan/Northern Indiana Drift Plains*) occurs in Indiana.

Figure 8 on the following page shows how the Level II ecoregions of Indiana are subdivided into Level III ecoregions.

The Level III Ecoregions can be divided even further into Level IV Ecoregions. Ecologists and wildlife biologists find these finer ecoregion divisions useful in the study of the natural history of organisms. Some species are dependent upon a specific habitat or ecoregion for survival. Thus, an understanding of the various ecoregions and what factors are important in the designation of that ecoregion are imperative to wildlife management and conservation efforts. To see how the Level III Ecoregions above are further divided into Level IV Ecoregions consult the Environmental Protection Agency's Ecoregions of North America website.

— PART 2—HABITATS —

In this book, as in many discussions about the natural environments of America, the terms habitat and ecoregion are frequently used interchangeably. But strictly speaking, there are differences between the two. The term "ecoregion," as defined by the World Wildlife Fund, means "a large unit of land or water containing a geographically distinct assemblage of species, natural communities, and environmental conditions." A habitat meanwhile is usually defined simply as "where an organism lives." Thus, an area of mesic (moist)

Figure 8.
The Level III Ecoregions in Indiana.
The bright yellow lines depict the boundaries of the Level II Ecoregions.

forest, or xeric (dry) forest, are both *habitats* that are contained within the larger forest *ecoregion*. In many publications, the word biome is sometimes used synonymously with both the term habitat and the term ecoregion.

A description of the habitat types found in Indiana is as follows:

Woodlands

Given that the Level I Ecoregion of Indiana is the Eastern Temperate Forest, it comes as no surprise that woodlands are one of the most widespread naturally occurring habitat types in the state. Some estimates put the original amount Indiana land covered in forest at 88 percent. Today that amount is less than 20 percent. Nearly all of the woodland habitats in Indiana today are regenerative woodlands, i.e. woodlands that have been logged for timber at some time during the last 150 years. A few enclaves of mature woodlands remain in the state, but they are tiny, highly fragmented remnants of what once was a mature forest ecosystem. As rare as mature forest habitat is in the state, virgin forests are even rarer. Virgin forests are forests that have not been impacted by human activity and remain in a completely natural state. These forests can contain trees that are several hundred years old. Alas, almost no virgin forests remain in Indiana today except for a few widely scattered locales containing only a few acres each.

Although professional biologists and ecologists recognize a large number of different woodland habitat types, in this volume woodland habitats have been simplified and combined into two major types of woodland habitats that can occur in all of Indiana's ecoregions. These two woodland habitat types are as follows:

Xeric (dry) Woodlands

These woodlands are usually found at the tops of ridges where the soil is thin and runoff is high. They can also occur on the sides of south or west south facing slopes of hills and ridges and steep slopes subject to a high rate of rainfall runoff and/or extensive sunlight. Drought tolerant plant species dominate these habitats. In some xeric woodlands where trees are widely spaced and shrub growth is reduced, grasses and herbs normally associated with savannas and grasslands can be found on the forest floor. Pines and Red Cedar are the representative conifers in dry woodlands while a variety of oaks and hickories dominate the deciduous tree community. Dry woodlands are also common in areas where rocky substrate may be near the surface and topsoils are thin or very poor. Many of the tree species are the same as those found in mesic woodlands, but in the xeric woods they are often stunted and gnarly. Xeric Woodland is least common in bottomlands and river valleys but can occur in upland areas such as bluffs that border the river floodplain, or in areas with sandy soils.

Mesic (moist) Woodlands

Mesic woods are found on north or east facing slopes, at the bottoms of deep gorges, and in protected coves and valleys where prolonged direct sunlight is limited and evaporation is low. Mesic Woodlands also are common in lowlands along major river valleys and in smaller creek bottomlands. Tulip Poplar, Sugar Maple, Beech, Basswood, oaks, hickories and in historical times the American Chestnut are just a few of the deciduous tree species found in these diverse woodlands. Extremely wet (swamp) forests are often dominated by species such as Baldcypress, Tupelo, gum, and Red Maple.

Wetlands

Wetlands were once a very significant part of the wildlife habitat of Indiana. Much of the northwestern portion of the state was once covered with seasonal and permanent swamps, marshes, bogs and lakes. Wetlands also commonly occurred in the major river valleys in the state. Wetlands can be areas that are seasonally flooded or contain permanent standing water. In this book, wetlands are characterized by two basic types, swamps and marshes. Both swamps and marshes are very important habitats for many types of wildlife in Indiana. Today very few of the original wetland habitats remain in the state. The two most important types of wetlands in Indiana are swamps and marshes.

Swamps

A swamp is best defined as a wetland area that is permanently or seasonally inundated in which the dominant plants are trees. Most of Indiana's swamplands have always been found in southern Indiana or in low-lying areas adjacent to rivers and streams. Baldcypress, willows, gums and Red Maple are common tree species of Indiana swamps. Generally speaking swamps are permanently flooded, but some habitat models may include seasonally flooded bottomland forest. Swamps are important areas of biodiversity and are critical to the survival of many vertebrate wildlife species in Indiana. Swamps are sometimes categorized by the dominant tree species present (as in Baldcypress Swamp, Tamarack Swamp, etc.).

Marshes

Marshes are wetlands in which the main plant species are grasses, sedges, and shrubs. Some small trees like willows may be present, but they are never dominant. Cattails, Pickerel Weed, Buttonbush, Rose Mallow, and Water Lily are common plants in marshes. Some marshes may be only seasonally flooded, while others have permanently standing water. As with swamps, marshes enjoy significant diversity and are vital habitats to many of Indiana's vertebrate wildlife species. Marshes were historically widespread in much of the state, especially in northwestern portions of the state.

Bogs

Bogs are shallow depressions that are permanently moist and often contain standing water. The vegetation often consists of mosses, ferns, sedges, Jewelweed and other herbaceous plants. Wetland loving trees can also be present and in fact the distinction between a bog and a swamp is somewhat subjective.

It is believed that the original amount of wetlands occurring in Indiana was once as much as 5.5 million acres. Today that amount has been reduced by nearly 90 percent. Subsequently, the preservation of the state's remaining wetlands should be of paramount importance to those who care about the nature and wildlife of Indiana.

Grasslands

In Indiana most of the larger expanses of grassland occurred in the form of Tallgrass Prairies in the northwestern portion of the state. This region represented the easternmost extension of the great Tallgrass Prairies that extended from northwest Indiana across much of northern Illinois and well into Missouri and Iowa.

In addition smaller pockets of grasslands were also scattered throughout much of the glaciated regions of Indiana. Fire has always been an important element in maintaining grasslands and prevented them from being lost in the constant tug of war between forest and grassland. Historically, natural fires started by lightning helped maintain America's prairie habitats. When humans arrived in North America they set fires to maintain clearings and openings for hunting and for primitive agricultural activities. These actions probably increased the amount of prairie habitat in places like Indiana where forests were the dominant habitat.

There are two main types of grassland habitats in Indiana, dry and wet. Wet grasslands are similar in many ways to marshlands. But marshes are much wetter and are inundated most or all of the time, whereas a wet grassland (or wet prairie) tends to be either only seasonally flooded or just contains soils that remain moist throughout most of the year.

Today, nearly all of this type of naturally occurring habitat is gone from Indiana. Most has been converted to agricultural use or swallowed up by urban sprawl. The few tiny pockets of natural grasslands left in the state are now protected in nature preserves.

Grasslands are a complex community of various grasses, forbs, and shrubs and provide habitat for a wide variety of wildlife species. Many species that are grassland specialists are now regarded as threatened or endangered in much of their former range where the natural prairies habitats have disappeared.

In fact all three of the major habitat types in Indiana, Woodlands, Wetlands, and Grasslands have seen a precipitous decline since the European invasion of North America. At least 85 percent of Indiana's wetlands have been lost, and as much as 99 percent of the original grassland habitats have disappeared. Deciduous forests once covered about 90 percent of the state, but today make up less than 20 percent of the land cover. Most of these habitats have been converted to agricultural use, but urbanization has also been responsible for much habitat loss in Indiana.

Throughout the world today the most significant threat to wildlife is *loss of habitat*. The two maps shown in Figure 9 on the following page graphically depict how thoroughly the natural habitats of Indiana have been ravaged by modern humans. These two images should be a wake-up call to all who care about the nature and wildlife of Indiana.

Universal Habitats

Universal habitats occur in virtually all ecoregions throughout North America. The term "universal habitat" is not a commonly used scientific denotation, but rather it is a term created by the author for this book as a way to designate those types of habitats that can and do occur almost everywhere. However, the three types of universal habitats listed immediately below (ecotones, successional areas, and riparian zones) are scientifically recognized terms.

Ecotones

Ecotones are defined as areas of transition between two or more habitats. The term "edge area" is often used synonymously with ecotone. Classic examples of ecotone

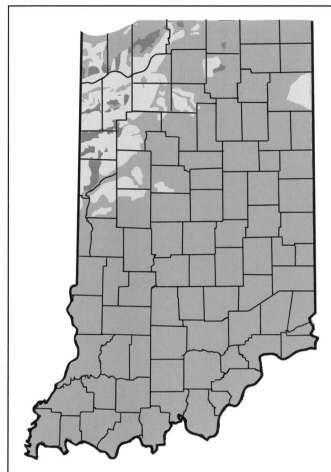 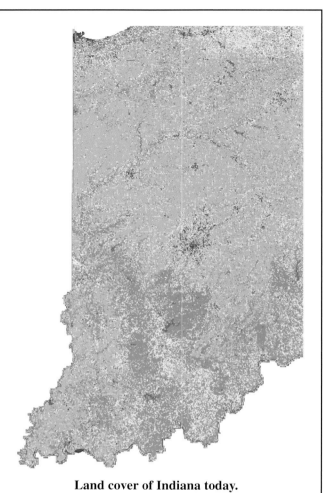

Land cover of Indiana prior to European settlement.
Green represents forests, pale blue is wetlands and brown is grasslands.

Land cover of Indiana today.
Tan is croplands, green is forests, yellow flecking is pasture and pink is urban/developed lands.

Figure 9.
Indiana Then and Now
The map on the left depicts the wildlife habitats of Indiana prior to European settlement. The map on the right shows those habitats today. Note that remaining wetland and grassland habitats are too small to be seen on the modern day map, and forested areas are greatly reduced. Meanwhile agricultural lands dominate the map of modern day Indiana. Maps adapted from original produced by US Geological Survey/US Environmental Protection Agency and Indiana Department of Natural Resources.

areas would be a place were a woodland meets an open field or where a swamp or bottomland abuts against a ridge of upland woods. Ecotones are universal habitats found in all regions. These are very productive areas for wildlife, as species from varying habitats can often be found together around ecotones.

Successional Areas
This is another type of habitat that can occur anywhere. Nature is never static. Grasslands are always in the process of becoming woodlands unless the successional process is altered by fire or mowing. Woodlands destroyed by fire may become grassland. A lake subject to sedimentation can become a swamp or marsh. In time a marsh can fill and become a meadow. Beavers can create a new wetland where before there was a meadow with a small stream. In Indiana, the most familiar successional habitat is the regeneration of a woodland following logging or the reversion to a weedy field of a neglected cropland. These last two types of successional areas are

favored by wildlife species like the Whitetail Deer and the Eastern Cottontail.

Riparian Zones

A riparian zone is a narrow band of habitat bordering a stream or river. Technically, the term is used to describe the narrow zone of lush growth that accompanies a stream coursing through an otherwise arid landscape (as in the riparian habitats of the desert southwest). In Indiana, where so much of the natural landscape has disappeared, stream courses through open farmlands with their associated ribbon of trees, shrubs, and forbs are significant zones of natural habitat which can become very important corridors for the movement and dispersal of vertebrate wildlife. Riparian habitats can occur throughout the state.

Man-Made Habitats

Man-made habitats usually receive no attention in most scientific discussions regarding natural habitats. However, humans have so altered the natural condition of the land that much of the wildlife habitat that exists in America today has been created by human activities. Although the loss of natural habitats has contributed to the disappearance of many species and continues to be the greatest threat to wildlife worldwide, many species have been able to adapt to man-made habitats and a few actually thrive in these new habitats.

Agricultural Areas

Although some may find it difficult to envision a harvested soybean field as a wildlife habitat, in truth many of Indiana's wildlife species have adapted to occupy or use on a part-time basis the state's abundant agricultural areas. A harvested soybean field in winter is one of the best places to see winter migrant birds like the Snow Bunting or Lapland Longspur. A cattle pasture in summer is home to the Eastern Meadowlark and flocks of Common Grackles, Starlings, and Red-winged Blackbirds will use both habitats throughout the year. Some species like the White-tailed Deer and the Wild Turkey in part owe their present day abundance to the ever present food supply provided by grain farmers. In fact, most mammals and many birds found in Indiana have adapted to include agricultural areas in their habitats.

Urban Habitats

As is the case with Agricultural lands, it is sometimes difficult to think of urban landscapes as wildlife habitat. Again however, many species adapt well to towns and cities and in fact some will thrive there. The Chimney Swift experienced a population boom in the days when every building in America had a chimney. The Common Nighthawk frequently nests on the flat rooftops of downtown buildings, and everyone is familiar with the sight of a Robin plucking worms from a well-manicured suburban lawn or a Rock Dove (Pigeon) strolling the sidewalks of a large city.

Today most of Indiana's land mass is held in private ownership. Less than 5 percent of the land mass of the state is held in public trust by state or federal agencies. Meaning over 95 percent is privately owned. Very little of these private lands are managed for wildlife or set aside as areas for the conservation of natural habitats. Fortunately, there are a number of agencies that hold land in public trust with the goal of providing and maintaining natural wildlife habitats. Among these are federal agencies like the US Forest Service, the US Fish & Wildlife Service and the Indiana Department of Natural Resources.

A quick look at the maps in Figure 9 provides a profound picture regarding the scope of the loss of Indiana's original vegetative habitats. To anyone with an appreciation of wilderness and nature in its pristine condition, Indiana has become an impoverished place. Many of the state's wildlife species face a perilous and uncertain future. Happily, many species continue to adapt and some to thrive in the state's new environments. Thankfully, agencies like the Indiana Department of Natural Resources and the US Fish & Wildlife Service work unceasingly to protect, manage, and enhance the state's wildlife and remaining wild habitats. But there is only so much that these organizations can accomplish. Today only a tiny fraction of Indiana's 36,418 square miles of land area is publicly owned. That means that the real responsibility for stewardship of nature in Indiana falls to individual landowners.

We humans, to a very great degree, have succeeded in altering our natural landscapes so much that we no longer feel an intimate connection to the land. We consider ourselves to be residents of an artificially created locality. We are Indianans rather than residents of the formerly great Eastern Deciduous Forest. If asked what part of the state in which our town is located we may say "Brown County" rather than reply that our town is located within rolling uplands of the Interior Plateau.

To some extent, natural boundaries have always been utilized by man when creating political boundaries. A prime example is the Ohio River that serves as the southern border of Indiana. Additionally, smaller creeks and rivers regularly serve as county lines.

But we humans have a strong tendency to create regions and boundaries which ignore natural boundaries and instead serve our personal, social and political needs. While this mindset serves our society well in many ways, it often does a disservice to our environment. If we could learn to think of ourselves more as a part of the larger ecosystems we would perhaps show more concern for the stewardship of those ecosystems. At this stage in human history, with our population rapidly approaching *9 billion people*, our natural resources being pushed to the point of exhaustion, our ocean ecosystems possibly on the verge of collapse, mass extinctions of wildlife species just around the corner, and global climate change the immediate future, a new understanding and appreciation of the natural world by all citizens seems to be the only hope for a promising future.

CHAPTER 3

THE MAMMALS OF INDIANA

TABLE 1

— THE ORDERS AND FAMILIES OF INDIANA MAMMALS —

Class—**Mammalia** (mammals)

Order—**Didelphimorphia** (opossums)

Family	**Didelphidae** (opossum)

Order—**Xenarthra** (armadillos, anteaters, sloths)

Family	**Dasypodidae** (armadillos)

Order—**Carnivora** (carnivores)

Family	**Procyondidae** (raccoon family)
Family	**Felidae** (cat family)
Family	**Canidae** (canines)
Family	**Mustelidae** (weasel family)
Family	**Mephitidae** (skunks)

Order—**Artiodactyla** (hoofed mammals)

Family	**Cervidae** (deer family)

Order—**Lagamorpha** (rabbits & hares)

Family	**Leporidae** (rabbits)

Order—**Rodentia** (rodents)

Family	**Sciuridae** (squirrel family)
Family	**Geomyidae** (gopher family)
Family	**Castoridae** (beaver)
Family	**Muridae** (rats & mice)
Family	**Zapodidae** (jumping mice)

Order—**Soricimorpha** (moles & shrews)

Family	**Sorcidae** (shrews)
Family	**Talpidae** (moles)

Order—**Chiroptera** (bats)

Family	**Vespertilionidae** (typical bats)

Class—**Mammalia** (mammals)

Order—**Didelphimorphia** (opossums)	Order—**Cingulata**
Family—**Didelphidae**	Family—**Dasypodidae** (armadillos)
Virginia Opossum *Didelphis virginiana*	**Armadillo** *Dasypus novemcinctus*

Size: About 2.5 feet from nose to tail tip. Males can weigh up to 14 pounds, females are smaller.

Abundance: Very common. In fact this is one of the most common medium-sized mammals in Indiana.

Variation: Opossums are quite variable. In most the fur is grizzled gray (as in photo above). All white or all black individuals can occur, along with a cinnamon color.

Presumed range in Indiana

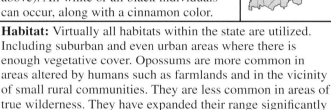

Size: About 30 inches from snout to tail tip. Adult can weigh up to 17 pounds. Babies are about 3 or 4 ounces at birth.

Abundance: Still fairly rare in Indiana, but increasing numbers of Armadillos are being seen in the southwestern tip of the state.

Variation: There is no significant variation in Armadillos and no subspecies in America. The sexes look alike but males are somewhat larger than females.

Presumed range in Indiana

Habitat: Virtually all habitats within the state are utilized. Including suburban and even urban areas where there is enough vegetative cover. Opossums are more common in areas altered by humans such as farmlands and in the vicinity of small rural communities. They are less common in areas of true wilderness. They have expanded their range significantly since the European settlement of America.

Habitat: This wide-ranging animal's habitat includes everything from tropical rain forest to arid semi-desert, grassland, and temperate forests. Moist or sandy soils are preferred as they facilitate easier digging of denning burrows as well as rooting for soil invertebrates. In Indiana presently restricted mostly to the southwestern part of the state but they appear to be expanding their range northward.

Breeding: This is America's only member of the mammalian subclass Marsupialia. Young opossums are born as embryos only twelve days after conception. The newborn babies are just over one-half inch in length. At one month they are about the size of a mouse. Litters are large (up to 13) and two litters per year is not uncommon.

Breeding: Females always give birth to four identical twins, all derived from a single fertilized egg that divides in two, then divides again to form four zygotes before beginning to then develop into individual embryos. The young are well developed at birth which reduces mortality among immatures. One litter per year is typical.

Natural History: Opossums are one of the most successful medium size mammals in America, which is somewhat surprising given that they are slow moving, rather dim-witted animals that rarely survive beyond two years in the wild. They are mainly nocturnal and eat most any palatable plant matter (seeds, grains, fruits, berries); and any type of meat they can catch or scavenge. They are known to kill and eat venomous snakes and have a strong resistance to pit viper venoms. They are well known for faking death (playing possum) when stressed. They have strong nocturnal tendencies but they are sometimes active during the day, especially when breeding. When hard pressed they will climb to escape. In trees they use their prehensile tail to compensate for their somewhat clumsy climbing. They will forage for road killed carrion along highways and their greatest enemy today is the automobile. Thousands are killed nightly on highways across America.

Natural History: Armadillos first began their northern expansion into the US from Mexico about 150 years ago. One hundred years later there were still no records from Indiana, although they were then found as far north as west Tennessee. The first documented sighting in Indiana was in 2003. Today increasing numbers are being seen in southern Indiana. Occasional road killed specimens from more northerly regions of the state may represent stowaways on trains or trucks, or more likely, individuals that have been purposely transported by people. How far north they will spread is unknown. Cold climates may be a limiting factor to their spread, and they may be benefiting from a warming climate. Surprisingly, Armadillos are capable of swimming and they are also known to hold their breath and "bottom walk" short distance across small streams. They are known to sometimes carry the ancient disease of leprosy and have been used in leprosy research.

Class—**Mammalia** (mammals)

Order—**Carnivora** (carnivores)

Family—**Procyonidae** (raccoon, ringtail, coati)	Family—**Felidae** (cats)

Raccoon *Procyon lotor*	**Bobcat** *Lynx rufus*

Size: Up to 2.5 feet in length. Weights of 15 to 30 pounds. Record 62 pounds. Females are smaller than males

Abundance: Common to very common. Can even be found in urban and suburban environments with sufficient cover in the form of trees and shrubs.

Variation: There is little variation in Indiana specimens. A few black individuals occur occasionally. Most resemble the photo above. As many as 25 subspecies range from northern Canada to Panama.

Presumed range in Indiana

Habitat: Found in virtually every habitat in the state except for very large and extensive croplands. Wetlands, stream courses and lake shores are favorite haunts.

Breeding: Breeds in late winter with an average of 4 (maximum of 8) young born two months later (April or May). Young begin to accompany the mother on foraging trips at about 2 months. They are on their own by 5 months.

Natural History: Raccoons are omnivores that feed on a wide variety of crustaceans, insects, amphibians, reptiles, small mammals and eggs as well as grains, berries, fruits, acorns, weed seeds and some vegetables. Although they are mainly nocturnal, they are often active by day, especially in morning and late afternoons. During particularly harsh weather they may den for days at a time. Summer dens are often tree hollows while old groundhog burrows may be used during the winter. The Raccoon is an important game animal harvested for its fur and to a lesser extent as food. More often they are hunted just for sport and released unharmed after being treed by hounds. Like many other mammals, Raccoons are subject to an interesting phenomena known as "Bergman's Rule." Bergman's rule states that the body size of mammals tends to be larger the farther north the species is found. This phenomena is the result of the fact that larger bodies are capable of retaining more heat. A really big male Raccoon from northern Canada may top the scales at 40 pounds. Meanwhile an adult male Raccoon in Florida may weigh only 10 to 12 pounds.

Size: Length up to 3 feet. Weighs 15 to 35 pounds. Maximum of about 45 pounds. Females are smaller than males.

Abundance: Uncommon in Indiana, but recently increasing in numbers. Most common in southern Indiana but could possibly be seen statewide in suitable habitat.

Variation: At least two subspecies are recognized but some experts recognize up to 12. There is little variation in Indiana, but some specimens have more pronounced spotting to their fur than others.

Presumed range in Indiana

Habitat: Rugged, remote woodlands and impenetrable swamps are preferred sanctuaries. Regions with a mosaic of farmlands and scattered woodlands are also used.

Breeding: Most breeding occurs in winter or spring with an average of 3 or 4 young born two months later. Young Bobcats begin to forage with the mother by late summer and may stay with her for up to a year while perfecting hunting skills.

Natural History: Strictly a meat eater, the Bobcat's food items range from mice to deer. Cottontail Rabbits are a favorite prey as are squirrels and songbirds. Bobcats hunt by ambush or by stalking to within close range and making an explosive attack. Although mainly nocturnal, Bobcats can be abroad at any time of day. Their home range can be from one to several square miles and males have larger ranges than females. Juveniles may disperse up to 100 miles. Scent marking territory with urine and feces is common. In captivity Bobcats have lived for over 20 years, but the estimate for wild cats is 12 to 14 years. This species has just begun to return to much of Indiana after being nearly extirpated over a hundred years ago. In recent years they have been recorded from almost every county and they may rarely be seen almost statewide in rural regions. They do require large tracts of woodland, swampland, or other protected natural habitats and they are least likely to be seen in urban areas or regions of extensive row crop agriculture. The core of their range in Indiana is in the level 3 ecoregions of the Interior Plateau and the Interior Lowlands (see Figure 8 on page 11).

Class—**Mammalia** (mammals)

Order—**Carnivora** (carnivores)

Family—**Canidae** (canines)

Gray Fox *Urocyon cinereoargenteus*	**Red Fox** *Vulpes vulpes*	**Coyote** *Canis latrans*

Size: Length 32 to 45 inches. Weighs 8 to 12 pounds. Max 15 pounds.

Presumed range in Indiana

Size: Length 33 to 43 inches. Weight up to 15 pounds.

Presumed range in Indiana

Size: Length up to 49 inches. Average about 35 pounds.

Presumed range in Indiana

Abundance: Fairly common.

Abundance: Fairly common.

Abundance: Fairly common.

Variation: There are several subspecies but only one occurs in Indiana with no significant color variation.

Variation: Indiana specimens are invariably the classic red phase, but other color morphs occur.

Variation: Very dark and reddish specimens are known to occur. Photo above is typical.

Habitat: Primarily a woodland animal that is more common in forested regions of the state. Tends to avoid expansive open regions like farmlands and prairies.

Habitat: Although habitat generalists, Red Foxes show a preference for open and semi-open country over deep woods. May occur in agricultural regions.

Habitat: Coyotes have adapted to all habitats, but they are most common in Indiana in more open agricultural areas. Occasionally adapts to urban parks.

Breeding: Dens in a burrow, hollow log or rock cave. Four pups is usual but up to seven is known.

Breeding: About 4 to 5 young are born underground, often in an old groundhog burrow, but they will dig their own hole.

Breeding: Coyotes are able to breed before their first birthday. Litter size (2 to 10) varies with availability of prey.

Natural History: The Gray Fox is the only American canine with the ability to climb trees. Insects are important food items in summer with mice and rabbits becoming more important in winter. When grapes, persimmons and other fruits are ripe they will eat them almost exclusively and in fact this is the most omnivorous canine in America. Home range can vary from a few hundred acres to over a square mile, depending upon habitat quality. Unlike the Red Fox that can be found as far north as the arctic circle, the Gray Fox is a more southerly animal and ranges southward into South America. Gray Foxes have lived for up to 14 years in captivity, but the average lifespan in the wild is only a few years. Contrary to popular belief, Gray Foxes never interbreed with Red Foxes. In Indiana more common in the more heavily forested southern portions of the state.

Natural History: The Red Fox is one of the world's most widespread mammals and is found in Europe, Asia, north Africa, and Australia (introduced) as well as throughout North America. They are adaptable, opportunistic omnivores that will eat everything from grasshoppers to grapes. Scavenging carrion is also common. Their fur is such a good insulator that they can sleep atop a snow bank without melting the snow beneath their body. These are important fur-bearing animals and are today often reared in captivity on "fur farms." Red Fox populations in Indiana have increased since European settlement and subsequent clearing of forests for agriculture. The short, summer coat is paler than the luxurious winter fur. Three distinct color phases are the Red, Silver, and Cross Fox. All color phases have a white tail tip.

Natural History: The Coyote is a relative newcomer to Indiana, having begun their invasion from the west about a half century ago. Today they range all the way to the Atlantic. They are the top predator in much of the state, occupying a niche once held by the wolf and the Cougar. They are extremely intelligent, adaptable canines that quickly learn to thrive in almost any environment. In rural areas where hunters abound they are extremely wary, but in urban areas or protected lands they may become quite bold around humans. The characteristic yipping and howling of these vocal canines has become a common nighttime sound throughout rural America and at times in suburban areas as well. Mostly nocturnal, but also active by day. The longevity record is 18 years for a specimen in captivity.

Class—**Mammalia** (mammals)

Order—**Carnivora** (carnivores)

Family—**Mustelidae** (weasel family)

Mink *Mustela vison*	**Long-tailed Weasel** *Mustela frenata*	**Least Weasel** *Mustela nivalis*

Mink		Long-tailed Weasel		Least Weasel	
Size: 20 to 27 inches in length. Weighs 2 to 3 pounds.	Presumed range in Indiana 	**Size:** 12 to 15 inches from snout to tail tip. Weighs 6 to 11 ounces.	Presumed range in Indiana 	**Size:** 7 inches. Weighs about 1.5 ounces.	Presumed range in Indiana 
Abundance: Fairly common.		**Abundance:** Uncommon.		**Abundance:** Uncommon to rare.	
Variation: Males are twice as large as females. Pelage color varies from light brown to very dark brown.		**Variation:** Males are nearly twice the size of females. Specimens in the northern portions of their range turn white in winter.		**Variation:** Specimens from farther north turn white in winter. Males are about one-third larger than females.	
Habitat: Swamps and marshes are the primary habitat. Also frequents creeks, rivers and lake shores.		**Habitat:** Occupies a wide variety of habitats but favors being near stream courses.		**Habitat:** Avoids deep woods and lives mostly in or around the edges of fields and marshes.	
Breeding: Three to six young are born in an underground den that is often an old muskrat house. Young begin to hunt with mother at about 2 months.		**Breeding:** Mating occurs in mid-summer but embryo development is delayed until the following spring. 4 to 5 young is typical and babies have white fur.		**Breeding:** Breeds throughout the year and can produce two litters per year of 1 to 6 young. Young develop quickly and can hunt on their own in 6 weeks.	
Natural History: Mink are well known for their luxurious fur. Most mink fur sold in America today is from captive, farm raised mink. Mink are excellent swimmers and will catch fish in stream pools. They are strict carnivores that feed heavily on amphibians and crayfish during the summer. In winter their diet turns to mammal prey such as rabbits and rodents. Muskrats are a favorite winter food of the large males who kill their formidable prey with a bite to the back of the neck. As with other members of the Mustelidae family, mink have well-developed musk glands that produce a distinct musky odor when the animal is excited, breeding, or marking territory. The range of the mink extends from the southeastern United States all the way to Alaska, and includes most of Canada.		**Natural History:** Weasels are known for being, on a pound per pound basis, one of the world's most ferocious predators. Although their prey includes animals as small as insects, they will also take prey the size of a grown Cottontail Rabbit. Mice, voles, and other rodents, along with shrews and small birds make up the bulk of their non-invertebrate diet. Of these, voles are a favorite prey and may make up as much as one-third of the diet. They have also been known to scavenge the dead bodies of large animals such as deer. These highly active mammals have a high metabolic rate and they are active by both day and night, consuming up to one-third of their body weight in a day. When an animal is killed that is too large to consume at one meal, they will cache the remains and return to finish it later. The most widespread weasel in America.		**Natural History:** This is one of the world's smallest carnivores. Their tiny, elongated bodies allow them to maneuver easily into rodent burrows and mice and voles are their primary prey. They hunt day and night, alternating hunts with short naps. They are active year-round and their rapid metabolism means they must consume one-half of their body weight each day. When the opportunity presents they will kill more than they can eat and store the extra food for later. They are known to line their nest with mouse fur or bird feathers from their prey. Few will ever see this tiny, secretive little predator. In Indiana they are found only in the northern portion of the state. Winter pelage in Indiana varies from solid white to white with patches of brown. Summer pelage is brown.	

Class—**Mammalia** (mammals)

Order—**Carnivora** (carnivores)

Family-**Mustelidae** (weasels)		Family—**Mephitidae (skunks)**

River Otter
Lutra canadensis

Size: Length 35 to 45 inches. Up to 25 pounds.	Presumed range in Indiana
Abundance: Uncommon.	
Variation: There is very little variation in Indiana. Males are slightly larger.	

Habitat: Any unpolluted aquatic habitat in the state may be suitable for River Otters. They are always in association with rivers, lakes, swamps, or creeks.

Breeding: Two or three young are born in an underground den often dug in a stream bank. Births are usually in the spring or summer.

Natural History: River Otters are semi-aquatic mammals that possess fully webbed toes and waterproof fur. They are excellent swimmers that prey on fish, frogs, crayfish, turtles and small mammals. Their fur is highly valued, a fact that lead to their extirpation from most of the eastern United States by the late 1800s. Restocking programs by state wildlife agencies throughout the Midwest have been successful and today these endearing animals can once again be found in most of Indiana. Although there may still be parts of the state where they may not yet have colonized, it is reasonable to consider their range today as being nearly statewide in suitable habitats along major river drainages. They sometimes wander into farm ponds where they can deplete fish populations. The species appears to be secure and increasing in the state today.

Badger
Taxidea taxus

Size: To 30 inches. Males to 24 pounds, females smaller.	Presumed range in Indiana
Abundance: Uncommon.	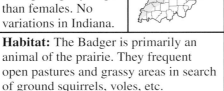
Variation: Males average slightly larger than females. No variations in Indiana.	

Habitat: The Badger is primarily an animal of the prairie. They frequent open pastures and grassy areas in search of ground squirrels, voles, etc.

Breeding: Breeds in mid-summer with young born in early spring. Average number of young is two or three but can be as many as six or seven.

Natural History: The Badger is a digging machine. It possesses long claws, powerful forelegs and a specialized structure of the eye known as a "nictitating membrane" which keeps dirt from entering the eye sockets. Badgers feed mostly by digging small mammals from their underground burrows. Ground squirrels and gophers are the favorite prey, but almost any type of animal may be eaten, including carrion. In the western US, Badgers have been observed hunting cooperatively with Coyotes. The Coyote guards the escape holes (and catches a few fleeing animals), while the Badger benefits from having the Coyote blocking the escape route long enough for the Badger to dig out a hapless ground squirrel or gopher. Abandoned Badger dens are utilized by a wide variety of other animals. Most common in northern and central Indiana.

Striped Skunk
Mephitis mephitis

Size: Length 23 to 31 inches. Weighs about 8 to 10 pounds.	Presumed range in Indiana
Abundance: Common.	
Variation: Varies in the amount of white in the stripes. Can be all white or solid black.	

Habitat: Striped Skunks are found in all habitats in Indiana, but they are most common in semi-open habitats, successional areas and edge areas.

Breeding: Breeding occurs in late winter. Litter size averages 3 or 4 but can be as many as ten. Weanlings follow the mother in single file while foraging.

Natural History: The Striped Skunk's distinctive black and white color is almost as well known as its primary defense, which of course is to spray an attacker with its pungent, foul-smelling musk. The musk can burn the eyes and membranes and its odor is remarkably persistent. They can effectively project the musk up to about 15 feet and the odor can be detected hundreds of yards away. A direct hit to the face from the musk glands can cause debilitating nausea and temporary blindness. Striped Skunks dine mainly on invertebrates and as much as three-fourths of their diet consists of insects and grubs. They possess well-developed front claws for digging and a powerful sense of smell for locating buried grubs, worms, turtle eggs, etc. They will also eat baby mice, eggs and the young of ground nesting birds.

Class—**Mammalia** (mammals)
Order—**Artiodactyla** (hoofed mammals)
Family—**Cervidae** (deer family)
Whitetail Deer—*Odocoileus virginianus*

Buck	Doe	Fawn

Size: Males up to 40 inches high at shoulder. Females about 20 percent smaller. Mature males can weigh over 200 pounds, females up to 150, though most are smaller. Deer from the northernmost regions have larger body size than those in the southern parts of country. This is due to a phenomena known as "Bergman's Rule." Larger bodies lose heat less rapidly due to the ratio of body volume to surface area, thus in colder regions mammals with a larger body size tend to survive better.

Presumed range in Indiana

Abundance: Very common. Least common in urban regions and areas of extensive agriculture.

Variation: There are as many as thirteen different subspecies of Whitetail Deer recognized in mainland North America, plus several more island races. The Indiana subspecies is the Northern Woodland Whitetail Deer, *Odocoileus virginianus borealis*. Young (fawns) exhibit a pattern of white spots that fade with age. Adults have reddish brown color in the summer and grayish in the fall/winter. Deer from northern regions can be considerably larger than those from southern regions.

Habitat: Found in virtually every habitat within the state and increasingly common in urban areas. Favorite habitats are a mix of woodland, brushy areas and weedy fields, especially near farmlands. Successional areas, such as regrowth of woodlands after fires or logging is also a prime habitat. Throughout America Whitetail Deer are more common where there is a mixture of agricultural land and woodlands. They are least common in mature, unbroken forests and in areas of intensive agriculture or major urbanization.

Breeding: Breeding begins in early fall and may continue into the winter, with the peak breeding season occurring in November. One to two (rarely three or even four) young are born in the spring or early summer following a six and a half month gestation. Females (does) usually bear their first offspring at two years of age. The first pregnancy typically results in a single fawn, the second pregnancy usually is twins and the third through fifth twins or triplets (rarely quadruplets). Young lie hidden for the first few weeks and are left alone much of the time. The female will visit the hidden fawn about once every four hours to allow nursing, then moves away to avoid attracting predators. At about one month of age the young will begin to follow the mother and stay close through the summer and into the fall.

Natural History: Bucks (males) shed their antlers each year in late winter and regrow a new set by fall. Growing deer antlers are among the fastest growing animal tissue known. While growing the antlers are covered in a spongy, fuzzy skin called "velvet." Antlers grow larger each year up to about six or seven years of age, when they begin a gradual decline. Whitetail Deer are browsers and they feed on a wide variety of forbs, leaves, twigs, buds, crops and mast (especially acorns). Although they are sometimes destructive to farm crops like corn or soybeans, they are an important game animal in America with as many as seven million harvested annually for food and sport. The maximum life span is 20 years, but most are dead by age 10. State wildlife agencies like the Indiana Department of Natural Resources are charged with the responsibility of protecting and managing the state's wildlife populations. This means taking into consideration not only the health and well-being of the state's deer herd, but also the cultural aspect of providing food and recreation for the state's hunting population. Additionally, considerations such as crop depredation by deer to the state's farmers, impacts on auto insurance rates by deer-auto collisions, etc. Thus determining how many deer of what sex should be harvested annually involves taking into consideration many factors. Happily, this animal represents one of the world's great wildlife conservation stories. Nearly wiped out by the early 1900s, the Whitetail Deer is today as numerous in America as it was during the time of Daniel Boone. At present, the population in North America averages around 30 million deer. In recent years these animals have begun to invade urban areas where deer hunting is restricted. In towns and cities they can become a nuisance as they feed in suburban gardens and devour landscape plants. Still, many urban dwellers enjoy their presence.

Class—**Mammalia** (mammals)
Order—**Lagomorpha** (lagamorphs)
Family—**Leporidae** (rabbits, hares)

Eastern Cottontail *Sylvilagus floridanus*	**Swamp Rabbit** *Sylvilagus obscurus*

Size: Adult length about 17 inches. Average weight about 2.5 pounds.

Abundance: Typically very common, but populations fluctuate on about a 10-year cycle. During years of high abundance they can be extremely common.

Variation: No variation in Indiana, but at least 12 very similar subspecies of this wide-ranging rabbit are recognized across the United States.

Presumed range in Indiana

Size: Adults reach about 20 inches and weigh as much as 5 pounds.

Abundance: Swamp Rabbits barely range into Indiana in the southwestern tip of the state. They are an endangered species in Indiana and may not be hunted.

Variation: No variation in Indiana. There is one other subspecies that inhabits the southwestern gulf coastal plain.

Presumed range in Indiana

Habitat: May be found in virtually any habitat within the state except for permanent wetlands. Most common in overgrown fields and edge areas. Fond of briers, honeysuckle, and tall weeds.

Habitat: Swamps, marshes and bottomlands in the southern tip of the state. Most common in the deep south, the Swamp Rabbit's range barely enters Indiana in the southwestern tip of the state where it hangs on in a few remaining wetlands.

Breeding: Has an amazing reproductive capacity. In fact, this is the most prolific of the several rabbit species in America, producing up to seven litters per year with as many as five young per litter.

Breeding: Much less prolific than its smaller cousin the Cottontail. Breeds January through August. Three young is typical after a 37-day gestation period. Averages two litters per year.

Natural History: In the spring and summer Eastern Cottontails feed on a wide variety of grasses, legumes and herbaceous weeds. Briers, sapling bark and other woody materials may make up the bulk of the diet in winter. They can become a nuisance in fruit orchards, where they will eat the bark of sapling fruit trees during the winter. These rabbits are prey for many predators including foxes, coyotes, bobcats, and hawks and owls, especially the Great Horned Owl. Humans hunt them as well and they are one of the most sought after small game animals in America. But there are fewer rabbit hunters today than there were years ago. Many people regard their flesh as highly palatable, and the German dish known as "Hasenpfeffer" is made from rabbit. The life expectancy for a Cottontail is not high, and only about one in four will live to see their second birthday. Maximum life span is probably about 5 years. Populations are known to fluctuate and during years when their numbers are highest there may be as many as nine rabbits per acre in good habitat.

Natural History: An excellent swimmer, the Swamp Rabbit will elude hunters' hounds by diving into water and swimming for a long distance. They sometimes dive under water and swim submerged. This is the largest of the "true" rabbits in America (not including jackrabbits and hares). They are nearly twice as large as the various species of Cottontails. The range of this species has diminished with the loss of wetlands both in Indiana and throughout its core range in the southern US. The occurrence of the Swamp Rabbit in wetlands is easily detected by the presence of droppings on floating logs within the swamp. They are mostly nocturnal but will be active at dusk or even afternoon in warm weather. These large rabbits have correspondingly larger ranges than the small Eastern Cottontail and their home range can exceed 10 acres. By contrast the Eastern Cottontail will typically have a home range of less than 3 acres. Bobcats and Great Horned Owls are probably the biggest predator of swamp rabbits in most areas of their range.

Class—**Mammalia** (mammals)

Order—**Rodentia** (rodents)

Family—**Sciuridae** (squirrels)

Gray Squirrel *Sciurus carolinensis*	Fox Squirrel *Sciurus niger*

Typical adult | Albino

Melanistic morph | Typical adult

Size: 19 inches and weighs about 18 ounces.

Presumed range in Indiana

Abundance: Very common.

Variation: At least six subspecies occur in the US and some are quite variable. Melanistic (black) populations can be found in some areas of the northern US and albino individuals occur rarely throughout the range. Some individuals may have reddish-brown tails but most resemble the typical adult above.

Size: 23 inches and weighs about 28 ounces.

Presumed range in Indiana

Abundance: Common.

Variation: There are a total of ten subspecies nationwide and they range in color from solid black to reddish to silver-gray. *S. n. rufiventer* occurs in Indiana. Most are like the specimen show above, but solid black color morphs are widespread throughout their range (see inset photo).

Habitat: Prefers mature deciduous forests but also found in mixed coniferous forests and second growth areas as well as urban parks. They are strictly a woodland animal but will persist in small woodlots and where ribbons of trees border streams. They will thrive in urban areas as well if there are mature mast trees present in any significant amount.

Habitat: Although they can be found in large expanses of unbroken forest the preferred habitat is more open forests with trees widely spaced. Small woodlots and woodland/field edge areas, overgrown fence rows, and riparian habitats are also utilized. Like the Gray Squirrel they can also exist in urban parks. They can sometimes be common in swamps.

Breeding: Breeds December through February and again in June/July. Four to six young per litter. Young females may breed as early as six to eight weeks of age. Males are polygamous and will breed with many females.

Breeding: Produces four to six young twice annually, breeding in winter and again in summer. Males quarrel for territorial dominance during the breeding season. Females may mate with more than one male. Young wean at about 8 weeks.

Natural History: Feeds on nuts, seeds, fungi, tree buds and the inner bark of trees as well as bird eggs and hatchlings. May sometimes even eat carrion. Like most rodents they will gnaw bones or shed deer antlers for calcium. Well known for burying and storing nuts. Frequently calls with a raspy "bark," especially when alarmed. Builds summer nests of leaves in tree crotches or in the forks of limbs. Winter dens are typically in tree hollows. During severe weather they may be inactive for several days. Poor mast years may produce mass migrations as they roam in search of food sources. Gray Squirrels are extremely athletic little animals and exhibit remarkable agility in trees. They also seem quite resistant to injury when on rare occasions they may fall from considerable heights. They are preyed on by a variety of predators. One of their main enemies is the Bobcat.

Natural History: Fox Squirrels wander frequently into open areas and spend more time on the ground than Gray Squirrels. Their home range is much larger. They are generally less common than the Gray, rarely reaching the population densities of their smaller cousins. In some areas of Indiana, however, they may be more common than the Gray Squirrel, especially in semi-open country. They feed on the same foods of nuts, seeds, buds, berries, etc. But the diet of Fox Squirrels also often includes the seeds of pine cones. Barks and chatters when disturbed but is overall less vocal than the smaller squirrel species which occur in the state. Like most squirrels they are diurnal in habits, retiring at night to leaf nests or tree hollows. During inclement weather they may remain in their dens for several days. Along with the Gray Squirrel they are an important game animal in Indiana.

Class—**Mammalia** (mammals)

Order—**Rodentia** (rodents)

Family—**Sciuridae** (squirrel family)

Eastern Chipmunk *Tamias striatus*	**Red Squirrel** *Tamiasciurus hudsonicus*	**Flying Squirrel** *Glaucomys volans*

Eastern Chipmunk		Red Squirrel		Flying Squirrel	
Size: About 10 inches and 4.5 ounces.	Presumed range in Indiana 	**Size:** 12 inches and about 6 ounces.	Presumed range in Indiana 	**Size:** 10 inches and 2 to 3 ounces.	Presumed range in Indiana 
Abundance: Fairly common.		**Abundance:** Fairly common.		**Abundance:** Fairly common.	
Habitat: Deciduous forests in upland areas. Fond of rock outcrops, stone fences, etc. Can often be common in urban parks.		**Habitat:** Like most tree squirrels this is a forest species. Uses a variety of woodlands but boreal forests are where they are most common.		**Variation:** There is little variation and the sexes are alike. As many as 8 subspecies nationwide but differences are very subtle.	

Eastern Chipmunk — Variation: There are between five and eight subspecies nationwide (experts disagree on the exact number). The differences between the subspecies are very subtle and apparent only to trained mammologists. Thus there is no significant variation and the specimen shown above is a good representative example.

Red Squirrel — Variation: Summer pelage is duller and less red and the prominent "ear tufts" are only seen in fall and winter squirrels. Some mammologists recognize up to 25 subspecies of this widespread squirrel. The subspecies that occurs in Indiana is *T. h. loquax*, the Southern Red Squirrel.

Flying Squirrel — Habitat: These little squirrels are totally dependent upon trees and make their home in woodlands. Primarily hardwoods but also in mixed pine-hardwood forests. They will live in suburbs and urban areas if sufficient mature trees are present. Dens in tree hollows and old woodpecker holes.

Eastern Chipmunk — Breeding: May breed twice per year, first in February and again in April. Females may mate with more than one male. Produces 4 to 5 young per litter.

Red Squirrel — Breeding: Capable of producing two broods per year. 3 to 5 young is typical. In years of good mast crops they may produce larger litters of 7 or 8.

Flying Squirrel — Breeding: Only one litter per year with up to six young. Nest is usually within a hollow in a tree. Bluebird boxes and other artificial nest sites are also used.

Eastern Chipmunk — Natural History: While they are excellent climbers, chipmunks are true "ground squirrels," sleeping, rearing young and wintering in an underground burrow which they dig themselves. They also will use rock crevices or hollow logs. They become less active in winter and will remain below ground living on stored nuts and seeds for long periods during harsh weather. Although Chipmunks are fairly common in much of Indiana they are usually absent from expansive open areas and areas of extensive agriculture. Chipmunks are a vocal animal and their voice sounds like the chirping of a bird.

Red Squirrel — Natural History: While most people find Red Squirrels to be endearing little animals, others regard them as pests that raid bird feeders and consume prodigious amounts of expensive bird seed. Red Squirrels will store huge piles of conifer cones, usually at the base of a large tree. These piles are known as "middens" and they can attain an enormous size. Piles 15 feet across and 3 feet high have been recorded. The range of the Red Squirrel in Indiana is not well understood but they are presumed to occur nearly statewide in suitable habitat, although they are absent from many areas of the state.

Flying Squirrel — Natural History: Our only nocturnal squirrel. Leaps from tree to tree and glides using flaps of skin between front and hind legs like a parachute. Flattened tail serves as a rudder while gliding. Feeds on nuts, seeds, fruits, fungi, lichens, tree buds, insects, bird eggs and nestling birds as well as mice. Flying Squirrels are gregarious animals and several may share a den. They can live up to ten years and will become quite tame in captivity, making reasonable pets. Wild squirrels in rural areas sometimes invade homes and attics where they can become a noisy nuisance as they scramble about in the wee hours.

Class—**Mammalia** (mammals)

Order—**Rodentia** (rodents)

Family—**Sciuridae** (squirrel family)

Groundhog *Marmota monax*	**Thirteen-line Ground Squirrel** *Ictidomys tridecemlineatus*	**Franklin's Ground Squirrel** *Poliocitellus franklinii*

Size: 16 to 26 inches and 6 to 9 pounds.

Presumed range in Indiana

Abundance: Common.

Variation: Individuals vary in color from brown to grayish, reddish, or rarely, nearly black. Most resemble the specimen shown.

Size: 12 inches and 5 to 8 ounces.

Presumed range in Indiana

Abundance: Fairly common.

Variation: No variation. They are remarkably similar throughout their range in the Midwest and the Great Plains.

Size: To 15 inches and 34 ounces.

Presumed range in Indiana

Abundance: Rare in Indiana.

Variation: No significant variation and apparently no subspecies. Males are slightly larger than females.

Habitat: Fields and woodland edges. The main habitat requirements are some open ground within the vicinity of the burrow for foraging, as well as some higher ground that is above the floodplain for locating the burrow. They avoid swamps and permanent wetlands.

Habitat: Inhabits prairies and sandy grasslands. Today pastures, golf courses, cemeteries, lawns, and even highway right of ways are often utilized. Prefers areas of short, sparse grass. Restricted mostly to the northern half of the state. The range map above is an estimate.

Habitat: Prefers taller grasses than the smaller Thirteen-lined Ground Squirrel. In Indiana this species is restricted to the Central Corn Belt Plains Level III Ecoregion (see Figure 8) where they inhabit remnant dry grasslands. They are an endangered species in Indiana.

Breeding: Mating occurs in spring with two to four young typical. One litter per year. Young remain below ground for about 6 weeks.

Breeding: Mating takes place soon after emerging from hibernation. The average of 6 to 8 young are blind and naked at birth. They wean at 6 weeks.

Breeding: Produces an average of 7 or 8 young born in May. Baby squirrels are born hairless and with eyes closed but will be mature by October.

Natural History: These large ground squirrels dig extensive underground burrows where they retreat from danger, spend the night, and overwinter. They accumulate huge deposits of fat during the summer and fall, which sustains them during winter hibernation. During this time their metabolism slows dramatically with as few as four heartbeats per minute. They will sometimes climb small trees and bushes in springtime to eat swelling tree buds, but their primary diet is forbs and grasses. Except during breeding or when rearing young they are solitary animals and typically only one adult occupies a burrow. They can become pests in rural gardens or farmers' croplands.

Natural History: Although they often go by the nickname "Striped Gopher," the Thirteen-lined Ground Squirrel is a member of the Squirrel Family and not very closely related to the true gophers that inhabit much of America. This species may have expanded its range from presettlement days. Cutting of forests and clearing of land for agriculture and other human uses seems to have benefited this open country species. They are confirmed burrowers that may excavate several tunnels which can be six feet in length and over a foot deep. Below ground hibernation begins in October and lasts about 6 months. In addition to grasses and clovers they will eat seeds and some insects.

Natural History: The Franklin's Ground Squirrel is a rare species with spotty distribution. It is often most common along old railroad tracks where the elevated road bed provides a bit of high ground for the burrow. They are diurnal in habits and are primarily vegetarians, but they will eat a wide variety of insects and animal matter, including carrion, even roadkills. These squirrels are not commonly observed in part because they spend so much time in their burrow. They have a rather long period of hibernation that may be more than half the year. In Indiana they are active from April to early September. Even in summer they will spend much time underground.

Class—**Mammalia** (mammals)

Order—**Rodentia** (rodents)

Family—**Geomyidae** (gophers)	Family—**Castoridae** (beaver family)

Plains Pocket Gopher
Geomys bursarius

Beaver
Castor canadensis

Size: 10 inches and 6.5 ounces.	Presumed range in Indiana 

Abundance: Rare in Indiana.

Variation: There is no significant variation in Indiana specimens. The subspecies *illinoenis* occurs in Indiana.

Habitat: Pocket Gophers require loose, loamy or sandy soils which facilitate easy burrowing. They avoid wet soil regions and fields that are regularly plowed. They will utilize pastures, hayfields, railroad beds and roadsides.

Breeding: Litter size is reported to be as many as 7 or as few as single baby. Young are mature in about three months.

Natural History: Pocket Gophers are truly fossorial mammals that spend nearly all their life in their elaborate underground burrow systems. Burrows up to 500 feet in total length have been recorded. They have well-developed claws on their front feet and very powerful forelimbs for excavating their burrows. Their enlarged incisor teeth are used mainly to sever roots, but are also adapted to allow them to literally chew their way through harder soils. Foods are mostly tuberous roots of a wide variety of forbs, but some leaves are also eaten. These rodents are quite rare in Indiana today as much of their original habitats have been converted to row crops like corn and soybeans. Regarded as a species of Special Concern.

Size: Up to 43 inches in total length. The largest adults can weigh up to 65 pounds.

Presumed range in Indiana

Abundance: Common. Most common in river valleys and lowlands.

Variation: The American Society of Mammologists recognizes twenty-four subspecies in North America. The status of Beavers in the eastern US is difficult to determine due to re-introduction programs using transplanted beavers that may have come from many locations across America. Re-introduction programs in Indiana began back in 1935 with animals from Wisconsin.

Habitat: Beavers are thoroughly aquatic mammals that to a great extent create their own wetland habitats. To construct their ponds and waterways they require the presence of a stream or spring run with constant or near constantly flowing water which can be dammed. Streams that are subject to fierce flooding or with exceptionally powerful flows are avoided in preference for more easily contained water flows. In addition they will use lakes, rivers, swamps, marshes, and large creeks.

Breeding: Mating takes place in mid-winter with the young being born about 4 months later. There is only one litter per year. Baby beavers are quite precocious and are born with well-developed fur and eyes that open immediately. Four or five young, called kits, is typical.

Natural History: Beavers are primarily nocturnal in habits, but they may be active at dawn and dusk. In remote locations where human intrusion is absent, they are observed active during the day as well. They feed mostly on the inner bark of trees, with willow being a dietary mainstay. They will also consume sedges and other aquatic vegetation, but in winter live exclusively on bark. The dorsal-ventrally flattened tail is hairless and scaly and along with the webbed hind feet provide these animals with powerful swimming tools. They also possess enlarged incisors which grow continually throughout life and are used to gnaw through trunks and fell trees. Most trees cut by Beavers are small saplings which are used as food, but they will also cut large trees up to two feet in diameter to open the canopy and promote the growth of new food sources. They are famous for their dam building abilities and they will also build elaborate living quarters known as "lodges." After many years of use these lodges may become up to 15 feet across and can house an entire extended family. They have underwater entrances for protection and a hollow "room" that is above the water-line and lined with wood chips or grasses. Other species such as Muskrats and mice may take up residence within these lodges. At one time Beaver fur was one of the most valuable natural resources in America and the pursuit of Beaver fur led to the exploration of much of the continent. Within a few decades they were nearly exterminated by trappers in much of America, including Indiana.

Class—**Mammalia** (mammals)

Order—**Rodentia** (rodents)

Family—**Muridae** (rats & mice)

Muskrat	Allegheny Woodrat	Norway Rat
Ondatra zibethicus	*Neotoma magister*	*Rattus norvigicus*

Muskrat
Ondatra zibethicus

Size: Reaches 20 inches in length and will weigh about 2.5 pounds.

Presumed range in Indiana

Abundance: Common in marshes throughout Indiana.

Variation: No significant variation occurs in Indiana.

Habitat: Aquatic. Prefers marshland but also inhabits swamp, ponds and lakes; even roadside ditches. Rarely in rivers or large streams. Often sympatric with the Beaver.

Breeding: Prolific. Capable of multiple litters annually and may produce as many as 6 young per litter. Young are weaned in about a month.

Natural History: Primarily nocturnal but often active during daylight hours in the spring. With webbed hind feet and a laterally flattened tail muskrats are excellent swimmers. They feed on a variety of aquatic vegetation. The name comes from the presence of well-developed musk glands. These rodents are an important fur-bearer and in the recent past millions were trapped annually across America for their fur. Life span is only 3 to 4 years in the wild. The Mink may be the most important predator on muskrats, especially of the young. Adults build lodges similar to the Beaver, but use grasses rather than sticks. The entrance to the Muskrat lodge is below water level while the chamber of the lodge itself is above the high water mark. Sometimes burrows into banks.

Allegheny Woodrat
Neotoma magister

Size: Adults reach 17 inches total length and up to about 12 ounces.

Presumed range in Indiana

Abundance: Very rare. Endangered in Indiana.

Variation: There are no subspecies and no variation in Indiana.

Habitat: Woodrats usually associate with rocks and cliff faces where they make their dens in crevices. They will also use logs, derelict buildings, etc. In Indiana uses limestone/sandstone bluffs.

Breeding: Breeds spring through fall. 3 to 4 litters per year is possible with 2 young being typical. Litter sizes of up to 6 young have been recorded.

Natural History: The range of this species in Indiana has shrunk to a very small area of rocky bluffs along the Ohio River. Woodrats favor rocky outcrops, talus slopes, boulder piles and cliff faces where they make their den in crevices or small caves. They are sometimes known as "packrats," a name derived from their habit of collecting shiny objects that range from aluminum cans to eating utensils. They cache food in large quantities in what are known as "middens." Ancient woodrat nests in caves can persist for centuries and are studied to gain insight into the historical natural history of a region. Dens are occupied by one adult (and young). This species has been extirpated from much of its historical range and appears to be declining in most of its remaining range.

Norway Rat
Rattus norvigicus

Size: Length can be up to 15 inches and weigh up to 12 ounces.

Presumed range in Indiana

Abundance: Very common. Especially in urban areas.

Variation: The laboratory rat is an albino of this species.

Habitat: This highly adaptable rodent can live virtually anywhere, including as a stowaway on ships, which is how it immigrated to America from Europe. They are least common in wilderness.

Breeding: The fecundity of the Norway Rat is legendary. From 6 to 8 litters per year with up to a dozen young per litter.

Natural History: Also called the Brown Rat, this species has followed man to every corner of the globe. They are responsible for an almost unimaginable degree of human suffering. Throughout the history of human civilization these rodents have destroyed crops and stored foods while spreading devastating diseases, most notably Bubonic Plague. Though less of a threat to modern societies, these rats still shadow the human species. They are common in both urban and rural settings. In cities they live on human garbage, in rural areas livestock food and crops. The common laboratory rat is a domestic version of this animal that has somewhat redeemed the species for humans as an experimental animal for medical and scientific research.

Class—**Mammalia** (mammals)		
Order—**Rodentia** (rodents)		
Family—**Muridae** (rats & mice)		

House Mouse *Mus musculus*	**Deer Mouse** *Peromyscus maniculatus*	**White-footed Mouse** *Peromyscus leucopus*

Size: 6.5 inches and 0.75 of an ounce.	Presumed range in Indiana 	**Size:** 5 to 8 inches and about 1 ounce.	Presumed range in Indiana 	**Size:** 7 inches and about 1 ounce.	Presumed range in Indiana 
Abundance: Very common.		**Abundance:** Fairly common.		**Abundance:** Very Common.	
Habitat: A highly adaptable, successful rodent that usually associates with human habitations and man-made structures.		**Habitat:** Deer Mice use open fields and agricultural land. Can sometimes be found in wide-open, harvested crop fields.		**Habitat:** White-footed Mice prefer the woods but may also be found in overgrown fields, fence rows, etc.	

Variation: Wild specimens show surprisingly little variation throughout the world, but domesticated laboratory mice come in a variety of colors and patterns. The most well-known color is solid white, and the "white mice" seen in labs and pet stores are albinos of this species.

Variation: These two species are so similar that most people will not be able to tell them apart. Both have several subspecies nationwide (over a dozen in the White-footed Mouse and over 50 in the Deer Mouse). In the Deer Mouse, short-tailed, small eared forms are found in open fields and grasslands and a long-tailed, large eared variant occurs in woodland habits. A trait that further complicates differentiating between the two. Both species exhibit some age-related color variation, with younger mice being darker, more grayish in color.

Breeding: Broods can number from 5 to 12. Young females begin breeding at 6 weeks and produce 14 litters per year.

Breeding: Both these species are prolific breeders that can breed nearly year-round. A typical litter is four or five young, but can be more. The young mice develop rapidly and can be ready to breed when they are only two months old.

Natural History: The House Mouse has adapted to living in close proximity to humans and today they are found wherever there are people throughout the world. As their name implies they regularly enter houses where they can become both a pest and a health hazard. They live both in cities and farmlands, and despite their predilection for human habitations, they are quite capable of living in wilderness. Like the Norway Rat the House Mouse originated in Eurasia and traveled around the world as a stowaway on sailing ships, eventually populating the entire globe. These mice are primarily nocturnal and their food includes nearly everything eaten by humans plus insects and fungi. The "lab mouse" is an albino version.

Natural History: These common mice serve as prey for a variety of predators, from coyotes and bobcats to weasels, snakes and birds of prey. Both species are primarily nocturnal. They feed on a wide array of seeds, nuts and grain as well as berries, insects, snails, centipedes, fungi, and occasionally other mice. One important food item is a fungus known as *Endogone* that is ubiquitous in the soil. They will cache large stores of seeds and nuts in the fall and they remain active throughout the winter. Both species shown above can become a nuisance as they will regularly enter human dwellings, often nesting in a little used drawer or cupboard. Several species of *Peromyscus* mice are vectors for tick-borne Lyme disease and in the southwestern United States some can harbor the deadly Hanta Virus. Humans who experience close contact or prolonged exposure to their feces and urine may be at risk. Both species can be arboreal and they may den or nest well above the ground, or they may live beneath a rotted log or stump. Both are adaptable and successful native rodents. The Deer Mouse is found in every habitat type in America and ranges from near sea level to the high mountains. The White-footed Mouse is nearly as adaptable. Professional mammologists use measurements of the skull, tail, and hind foot to differentiate between these two similar and sympatrically occurring species. Together they constitute much of small mammal foods for many of America's predators and their role in local ecosystems is of great importance.

Class—**Mammalia** (mammals)

Order—**Rodentia** (rodents)

Family—**Muridae** (rats & mice)

Western Harvest Mouse *Reithrodontomys megalotis*	Woodland Vole *Microtus pinetorum*	Prairie Vole *Microtus ochreogaster*

Western Harvest Mouse
Reithrodontomys megalotis

Size: Length about 5.5 inches and weighs two-fifths of an ounce.

Abundance: Uncommon in IN.

Variation: No significant variation among adults. Young mice are darker and more grayish.

Presumed range in Indiana

Habitat: Favors areas of successional growth. Overgrown fields with rank growth of grass or weeds, remnants of prairie habitats, edge areas, etc.

Breeding: Average litter size is 4. Babies are born naked and with their eyes closed but will be weaned within a month.

Natural History: Harvest Mice are very similar to several other mice species found in the state. Mammologists can quickly recognize the Harvest Mouse by examining the front incisors, which possess a groove not seen in other species of mice. Their food is thought to be mostly the seeds from various grasses, but they are known to feed on insects and larva as well. There is some belief that these mice have recently expanded their range in some areas. They may have been rarer in the state prior to European settlement. The fact that their favorite habitat is successional areas means that human activities could have helped open habitat niches for the species throughout the eastern United States. Prior to European settlement, burning of grasslands by natives may also have helped this species by creating successional habitats.

Woodland Vole
Microtus pinetorum

Size: Length can reach 5 inches. Weight 1 ounce.

Abundance: Common.

Variation: Several subspecies are recognized, but differences are indistinguishable to the lay observer.

Presumed range in Indiana

Habitat: Primarily deciduous woodlands but also found in mixed hardwood/conifer forests. May sometimes be found in overgrown fields.

Breeding: Breeds spring through fall with up to four litters per year. 1 to 4 young per litter.

Natural History: Woodland Voles create networks of tunnels just below the ground or "runways" that are near the surface but beneath the leaf litter on the forest floor. These tunnel systems are utilized by other small mammals such as shrews. They rarely venture far from these tunnels, but do emerge to glean seeds, grasses and mast. They also eat roots, especially roots of grasses, and root crops like potatoes are also eaten. Active both day and night. Their subterranean habits render them less vulnerable to many predators, but they are prey for a wide variety of carnivores, raptors, and especially snakes which are able to enter the burrow systems. Owls are another significant predator. Young exhibit a dark gray color. Adults are more chestnut. They often go by the name Pine Vole, especially in the south where they are common in pine forests.

Prairie Vole
Microtus ochreogaster

Size: As much as 6 inches in length and 1.5 ounces.

Abundance: Fairly common.

Variation: No significant variation among adults. Young voles are usually darker in color.

Presumed range in Indiana

Habitat: This species generally avoids the woods and prefers open, grassy habitats and overgrown fields. Unlike the Meadow Vole, uses dry upland fields.

Breeding: Unlike most rodents, Prairie Voles are monogamous. 3 to 5 young is typical.

Natural History: Coarse, grizzled gray fur distinguish this species from the sympatrically occurring Woodland Vole. The similar Meadow Vole (also found throughout the state) has a longer tail. Although insects are eaten, these voles feed mostly on vegetation. Including but not limited to grasses, roots, herbaceous weeds, seeds, leaves, stems, etc. Like other voles they will create a system of shallow burrows. The North American range of this species approximates the occurrence of the original American prairies. It is probably less common today than in historical times, but it is still a widespread and fairly common species in Indiana. Like many small mammals native to Indiana, the population densities of these voles can fluctuate from year to year or even within a calendar year. The exact cause of these fluctuations is not understood.

Class—**Mammalia** (mammals)

Order—**Rodentia** (rodents)

Family—**Muridae** (rats & mice)

Family—**Dipodidae** (jumping mice)

Meadow Vole *Microtus pennsylvanicus*	**Southern Bog Lemming** *Synaptomys cooperi*	**Meadow Jumping Mouse** *Zapus hudsonius*

Size: About 6.5 inches in length and 1.75 oz.

Presumed range in Indiana

Abundance: Very common.

Variation: As many as 25 subspecies are recognized in America, but differences are insignificant.

Habitat: Primarily fields and meadows from the northern US to the Arctic Circle. Shows a preference for damp meadows.

Breeding: A remarkably fecund animal, young Meadow Voles can breed within 4 weeks after birth. Litter size is 4 to 6.

Natural History: Generally regarded as one of the world's most prolific mammals. They may produce a litter every three weeks. Populations in many areas are cyclical and during years of high population density there can be as many as several hundred per acre in prime habitat. Because they can be so common, these voles are an important food source for predatory species ranging from snakes and carnivorous mammals to birds of prey. They can also impact humans by eating crops, garden produce, young trees in orchards, etc. They feed on a wide variety of grasses and plants and will eat seeds, roots and even bark. They maintain surface runways hidden beneath rank grasses and they may be active both day and night. Although they may occur statewide, they are probably more common in northern Indiana than in southern tip of the state.

Size: Adult is about 5 inches in length and weighs 1.25 ounces.

Presumed range in Indiana

Abundance: Can be locally common.

Variation: There are a total of seven subspecies but differences are indistinguishable to the laymen.

Habitat: Although they can found in bogs, they occupy nearly all habitat types. The presence of grasses seems to be the only habitat requirement.

Breeding: Breeds most of year except for mid-winter. Typical litter is three with a maximum of eight.

Natural History: Bog Lemmings often use the same burrows as other mice and vole species. Primarily nocturnal and crepuscular, they feed on green plants and berries mainly, with grasses making up a significant portion of the diet. They often occur in colonies and their presence can be determined by piles of bright green droppings within their runways. Despite their common name they are not closely related to the famous lemmings of Alaska. Bog Lemmings are mainly northern mammals, and the southern Appalachians represent their southernmost distribution today. As with many small mammal species, the numerous subspecies can be told apart only by expert mammologists. The range map above may not be an accurate depiction of this species distribution in Indiana, although most publications do show it being found statewide.

Size: 8 inches (mostly tail, body less than one-third total length).

Presumed range in Indiana

Abundance: Uncommon.

Variation: No sexual dimorphism is noted and there are no subspecies within Indiana.

Habitat: Meadows and fields that contain dense cover. Generally avoids woodlands but may occur in edge areas or tree-line fence rows.

Breeding: 3 to 6 young are born after an 18-day gestation period. Breeds 3 times a year from spring to late summer.

Natural History: This rodent comprises one half of the North American representatives of the family Dipodidae. This unique family also ranges into the Old World. The Meadow Jumping Mouse is distinguished from the similar Woodland Jumping Mouse (not found in Indiana) by the uniformly dark tail (as opposed to a white-tipped tail). All Jumping Mice are mainly nocturnal and do not make runways of their own. But they do frequently use runways made by *Microtus* (voles) or other small rodents. Food items include fungi, insects, seeds, and berries. Jumping Mice put on heavy layers of fat just prior to their long hibernation, but mortality during hibernation is high and many will not survive their winter sleep. These mice are often found near streams or near the edges of marshes and wetlands.

Class—**Mammalia** (mammals)

Order—**Soricomorpha** (insectivorous mammals)

Family—**Sorcidae** (shrews)

Masked Shrew (Cinereus Shrew) *Sorex cinereus*	Southeastern Shrew *Sorex longirostris*	Smoky Shrew *Sorex fumeus*

Size: Maximum of 3.8 inches in length and 0.375 ounce in weight.	Presumed range in Indiana 	**Size:** Maximum of 3.5 inches in length and one-seventh ounce in weight.	Presumed range in Indiana 	**Size:** Maximim length 4.5 inches. Weight is only about 0.5 ounce.	Presumed range in Indiana 
Abundance: Fairly common.		**Abundance:** Fairly common.		**Abundance:** Uncommon in Indiana.	
Variation: Brownish in summer, grayish in winter. Eight subspecies, all appear very similar.		**Variation:** No significant variation occurs in Indiana. Three known subspecies, all very similar.		**Variation:** Winter pelage dark gray, summer pelage is lighter, more gray/ brown.	

Habitat: Found in virtually all wild habitats. Primarily a northern species. Prefers mesic micro-environments and may occur in wetlands.	**Habitat:** Found in a wide variety of habitats. Woods, fields, thickets, etc. May occupy both moist and dry environments.	**Habitat:** Moist woodlands. Especially where there is abundant ground cover. Can be found in both hardwood forests and coniferous forests.
Breeding: Breeds throughout the summer. At least 2 litters of 4 to 6 annually.	**Breeding:** Four to ten tiny (0.5 inch) young are born from spring to fall.	**Breeding:** Litter size averages 5 to 6. Two or three litters in warmer months.
Natural History: Although they are mainly nocturnal animals, these shrews are active both day and night. They dart in and out of leaf litter on the forest floor or move rapidly along runways in overgrown fields. They will make chirping noises as they forage and some believe these sounds are used to echo-locate. Known food items are snails/slugs, caterpillars, grubs, spiders, and ants. They will also eat carrion. Shrews do not hibernate, and must forage year-round. For an animal with such high food requirements, survival in winter would seem a daunting task. But dormant insects and other invertebrates are located and eaten in large quantities. In fact, shrews may be quite beneficial to man by consuming enormous quantities of injurious insects and grubs. The Masked Shrew also frequently goes by the name Cinereous Shrew.	**Natural History:** As with most tiny vertebrates, the Southeastern Shrew has a remarkable metabolic rate and must eat almost constantly to survive. Another characteristic of tiny mammals is a short life span. The maximum life span for the Southeastern Shrew is reported to be about one and a half years. Spiders are reported as the most important food item, but a wide variety of other invertebrates are also eaten. As the name implies, they are found throughout the southeastern United States. They can sometimes be discovered beneath cover boards, tin, or other material placed in suitable habitats to attract small, secretive vertebrates. Many locality records come from herpetologists seeking reptiles beneath cover. The range maps for all the shrews on this page are derived from originals created by Cudmore and Whitaker, Indiana Academy of Sciences.	**Natural History:** This is another primarily northern species that invades the southern United States as far south as northern Georgia in the Appalachian Plateau. Like other shrews it does not hibernate and will be active even in the coldest weather. Its diet is mostly insects and other invertebrates, but salamanders are also listed as prey. The Smokey Shrew, along with other shrew species, is undoubtedly a very beneficial species to man due to the large number of larva, pupae and adult insects consumed daily. Many of which are significant pests to forest trees. The average life span of this species is less than a year and half. The **Pygmy Shrew** (*Sorex hoyi*), not shown, is also found in Indiana and its range closely mimics that of the Smokey Shrew. It is a tiny animal barely more than 2 inches in length and is rarely seen.

Class—**Mammalia** (mammals)

Order—**Soricomorpha** (insectivorous mammals)

Family—**Sorcidae** (shrews)

Northern Short-tailed Shrew *Blarina Brevicauda*	Least Shrew *Cryptotis parva*

Size: Maximum length of about 5.5 inches and weighs 1 ounce.	Presumed range in Indiana 	**Size:** May reach 3 inches and weigh as much as one-fifth ounce.	Presumed range in Indiana 
Abundance: Very common. Probably the most common shrew species in much of its range.		**Abundance:** Probably fairly common but rarely seen due to its tiny size and secretive habits.	
Variation: Eleven known subspecies appear identical to lay persons.		**Variation:** Summer pelage is brownish, turns slate gray in winter.	
Habitat: Fond of damp woodlands and in fact can't tolerate excessively dry conditions. Avoids saturated soils however.		**Habitat:** Grassy areas and overgrown fields primarily, but also in woodlands. Uses rotten logs and old stumps.	

Breeding: Breeding is believed to occur in spring and fall. Up to four litters of 4 to 6 young annually.	**Breeding:** Several litters per year is common averaging 4 to 5 young per litter.

Natural History: This species is easily confused with the Least Shrew, from which it can be distinguished by examining the teeth with the aid of a magnifying glass or dissecting microscope (Least Shrews have three visible unicuspids, Short-tail Shrews have four). Northern Short-tail Shrews are primarily nocturnal animals and have very high metabolic rates. They are hyperactive animals that will eat as much as one-half their body weight daily! The ferocity of shrews is legendary among mammologists. Many have learned the hard way never to place a shrew in a container with a mouse if you want to keep both alive! This species is known to have periods of intense activity followed by periods of lethargy. Food is a variety of insects, snails, earthworms, millipedes, etc. as well as much larger prey including mice that are as large as themselves. The Northern Short-tailed Shrew is known to possess venomous saliva with which it kills its prey. It has tiny eyes and its vision is quite poor. Known to utilize echolocation. Some sounds they produce are audible to humans, but others are not. It is believed that these "ultrasonic" sounds act like a form of radar to detect objects in their path, rather like what is known in bats. Except when breeding and rearing young these are solitary animals. They forage beneath the leaf litter in runways and tunnels and will dig their own tunnels or use those of other small rodents.

Natural History: Possessing an extremely high metabolism, this tiny mammal can consume its own weight in food daily. Known food items are caterpillars, beetles, other insects, snails, spiders and earthworms. Like many other shrews they are known to cache food items. Although these shrews are rarely seen due to their diminutive size and reclusive habits, they are usually a fairly common mammal. Owls are a major predator and in fact the presence of these tiny shrews in a given area is often confirmed by examining owl pellets for skeleton remains. When owls catch a small animal like a shrew they typically swallow it whole. All the soft body parts are digested but the bone and fur is regurgitated in a compact pellet know as a "casting." Biologists studying shrews will look for owl roosts where they can search ground below for these castings and retrieve the skulls of the small mammals eaten by the owl. Using this technique biologists can easily determine what small mammal species exist in the area and how common each species may be. Very small mammals like the Least Shrew can be difficult to trap since they don't weigh enough to trip the mechanism on most small mammal traps. Thus owls have unwittingly contributed to our understanding of several species of small, secretive mammals. This species, along with the Pygmy Shrew are among the smallest mammals in North America.

Class—**Mammalia** (mammals)	
Order—**Soricomorpha** (insectivorous mammals)	
Family—**Talpidae** (moles)	

Eastern Mole *Zapus hudsonius*	**Star-nosed Mole** *Condylura cristata*

 |

Close-up of snout

Size: 6 inches in length and weighs about 2 ounces.	Presumed range in Indiana 	**Size:** Total length 7 inches. Weight 2 ounces.	Presumed range in Indiana 
Abundance: Very common. This is the mole that is typically the bane of gardeners in Indiana.		**Abundance:** Uncommon. The IDNR lists this mole as a Species of Concern in Indiana.	
Variation: No significant regional variations noted. Males are slightly larger than females.		**Variation:** No sexual dimorphism or regional variation noted. Juvenile specimens have darker pelage.	
Habitat: Except for wetlands these moles can be found anywhere soils are suitable for burrowing.		**Habitat:** Wet meadows, swamps, mesic woodlands and stream courses. Even inhabits muddy habitats.	

Breeding: One litter per year in early spring. 2 to 5 young. Underground nest chamber is lined with dried grass.	**Breeding:** Breeds in late winter and litters of 2 to7 are born in early spring.

Natural History: The most wide-ranging mole in America. Although considered a pest in suburban lawns and rural gardens, Eastern Moles actually perform some helpful tasks. The tunnels they dig help to aerate the soil and allow rainfall to penetrate more easily. They also prey heavily upon destructive grubs such as the Japanese Beetle. The pelage of the Eastern Mole is "reversible" and will lie smoothly against the skin whether mole is moving forward or backward in tight tunnels. The powerful forelegs allow this animal to burrow at an astonishing pace, and the webbed toes help move dirt aside. The eyes are tiny and covered with skin, and there are no external ears. This is an animal that is superbly adapted to a subterranean lifestyle and Eastern Moles will spend 99 percent of their lives below ground. They are sometimes found above ground following heavy rains when their tunnels may become flooded. They will share their territory and their tunnels with other moles. The surface tunnels seen as lines of raised earth in lawns and gardens are primarily dug as the mole forages for food. Permanent travel tunnels are deeper underground and this is where they will spend most of their time during winter. Hard clay soils can be a barrier to their dispersal. Although they can swim well they usually avoid permanent wetlands and swamps. For all practical purposes moles are blind, but they can probably detect light.	**Natural History:** Morphologically speaking, this is surely one of America's most unusual animals. The tip of the snout is adorned with fleshy tentacles. At first glance it resembles a mole with a sea anemone (or perhaps a small octopus) attached to its nose! The fleshy tentacles are most likely tactile in function, and some experts cite evidence that they may also serve to detect electrical impulses emitted by fish and other aquatic animals (Whitaker & Hamilton, 1998). In habits this mole is also unique among the Talpidae of the eastern US in that they are decidedly aquatic animals. Their tunnels sometimes open directly into streams and they are excellent swimmers. Aquatic insects, worms, and even crustaceans and small fish are frequently captured underwater. Their primary food appears to be earthworms and the unusual tentacled "star" on the snout undoubtedly plays an important role in locating the moles' food. While this species is generally regarded as rare or uncommon in Indiana, Whitaker and Mumford in their essential reference book *The Mammals of Indiana* state that "We feel that this species is probably common in some parts of its northeastern Indiana range and has a wider distribution than previously known." The map above may not be exactly accurate for its range in the state. There is obviously still much to be learned about this fascinating species in the state of Indiana.

Class—**Mammalia** (mammals)

Order—**Chiroptera** (bats)

Family—**Vespertilionidae** (mouse-eared bats)

Hoary Bat *Lasiurus cinereous*	**Eastern Red Bat** *Lasiurus borealis*	**Big Brown Bat** *Eptisicus fuscus*

Size: Maximum 5.5 inches. Wingspan to 16 inches.	Presumed range in Indiana	**Size:** Maximum 5 inches. Up to 0.5 oz. Wingspan 13 inches.	Presumed range in Indiana	**Size:** 4.5 inches and nearly 1 oz. Wingspan 14 inches.	Presumed range in Indiana
Abundance: Uncommon. IDNR Species of Special Concern.		**Abundance:** In decline and considered a species of Special Concern by IDNR.		**Abundance:** Common. These bats are widespread in the United States.	
Variation: Females average slightly heavier than males.		**Variation:** Males are red, females are chestnut or yellowish.		**Variation:** No significant variation in Indiana.	

Habitat: Forest species primarily. Also occurs in towns and farmlands.	**Habitat:** Woodlands and edge areas. Large trees widely spaced, urban parks.	**Habitat:** Open fields, vacant lots. Large and small towns and farmlands.
Breeding: Averages two pups born in mid-May to mid-June.	**Breeding:** Litter size is 1 to 4 with the pups born in late May or early June.	**Breeding:** Several litters per year is common averaging 4 to 5 young per litter.

Natural History: With a wingspan of 16 inches, this is the largest bat species in Indiana. Its name comes from the white-tipped hairs of the fur on its back. Hoary Bats have the greatest distribution of any American Bat. They summer as far north as Canada and winter in the coastal plain of the southeastern United States or in the desert southwest. Most of the Hoary Bats seen in Indiana are migrating to and from summer/winter residences. Although they are not rare during spring and fall migrations, they are not usually seen at other times of the year. Oddly, the sexes segregate themselves following breeding and most of those seen in the eastern United States in summer are females. Males summer farther west in the great plains, Rocky Mountains, or west coast. Like the Red Bat these bats are mostly solitary and roost among the foliage in trees. Moths are reported to be their primary food. Likes open woodlands with widely spaced trees or urban parks.

Natural History: In summer this species usually roosts in trees by hanging from a limb. Usually solitary but sometimes more than one bat will roost together. Roosting bats resemble dead leaves. Trees chosen for roosting are often at the edge of a woodland bordering an open field. Red Bats are migratory and summer in Indiana while wintering farther to the south. They may linger well into the fall and begin arriving in as early as late March. Their total range in America is quite large and includes most of the United States east of the Rocky Mountains and much of southeastern Canada. Hibernation takes place in hollow trees or beneath leaf litter on the forest floor, a very unusual tactic for a bat! Though mainly nocturnal, this species often flies in daylight, especially in late afternoon or early evening. Their habit of roosting on low hanging branches at woodland edges makes them fairly conspicuous. They like open woodlands with widely spaced trees.

Natural History: More cold tolerant than most bats. Winters in caves or derelict buildings. Summer roosts are usually associated with human structures (buildings, eaves, bridges). Also known to use hollow trees and abandoned mines. The primary food is reported to be beetles. These are the large, brown bats that are common around human habitations and they range throughout the state. These bats seem to tolerate cold fairly well and they remain active well into the fall. They can sometimes even be seen flying around on warm days in winter. Small flying beetles are a favorite food item, but a wide variety of insects are eaten. This bat is a useful consumer of insect pests and is thus a valuable friend to man. Like many bats in America, it has been hard hit by the fungal infection known as "White-nose Syndrome." The impact of this devastating disease on ecosystems is yet to be determined, but it will almost certainly be detrimental.

Class—**Mammalia** (mammals)
Order—**Chiroptera** (bats)
Family—**Vespertilionidae** (mouse-eared bats)
Genus—*Myotis* (myotis bats)

Gray Bat *Myotis grisescens*	**Northern Bat** *Myotis septentrionalis*	**Little Brown Bat** *Myotis lucifugus*

Size: All *Myotis* are somewhat small bats, ranging in size from 3 to 3.5 inches and weighing from one-fifth to one-third of an ounce. The Gray Bat is the largest (3.5 inches), with one of America's smallest being the Eastern Small-footed Bat (3 inches in length and about one-fifth of an ounce).

Abundance: The Myotis Bats found in Indiana range in abundance from common to rare. The rarer species are the Gray Bat (federally endangered, restricted to southern tip of the state) and the **Indiana Bat**, *M. sodalis*, (not shown, widespread but federally endangered). The Northern Bat and the Little Brown Bat are both widespread but are both regarded as state endangered. One other *Myotis* species, the Southeastern Bat, once occurred in southern Indiana but is today apparently extirpated. Nearly all these bats were until recent times fairly common in America but they have been hard hit by the deadly fungal disease known as "White-nosed Syndrome."

Variation: Most bats present an identification problem for the average person, but the Myotis Bats can be especially confusing. Confirming the exact species usually requires looking very closely and may sometimes mean having the bat in hand. An exception would be the Gray Bats, that can be told from *other myotis bats* by their decidedly grayish coloration.

Presumed collective range of the Myotis Bats in Indiana

Habitat: Gray Bats are true cave dwellers, using caves for hibernation, roosting and rearing young. Other *Myotis* species may hibernate in caves but will also use other places such as hollow trees or buildings for summer-time roosts. Some species are sometimes seen roosting in clumps by day beneath the shelter of roof overhangs, roofs of picnic pavilions, inside old barns, etc. A wide variety of habitats are utilized by these bats during warmer months including forests, fields, wetlands, and especially stream courses. Some species, like the Little Brown Bat will sometimes roost in buildings, including attics of inhabited houses. The Northern Bat has been known to use buildings as a winter refuge.

Breeding: Mating occurs in the fall with fertilization delayed until early spring. Young are born in late spring or early summer and all species form "maternity colonies" of females with young which may be in caves, buildings, hollow trees, or other structures. *Myotis* bats produce a single baby annually, except for the Southeastern Bat which can give birth to twins.

Natural History: Virtually the entire population of Gray Bats in America hibernate in a handful of caves scattered across the southeastern United States. Indiana Bats (*Myotis sodalis*-not shown) are also known for their huge hibernating colonies that tend to concentrate in only a few select caves during winter. Both species are thus vulnerable to human or natural disturbance of their select hibernating locales. Some *Myotis* Bats are migratory, moving south during winter months. Most feed in flight on flying insects but one species (Northern Bat) feeds by gleaning insects from leaves while hovering. Some like to forage primarily over water above ponds, creeks, and wetland areas (Little Brown Bat, Gray Bat). Throughout America, many bat species are in steep decline and many once common species have been hard hit by a fungal disease known as "White Nose Syndrome." The Little Brown Bat, once perhaps the most common *Myotis* in America, has been especially hard hit by this disease. All bats are remarkable little animals that consume untold numbers of injurious insect species, including many millions of mosquitoes, and they are thus extremely useful to man. Their reputation for harboring the rabies virus is factual, but the threat to the average person is grossly overstated. There is a common myth that any bat seen abroad during daylight is rabid. In fact, some bats will fly in late afternoon or on warm days in winter, and their appearance in daylight does not mean a rabid bat. Bats found on the ground however, should not be handled. Though some bats will roost or even hibernate beneath leaf litter on the forest floor, bats on the ground and out in the open may in fact be sick and infected and should thus be left alone. Two other *Myotis* bats occur in Indiana. They are the **Southeastern Bat** (*M. austroriparius*) and **Small-footed Bat** (*M. leibii*).

Class—**Mammalia** (mammals)
Order—**Chiroptera** (bats)
Family—**Vespertilionidae** (mouse-eared bats)

Silver-haired Bat *Lasionycterius noctivagans*	**Tri-colored Bat** *Pipistrellus subflavus*	**Evening Bat** *Nycticeius humeralis*

Size: Maximum length of 4 inches and one-third ounce.	**Size:** 3.5 inches. Weight about 0.25 oz. Wingspan 9 inches.	**Size:** Maximum length 4 inches. Weighs 0.5 ounce.
Presumed range in Indiana	Presumed range in Indiana	Presumed range in Indiana 
Abundance: Species of Concern in Indiana.	**Abundance:** Declining. Endangered in Indiana.	**Abundance:** Declining. Endangered in Indiana.
Habitat: Mainly a species of forests and woodland edges. Roosts under bark.	**Habitat:** Woodlands. Hunts along stream courses and edge areas.	**Habitat:** Swamps, stream corridors, wooded bottomlands.
Variation: Mostly grayish, rarely brownish.	**Variation:** Various shades of brown. Immatures grayish.	**Variation:** Adults are brown, juveniles darker.
Breeding: Young are born in late spring. Two pups is typical.	**Breeding:** Litter size is 1 to 4 with the pups born in late May or early June.	**Breeding:** Several litters per year is common averaging 4 to 5 young per litter.
Natural History: This is a widespread species that ranges from coast to coast in North America. In summer this species ranges as far north as Canada and southeastern Alaska. In fact this species is more common in summer months in northern regions. In Indiana this is apparently a migrant species that leaves the state in summer for more northerly forests. It is probably most common in spring and fall and may overwinter in the southern part of the state. Unlike many bat species the Silver-haired Bat is mostly a solitary animal that roosts singly, although some colony activity is reported among females with young. Silver-haireds derive their name from the "frosted" appearance of their pelage, a unique and identifying characteristic among Indiana's bats. Feeding flights are mostly near water.	**Natural History:** Also known as the Eastern Pipistrelle, this bat ranges throughout the eastern US. They will leave the roost before dark and are often seen hunting at dusk. Like many bats the females form maternal colonies where young are reared, often in buildings or sheds. Unlike many other species however, these maternal colonies are usually small, numbering only one or two dozen individuals. Hibernation begins in late fall (October) and lasts until April or May. Hibernating bats may lose as much as 25 to 30 percent of their body weight before emerging in the spring. Uniquely among bats, hibernating *Pipistrellus* bats accumulate water droplets on their fur. Why this happens is not fully understood. When flying these little bats move slowly in a very erratic manner and in flight they resemble a large moth.	**Natural History:** Evening Bats in Indiana are summer residents that winter farther south where hibernation is not necessary. Most leave by early fall, but some may stay into late fall. Summer roosts include hollow trees as well as buildings, and they do not seem to utilize caves as is the habit of many bat species. A wide variety of small insects are eaten, including species that are injurious to farm crops. Though widespread across much of the southeast, these are lowland and low plateau animals that avoid the higher elevations of the Appalachian Mountains. Most of these bats found in the northern portions of their range in summer are females, with the males apparently staying farther to the south. This separation of sexes during certain times of the year is not an uncommon trait among bats.

CHAPTER 4

THE BIRDS OF INDIANA

TABLE 2

— THE ORDERS AND FAMILIES OF INDIANA BIRDS —

Class—**Aves** (birds)

Order—**Passeriformes** (songbirds)

Family	**Tyrannidae** (flycatchers)
Family	**Turdidae** (thrushes)
Family	**Lanidae** (shrikes)
Family	**Aluidae** (larks)
Family	**Mimidae** (thrasher family)
Family	**Motacillidae** (wagtails & pipits)
Family	**Bombycillidae** (waxwings)
Family	**Certhidae** (creepers)
Family	**Paridae** (chickadee family)
Family	**Regulidae** (kinglets)
Family	**Sittidae** (nuthatches)
Family	**Troglodytidae** (wrens)
Family	**Polioptilidae** (gnatcatchers)
Family	**Hirundinidae** (swallows)
Family	**Corvidae** (crows & jays)
Family	**Vironidae** (vireos)
Family	**Parulidae** (warblers)
Family	**Icturidae** (blackbirds)
Family	**Sturnidae** (starling)
Family	**Passeridae** (european sparrows)
Family	**Emberzidae** (sparrows)
Family	**Calcaridae** (longspurs & snow bunting)
Family	**Cardinalidae** (tanagers & grosbeaks)
Family	**Fringillidae** (finches)

Order—**Apodiformes** (swifts & hummingbirds)

Family	**Apodidae** (swifts)

Family	**Trochylidae** (hummingbirds)

Order—**Coraciiformes**

Family	**Alcedinidae** (kingfishers)

Order—**Piciformes**

Family	**Picidae** (woodpeckers)

Order—**Cuculiformes**

Family	**Cuculidae** (cuckoos)

Order—**Columbiformes**

Family	**Columbidae** (doves)

Order—**Galliformes** (chicken-like birds)

Family	**Phasianidae** (grouse)
Family	**Odontophoridae** (quail)

Order—**Caprimulgiformes**

Family	**Caprimulgidae** (nightjars)

Order—**Strigiformes** (owls)

Family	**Tytonidae** (barn owl)
Family	**Strigidae** (typical owls)

Order—**Falconiformes** (raptors)

Family	**Accipitridae** (hawks, eagles, kites)
Family	**Falconidae** (falcons)

Order—**Cathartiformes** (vultures)

Family	**Cathartidae**

Order—**Ciconiiformes** (wading birds)

Family	**Ardeidae** (herons)
Family	**Ciconiidae** (storks)

Order—**Gruiformes** (rails & cranes)

Family	**Rallidae** (rails)
Family	**Gruidae** (cranes)

Order—**Charadriiformes** (shorebirds)

Family	**Charadriidae** (plovers)
Family	**Scolapacidae** (sandpipers)
Family	**Laridae** (gulls & terns)

Order—**Suliformes**

Family	**Phalacrocoracidae** (cormorants)

Order—**Pelicaniformes**

Family	**Pelecanidae** (pelicans)

Order—**Gaviiformes**

Family	**Gaviidae** (loons)

Order—**Podicipediformes**

Family	**Podicipedidae** (grebes)

Order—**Anseriiformes** (waterfowl)

Family	**Anatidae** (ducks, geese & swans)

Class—**Aves** (birds)

Order—**Passeriformes** (songbirds)

Family—**Tyrannidae** (flycatchers)

Eastern Wood Pewee *Contopus virens*	**Olive-sided Flycatcher** *Contopus cooperi*	**Eastern Phoebe** *Sayornis phoebe*

Size: 6.5 inches.

Abundance: Common.

Variation: None. Sexes are alike.

Habitat: Wood Pewees are forest birds but they favor small openings in the woods or edge areas.

Presumed range in Indiana

Migratory Status: Wintering in South America, the Eastern Wood Pewee arrives in North America in late spring (peak arrival in mid-May). They are a summer/breeding resident across the eastern half of America that stays throughout the summer. They begin leaving in late August with a few lingering into early October.

Breeding: Nests are usually built high in trees in a terminal fork. Nest material consists of grasses and lichens. 2 to 4 eggs are laid.

Natural History: These nondescript little brown birds often go unnoticed except for the distinctive call from which they derive their name. Their "pee-a-weee" song is a common summer sound in the woodlands throughout the eastern US. Like other members of the flycatcher family, they hunt flying insects from high perches, swooping out to catch their food on the wing. They are typically fairly tolerant of humans and can sometimes be closely approached. They are very similar to Eastern Phoebe, but note orange lower bill and pale wing bars on the Eastern Wood Pewee.

Size: 7.5 inches.

Abundance: Uncommon to rare.

Variation: None. Sexes are alike.

Habitat: The summer habitat is coniferous forests of mountains and northern North America.

Presumed range in Indiana

Migratory Status: A spring and fall passage migrant in Indiana. Birds that pass through the state spend the summer in the boreal forests of Canada and winter from southern Mexico to South America. Spring migrants begin to arrive in state in May and have moved on by mid-June. Fall migration through state is mid-August through September.

Breeding: Nest is typically on a branch of a conifer and built of sticks, lichens and rootlets. One clutch per year. 3 to 4 eggs per clutch.

Natural History: These flycatchers are quite acrobatic in the air. They feed in typical flycatcher fashion by sallying forth from a high perch to snatch flying insects. Bees and wasps are reportedly a favorite food. This species avoids deep forest in favor of openings such as bogs, meadows or second growth and may benefit from forest fires or human activities such as logging. Paradoxically, the species has been declining in recent decades. This decline is possibly tied to changes in the winter habitat in tropical America. They are federally listed as Species of Concern by the USFWS.

Size: 7 inches.

Abundance: Common.

Variation: None. Sexes are alike.

Habitat: Woodlands and woods openings. Also in rural yards or parks in wooded regions.

Presumed range in Indiana

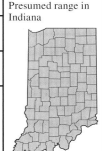

Migratory Status: Eastern Phoebes begin to arrive in the Midwest as early as March, perhaps a little later in the northernmost portion of Indiana. They are summer residents that will nest in the state. Fall migration begins late September through October and in the southernmost region of the state a few may linger into the winter.

Breeding: Phoebes are early nesters. Nesting can occur by early April and there will often be a second nesting later in the summer.

Natural History: The Eastern Phoebe is most easily told from other Flycatchers by its habit of constantly wagging its tail down and up. Its nests are also distinctive, being constructed of mud and lined with mosses. Nests are placed beneath some form of overhang, most often the eaves of buildings. The cup-shaped nest is plastered to the surface in the manner of many swallows. These are normally tame little birds that will allow humans to approach to within a few yards before flying off only a short distance. Similar to the Wood Pewee but has a dark bill and lacks wing bars.

Class—**Aves** (birds)

Order—**Passeriformes** (songbirds)

Family—**Tyrannidae** (flycatchers)

Empid Flycatchers
genus—*Empidonax* (5 nearly identical species in Indiana)

Acadian Flycatcher *Empidonax virescens*	**Willow Flycatcher** *Empidonax traillii*	**Least Flycatcher** *Empidonax minimus*

Alder Flycatcher *Empidonax alnorum*	**Yellow-bellied Flycatcher** *Empidonax flaviventris*	Combined range of all five *Empidonax* Flycatchers in Indiana
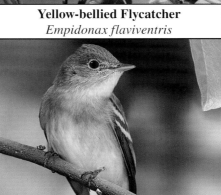		

Size: Range in size from 5.25 to 5.75 inches.

Abundance: Least Flycatcher is fairly common throughout its broader range but has declined in some regions of the Midwest. Alder Flycatcher may be the least common of the group. Acadian is probably the most common. Willow and Yellow-bellied are probably fairly common.

Variation: Five species of *Empidonax* flycatchers may be seen in Indiana. All five species are so similar in appearance that even expert bird watchers have trouble identifying individual species. Most people must content themselves with calling them all "Empid Flycatchers."

Migratory Status: The Yellow-bellied Flycatcher and the Alder Flycatcher are spring and fall migrants that merely pass through the state. The other three *Empidonax* flycatchers all probably breed in the state. All winter far to south, some as far as South America. They return mid-May to mid-June. All begin to leave in August and are gone by mid-September.

Habitat: All are woodland species. Acadian and Willow Flycatchers are fond of stream-side habitats, swamps and marshes. Least Flycatchers prefer regenerative woodlands and edge areas. Yellow-bellied Flycatchers summer in the boreal forests of the far north. Both the Alder Flycatcher and the Least Flycatcher also range well to the north into Canada. All five species may be seen throughout the state during migration.

Breeding: The Acadian Flycatcher weaves a flimsy nest of grass on a low branch and lays 2 to 4 eggs. Willow Flycatchers build their nest in the fork of a low branch or bush and lay 2 to 4 eggs. Least Flycatcher breeds mostly to the north of Indiana but a few will breed in the northern part of the state. They usually lay 4 eggs in a nest woven of grasses and fibers and placed in a fork of a tree branch. Alder Flycatcher nests are coarsely woven cups typically placed in low bushes with 4 eggs.

Natural History: Some species, like the Acadian Flycatcher, may be less numerous today due to the decline in forested habitats. The Willow Flycatcher on the other hand may be helped by the regeneration of successional forests. Serious birdwatchers find that the most reliable way to identify these small flycatchers is to learn their songs. In fact, Willow and Alder Flycatchers are so similar in appearance that visual identification alone is usually unreliable.

Class—**Aves** (birds)
Order—**Passeriformes** (songbirds)
Family—**Tyrannidae** (flycatchers)

Eastern Kingbird *Tyrannus tyrannus*	**Great Crested Flycatcher** *Myiarchus crinitus*

Size: 8.5 inches.	Presumed range in Indiana	**Size:** 8.75 inches.	Presumed range in Indiana
Abundance: Common.		**Abundance:** Fairly common.	
Variation: None. Sexes alike.		**Variation:** None. Sexes alike.	
Migratory Status: A summertime resident that nests in the state. Winters entirely in South America, mainly in Amazonian regions of Columbia and Ecuador. Movement north begins in late April with some birds not arriving until early May. Departs in September.		**Migratory Status:** A summertime resident. Arrives in the state in April or early May. Some birds will winter in peninsula Florida, but most winter in Central America or Mexico. Some migrate through the Caribbean. Others up the coast of Texas or across the Gulf of Mexico.	

Habitat: Prefers open fields and pastures in rural areas. In urban settings it likes open parks and large empty lots. Commonly seen perched on fences or power lines.	**Habitat:** Openings in deciduous and mixed woodlands. Edge areas and open woodlands are also used. Winter habitat is tropical forests of many types.
Breeding: The nest is built of twigs and grass high in trees. The average clutch size is 3 to 5 eggs. One clutch per year. Sturdy nest is placed on limb near the top of large tree.	**Breeding:** Unlike most flycatchers this bird is a cavity nester, often using old woodpecker holes or natural knotholes in trees. 3 to 5 eggs, laid in mid-May, is typical.
Natural History: The name "Kingbird" is derived from this species aggressive defense of territory against other birds, including even large hawks! They hunt flying insects from an open perch, which is frequently a fence or power line. When flying insect prey is spotted they will launch themselves into an attack that often results in an aerial "dogfight" between bird and insect. They will also hunt flying insects by hovering. Berries are an important food item, especially mulberries. Serviceberries, blackberries, and elderberries are also eaten. These are conspicuous birds. Their charcoal gray upper parts contrast strongly with a whitish breast and belly. The bright reddish-orange blaze on the top of the head is usually not visible to the casual observer. Winters in South America, as far south as Argentina. Some populations in the eastern United States have shown declines in the last few decades.	**Natural History:** The name comes from the "crested" look of the head, which may not be readily apparent. Reddish underside of the tail and wing primaries along with the distinctly yellowish belly contrasting with gray breast is unique among Indiana flycatchers. These features plus large size make it one of the more recognizable members of the flycatcher family. However, they are a rather unobtrusive species that can be easily overlooked. Food is large insects captured in flight from its perch, which is often high in the canopy. Typically returns in late April from wintering grounds in Central America. Forages for insects in treetops and catches flying insects on the wing. Also consumes some berries. More common in the southeastern United States than in the Midwest. Breeding success may be tied to woodpecker populations since old woodpecker holes are a favorite nesting site.

Class—**Aves** (birds)

Order—**Passeriformes** (songbirds)

Family—**Turdidae** (thrush family)

American Robin *Turdus migratorius*	**Eastern Bluebird** *Siala sialis*	**Wood Thrush** *Hylocichla mustela*

American Robin	Eastern Bluebird	Wood Thrush
Size: 10 inches.	**Size:** 7 inches.	**Size:** 7 inches.
Abundance: Very common.	**Abundance:** Fairly common.	**Abundance:** Uncommon.
Variation: Male is more brightly colored than female.	**Variation:** Significant sexual dimorphism. See photo above.	**Variation:** No significant variation and no sexual dimorphism.
Migratory Status: Migratory but can be seen year-round in Indiana.	**Migratory Status:** Mostly a summer resident in Indiana.	**Migratory Status:** A summer resident. Winters to South America.
Presumed range in Indiana	Presumed range in Indiana	Presumed range in Indiana
Habitat: Virtually all habitats in the state may be utilized. Most common in areas of human disturbance, especially older suburbs. They are fond of hunting earthworms in suburban lawns.	**Habitat:** Field edges, woods openings, and open fields, marshes, and pastures. Savanna like habitats, (i.e. open spaces interspersed with large trees), are a favorite habitat.	**Habitat:** Woodlands. May be found in both mature forests and successional areas. In both it likes thick undergrowth. On wintering grounds uses tropical rainforests.
Breeding: The 3 to 4 "sky blue" eggs are laid in a nest constructed of mud and grass, often in the crotch of a tree in an urban yard.	**Breeding:** Bluebirds are cavity nesters that readily take to man-made nest boxes. Two broods per summer is common. 3 to 6 eggs per clutch.	**Breeding:** Nest is mud, twigs, and grass similar to that of the Robin. Nest may be in under story or at mid-level. Lays 2 to 5 blue-green eggs.
Natural History: Despite the fact that the Robin is a migratory species, individuals are seen in Indiana year-round. It is likely that the state's summer residents retreat south during winter and are replaced by southward moving individuals that have summered much farther to the north. In winter they are sometimes seen in large migratory flocks numbering over 100 birds. Certainly one of the best known of America's bird species, Robins are commonly seen on both urban and rural lawns throughout the America. They may also be seen in remote wilderness areas. Their overall range coincides almost precisely with that of the North American Continent. The Latin name *migratorius* is appropriate for this species and its summer range extends all the way to the Arctic. Feeds heavily on earthworms.	**Natural History:** The Eastern Bluebirds habit of readily adapting to artificial nest boxes has helped bring them back from alarmingly low numbers decades ago, when rampant logging of eastern forests depleted nest cavities. They are primarily insect eaters and are vulnerable to exceptionally harsh winters. Harsh winter weather will prompt a mass movement south and prolonged periods of very cold weather can literally wipe out entire populations that are caught too far north. A few will overwinter in the southern parts of the state but most will move farther south. In winter Bluebirds eat many types of berries and will readily eat raisins from feeders. Their popularity among humans has lead to the establishment of The North American Bluebird Society, dedicated to Bluebird conservation.	**Natural History:** The Wood Thrush feeds on insects, spiders, earthworms and other invertebrates found by foraging beneath leaf mold on the forest floor. They will also feed on berries which can be an important food during fall migration. Like many songbirds this species is threatened by the fragmentation of forest habitats throughout North America. Smaller forest tracts make it easier for Cowbirds to find Wood Thrush nests. Consequently nest predation by Cowbirds is increasing and may be one reason for recent population declines. This threat is especially pronounced in the Midwest where so much of the forest habitats have been depleted. The exceptional song of the Wood Thrush is usually described as "flute-like," or "ethereal" and is heard mostly at dawn and dusk.

Class—**Aves** (birds)

Order—**Passeriformes** (songbirds)

Family—**Turdidae** (thrush family)

Hermit Thrush *Catharus guttatus*	**Veery** *Catharus fuscescens*	**Swainson's Thrush** *Catharus ustulatus*

Size: 7 inches.	**Size:** 7 inches.	**Size:** 7 inches.
Abundance: Fairly common.	**Abundance:** Uncommon.	**Abundance:** Fairly common.
Habitat: Damp woodlands, thickets, and successional areas with heavy undergrowth of bushes and shrubs. Also in urban parks.  Presumed range in Indiana	**Habitat:** Under story of deciduous woodlands. Most common in second growth forest with thick undergrowth. Rare in urban parks.  Presumed range in Indiana	**Habitat:** Moist to wet woodlands and swamps with heavy underbrush and cool, heavily shaded woods. Can be seen in suburbs and parks.  Presumed range in Indiana
Variation: Varies slightly from reddish brown to grayish brown.	**Variation:** Eastern birds are reddish, those from farther west are duller.	**Variation:** Varies from grayish brown to olive brown.
Migratory Status: Mostly a spring fall migrant. Lingers in northern Indiana in fall. May be seen throughout the winter in extreme southern Indiana.	**Migratory Status:** Spring and fall migrant throughout most of the state. A few will summer in northern Indiana, mostly in the northernmost portion.	**Migratory Status:** Spring and fall migrant. Winters in South America and summers quite far to the north in Canada and even Alaska.
Breeding: 3 to 5 bluish-green eggs are laid in a nest built just above ground level. Most will nest in the boreal forests of Canada. No nesting in Indiana.	**Breeding:** Breeds mostly farther north, but some nesting in northern Indiana. Nest is hidden in thickets on or near the ground. From 3 to 5 eggs are laid.	**Breeding:** Builds its moss-lined nest in a coniferous tree in boreal forest well to the north of Indiana. Lays 3 to 5 eggs that are blue with brown spots.
Natural History: Any Thrush seen in Indiana during the winter is most likely to be this species. They are rather shy but less so than other *Catharus* and they will sometimes visit feeders for suet or raisins. They feed mainly on insects found on the forest floor and beneath leaf mold, but berries are also an important element in the diet, especially in winter. The song of the Hermit Thrush is regarded by many as one of the more beautiful summer sounds in the northern forests. Although secretive their presence during winter makes them more conspicuous. Unlike most other thrush species, populations of the Hermit Thrush appear stable. As with other thrush species the Hermit Thrush is known for the quality of its song which is often describe as melancholy.	**Natural History:** Although the Veery is widespread during migration, they are hard to observe in much of the eastern US since most are usually just passing through and they migrate mostly at night. One of the more secretive of the thrushes, they stay mostly in thick undergrowth where they feed on a variety of insects, earthworms, spiders and berries. Bird watchers often confirm this bird's presence by recognizing its distinctive call, which has been described as "hauntingly beautiful." This species has shown a downward population trend in many regions of its range in North America. Factors cited as possibly contributing to this trend are loss of wintering habitat in South America and fragmentation of breeding habitats in North America.	**Natural History:** Another secretive, difficult to observe thrush that in migration flies by night and spends its days resting and feeding in heavy undergrowth. As with many of the thrushes, positive identification can be difficult. This species and the Gray-cheeked Thrush are easily confused. The buff colored cheeks are a good identification character. Like others of its kind the Swainson's Thrush feeds on insects and invertebrates as well as berries. Unlike others of its genus however this thrush is known to feed higher in trees (most other thrushes feed mostly on the ground). Spring migration in the Midwest begins in late April and runs through mid-May. Fall migration peaks in September. Like other thrushes this bird is easier heard than seen.

Class—**Aves** (birds)

Order—**Passeriformes** (songbirds)

Family—**Turdidae** (thrush family)	Family—**Lanidae** (shrikes)	Family—**Alauidae** (larks)

Gray-cheeked Thrush
Catharus minimus

Size: 7.25 inches.

Presumed range in Indiana

Abundance:
Uncommon. Our least common thrush.

Variation: Overall coloration varies from grayish to brownish.

Migratory Status: A secretive night-time spring and fall migrant that is easily missed.

Habitat: Summer habitats are boreal forests. Winters in South America. May be seen in woodlands throughout the state during migration.

Breeding: Breeds in remote tundra and taiga in northern Canada and Alaska. Lays 3 to 6 eggs.

Natural History: Secretive and uncommon, the biology of the Gray-cheeked Thrush is poorly known. Its summer habitats are dense spruce forests and willow/alder thickets in the far north. Breeding range extends well into the Arctic Circle and winter range is at least as far south as northern South America. Differentiating between the various thrush species can be challenging. The Gray-cheeked Thrush is easily confused with both the Swainson's Thrush and the Hermit Thrush but can be told by the gray color of the cheek. Another similar thrush, the Bicknell's Thrush (not seen in Indiana), is one of America's newest described bird species and was once regarded as being the same species as the Gray Cheeked Thrush. This is the least common of the thrushes in Indiana.

Loggerhead Shrike
Lanius

Size: 10 inches.

Presumed range in Indiana

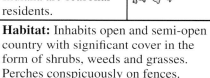

Northern Shrike

Loggerhead Shrike

Abundance:
Endangered in Indiana.

Variation: Sexes alike. Juveniles show faint barring below.

Migratory Status: Both Shrike species in Indiana are seasonal residents.

Habitat: Inhabits open and semi-open country with significant cover in the form of shrubs, weeds and grasses. Perches conspicuously on fences.

Breeding: Nest is built low to the ground (3 to 5 feet) in thick shrubs or small trees in thickets. Lays 4 to 6 eggs.

Natural History: These fierce little birds are much like a miniature raptor. They hunt mostly insects, but will also attack and kill lizards, mice, small snakes and birds as large as themselves. Sometimes called "Butcher Bird," they kill with a powerful beak and have the unusual habit of caching food items by impaling the bodies of prey onto a thorn or fence barb. There are actually two nearly identical Shrike species in Indiana. The other species is the **Northern Shrike,** *Lanius excubitor.* While the Loggerhead Shrike is a southern species that moves north into the southern portion of Indiana in summer, the Northern Shrike lives in the far north and moves south into northern Indiana in winter (see range map above). Both species are uncommon in the state and Indiana represents the periphery of their range.

Horned Lark
Eremophila alpestris

Size: 7.5 inches.

Presumed range in Indiana

Abundance:
Fairly common, especially in winter.

Variation: Sexes similar. Males more vividly colored.

Migratory Status: Year-round, but more common during spring and fall.

Habitat: This is a prairie species that is seen only in expansive, open fields. Large, harvested crop fields are the primary habitat for this bird in winter.

Breeding: Nests on barren ground. Lays 3 to 5 eggs. Breeds in open regions throughout most of Indiana.

Natural History: This prairie species needs open ground and has probably benefited from human activity in the eastern United States as a result of land clearing and agricultural operations. Closely cropped pastures or tilled lands are primarily used habitats in the eastern US. Except during nesting, these are gregarious birds that are nearly always seen in flocks. They feed on small seeds and tiny arthropods gleaned from what may appear to be nearly barren ground. In winter when insect food is unavailable they eat seeds of weeds and grasses and will take cracked corn around feeders and farm lots. Harvested agricultural fields, gravel bars, mudflats and other open lands are utilized, especially in winter. During outbreaks of severe winter weather flocks may move farther south.

Class—**Aves** (birds)

Order—**Passeriformes** (songbirds)

Family—**Mimidae** (thrasher family)

Northern Mockingbird *Mimus polyglottis*	Gray Catbird *Dumetella carolinensis*	Brown Thrasher *Toxostoma rufum*

Size: 10.5 inches.

Abundance: Common.

Variation: None.

Migratory Status: Summer only resident in Northern Indiana, but is a year-round resident in most of the rest of the state.

Presumed range in Indiana

Size: 8.5 inches.

Abundance: Fairly common.

Variation: None.

Migratory Status: Spring, summer and fall only. A few reach the shores of Lake Michigan by late April, most arrive in early May.

Presumed range in Indiana

Size: 11.5 inches.

Abundance: Fairly common.

Variation: None.

Migratory Status: A summer resident in most of Indiana. A few will winter in the southern tip of the state if the weather is mild.

Presumed range in Indiana

Habitat: Prefers semi-open habitats with some cover in the form of bushes and shrubs. Found in both rural and urban environments. During colder months they are usually found in the vicinity of berry-producing plants.

Habitat: Edge areas, thickets and overgrown fence rows are this bird's preferred habitat. In urban areas it is often found in older neighborhoods containing landscapes overgrown with large bushes and shrubs.

Habitat: Edges of woods, thickets, fence rows, overgrown fields and successional areas. Suburban lawns that have adequate cover in the form of bushes and shrubs may also be used. Avoids deep woods.

Breeding: The nest is made of sticks and is usually in a thick bush or small tree. 3 to 4 eggs are laid and more than one nesting per season is usual.

Breeding: The loosely constructed nest is made of sticks, vines, and leaves placed in dense bushes. Three to four eggs is common.

Breeding: Builds a stick nest in the heart of a dense shrub, usually within a few feet of the ground. Lays two to five eggs in late spring.

Natural History: The name "Mocking Bird" is derived from this bird's habit of mimicking the calls of other birds, and they have a huge repertoire of songs. They are known to mimic the calls of everything from warblers to blue jays and even large hawks. New songs are learned throughout their life and the number of different songs recorded by this species is up to 150. They feed largely on insects, but in the winter will switch to berries and fruits. Mockingbirds have a reputation among rural folk as a useful bird that will chase away other pesky birds such as blackbirds and other species that can be garden pests. They will aggressively defend food sources. Appears to be expanding its range northward into southern Canada.

Natural History: The Gray Catbird is much more secretive than its relative the Mockingbird. Food includes all manner of insects, spiders, larva and berries. Feeds both in the trees and on the ground. When feeding on the ground will use the bill to flip over dead leaves. Named for their call which sounds remarkably like a meowing cat, these shy birds are often heard but unseen as they "meow" from beneath a dense shrub. Like their cousins the Mockingbirds, Gray Catbirds have a large repertoire of songs and they are accomplished mimics of other bird species. They winter along the lower coastal plain of the US, Florida, the Caribbean, Mexico, and Central America. This species longevity record is just under 18 years!

Natural History: During warm weather the Brown Thrasher feeds on insects and small invertebrates of all types. It uses its long bill to overturn leaves and debris beneath trees and shrubs and also actively hunts in the grass of urban lawns. In winter they will eat berries and sometimes come to feeders for raisins or suet. During the breeding season males perch atop bushes or small trees and serenade all within earshot with their song. Though the Brown Thrasher lacks the repertoire of its cousin the Mockingbird, it does possess one of the most varied song collections of any bird in America. Migrates at night. A few will remain in southern Indiana throughout the winter if the winter is not too harsh.

Class—**Aves** (birds)

Order—**Passeriformes** (songbirds)

Family—**Motacillidae** (wagtails)	Family—**Bombycillidae** (waxwings)	Family—**Certhiidae** (creepers)
American Pipit *Anthus rubescens*	**Cedar Waxwing** *Bombycilla cedrorum*	**Brown Creeper** *Certhia americana*

Size: 6.5 inches.

Presumed range in Indiana

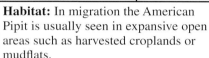

Abundance: Uncommon.

Variation: Non-breeding birds are browner.

Migratory Status: Seasonal migrant seen during spring and fall and rarely in winter.

Habitat: In migration the American Pipit is usually seen in expansive open areas such as harvested croplands or mudflats.

Breeding: Breeds in tundra areas and southward into the higher altitudes of the Rocky Mountains. Lays 3 to 7 eggs in a nest on the ground.

Natural History: The American Pipit is a hardy species that nests in America's coldest climates. They move south in the winter where they are easily overlooked. Their brown winter plumage is highly cryptic, especially where they usually reside in expansive, open fields or mudflats. During migration and in winter they may be seen in the company of flocks of Horned Larks or rarely with Lapland Longspurs (another winter migrant from the far north). Characteristically wags its tail up and down. Despite being widespread (their range includes all of North America) they are relatively unknown birds to many. The specimen shown is in spring breeding plumage. Fall and winter birds are browner and have heavy brown streaks on the breast. Sometimes go by the name "Water Pipit," but that name belongs to the similar Eurasian species.

Size: 7 inches.

Presumed range in Indiana

Abundance: Fairly common.

Variation: No variation. Sexes alike.

Migratory Status: Year-round resident but usually more common during migration.

Habitat: Found both in forests and semi-open country including overgrown fields, orchards, etc. May be seen in both rural and urban settings.

Breeding: Builds a nest of grasses. Nest site is typically high on a tree branch. Nesting occurs in June. Lays 3 to 5 eggs.

Natural History: Waxwings are named for the peculiar red-colored waxy feathers on their wings. The name "Cedar" Waxwing comes from their propensity for Eastern Red Cedar trees where they consume large quantities of cedar berries. These birds are highly social and are usually seen in large flocks. They are rarely seen singly or in pairs. They feed mostly on berries and wander relentlessly in search of this favored food item. In summer insects, mulberries and serviceberries are important food items. Crabapples and other fruiting trees are also favored. They are highly irregular in occurrence but are frequently seen across the state as they rove around in search of food sources. Large flocks are known to descend on a fruiting bush and consume every berry. Instances of these birds becoming intoxicated after feeding on fermented fruits have been recorded.

Size: 5.25 inches.

Presumed range in Indiana

Abundance: Uncommon.

Variation: No variation, sexes alike.

Migratory Status: In Indiana this is a winter resident that summers as far north as Alaska.

Habitat: This is a forest species that prefers mature woodlands with large trees for breeding. In winter they are seen in a variety of wooded habitats.

Breeding: The nest is nearly always built behind a piece of loose bark on the trunk of a large dead tree. Five or six eggs is typical.

Natural History: Brown Creepers feed on small insects, spiders, etc., found in tree-trunk bark crevices. They have the peculiar foraging habit of landing on the trunk at the base of the tree and "creeping" upward, spiraling around the tree as they go. When they reach a certain height, they fly down to the base of another nearby tree and begin again. Generally speaking the Brown Creeper is a bit of a loner, and it is rare to see more than one or two in any one area. This is the only representative of the creeper family (Certhidae) found in North America. Several other species occur in Eurasia and Africa. Population declines in regions where mature forests have been reduced suggests a dependence upon that habitat type. Has probably declined in the eastern US since European settlement and the subsequent rampant deforestation.

Class—**Aves** (birds)		
Order—**Passeriformes** (songbirds)		
Family—**Paridae** (chickadee family)		

Carolina Chickadee *Poecile carolinensis*	**Black-capped Chickadee** *Poecile atricapillus*	**Tufted Titmouse** *Baeolophus bicolor*

Size: 4.75 inches.

Abundance: Very common.

Variation: None. Sexes alike.

Migratory Status: A year-round resident in the southern three quarters of the state.

Presumed range in Indiana

Size: 5.25 inches.

Abundance: Common.

Variation: None. Sexes alike.

Migratory Status: A year-round resident in the northern quarter of the state.

Presumed range in Indiana

Size: 6 inches.

Abundance: Very common.

Variation: None. Sexes alike.

Migratory Status: A year-round resident. Common at feeders during winter.

Presumed range in Indiana

Habitat: Carolina Chickadee is primarily a deciduous woodland species but may be found anywhere so long as at least a few trees are present. Black-capped Chickadee adds coniferous woodlands to its habitat types. Both may be found in urban and rural areas, and both show a preference for edge areas.

Habitat: Small woodlots and successional areas. Favors edge habitats. Common in both rural and urban habitats.

Breeding: Both species are cavity nesters that will use hollows in limbs, rotted fence posts, etc. or very often, old woodpecker holes. Man-made nest boxes may also be used but natural cavities are preferred. Carolina Chickadee lays 4 to 6 eggs in April or May. Black-capped lays 6 to 7 eggs from late April to early June.

Breeding: This species is a cavity nester that will utilize natural cavities as well as old woodpecker holes. Average of 5 eggs.

Natural History: Among our smallest songbirds, the Chickadees are a familiar bird at feeders throughout the state. They will become quite acclimated to people and with some patient coaxing they may be induced to land upon an outstretched hand containing sunflower seeds. An acrobatic little bird when searching for insect prey, they can dangle upside down from tiny branches. Their whistling song and their "chick-a-dee-dee-dee" call is distinctive and they can be quite noisy at times. In winter they will form mixed flocks with other small birds. They are hyperactive, tiny birds that have high energy requirements. Winter mortality can be high. The ranges of these two very similar species are generally mutually exclusive, with the Black-capped occupying the more northerly regions. In fact, the Black-capped ranges as far north as northern Canada and Alaska. The Carolina on the other hand is a southern bird that ranges across the southeastern United States (except for the highest elevations in the Appalachian Mountains). In harsh winter weather Black-cappeds may move a little farther south into the range of the Carolina Chickadee. Additionally some evidence suggests that the Carolina Chickadee may be expanding its range northward. Hybrids between these two species are known to occur where the ranges meet in some areas of the eastern United States. It is unclear if hybridization occurs in Indiana, but it is reasonable to assume that occasional hybrids may appear in the state. Of the two, the Black-capped is slightly larger and has more of a white "frosting" on the wings. The range maps above are at best close approximations of the ranges of these two species rather than exact depictions of where they might occur in the state.

Natural History: Primarily a seed eater in winter, the Tufted Titmouse is one of the first birds to find a new bird feeder. Sunflower seeds are favored, but they also love peanuts. Like Chickadees they are sometimes quite bold around humans servicing feeders. In warm months they forage for small insects and spiders among the foliage of trees. They can sometimes be seen hanging upside down on a small branch or leaf as they search for prey. Their familiar song is a melodic "birdy-birdy-birdy." In winter they mix readily with Chickadees and other small birds. Their range corresponds closely to the Eastern Temperate Forest Level I Ecoregion. Old reports suggest this species has only expanded its range into northern Indiana in the last century. They are still more common in the southern half of the state, especially in winter.

Class—**Aves** (birds)

Order—**Passeriformes** (songbirds)

Family—**Regulidae** (kinglets)

Ruby-crowned Kinglet *Regulus calendula*	**Golden-crowned Kinglet** *Regulus satrapa*

Male / Female

Size: 4.25 inches.

 Presumed range in Indiana

Abundance: Fairly common. During periods of peak migration they can be quite common, especially during fall cold fronts.

Variation: Male has red stripe on head that is most visible when the male is excited. Females lack this red stripe on the crown. Otherwise sexes are very similar. Spring birds and juveniles are grayer above and less yellowish below.

Migratory Status: Spring and fall migrant that passes through the state. They summer well to the north. A few may spend the winter in the southernmost parts of the state, but will move south if the weather gets too harsh.

Habitat: Summer habitat is undisturbed boreal forest across all of Canada from the Atlantic to the Pacific and well into Alaska. Also summers in the higher elevations of the Rocky Mountains. Winter habitats much more generalized to include deciduous and mixed woodlands as well as swamps and lowlands.

Breeding: Breeds in old growth conifers in the far north. Produces enormous clutches of up to 12 eggs. Nest is built near the tops of spruce trees or fir trees. Nest is constructed of a wide variety of materials including mosses, lichens, blades of grass and conifer needles. Fur, feathers, or animal hair are used to line the nest.

Natural History: This is one of America's smallest songbird species, smaller even than the Chickadee. The bright red blaze on the top of the head of the male is usually not visible unless the feathers of the crown are erected. Males most often display the red feathers on the crown when issuing a challenge to other males, displaying to females, or singing their territorial song. Otherwise their bright red crown feathers will remain hidden from view. In summer they prey on arthropods and their eggs. In winter they will also feed on berries and some seeds. They are hyperactive little birds that forage throughout the canopy as well as along lower branches. Clumps of dead leaves hanging from a tree limb are like magnets to these tiny hunters who will find small spiders, insects and other diminutive arthropods hiding within the clumps. They are constantly in motion and regularly flick the wings open as they hop quickly from tiny branch to tiny branch at the terminal end of boughs of trees and bushes. Hunts mostly along the tips of smaller branches. Some studies suggest this species may be declining in the eastern United States. Some suggest this decline may be due to logging and forest fragmentation in the breeding range. Birds that pass through Indiana are true latitudinal (north-south) migrants. Populations living in the Rocky Mountains of the western United States migrate from high elevations to lower elevations (altitude migration). These delightful little birds are not common at bird feeders but they can be lured to feeders with suet, sunflowers or especially mealworms.

Size: 4 inches.

  Presumed range in Indiana

Abundance: Fairly common.

Variation: Males have orange crown, females (shown) have yellow crown.

Migratory Status: A winter resident that usually arrives in September or October.

Habitat: This is a forest species that prefers mature woodlands with large trees for breeding. In winter they are seen in a variety of wooded habitats.

Breeding: Builds its nest in the top of a spruce or fir in northern woodlands. Lays a large clutch of up to 11 eggs and may produce two broods per year.

Natural History: Even smaller than its cousin the Ruby-crowned Kinglet, the Golden-crowned is a hardier bird that can tolerate colder winter weather. However, severe winter conditions can lead to near 100 percent mortality in localized areas. Amazingly, this little carnivore manages to find arthropod prey throughout the winter and does not switch to seeds and berries in colder weather. Hyperactive and always in motion. They often feed by "leaf hawking" (hovering while picking tiny insects from beneath a leaves). In winter they are often seen in small groups or mixed flocks. Although these little birds may be seen throughout the winter in the state, they are probably most common during fall migrations. They can be quite tolerant of human presence.

Class—**Aves** (birds)

Order—**Passeriformes** (songbirds)

Family—**Sittidae** (nuthatches)

White-breasted Nuthatch	Red-breasted Nuthatch
Sitta carolinensis	*Sitta canadensis*

Size: 5.75 inches.

Abundance: Fairly common.

Variation: None. Sexes alike.

Migratory Status: A year-round resident that sometimes migrates.

Habitat: This is a bird of deciduous and mixed woodlands. Mature forests are preferred, but they also occupy re-growth.

Breeding: Nests in natural tree cavities or woodpecker holes. Averages 6 eggs per clutch. Only one brood per year is produced and young fledge in late May.

Presumed range in Indiana

Size: 4.5 inches.

Abundance: Fairly common.

Variation: None. Sexes alike.

Migratory Status: Mostly a fall and winter resident in Indiana.

Habitat: Summers in the spruce-fir forests of the north and west. Occupies deciduous woodlands in winter range.

Breeding: Cavity nester that excavates their own nest holes in the manner of woodpeckers. Average of 6 eggs. Breeds in northern forests and high mountains.

Presumed range in Indiana

Natural History: Nuthatches are famous for foraging tree trunks in an upside down position. This behavior gives them the opportunity to occupy a different feeding niche from woodpeckers and other bark-hunting birds that hunt from an upright position. By creeping down the trunk in an upside down position the nuthatches may see tiny prey hidden in crevices visible only from an above perspective and therefore missed by woodpeckers and creepers. This is an example of different species partitioning the same feeding habitat by exhibiting different foraging behavior. In addition to insects they also eat seeds and are regulars at most bird feeders in the state. They will cache seeds in bark crevices and they tend to be quite territorial. Pairs will stake out a territory and typically live within that area throughout the year. One of four species of nuthatch found in North America and the only one that is a full time inhabitant of deciduous woodlands. Other species occupy boreal forests, southern pine forests, and western pine forests. Regularly visits bird feeders for seeds like sunflowers or peanuts.

Natural History: These birds have a tendency to make "irruptive" migrations far to the south in winter every few years and the exact mechanism of their irruptive movements remains something of a mystery. It is believed to be related to cone production in northern coniferous forests where this species usually lives. During the spring and summer the Red-breasted Nuthatch feeds entirely on small arthropods. Seeds are the staple food during winter and Sunflower seeds are a favorite item at bird feeders. They will wedge seeds into bark crevices to hold them fast while using the beak to hammer open the shell in characteristic "nuthatch" fashion. They will glean insects from bark in the same upside down manner as their larger cousin the White-breasted Nuthatch. Unlike many cavity nesters the Red-breasted Nuthatch seems to avoid using man-made nest boxes. Instead they insist on creating their own nest holes. It may take over two weeks to excavate their nest hole. They will reportedly line the entrance of the nest cavity with resin from conifers, possibly to deter other cavity nesters or potential predators.

Class—**Aves** (birds)		
Order—**Passeriformes** (songbirds)		
Family—**Troglodytidae** (wrens)		

Carolina Wren *Thryothorus ludovicianus*	**Marsh Wren** *Cistothorus palustris*	**Sedge Wren** *Cistothorus platensis*

Size: 5.5 inches.	Presumed range in Indiana 	**Size:** 5 inches.	Presumed range in Indiana	**Size:** 4.25 inches.	Presumed range in Indiana 
Abundance: Common.		**Abundance:** Uncommon.		**Abundance:** Uncommon.	
Migratory Status: Carolina Wrens are a year-round resident in all of the state.		**Migratory Status:** Summer resident in all but southern Indiana where it is a migrant.		**Migratory Status:** Migrant in southern Indiana. Summer resident elsewhere in the state.	
Variation: No population variations and the sexes are alike.		**Variation:** No population variations and the sexes are alike.		**Variation:** No population variations and the sexes are alike.	

Habitat: Carolina Wrens are very flexible in habitat choices. They can be seen in remote wilderness or in suburban back yards.	**Habitat:** Pastures, marshes, and lowland meadows as well as open, grassy edges of wetlands or ponds. Coastal salt marshes are widely used in winter.	**Habitat:** This is a wetland species that enjoys marshes and wet meadows. Unlike the Marsh Wren it does not occupy cattail marsh but prefers grassy areas.
Breeding: A nest of fine twigs and grass is built in a sheltered place, often provided by man. Eggs number 3 to 6. Females will produce at least two clutches per year.	**Breeding:** Nest is low in grasses or small bush. Nest is built of grasses woven into a ball with an entrance hole in the side. Several unused "decoy" nests are built. 7 eggs is typical.	**Breeding:** Nest is built low to the ground, often in a clump of sedges or a small bush. 6 or 7 eggs is typical and some may produce two broods per year. Most common in northern Indiana.
Natural History: Along with the House Wren, this is one of the most common wrens in the Eastern US. The Carolina Wren adapts well to human influenced habitats and is well known for building its nest in an old pair of shoes or in a vase of flowers left on the back porch for a few days. They will become quite tame around yards and porches and frequently endear themselves to their human neighbors. They are voracious consumers of insects, spiders, and caterpillars and help control insect pests around the home. They are also incessant singers whose musical song serves as a dawn alarm for many residents throughout the state. They are most common in the southern half of the state. In more northern regions they are vulnerable to harsh winters.	**Natural History:** Marsh Wrens winter to the south of Indiana but they are an uncommon summer resident in the much of the state. They may be seen anywhere in the state where suitable habitat exists during migration periods. These are secretive birds that can be very difficult to observe, even in areas where they are common. They spend most of their time hidden in thick stands of cattails or other vegetation deep in the marsh. Like most wrens they will sing continuously in the breeding season and most birdwatchers confirm their presence by learning to recognize their song. They will build one or more "decoy" nests that are never used and they are also known to destroy the eggs of other birds that may be nesting in the vicinity of their own nests.	**Natural History:** This is another secretive species that is difficult to observe. Like the Marsh Wren it winters well to the south of Indiana but it is an uncommon summer resident in the state. The natural history of this species is poorly known, but it is known that nesting dates vary considerably from one region of the country to another. Nesting can occur from May to as late as September. Some birds may produce two broods per year in two different regions. The diet is spiders and insects. Sedge Wrens winter in coastal plain of the southeastern United States from the Carolinas all the way to northwestern Mexico. Fall migration begins in September and most birds are usually gone from the northern portions of their range by late October. Spring migration is in April and May.

Class—**Aves** (birds)

Order—**Passeriformes** (songbirds)

Family—**Troglodytidae** (wrens)		Family—**Poliptilidae** (gnatcatchers)

House Wren
Troglodytes aedon

Size: 4.75 inches.

Abundance: Very common.

Variation: Sexes are alike.

Migratory Status: A spring/summer resident that begins to arrive in April and departs in the fall.

Presumed range in Indiana

Habitat: Prefers open and semi-open habitats. These wrens readily associate with humans and are most common in small towns and suburbs. They can also be common in more natural habitats.

Breeding: A cavity nester, the House Wren readily takes to artificial nest boxes. In fact, this species may owe its increase in population to man-made "bird houses." Lays up to 8 eggs.

Natural History: Although the House Wren may be seen anywhere in Indiana, it may be more common in the northern portions of the state during the breeding season. It is perhaps least common in the southern tip of the state, but it does breed statewide. They are more common today than in historical times, as they favor open and semi-open habitats over dense forests. They also have a strong affinity for human altered habitats and settlements. They feed on a wide variety of insects, spiders, snails, caterpillars, etc. When feeding large broods of young they catch huge quantities daily. House Wrens range from coast to coast across America and northward into the prairie provinces of Canada.

Winter Wren
Troglodytes hiemalis

Size: 4 inches.

Abundance: Uncommon.

Variation: No variation, sexes alike.

Migratory Status: A winter resident and migrant. Lingers then moves farther south in harsh winter weather.

Presumed range in Indiana

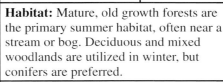

Habitat: Mature, old growth forests are the primary summer habitat, often near a stream or bog. Deciduous and mixed woodlands are utilized in winter, but conifers are preferred.

Breeding: Breeds to the north of Indiana, mainly in the boreal forests of Canada. Nest is often constructed in the root wad of an upturned tree. Lays 5 to 9 eggs.

Natural History: Much shyer and more secretive than other wrens, the Winter Wren skulks about under dense bushes and shrubs where it tends to stay close to the ground. This species has likely declined since presettlement times due to the destruction of ancient forests. Like other wrens, these birds are strictly carnivorous and feed on a wide variety of small insects, larva, arachnids, amphipoda, etc. As with many other invertivorous birds, they are vulnerable to exceptionally harsh winters. Their stubby, upturned tail makes identification easy, but they are more often heard than seen as they are persistent, loud singers. Winter Wrens are holarctic in distribution, being found in Europe and northern Asia as well as North America.

Blue-gray Gnatcatcher
Polioptila caerulea

Size: 4.25 inches.

Abundance: Common.

Variation: No significant variation.

Migratory Status: One of the earliest returning summer migrants, arriving in southern Indiana as early as late March.

Presumed range in Indiana

Habitat: Occupies a wide variety of forested or successional habitats. Most common along wooded streams and bottoms. Shows a definite preference for deciduous woodlands.

Breeding: Nest is a cup-like structure built with lichens and plant fibers glued together with spider web. Nest usually placed at mid-level near the terminus of a branch. 4 to 5 eggs is average.

Natural History: As their name implies gnatcatchers feed on tiny prey. Any type of small arthropod is probable food item. They hunt the tips of tree branches and sometimes pick off prey while hovering. Despite their small size they will chase away larger birds and will mob predators such as hawks, snakes, or house cats. The gnatcatchers are a unique family that is probably most closely related to the wrens. Like many small songbird species the Blue-gray Gnatcatcher is often the victim of nest parasitism by the Brown-headed Cowbird, which lays its eggs in other birds' nests. Despite cowbirds, they seem to be a thriving species and their range has been expanding northward in recent times.

Class—**Aves** (birds)

Order—**Passeriformes** (songbirds)

Family—**Hirundinidae** (Swallows)

Barn Swallow *Hirundo rustica*	**Cliff Swallow** *Petrochelidon pyrrhonota*	**Bank Swallow** *Riparia riparia*

Barn Swallow — *Hirundo rustica*

Size: 7 inches.

Abundance: Very common throughout most of the state.

Variation: Males are slightly more vivid.

Migratory Status: A summer resident that returns to the state in April.

Presumed range in Indiana

Habitat: Open and semi-open habitats. Most common in agricultural areas but found virtually everywhere in the state. Least common in forest areas.

Breeding: Nest is bowl shaped and made of mud and grasses plastered to roof joists of a barn or eaves of buildings, beneath concrete bridges, etc.

Natural History: A familiar bird to all who grew up on rural farmsteads. Barn Swallows are common throughout most of North America in summer, and birds that summer in the US winter in Central and South America. European breeders winter in the Mediterranean, Africa and the Middle East while Asian breeding birds winter throughout southeast Asia to Australia. Thus this is one of the most widespread bird species in the world. Its long association with humans throughout the world has led to the invention of many legends. Barn Swallows nesting in your barn was considered by pioneers as good luck, while destroying a nest in the barn would cause the milk cow to go dry. Flying insects are the main food including pesky flies and even wasps. This is the world's most common swallow species.

Cliff Swallow — *Petrochelidon pyrrhonota*

Size: 5.5 inches.

Abundance: Fairly common in most of the state.

Variation: No variation. Sexes alike.

Migratory Status: Summer resident. Seen in Indiana from April to September.

Presumed range in Indiana

Habitat: Open areas near large bodies of water are the preferred habitat for this species. Breeding habitat was historically limited to regions with cliff faces.

Breeding: Conical mud nests are plastered beneath sheltered overhangs of concrete structures such as bridges or dams. Four eggs is typical.

Natural History: The Cliff Swallow is primarily a western species that nested historically on cliff faces in the Rocky Mountains. They are more numerous today than even a few decades ago. Man-made structures such as dams and bridges have likely helped this species expand its range in the eastern United States. These birds are colony animals that seem to always nest in groups. A source of mud for building nests is required and there seems to be a preference for nesting near water. Colony size varies from a few dozen to a few hundred nests. Farther west, where the species is more common and widespread, colonies consisting of several thousand nests are known. Like other swallows they feed almost entirely upon airborne insects, and they are adept at locating swarms of airborne prey.

Bank Swallow — *Riparia riparia*

Size: 5.25 inches.

Abundance: Uncommon in most of Indiana.

Variation: No variation. Sexes alike.

Migratory Status: Summer resident. Seen in Indiana from April to September.

Presumed range in Indiana

Habitat: Open country near large rivers. In migration may be seen in a wide variety of habitats but most often observed in valleys, near lakes, etc.

Breeding: Historically nested in high steep banks along major rivers. Nest hole is dug by the parents and may be as much as 2 to 3 feet deep. 4 to 6 eggs.

Natural History: Although widespread across America during migration, this species is rather rare in much of the state. Like many swallows the Bank Swallow nests in large communities. Nest colonies are usually associated with large river systems with exposed cliff faces. Despite being somewhat uncommon in Indiana, these birds are found throughout the world, in fact they are one of the most widespread bird species on earth. The natural nesting habitat has always been riverbanks and bluffs, but today they utilize the banks created by man-made quarries or road cuts through hillsides. During migration Bank Swallows can be seen in the company of other species of migrating swallows. Food is exclusively flying insects caught on the wing. Mostly flies, flying ants, small beetles, and mayflies.

Class—**Aves** (birds)

Order—**Passeriformes** (songbirds)

Family—**Hirundinidae** (Swallows)

Northern Rough-winged Swallow *Stelgidopteryx serripennis*	Tree Swallow *Tachycineta bicolor*	Purple Martin *Progne subis*

Size: 5.5 inches.

Abundance: Fairly common.

Variation: No variation, sexes alike.

Migratory Status: Summer resident. Winters in south Florida and in Central America.

Presumed range in Indiana

Size: 5.75 inches.

Abundance: Fairly common.

Variation: Immatures are gray. Sexes alike.

Migratory Status: A warm-weather bird. Seen from spring to fall. Arrives as early in Indiana as March.

Presumed range in Indiana

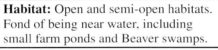

Size: 8 inches.

Abundance: Fairly common.

Variation: Sexually dimorphic (see photo).

Migratory Status: Summer resident. Males are the first to appear and may arrive as early as late March.

Presumed range in Indiana

Habitat: Mainly open and semi-open areas, but can be found in forested regions along rivers or cliffs.

Habitat: Open and semi-open habitats. Fond of being near water, including small farm ponds and Beaver swamps.

Habitat: Inhabits both rural areas and suburbs. Artificial nest boxes near water in open areas are attractants.

Breeding: Nests in crevices in rock faces, cliffs, etc. Today often uses man-made situations such as road cuts, quarries, etc. Not a colony nester. Lays 4 to 8 eggs.

Breeding: A cavity nester, Tree Swallows will use old woodpecker holes or tree hollows. They also use artificial nest boxes and sometimes nest in close proximity to Purple Martins.

Breeding: Originally nested in natural cavities but today nearly all use artificial nest sites. 3 to 6 eggs is typical but may lay as many as 7 or 8. Purple Martins are colony nesters.

Natural History: As with other swallows the Rough-winged Swallow feeds by catching flying insects in mid-air. All swallows in America are diurnal hunters whose predatory role is replaced at dusk by the bats. Although this swallow is found from coast to coast across America it is not extremely common anywhere. Unlike the similar Bank Swallow, Rough-winged Swallows are not known to dig their own burrow and availability of nest burrows may be one reason why these swallows tend to be solitary nesters. They will use burrows dug by other species of birds or small mammals as well as natural cavities in cliff faces. They are also known to use man-made structures. In mountainous regions this species is usually associated with river valleys. The name comes from the rough feel of the wing feathers.

Natural History: Tree Swallows are more numerous today than in historical times and are increasing in numbers in the state. Human activities have benefited this species by creating more open lands and also by creating more ponds and lakes throughout the landscape. The proliferation of artificial nest boxes has also helped (they take readily to Bluebird Boxes) and the resurgence of Beaver populations is also credited with helping this species. Flying insects are the primary food items, but the species also eats bayberries during the winter. They are also known to eat snails during the breeding season to obtain calcium for eggshell production. The Tree Swallow winters along the southeastern coastline of the US, Florida, Mexico, and the Caribbean. In summer look for them in open meadows near a pond.

Natural History: Our largest swallow and perhaps the most beloved bird in America. Many people anxiously await the return of Purple Martins each spring to nest boxes erected in their yard. This bird's relationship with humans extends at least as far back as the 18th century and today there are at least two national organizations dedicated to Purple Martin enthusiasts. House Sparrows and Starlings sometimes take over "martin houses" unless the landowner is vigilant. Mainly a warm weather species that is dependent upon flying insect prey, Purple Martins are vulnerable to spring cold fronts in the more northern reaches of the summer range. This species is so adapted to nesting in man-made nest boxes that today it is rare to find one nesting in natural cavities. A useful consumer of flying insect pests.

Class—**Aves** (birds)

Order—**Passeriformes** (songbirds)

Family—**Corvidae** (jays & crows)

Blue Jay *Cyanocitta cristata*	**American Crow** *Corvus brachyrhynchos*	**Fish Crow** *Corvus ossifragus*

Size: 11 inches.

Presumed range in Indiana

Abundance: Common.

Variation: No variation, sexes alike.

Migratory Status: Although some populations may migrate, Blue Jays can be seen in Indiana year-round.

Habitat: State-wide from dense woodlands to semi-open farmlands. They can also be common in suburban and urban neighborhoods.

Breeding: Builds a stick nest fairly high up on a tree branch, often in a fork. Lays an average of four eggs usually in April. Blue Jays in the southern United States may produce two clutches.

Natural History: The Blue Jay's handsome blue, black, and white feathers and distinctive crest make it one of the most recognizable birds in the state. They mainly eat insects, acorns and grains, but also eat eggs and young of other songbirds. They will aggressively mob much larger birds like hawks and owls, as well as snakes and house cats. Members of this family are relatively long-lived. The record life span for a wild Blue Jay is 18 years, but a captive specimen was reported to have lived for 26 years. An endemic American bird, Blue Jays are found throughout the eastern half of the United States from about the Rocky Mountains eastward. They also range northward into Canada but well below the Arctic Circle. They may be very common in suburban areas.

Size: 17.5 inches.

Presumed range in Indiana

Abundance: Common.

Variation: No variation, sexes alike.

Migratory Status: This is a year-round bird, but migrant crows from farther north increase the population in winter.

Habitat: Occurs in virtually all habitats including urban areas. Favors regions where there is a patchwork of woods and open spaces.

Breeding: Crows build a bulky stick nest high in the fork of a tree, usually well hidden by thick foliage. The nest is quite large and may be 2 feet across. 4 eggs is a typical clutch.

Natural History: Crows are omnivores that will eat virtually anything, including the young and eggs of other birds. They are among the most intelligent and resourceful of birds. They may be seen in pairs, small groups, or large flocks numbering in the hundreds. Highly adaptable, crows have fared well in human altered habitats and the species is more common today than prior to European settlement. It is almost certain to remain a common species. As a testament to the crow's intelligence, in rural areas where hunting is commonplace, they are extremely wary of humans; while in protected parks and urban regions they will become quite accepting of the presence of humans. In such environments they will raid suburban yards for pet food and garbage.

Size: 15 inches.

Presumed range in Indiana

Abundance: Rare in Indiana.

Variation: No variation, sexes alike.

Migratory Status: Summer migrant that winters in the lower coastal plain. Restricted to extreme SE Indiana.

Habitat: Restricted to the floodplains of the Wabash and Ohio Rivers, as well as near the mouths of tributaries. May be expanding range northward.

Breeding: Large stick nest is placed in a tree crotch. Average clutch size is about 4 eggs. Only a single clutch is produced annually. Breeding range may be expanding into southeastern Indiana.

Natural History: Identical to the America Crow but smaller (15 inches), the Fish Crow occurs in Indiana mostly along the major rivers in the southeastern tip of the state. They are often seen in the company of their larger cousin and when seen together the Fish Crow can be distinguished by its smaller size. Expert bird watchers can identify this species by its call, which is higher pitched than that of the American Crow. A southern species that historically was found in coastal areas and lowlands of the lower coastal plain, the Fish Crow has expanded its range northward over the last few decades. They were first recorded in the Mississippi Alluvial Plain of Kentucky about fifty years ago. Today they range all the way up into southeastern Indiana during summer.

Class—**Aves** (birds)		

Order—**Passeriformes** (songbirds)

Family—**Vironidae** (vireos)

Yellow-throated Vireo *Vireo flavifrons*	**White-eyed Vireo** *Vireo griseus*	**Blue-headed Vireo** *Vireo solitarius*

Size: 5.5 inches.	Presumed range in Indiana	**Size:** 5 inches.	Presumed range in Indiana	**Size:** 5.5 inches.	Presumed range in Indiana
Abundance: Fairly common statewide.		**Abundance:** Most common in southern IN.		**Abundance:** Fairly common in migration.	
Variation: No variation, sexes alike.		**Variation:** No variation, sexes alike.		**Variation:** No variation, sexes alike.	
Migratory Status: A long-range migrant that winters as far away as northern South America. Returns in April.		**Migratory Status:** Winters from the lower coastal plain into Mexico, Cuba and Bahamas. Returns in April.		**Migratory Status:** A spring/fall migrant that passes through the state in April and again in September.	

Habitat: A woodland bird that will inhabit a wide variety of forest types excluding stands of pure conifers. More common in areas of extensive forest where it prefers edge areas.	**Habitat:** Dense thickets and early successional hardwoods are favored. May also be seen in later stage successional deciduous woodlands and in overgrown fields with small saplings and thickets.	**Habitat:** This vireo likes expanses of mature forests, and is also partial to conifers for its summer habitat. It thus summers mostly well to the north of Indiana in the boreal forests of Canada.
Breeding: The nest is a woven basket usually suspended from the fork of a small branch at the mid-story level. Four eggs is typical.	**Breeding:** Nest is a woven, hanging basket held together with silk from caterpillars or spiders placed in a fork very low to the ground. Three to five eggs.	**Breeding:** Nest construction is similar to other vireos. A tightly woven cup is suspended from a horizontal fork. Four eggs is typical.
Natural History: The nest is usually located in a branch overhanging a forest opening such as a lane or a stream. Feeds on a wide variety of arthropods with caterpillars being a mainstay. Also eats small amount of berries and seeds in the fall. The biology of this species is not as well understood as with many other vireos, but it is known that it has decreased in numbers in areas of deforestation. As with many small woodland songbirds, the nest of the Yellow-throated Vireo is subject to parasitism by cowbirds. The summer range of this species coincides closely with the Eastern Temperate Forest Level I Ecoregion. The winter range is from southern Mexico to northern South America. Migrants regularly cross the Gulf of Mexico.	**Natural History:** This is the only vireo with a white iris, making identification easy. Nest parasitism by Brown-headed Cowbirds is estimated to be as high as fifty percent, with no young surviving in parasitized nests. Highly insectivorous. Caterpillars are a favorite food item. Will also eat fruit. White-eyed Vireos winter along the lower coastal plain of the US, the Caribbean, and the Yucatan Peninsula. Like the previous species, nest parasitism by Brown-headed Cowbirds poses a potential threat. Deforestation contributes to the problem. Brown-headed Cowbirds tend to avoid deep woods in favor of more open habitats. Loss of large tracts of woodland makes life easier for the cowbirds and more difficult for the species which they parasitize.	**Natural History:** Also known as the Solitary Vireo. Blue-headed Vireos breed and rear their young mostly in Canada and in the Appalachian Mountain range. They winter from the lower coastal plain of the southeastern US all the way to Central America and they are quite common in peninsular Florida throughout the winter. Food is mostly insects, with moths and butterflies and their larva being a major portion of the diet. Most foraging is done in trees well above the forest floor. As is the case with many of America's migrant songbirds, the Blue-headed Vireo is highly dependent upon large tracts of forest. Deforestation negatively impacts local populations; but forest regeneration in many areas of its summer range has helped this species in recent years.

Class—**Aves** (birds)

Order—**Passeriformes** (songbirds)

Family—**Vironidae** (vireos)

Red-eyed Vireo *Vireo olivaceus*	**Warbling Vireo** *Vireo gilvus*	**Philadelphia Vireo** *Vireo philadelphia*

Size: 5.25 inches

Abundance: Very common.

Variation: The sexes are alike but the males may be slightly larger.

Migratory Status: A summer resident that arrives in early to late April.

Presumed range in Indiana

Habitat: Although a woodland species, the Red-eyed Vireo is very generalized in its habitat requirements. Mature forests, regenerating woodlands and forest fragments are all occupied.

Breeding: 2 to 4 eggs are laid in May. May have two broods per summer with second brood fledging in late August.

Natural History: This is one of the most common summer songbirds in American forests and woodlots, but it is not readily observed due to its habit of staying high in the forest canopy. It is however regularly heard, as it sings incessantly throughout the spring. While on their breeding grounds they are primarily insectivorous feeders, but they do consume some fruits while wintering in the tropics. The population health of the Red-eyed Vireo may be due to its less stringent dependence upon large tracts of forest. This species can subsist happily in small woodlands and regenerative areas. However, in these habitats it is more susceptible to the parasitic nesting of the Brown-headed Cowbird. Winter range is in South America. Their red eye color is unique among vireos.

Size: 5 inches.

Abundance: Fairly common.

Variation: No variation between sexes or in annual molts.

Migratory Status: A summer resident that arrives in Indiana in late April to early May.

Presumed range in Indiana

Habitat: Although this species likes mature trees in its habitat, it avoids dense forest in favor of areas with a mosaic of small woodlands. Riparian woodlands are also utilized.

Breeding: Nesting takes place in mid-summer. Nests are placed high in trees. Four eggs is typical.

Natural History: The Warbling Vireo is less common than the Red-eyed Vireo in Indiana. But, like the similar Red-eyed Vireo, they are persistent singers that are more often heard than seen. They are browner in color and lack the distinctive red iris of the Red-eyed Vireo, They feed by gleaning small insects and other arthropods from canopy foliage. A few seeds and berries are also sometimes eaten. This is one of the most widely distributed members of the North American Vironidae family. Their breeding range extends from coast to coast across the northern two-thirds of the United States as well as much of Canada. By contrast, the winter range is much smaller and restricted to the western half of Mexico and western Central America from northern Costa Rica northward.

Size: 5.5 inches.

Abundance: Fairly common.

Variation: Sexes alike. Juveniles brownish above.

Migratory Status: Migrant. Passes through in late spring or very early summer.

Presumed range in Indiana

Habitat: Philadelphia Vireo can be found in large tracts of forest, but it seems to favor successional woodlands over mature. Uses mixed conifer and deciduous woodlands.

Breeding: The breeding range of the Philadelphia Vireo is contained mostly in Canada. Four eggs is typical.

Natural History: The Philadelphia Vireo migrates through most of the state each spring but it does not nest in here. They are a somewhat rarely observed bird and are difficult to distinguish from the more common Warbling Vireo. They usually have more yellowish wash below. They are also very similar to the Red-eyed Vireo and their song also closely resembles that species. Their food is mostly caterpillars. As with many other neotropical migrant songbirds that can be seen in Indiana, this species is a trans-gulf migrant that makes epic non-stop flights across the Gulf of Mexico during migration. The **Bell's Vireo** (*V. belli*) is a similar species of *Vireo* that although generally less common than the Philadelphia Vireo it will spend the summer in Indiana and may breed widely in the state.

Class—**Aves** (birds)

Order—**Passeriformes** (songbirds)

Family—**Parulidae** (warblers)

Canada Warbler *Cardellina canadensis*	Wilson's Warbler *Cardellina pusilla*	Yellow-breasted Chat *Icteria virens*

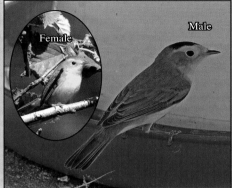

Size: 5.5 inches.

Presumed range in Indiana

Abundance: Uncommon.

Variation: Females have less black.

Migratory Status: A seasonal migrant that passes through the state in spring and fall.

Habitat: Favors moist northern forests with thick under-story shrubs. Known to associate with conifers on breeding grounds.

Breeding: Nest is on the ground and hidden amid dense vegetation. In Canada nest is often placed amid carpet of moss. Four or five eggs is typical.

Natural History: A few will nest in parts of the midwestern US or in the Appalachians but most (over 80 percent) will nest in Canada. Although they do migrate through most of Indiana they do so mostly at night and pass through quickly en route to breeding grounds farther to the north. The Canada Warbler has been in decline for several decades. Loss of breeding habitat in North America as well as degradation of wintering habitat in South America is probably to blame. Unlike many warblers that fly across the Gulf of Mexico, this species migrates along the coast of Texas and passes through Indiana in late April of early May. Fall migration begins in August. Future threats include the Woolly Adelgid, an alien insect that is decimating hemlock forests. Formerly this species was placed in the genus *Wilsonia*.

Size: 4.75 inches.

Presumed range in Indiana

Abundance: Uncommon.

Variation: Black "cap" more prominent in males.

Migratory Status: Seasonal migrant. Passes through state in spring and again in the fall.

Habitat: Summer breeding habitat is in the boreal forests of Canada, Pacific northwest, northern Rockies, and Alaska. Winter habitat is tropical forests.

Breeding: Nest is on the ground. Uniquely, the nest of this warbler is usually placed in a small depression. From 2 to 7 eggs may be laid.

Natural History: Wilson's Warbler is not a common species in Indiana. Although they may migrate through any part of the state, the bulk of this species population occurs and migrates throughout the western United States. They migrate later in spring than most other warblers and they can be seen well into the month of May. They are more numerous in the Rocky Mountain states and the Pacific states than they are in the eastern United States. However some studies indicate that they are declining in the west. In western regions they are fond of streamside habitats and some biologists blame the loss of riparian habitat for decline in western populations. They range as far north as the Arctic Ocean in summer and as far south as Panama in winter. The common name honors early naturalist and ornithologist Alexander Wilson.

Size: 7 inches.

Presumed range in Indiana

Abundance: Fairly common.

Variation: None. Sexes alike.

Migratory Status: Summer resident. Winters in southern Mexico and Central America.

Habitat: This warbler likes overgrown fields, second growth areas and early successional regenerating woodlands. It avoids the deep woods.

Breeding: Nests low to the ground in brier thickets or a dense shrub such as a Multiflora Rose. Nest is cup-like. Lays 2 to 5 eggs.

Natural History: The Yellow-breasted Chat is America's largest wood warbler and some question its status in the family Parulidae. They are fairly common in suitable habitats in southern Indiana in summer months but are not easily observed due to their secretive nature and preference for dense vegetation. They are becoming increasingly scarce from about central Indiana northward, but do occur statewide in summer months. Foods are a wide variety of arthropods with a preference for crickets, grasshoppers, caterpillars and spiders. They are also known to eat some fruits and berries. These birds are probably more numerous today than prior to deforestation. Their breeding range in eastern North America corresponds closely to the Eastern Temperate Forest level I ecoregion. The longevity record for the species is 11 years.

Class—**Aves** (birds)

Order—**Passeriformes** (songbirds)

Family—**Parulidae** (warblers)

Black-and-white Warbler *Mniotilta varia*	**Hooded Warbler** *Setophaga citrina*	**Northern Parula** *Setophaga americana*

	Black-and-white Warbler		Hooded Warbler		Northern Parula

Size: 5 inches.

Abundance: Fairly common.

Variation: Female has more white on face and breast.

Migratory Status: Summer resident in most of Indiana.

Presumed range in Indiana

Size: 5 inches.

Abundance: Uncommon in Indiana.

Variation: Black "hood" on head and face is reduced in females.

Migratory Status: Summer resident in most of state.

Presumed range in Indiana

Size: 4.5 inches.

Abundance: Fairly common.

Variation: Females lack black on breast but otherwise sexes are similar.

Migratory Status: Summer resident in southern IN. Migrant in north.

Presumed range in Indiana

Habitat: Found in a wide variety of forest types, but mature and second-growth deciduous forests are the primary habitat. Mixed conifer-hardwood forests are also used. Likes woodlands with dense under-story.

Habitat: A forest species. Most common in heavily forested regions but may be found anywhere that there is significant woodlands. In Indiana this species is most common in the southern tip of the state.

Habitat: Habitat is forest. Mostly bottomland woods or swamps or along streams and rivers. In Indiana this species is seen mostly in the southern half of the state where it stays all summer. Migrants can be seen statewide.

Breeding: Nest is constructed of dry leaves, dead grasses, and the bark of grapevines. Placed in a depression on the ground at the base of tree or stump. Lays 3 to 5 eggs.

Breeding: Cup-shaped nest of grasses, bark, and dead leaves is woven into two or more upright limbs of a small bush near the ground. Nest sites are usually associated with dense shrubs. 4 eggs.

Breeding: Nests high in trees. In Kentucky Sycamores, Baldcypress, and Hemlocks are reported as favorite nest trees. In the deep south nests are often built in Spanish moss. 4 or 5 eggs.

Natural History: Feeds by plucking tiny creatures from tree bark and branches. Its feeding habits are more similar to that of woodpeckers, nuthatches, and creepers than to most warblers. This species is dependent upon deciduous and mixed conifer forests, and it can be sensitive to deforestation. But overall it does not appear to have been significantly impacted throughout its wider range. While this species can be seen throughout the state during migration, it nests in Indiana mostly in the southern part of the state where ample woodlands still remain. Like many warblers it spends much of its time in the canopy which makes it difficult to observe. When seen its black and white color is distinctive.

Natural History: Like many small, woodland birds the Hooded Warbler is more likely to be heard than seen. On their breeding grounds in the eastern US they require large tracts of woodlands and they have declined in areas where intensive agriculture or development has resulted in the loss of this habitat. This handsome little warbler is a good example of why the protection of extensive tracts of forest can be so important in the conservation of neotropical migrant songbirds. With the largest eyes of any warbler, this species is adapted to a life spent in heavy shade. Unlike most warblers that tend to be treetop dwellers this species often feeds on the ground or in low shrubs. Spring migrants arrive in April and May.

Natural History: The Northern Parula feeds by gleaning tiny arthropods from tree branches. They tend to feed and spend much time in the middle and upper story of the forest. This habit coupled with their small size make them difficult to observe. These handsome little warblers are most common in deep forests and are least common in the northeast. They can be common breeding birds in the southern tip of Indiana and also far to north in Canada, but they seem to avoid most of the northern portions of the state for nesting. They are one of the smallest warblers, but are strikingly colored, especially the males. They are early spring migrators arriving as early as March. They winter from south Florida to Central America.

Class—**Aves** (birds)

Order—**Passeriformes** (songbirds)

Family—**Parulidae** (warblers)

Yellow Warbler *Setophaga petechia*	Black-throated Blue Warbler *Setophaga caerulescens*	Cerulean Warbler *Setophaga cerulea*

Size: 5 inches.

Presumed range in Indiana

Abundance: Common.

Variation: Male has bright chestnut streaks on breast.

Migratory Status: Summer resident. May through August.

Habitat: Thickets of willow or buttonbush in wet lowlands are the classic habitat for this species. Mesic upland woods may also be used.

Breeding: Nest is built in the upright fork of a sapling and averages four or five eggs. Nest is a cup-like structure made mostly from grasses. Breeds throughout the state.

Natural History: This is one of North America's most wide ranging of the warblers. Their summer breeding range encompasses the entire northern two thirds of North America, from the Atlantic to the Pacific and extends as far north as the Arctic Circle and they can be seen statewide in Indiana. Birds nesting in Indiana arrive in late April and early May. Fall migration is early. In fact this is one of the earliest fall migrators, leaving in mid-July. Feeds on a variety of insects and other arthropods and uses a variety of foraging techniques including gleaning of leaves and branches, flying from perch to seize airborne prey and picking insects from leaves and branches while hovering. Caterpillars are an important food item during breeding. Longevity record for the species is 11 years.

Size: 5 inches.

Presumed range in Indiana

Abundance: Uncommon in Indiana.

Variation: Female is olive brown above, drab olive-yellow below.

Migratory Status: A passage migrant seen mostly in April and May.

Habitat: Summer habitat consists of large, contiguous tracts of mature northern forests. During migration seen in a variety of habitats.

Breeding: Nest is strips of bark lined with finer materials such as moss. Usually placed in an upright fork of dense shrub. Clutch size typically 4. Does not breed in Indiana.

Natural History: Most of this warblers summer/breeding habitat is to the north and east of Indiana. Summers mostly in the northeastern US and eastern Canada. Departs breeding grounds in early fall and spends the winter in the Caribbean. A few will winter in the southern tip of Florida. In Indiana it is seen only as a migrant and then only in spring as the fall migration is usually to east of Indiana. This species forages mostly in shrubs and branches at the mid-story level for caterpillars and other small arthropod prey. Deforestation and forest fragmentation in both summer and winter habitats are the greatest threats. These threats may be compounded by habitat degradation from alien species like the Woolly Adelgid. The longevity record for this species is just under 10 years.

Size: 4.25 inches.

Presumed range in Indiana

Abundance: Uncommon in Indiana.

Variation: Female is bluish-green with faded gray streaks.

Migratory Status: A summer resident. Arrives in April or May.

Habitat: Summer habitat is primarily deciduous forests. Both bottomland forest and moist upland woods; requires mature forests.

Breeding: Nest is a tight cup woven around forked branches in the mid to upper canopy level. Average clutch size is 3 or 4 to as many as 5. Breeding habitat includes thick under-story.

Natural History: The Cerulean Warbler hunts high in the canopy, gleaning tiny invertebrates from small branches and leaves. Searches both upper and lower surface of leaves for food. Like many species dependent upon forests, this warbler experienced significant population declines following the European settlement of America. Today many states list it as a threatened species, including Indiana. Protection of large tracts of deciduous woodlands is probably the best conservation action that can be taken to help the species. Unfortunately, not enough of this type conservation takes place in America. Winters in the Andes Mountains. In spring migration it flies across the gulf to the southeastern US coast, often stopping to rest and feed on barrier islands before moving northward into interior.

Class—**Aves** (birds)

Order—**Passeriformes** (songbirds)

Family—**Parulidae** (warblers)

Magnolia Warbler	**Yellow-rumped Warbler**	**Blackpoll Warbler**
Setophaga magnolia	*Setophaga coronata*	*Setophaga striata*

Size: 5 inches.	**Size:** 5.5 inches.	**Size:** 5.5 inches.
Abundance: Common.	**Abundance:** Common.	**Abundance:** Uncommon.
Variation: Female has more subdued pattern.	**Variation:** Sexually dimorphic (see above).	**Variation:** Sexually dimorphic (see above).
Migratory Status: Migrant that passes through in spring and fall.	**Migratory Status:** A summer resident north, year-round in south.	**Migratory Status:** This is a springtime migrant in Indiana.

Presumed range in Indiana

Habitat: Summer habitat for most is in spruce forests in Canada. In Indiana it can be seen statewide in wooded areas during migration. Winters in Mexico, Central America and Caribbean.

Breeding: Nests in evergreen trees. The nest is usually well concealed amid dense vegetation. 4 eggs laid. Breeds in the far north across Canada, New England, and in the northern Appalachians.

Natural History: Feeds on insects (including large numbers of caterpillars) that are caught near the ends of branches in dense conifer trees. Known to feed on the Spruce Budworm and may enjoy greater survival of offspring during years of budworm outbreaks. This is an abundant species that appears to be stable in population numbers. Leaves Central American wintering grounds in February and passes through Indiana from mid-April to mid-May. They are fairly common migrants throughout the state in spring. Fall migration begins in September and may last into October. Fall migration routes generally more easterly than spring, thus they are usually observed in Indiana during spring migration. The longevity record for this species is just under 9 years.

Habitat: Outside its breeding range this warbler is a habitat generalist. It can be seen virtually anywhere in the state during spring or fall migrations. Summer habitat is boreal forests.

Breeding: Breeds in the boreal forest of Canada and Alaska. Nest is built on the branch of a conifer. Clutch size is usually 4 or 5 eggs. One clutch per year. Vulnerable to cowbirds.

Natural History: There are two morphologically distinct forms of this common warbler, one in the eastern US and one in the western US. The form seen in Indiana is sometimes called the "Myrtle Warbler." This species also exhibits seasonal plumage changes, with winter birds resembling females. In summer feeds mainly on insects, but if bad weather necessitates it is capable of surviving on berries during the winter. Unlike most warblers that will winter in the tropics, the Yellow-rumped is a hardy species and in mild winters can be seen as far north as southern IL, IN, and OH in the Midwest and NJ on the east coast. Populations of this bird seem fairly stable and it is probably in less jeopardy than many other warblers. Mostly a summer resident but year-round in the southern part of the state.

Habitat: Summer habitat is taiga and tundra-taiga transition zones; often well above the arctic circle. During migration they can be seen in a variety of woodland habitats.

Breeding: Nest is an open cup built on a branch near the tree trunk, usually in a spruce and often only a few feet off the ground. Eggs number 3 to 5. Young fledge as early as within 8 to 10 days.

Natural History: This is one of the great long distance migrants among America's songbird species. In fall migration some may travel non-stop over the Atlantic Ocean from Newfoundland (Canada) all the way to South America. Considering that this is a bird that weighs less than 0.5 ounce, that is a remarkable feat of endurance. To accomplish this remarkable flight they will pack on a heavy layer of fat during summer. Although some individuals will pass through Indiana during the spring, they tend to stay hidden high in the forest canopy. The fall migration is mostly along the east coast. Thus this is a rarely seen bird in the state except by those who train themselves to look for it during spring migration. The fall migration is generally well to the east of Indiana along the Atlantic coast.

Class—**Aves** (birds)

Order—**Passeriformes** (songbirds)

Family—**Parulidae** (warblers)

Bay-breasted Warbler *Setophaga castenea*	Pine Warbler *Setophaga pinus*	Black-throated Green Warbler *Setophaga virens*

Spring male

Fall male

Male

Male

Female

Size: 5.5 inches.

Abundance: Uncommon.

Variation: See photos above. Female resembles fall male.

Migratory Status: Spring migrant. Fall migration is mostly east of the Appalachians.

Presumed range in Indiana

Size: 5.5 inches.

Abundance: Uncommon in Indiana.

Variation: Males are brighter, females and immatures are drabber.

Migratory Status: Mainly a summer resident, a few may linger into late fall or winter.

Presumed range in Indiana

Size: 4.5 inches.

Abundance: Fairly common.

Variation: Females have less black, more yellow on throat.

Migratory Status: In Indiana this species is a seasonal migrant seen in spring and fall only.

Presumed range in Indiana

Habitat: Summer habitat is spruce/fir woodlands of Canada. During migration it is found in a variety of habitats. Winter habitats are tropical forests of Central and South America.

Habitat: Pine forests are the primary habitat, but they are also seen in deciduous and mixed woodlands, especially during migration. In Indiana they occur mostly in the southern part of the state.

Habitat: This warbler requires significant tracts of unbroken forests. Except for migration, it is an inhabitant of conifer and mixed conifer/deciduous forests, especially those containing hemlock.

Breeding: Nests in dense conifer trees on a horizontal limb. Nest is cup-shaped and made of woven twigs, pine needles and grasses. Average clutch size is 5 or 6 eggs.

Breeding: Builds its nest high in pine trees. This is one of the earliest nesting warblers, with 3 or 4 eggs laid as early as mid-April. Breeding range is limited to regions where pines occur.

Breeding: Does not breed in Indiana. Most nesting occurs in the northern Great Lakes and in the Appalachian Mountains. Lays 4 eggs in nest usually built in a conifer.

Natural History: This long distance migrant is not commonly seen by residents of Indiana, as they pass through rather quickly. They migrate later than most other warblers and don't appear in northern Indiana until mid to late May. Their primary food in summer is the Spruce Budworm caterpillar and their populations may rise and fall with the availability of this insect. In winter they will eat fruit. These birds are less common today than decades ago. Populations have declined possibly due to spraying of Canadian forests to control spruce budworms. Ironically, the best controller of destructive insect pests may be insect-eating birds. They winter from southern Central America to northwestern South America.

Natural History: As its name implies, this species is always found in association with pine trees. This is the only warbler whose range is contained entirely within the United States and Canada. It is also the only one of its kind to regularly change its diet from insects to seeds in the winter, thus it is one of the few warblers seen at bird feeders. These birds can reach high densities in winter in the southern pine forests, when resident populations are supplemented by northern migrants. Pine Warblers are much more tolerant of cold weather than other warblers, perhaps because they are able to switch from insects to seeds as a food source. In winter they will gather in large flocks, a characteristic unusual to other warblers.

Natural History: Like others of its kind, this small, handsome warbler faces many threats. Red Squirrels are reportedly an important nest predator in the boreal forests of Canada and New England. In places nesting threats may come from other birds like the Blue Jay and from common and widespread Woodland Rat Snakes. Sharp-shinned Hawks are always a threat to the adults, while Brown-headed Cowbirds parasitize the nest. Human activities such as forest fragmentation threaten populations as a whole. Add to that the impact of Woolly Adelgid insects on hemlock trees and you have an uncertain future for this and many other warbler species. Like many warblers they spend most of their time high in the treetops.

Class—**Aves** (birds)

Order—**Passeriformes** (songbirds)

Family—**Parulidae** (warblers)

Blackburnian Warbler *Setophaga fusca*	**Palm Warbler** *Setophaga palmarum*	**Yellow-throated Warbler** *Setophaga dominca*

Size: 4.5 inches.

Abundance: Fairly common migrant.

Variation: Bright orange of males reduced to yellowish wash on females and immatures.

Migratory Status: A spring/fall migrant.

Presumed range in Indiana

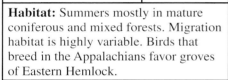

Size: 5.5 inches.

Abundance: Fairly common migrant.

Variation: Exhibits seasonal variation, but winter plumaged birds are not seen in Indiana.

Migratory Status: A spring and fall migrant.

Presumed range in Indiana

Size: 5.25 inches.

Abundance: Fairly common.

Variation: Sexes similar. No significant variation between adults and juveniles.

Migratory Status: A summer resident.

Presumed range in Indiana

Habitat: Summers mostly in mature coniferous and mixed forests. Migration habitat is highly variable. Birds that breed in the Appalachians favor groves of Eastern Hemlock.

Habitat: Summer habitat consists of bogs and woods openings in boreal forests. Transient in a variety of habitats during migration. Winter habitat is open woodlands, mangroves and thickets.

Habitat: In Indiana found mostly along wooded stream corridors. Also uses bottomland forest and mature woodlands with open under-story. Known to often associate with Sycamore trees.

Breeding: Does not nest in Indiana. Elsewhere nest is usually in a conifer and well concealed amid foliage. Average of 4 to 5 eggs.

Breeding: Nests of moss is on the ground in a northern bog, usually at the base of a conifer tree. Clutch size is 4 or 5. Many nest in remote wilderness.

Breeding: Nest is placed high in a tree, often a Sycamore. Nest is made of grasses and spider web and lined with soft materials. Four eggs is typical.

Natural History: The beautiful blaze orange coloration on the head, throat, and breast of the Blackburnian Warbler is unmistakable. They are probably fairly common during migration. However, this is a difficult species to observe due to the fact that it is primarily a treetop dweller. Thus few people who are not trained to look for them will see them. They feed mostly on caterpillars. Blackburnian Warblers seen in Indiana are merely passing through en route to boreal forests far to the north. Some will nest in the southern Appalachians as far south as northern Georgia, but those that pass through Indiana are on their way to more northerly regions in Canada. Forest fragmentation on wintering grounds in South America may pose a threat.

Natural History: This species nests in the boreal forests of Canada and winters along the southeastern US coast and throughout the Caribbean. Unlike most warblers that spend most of their time high in the canopy, the Palm Warbler is a decidedly terrestrial species that hunts primarily on the ground or in low shrubs. It is one of the most northerly wintering of the warblers and most winter in Florida (thus the name Palm Warbler). The winter range also includes the entire gulf coast region. Their summer habitats are very far to the north, well into northern Canada. Food is mainly insects, mostly caught on the ground. Includes grasshoppers, beetles, lepidopterans, flies and bee larva. Some berries and nectar may be consumed in winter.

Natural History: This warbler species can be seen all summer in southern Indiana and a few will nest well north of the area shown on the range map above. They arrive early to mid-April. Winter range is south Florida and the Caribbean. This is another "treetop" species that spends most of its time high in the canopy. It feeds on diminutive arthropods gleaned in a very deliberate fashion from branches, bark, leaves and petioles. This species retreated from the northern portions of its breeding range several decades ago, but is now showing a resurgence back into those areas. The cause of this population fluctuation is unknown but possibly relates to habitat alterations by man and a subsequent recovery of those habitats. They are a rare species in northern Indiana.

Class—**Aves** (birds)

Order—**Passeriformes** (songbirds)

Family—**Parulidae** (warblers)

Prairie Warbler *Setophaga discolor*	**Chestnut-sided Warbler** *Setophaga pensylvanica*	**American Redstart** *Setophaga ruticilla*

Size: 4.75 inches.

Abundance: Fairly common.

Variation: Sexes very similar but female colors more subdued.

Migratory Status: Summer resident in southern half of state.

Presumed range in Indiana

Habitat: Semi-open habitats. Old, overgrown fields, shrubby successional areas, second growth woodlands and cedar glades. Very rare to absent in intensive agricultural areas. Uses coastal dunes during winter.

Breeding: Breeds throughout the southern half of the state. An average of four eggs (3 to 5) are laid May to June.

Natural History: Insects, spiders, slugs and other soft-bodied arthropods are listed as food items. Feeds from the ground all the way up to tree-tops, but mainly gleans lower bushes and shrubs. Tail-bobbing is a common behavior in this species. The Prairie Warbler winters farther north than many warbler species. While some fly as far as the Yucatan Peninsula, others stay in the northern Caribbean or Florida. They can be fairly common in the Florida Everglades during winter. Despite having benefited from clearing of forests the last century, there are unexplained declines in some populations in recent years. Occurs sporadically in Indiana north of the area shown on map above. Males show fidelity to breeding areas and may return year after year.

Size: 5.25 inches.

Abundance: Fairly common migrant.

Variation: Female like male but colors more subdued.

Migratory Status: Mostly a spring/fall migrant in Indiana.

Presumed range in Indiana

Habitat: The Chestnut-sided Warbler is a bird of successional areas and shrubby second-growth. Forest edges, early regenerative timber harvest areas, and forest clearings are favored for nesting. In migration also seen in mature woods.

Breeding: Nests fairly low to the ground in thick cover of dense sapling growth. 3 or 4 eggs are laid in late spring or early summer.

Natural History: This is one of the few warbler species that has benefited from deforestation. They are probably more common now than they were in the days prior to the European settlement of America. Despite their overall increase in population, they are negatively impacted by modern agricultural practices. The clearing of fence rows and overgrown field corners, and conversion of successional habitats into cropland eliminates their preferred habitat. They are thus absent from most regions of intensive agriculture. As with many other migrant warbler species that travel through Indiana, the Chestnut-sided warbler breeds mostly far to the north in Canada or New England. However, there is some breeding that occurs in the northernmost regions of the state.

Size: 5 inches.

Abundance: Fairly common.

Variation: Sexually dimorphic (see photos above).

Migratory Status: Summer resident in forested regions.

Presumed range in Indiana

Habitat: Prefers deciduous woodlands over conifers. More common in second growth areas and riparian thickets. Larger woodlands are preferred over small woodlots. In winter range uses mangroves and tropical forests.

Breeding: The nest woven of thin fibers of grass or bark strips and placed in the crotch of an upright branch or trunk. Usually 4 eggs.

Natural History: The striking bright orange-on-black colors of the male flash like neon in the heavily shaded forests where this species makes its home. The females yellow and black colors are only slightly less evident. They are active little birds that display their bright colors by regularly spreading their tail feathers and drooping their wings. They hunt tiny insects among the foliage and often catch flying insects in mid-air. In Indiana this species is much more common in forested regions and it may be absent from expansive agricultural regions. Small numbers winter in coastal Louisiana, the lower Rio Grande valley and the Everglades region of south Florida. Most winter from northwestern Mexico to northern South America. Clearing of tropical forests is a threat.

Class—**Aves** (birds)

Order—**Passeriformes** (songbirds)

Family—**Parulidae** (warblers)

Cape May Warbler *Setophaga tigrina*	**Orange-crowned Warbler** *Oreothlypis celata*	**Nashville Warbler** *Oreothlypis ruficapilla*

Size: 5 inches.	**Size:** To 5.5 inches.	**Size:** To 5 inches.
Abundance: Fairly common.	**Abundance:** Rare in Indiana.	**Abundance:** Common migrant.
Variation: Females and immatures are less vividly colored.	**Variation:** Female slightly duller. Varies regionally.	**Variation:** Males, females and immatures are all similar.
Migratory Status: Transient spring migrant. Not seen in fall.	**Migratory Status:** Passage migrant in both spring and fall.	**Migratory Status:** A passage migrant in both spring and fall.

Presumed range in Indiana (three maps)

Habitat: This is another species that summers in boreal forests, primarily in the vicinity of spruce bogs and other forest openings. Winter habitat is mostly in the West Indies.	**Habitat:** Summers in northern woodlands (Canada and Rocky Mts.) where it prefers habitats with significant understory. Also found old weedy fields, brier thickets, etc. during migration.	**Habitat:** Summer habitat includes tamarack bogs and boreal forests. Prefers second growth and open woodlands with shrubby undergrowth. Avoids the deep woods.
Breeding: Nest is near the trunk in the top of a spruce or fir. Five or six eggs are laid in early to mid-June. One clutch per year.	**Breeding:** Breeds in northern Canada and as far north as Alaska and well into the Arctic Circle. Western subspecies breeds along west coast. Lays 4 to 5 eggs.	**Breeding:** Nests on the ground under bushes or in hummocks of grasses or sphagnum moss. Clutch size ranges from 3 to 6.
Natural History: On summer breeding grounds far to the north the Cape May Warbler spends its time high in the trees. Feeds heavily on Spruce Budworm caterpillars. Their breeding cycle corresponds to the timing of maximum availability of budworm caterpillars and the population density of this species is known to be closely tied to the presence of this food source. In years of heavy budworm infestations they will rear large broods. On wintering grounds they are known to feed heavily upon nectar and fruits and they have a specialized tubular tongue for extracting nectar from flowers and juices from fruit. The fall migration back to the Caribbean is mostly to the east of Indiana, thus they are only seen in the state for a short time each spring.	**Natural History:** Like most warblers, this species is highly insectivorous, but in winter it also eats some fruit and is known to feed at the sap wells created by sapsucker woodpeckers. Feeds deliberately in the lower branches of trees and in bushes. These can be very common birds on their northern breeding grounds, but they are uncommon in Indiana and seen only during migration. Their range coincides with the North American Continent. They sometimes linger well north of their summer range and have been seen very rarely in northern states in winter. Orange streak on crown from which it derives its name is not typically visible in the field. Winters across the southern US from the Carolinas to California, and south to northernmost Central America.	**Natural History:** This warbler species has benefited from human alterations to the American landscape (they prefer logged over, second-growth habitats). However, some human alterations have also had a very negative effect. As with many other migrant songbirds, they are vulnerable to towers, power lines, and antennas. No one knows exactly how many birds are killed during migration each year by flying into these obstacles, but some estimate the number to be in the millions. Insects are eaten almost exclusively by this warbler. Summers in northern US and Canada, winters in Mexico. Ornithologists recognize two distinct subspecies in North America. One migrates through the Rocky Mountain west, the other subspecies stays east of the Great Plains.

Class—**Aves** (birds)

Order—**Passeriformes** (songbirds)

Family—**Parulidae** (warblers)

Tennessee Warbler	Blue-winged Warbler	Golden-winged Warbler
Oreothlypis peregrina	*Vermivora cyanoptera*	*Vermivora crysoptera*

Size: 4.75 inches.

Abundance: Common migrant.

Variation: Females and fall plumages more greenish overall.

Migratory Status: Passage migrant in both spring and fall.

Presumed range in Indiana

Size: 4.75 inches.

Abundance: Uncommon.

Variation: Hybrids with Golden-winged produces 3 different variants.

Migratory Status: Summer resident in parts of the state.

Presumed range in Indiana

Size: 5 inches.

Abundance: Rare. A declining species.

Variation: Males are more vividly colored. Young resemble female.

Migratory Status: Passage migrant in both spring and fall.

Presumed range in Indiana

Habitat: Summer habitat is the boreal forest of Canada. Winter habitat in Central America is semi-open forest and forest edges. In migration may be seen anywhere.

Habitat: Overgrown weed fields with ample brushy undergrowth and early successional woodlands constitute this bird's primary habitat. Least common in areas of intensive agriculture.

Habitat: Second-growth woodlands and overgrown fields. Summer range is in the boreal forest of Canada and in the higher elevations of the Appalachian Mountains.

Breeding: Nest is on the ground at the base of a tree or among upturned roots. Nest is usually well hidden. Clutch size ranges from 3 to 8.

Breeding: Nest is near the ground in or under a low bush often at the edge of a woodland/field interface. From 4 to 6 eggs are laid in May.

Breeding: Nests on the ground near the ground at the base of a bush, hidden in thick grass and weeds. Nest is a cryptic bowl of dead leaves and grass. 4 to 5 eggs.

Natural History: The numbers of this species passing through Indiana each spring and fall fluctuates depending upon the previous year's abundance of its primary summer food, the Spruce Budworm. In the northern forests of Canada in good budworm years, this is one of the most common bird species. In years of diminished budworm populations, the population of these birds also crashes. This relationship provides a valuable insight into the intricate interdependencies of unrelated organisms. This is an inconspicuous bird as it feeds high in trees and migrates later in the spring after trees are fully leaved. Thus it is difficult to detect despite being common. The name comes from the fact that first scientifically collected specimen was from Tennessee. Can be seen April/May and Sept./Oct.

Natural History: A shrub land specialist, the Blue-winged Warbler experienced an upswing in populations as a result of deforestation by pioneering European settlers of eastern North America. In recent years there has been a decline in their numbers in the northeastern US as forests have begun recovering from the rampant logging of the last century. In North America they are most common in the Appalachian Plateau Province and rare in the agricultural regions of the Interior Lowlands Province (including in Indiana). These birds sometimes hybridize with the similar Golden-winged Warbler and produce at least 3 additional forms of difficult to identify hybrid birds. Populations of this species have declined in recent years due to loss of habitat. In Indiana they are more common in the south.

Natural History: This species may be seen anywhere in the state during migration. But actual sightings of this bird in Indiana may be difficult as they are increasingly rare. They are a highly sought species with the state's birdwatchers. Loss of winter habitat and nest parasitism by the Brown-headed Cowbird are possible reasons for a recent population decline. But hybridization with Blue-winged Warblers which are now expanding their range northward may be the main reason for the increasing rarity of the Golden-winged. They winter in a variety of forest habitats in Mexico, Central America and northern South America from sea level to 7,000 feet. Like many other warblers, this species makes the perilous journey across the Gulf of Mexico in spring.

Class—**Aves** (birds)
Order—**Passeriformes** (songbirds)
Family—**Parulidae** (warblers)

Ovenbird *Seiurus aurocapilla*	**Louisiana Waterthrush** *Parkesia motacilla*	**Northern Waterthrush** *Parkesia novaboracensis*

Ovenbird

Size: 5.5 inches.

Abundance: Fairly common.

Variation: Females and fall plumages more greenish overall.

Migratory Status: Mostly a migrant but a few summer residents.

Presumed range in Indiana

Habitat: Mature, contiguous forests. Seems to prefer upland woods. A substrate of abundant leaf litter is an important element to this bird's habitat. Probably absent from many areas of the state where forests no longer exist.

Breeding: Nest is on the ground and is constructed of leaves and grass. Nest is unique in that it has a domed roof with an opening in front. 3 to 6 eggs.

Natural History: This large warbler is a ground dweller, and is usually observed on the ground or in low foliage. Food is a wide variety of insects and arthropods taken mostly on the ground among the leaf litter. The song of the Ovenbird is distinctive and has been variously described as "emphatic" and "effervescent." Often two nearby birds will sing at once, with their overlapping songs sounding like a single bird. This species has experienced a decline in the last few decades. Forest fragmentation and Brown-headed Cowbird nest parasitism may be to blame. The name "Ovenbird" is derived from the fact that the nest is shaped rather like the old-fashioned brick ovens that had a domed roof and opened to the front. Winters from Florida and tropical Americas.

Louisiana Waterthrush

Size: 6 inches.

Abundance: Fairly common.

Variation: No variation. Sexes and juveniles are all alike.

Migratory Status: Louisiana Waterthrush is a summer resident.

Presumed range in Indiana

Habitat: Louisiana Waterthrush uses forested streams as the preferred habitat. In migration they may also be seen along the edges of swamps or small woodland ponds. More inclined to use streams and flowing waters.

Breeding: Nesting can occur as early as May in southern Indiana. 4 to 6 eggs are laid in a nest placed in tree roots along the banks of a stream.

Natural History: This species is famous for its incessant "tail bobbing" behavior. The entire rear half of the body constantly wags up and down when foraging in stream-side habitats. Requires ecologically healthy stream habitats and this species may be a barometer of overall stream health. Although current populations appear stable, stream degradation in its breeding range has probably reduced its numbers from historical times. Distinguishing between this species and the nearly identical Northern Waterthrush can be very difficult. Noting the range is the most reliable way to differentiate the two. The summer range of the Louisiana is generally south of the Great Lakes. The northern species summers to the north of the Great Lakes.

Northern Waterthrush

Size: 5.25 inches.

Abundance: Fairly common migrant.

Variation: No variation. Sexes and juveniles are all alike.

Migratory Status: This is a passage migrant in Indiana.

Presumed range in Indiana

Habitat: Northern Waterthrush is more inclined to use still water environments and bogs are a favored habitat in the summer breeding range. In migration they are often seen around the edge of woodland ponds or swamps.

Breeding: Breeds from northern Great Lakes and New England all the way to the Arctic Circle in Alaska. Nest is on the ground and well hidden.

Natural History: The Northern Waterthrush is so similar to the Louisiana Waterthrush that most casual observers will not be able to tell them apart. Of the two, the Northern is slightly smaller and has a narrower "eyebrow." The Northern Waterthrush just passes through Indiana while the Louisiana Waterthrush breeds in much of the state. Northern breeds in bogs and beaver ponds in boreal forests of Canada and Alaska. Both species associate with wetland habitats and in migration both can be seen in woodland habitats. Northern Waterthrush feeds in wet, soggy places and will wade in shallow water. It uses its bill to flip dead leaves and often feeds on the top of half submerged logs. Like the Louisiana Waterthrush this species "tail bobs" constantly while feeding.

Class—**Aves** (birds)

Order—**Passeriformes** (songbirds)

Family—**Parulidae** (warblers)

Prothonotary Warbler *Protonotaria citrea*	**Common Yellowthroat** *Geothlypis trichas*	**Kentucky Warbler** *Geothlypis formosus*
 Male	 Male	 Male

Size: 5.5 inches.		**Size:** 4.5 to 5 inches.		**Size:** 5 inches.	
Abundance: Fairly common.	Presumed range in Indiana	**Abundance:** Common.	Presumed range in Indiana	**Abundance:** Uncommon in Indiana.	Presumed range in Indiana
Variation: Females are slightly less vivid in their colors.		**Variation:** Female lacks the prominent black mask.		**Variation:** Female has reduced black mask, otherwise very similar.	
Migratory Status: A summer resident in most of the state.		**Migratory Status:** Summer resident throughout Indiana.		**Migratory Status:** A summer resident in southern Indiana.	

Habitat: Prothonotary Warblers always nest near water. They are most common in swamps and marshes but can also be seen along lake shores, riparian areas, and in the vicinity of small ponds. Most common in the southern tip of the state.	**Habitat:** Likes thick vegetation in wetland areas. Cattails and sedges in marshes and swamp edges are especially favored. Avoids deep woods but may be seen around edges of woods, especially near streams.	**Habitat:** Throughout its summer range the Kentucky Warbler enjoys deciduous bottomland forests and wooded riparian habitats. Within this macro-habitat it requires a micro-habitat of dense undergrowth.
Breeding: Unlike other warblers that build a nest, the Prothonotary Warbler nests in tree cavities. They will also use artificial nest boxes. Lays 4 or 5 eggs.	**Breeding:** The nest is woven from wetland grasses among cattails or sedges. Four to six eggs are laid in late May or early June. Cowbird parasitism occurs.	**Breeding:** A ground nester. The nest is constructed of dead leaves and grasses and is usually well hidden. Four to five eggs are laid by mid-May.
Natural History: The dredging and draining of swamplands throughout the eastern United States significantly reduced breeding habitat for this warbler in the first half of the 20th century. Loss of wetlands in the US has stabilized somewhat in the last few decades, but the species now faces threats from habitat loss on its wintering grounds in northern South America. Most of the swampland habitats in Indiana disappeared with European settlement. In Indiana today this warbler occurs sporadically throughout the state where suitable habitat still exists. In some areas of its range it has recently benefited from the placement of artificial nest boxes. Feeds on aquatic insects, snails and tiny crustaceans. In winter they will also eat fruits and nectar.	**Natural History:** The Common Yellowthroat is one of the more abundant warblers in America and their summer range includes most of North America south of the Arctic. They do avoid the desert southwest and dry southern plains. Not surprising since they are mainly a wetland loving species. They feed low to the ground on almost any type of tiny invertebrate. Their behavior when foraging is rather "wren-like" as they negotiate dense stands of cattails, reeds, and tall grasses. They tend to stick to heavy cover and when flushed make short flights into deep cover. Nearly all of Indiana's Common Yellowthroats move south in the fall, but a few have been been known to linger in the southern part of the state well into late fall.	**Natural History:** Kentucky Warblers are an abundant and widespread bird in suitable habitats throughout the southeastern United States. Although widespread across southern Indiana in summer, they become increasingly scarce northward and in regions of intensive agriculture. They are most common in the southernmost portion of the state. Like other small warblers they are easily overlooked. The Cornell Laboratory of Ornithology (birds online) website reports that this species appears to be in decline. Destruction of mature tropical forests may be to blame. It is also possible that fragmentation of large forest tracts in North America could be a threat. A handsome warbler, it feeds low to the ground on a wide variety of invertebrates.

Class—**Aves** (birds)

Order—**Passeriformes** (songbirds)

Family—**Parulidae** (warblers)

Mourning Warbler *Geothlypis philadelphia*	**Connecticut Warbler** *Oporonis agilis*	**Worm-eating Warbler** *Helmitheros vermivorus*

Mourning Warbler
Geothlypis philadelphia

Size: 5.5 inches.

Abundance: Uncommon in IN.

Variation: Female has less contrasting head color.

Migratory Status: Passsage migrant seen statewide.

Presumed range in Indiana

Habitat: The Mourning Warbler's summer/breeding habitat is mostly in the boreal forests and bogs of Canada. In migration they are most likely to be seen in dense regenerative woodlands. Usually seen on or near the ground.

Breeding: Nests on the ground in dense vegetation or a clump of grass. Lays an average four eggs. Does not breed in Indiana but passes through the state in route to more northerly regions.

Natural History: This warbler likes second growth areas with lush undergrowth. It prefers these conditions both in its summer breeding grounds in boreal forests as well as its wintering grounds in tropical forests. Thus it is one of the few neotropical migrant warblers that has actually benefited from man's insatiable appetite for wood products. They are not easily observed as they are a secretive bird that "skulks" in dense thickets. Unlike many neotropical migrant songbirds that make long distance flights across the Gulf of Mexico, this warbler follows the coastline north through Mexico, Texas and Louisiana before flying inland up the Mississippi Valley and dispersing across northern regions.

Connecticut Warbler
Oporonis agilis

Size: 5.75 inches.

Abundance: Rare in Indiana.

Variation: Females are duller without gray head of male.

Migratory Status: Moves quickly through the state in spring.

Presumed range in Indiana

Habitat: Summer/breeding habitat is boreal forest. There it prefers edges of coniferous woodlands bordering wetland habitats like tamarack bogs and muskeg. Winter habitat is forests in Central and South America.

Breeding: Nest is hidden in thick undergrowth on or near the ground. Three to five eggs are laid in late June. Young birds fledge in late July or early August. Does not breed in Indiana.

Natural History: This shy warbler is rarely observed. In part due to its secretive nature (migrating birds are typically observed low to the ground in dense undergrowth). In addition, it occurs in the state only briefly during migration. Finally, this is one of the rarest of America's warblers. Even on the breeding grounds they favor remote regions where they are difficult to locate. Most breeding is in Canada, but they do breed in parts of northern Wisconsin and Minnesota. Despite its name, this species is quite rare in Connecticut, where it may only occasionally be seen during fall migration. Due to its secretive nature and relative rarity, this is one of the least understood and least commonly observed of America's warbler species.

Worm-eating Warbler
Helmitheros vermivorus

Size: 5 inches.

Abundance: Uncommon in IN.

Variation: No significant variation and the sexes are alike.

Migratory Status: Summer resident and passage migrant.

Presumed range in Indiana

Habitat: This is a woodland species, but it seems to avoid lowland forests. It is more common in summer in rugged regions with steep slopes. It may occur in a wide variety of habitats during migration.

Breeding: Nests are built on the ground in deep woods and are often hidden beneath overhanging vegetation. 4 to 5 eggs is typical. They do breed in southern Indiana.

Natural History: Although the Worm-eating Warbler may be seen throughout Indiana during migration they are quite rare in the northern half of Indiana and uncommon in the southern half. This is a species that specializes in feeding amid low bushes, searching the dead leaf clusters and low hanging foliage for insects, spiders and primarily, caterpillars. Like many of America's neotropical migrant songbirds, the Worm-eating warbler is highly dependent upon deciduous forests for breeding habitat. They need large tracts of woodland. They winter in Mexico, Central America and the West Indies. Despite their name, earthworms are not an important item in their diet. Spiders and insects are their primary foods.

Class—**Aves** (birds)

Order—**Passeriformes** (songbirds)

Family—**Icturidae** (blackbirds)

Brown-headed Cowbird *Molothrus ater*	**Red-winged Blackbird** *Agelaius phoeniceus*	**Common Grackle** *Quiscalus quiscula*

Size: 7.5 to 8 inches.

Abundance: Very common.

Variation: Sexually dimorphic. See photos above.

Migratory Status: Year-round resident most conspicuous in winter.

Presumed range in Indiana

Habitat: Open fields and agricultural areas primarily, but can also be common in towns and suburbs. Inhabits edge areas and woods openings but avoids deep forest.

Breeding: Female cowbirds lay their eggs in the nest of other bird species, a unique nesting strategy known as "brood parasitism" (see below). As many as 40 eggs may be laid in dozens of songbird nests.

Natural History: This species is unique among Indiana birds in that the adults play no role in rearing their young. Instead the female lays an egg in another species' nest and the adoptive parents rear the young cowbird, usually to the detriment of their own offspring. The disappearance of extensive forest tracts has allowed the cowbird to parasitize many more woodland songbirds than was possible prior to settlement. As a result, this species has increased in numbers and now poses a real threat to many smaller songbird species, especially the warblers. In winter Cowbirds will join with mixed flocks of other blackbird species. They can become an unwelcome nuisance at backyard bird feeders during harsh weather.

Size: 9 inches.

Abundance: Common.

Variation: Sexual and seasonal plumage variations.

Migratory Status: Although migratory, seen year-round in Indiana.

Presumed range in Indiana

Habitat: The Red-wing Blackbirds favorite breeding habitat is marsh or wet meadows. They are also found along roadside ditches and the edges of ponds in open areas.

Breeding: The nest of the Red-winged Blackbird is a woven basket usually suspended from two or three cattail blades and is most often positioned over water. Two to four eggs are laid. Young are fed enormous quantities of insects.

Natural History: In winter Red-winged Blackbirds often join large mixed flocks that can include all the birds shown on this page. All together the blackbirds are probably the most numerous birds in Indiana in winter. Males sing conspicuously in spring. Like the other blackbirds on this page, the Red-winged has benefited from human alterations to Indiana's natural habitats, thriving in open land and agricultural areas. Food is almost entirely insects and along with other members of the blackbird family (Icturidae) this species plays an important role in insect control. The bright red and yellow "epaulets" on the wing of the male are greatly reduced in winter, but some color is still visible on the wing.

Size: 12.5 inches.

Abundance: Very common.

Variation: Female is slightly less vividly colored.

Migratory Status: Although migratory, seen year-round in Indiana.

Presumed range in Indiana

Habitat: Grackles favor agricultural areas and open fields/croplands. They are also common in urban areas where they inhabit lawns, parks, etc. In winter roosts in large flocks in small woodlots.

Breeding: Grackles often nest in groups that may consist of a dozen or more pairs. The nest is built in the upper branches of medium-size trees and several nests can be in the same tree, or in adjacent trees.

Natural History: Grackles are known for forming large flocks during the winter that will roost communally and can number in the thousands. When these large congregations move into a town or neighborhood they can become a messy nuisance, but their reputation for spreading disease is exaggerated. Throughout most of the year they are busy consuming millions of insect pests. In harsh winter weather they may descend on backyard bird feeders in large flocks that overwhelm the regular residents, creating consternation among backyard birdwatchers. The two color morphs known as "bronze" and "purple" reflect the color of the iridescence of the plumage. Indiana birds are typically purple morphs.

Class—**Aves** (birds)

Order—**Passeriformes** (songbirds)

Family—**Icturidae** (blackbirds)

Bobolink *Dolichonyx oryzivorus*	**Rusty Blackbird** *Euphagus carolinus*	**Brewer's Blackbird** *Euphagus cyanocephalus*

Size: 7 to 8 inches.

Abundance: Uncommon.

Variation: Females and winter males are sparrow-like in color.

Migratory Status: Summer resident in northern IN, migrant in southern IN.

Presumed range in Indiana

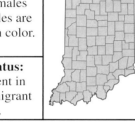

Size: 9 inches.

Abundance: Uncommon to rare.

Variation: Significant seasonal plumage variations. See photos above.

Migratory Status: Both a seasonal migrant and a winter resident. Most winter to the south of IN.

Presumed range in Indiana

Size: 9.5 inches.

Abundance: Uncommon in Indiana.

Variation: Females are drab brown. Males are iridescent blue-black.

Migratory Status: A winter/spring migrant visitor from the western United States.

Presumed range in Indiana

Habitat: Boblinks are open country birds and they are usually seen in pastures and hayfields. Their original habitats in the state were probably tallgrass prairies, which no longer exist in any significant amount.

Habitat: Wintering Rusty Blackbirds favor wetland habitats. Floodplain forests, edges of swamps and woods bordering marshes make up the bulk of this bird's winter habitat. Summers in wet boreal woodlands and tundra edges.

Habitat: Favors open country. It is often seen in harvested or plowed agricultural fields, pastures, etc. It may also frequent feedlots where it feeds on waste grain. In the bulk of its range out west it inhabits grasslands.

Breeding: Females breed with a number of males and a clutch of 5 eggs may have several fathers. Nest is woven of grasses and placed on the ground.

Breeding: Breeding occurs far to the north (as far as the arctic). An average of four eggs are laid in a bulky nest of twigs, lichens and grass.

Breeding: As many as 8 eggs may be laid, but 5 or 6 is probably average. Nests on the ground. Nesting has been recorded nearby in northern Illinois.

Natural History: Boblinks are one of the greatest migrators of any songbird seen in Indiana. They will nest in the northern US and Canada and winter in southern South America in the open grasslands of the Pampas region of Uruguay and Argentina. That's a round trip of nearly 20,000 miles! In Indiana they are more common in the northern half of the state where they are a nesting bird. They are migrants in southern Indiana. This species has experienced population declines in the last half century, but has recently benefited from CRP programs. Food items include seeds, grains and many invertebrates during breeding. Many people are surprised to learn that these handsome birds are in the blackbird family.

Natural History: In the last few years Rusty Blackbirds have garnered the attention of birdwatchers and conservationists concerned about an apparently significant decline in the population of this species. The loss of wet woodlands to agriculture throughout much of their wintering grounds in the southern US may be partly to blame. Unlike many blackbirds that regularly intermingle with other species, the Rusty Blackbird seems to remain mostly segregated from the large winter flocks of grackles, cowbirds, Starlings and Red-wingeds. These birds summer far to the north and are seen in Indiana mostly in winter. They will migrate farther to the south if the winter weather gets harsh. Food is insects, seeds, grains, etc.

Natural History: The Brewer's Blackbird is a western species that historically inhabited the Great Plains and Rocky Mountain Regions all the way to the Pacific Ocean. With the clearing of land brought on by human activities, the Brewer's Blackbird began to invade the Eastern Temperate Forest Level I Ecoregion in the early 1900s. Although they are still uncommon in Indiana compared to our other blackbirds, birdwatchers report sporadic sightings throughout the state. A few summer in extreme northern Indiana. Feeds mostly on grains and seeds of grasses or weeds in winter. Summer diet is largely insects, including prodigious numbers of grasshoppers. They are very common birds in western North America.

Class—**Aves** (birds)

Order—**Passeriformes** (songbirds)

Family—**Icturidae** (blackbirds)

Yellow-headed Blackbird *Xanthocephalus xanthocephalus*	Eastern Meadowlark *Sturnella magna*	Western Meadowlark *Sturnella neglecta*

Size: 9.5 inches.

Abundance: Very rare in Indiana.

Variation: Sexually dimorphic. See photos above.

Migratory Status: Rare summer resident in extreme northwestern Indiana.

Presumed range in Indiana

Habitat: A marsh specialist. Throughout their range in the western US they are common around "prairie potholes," lake-shores, marshes, beaver ponds and creeks where cattails and sedges dominate. They are very rare in Indiana.

Breeding: A cup-like nest is woven around several upright stalks of cattail or sedge. Averages 3 to 5 eggs and produces only one clutch per season.

Natural History: Feeds heavily on aquatic insects during the breeding season and feeds them to the young exclusively. In fall and winter switches to weed seeds and grains. When engaged in territorial displays and singing the males are quite conspicuous. Females are more discreet and sometimes difficult to observe. Adult males migrate separately from females and juveniles. They are seemingly less tolerant of cold than most other blackbirds as they will arrive on northern breeding grounds later and depart earlier than other blackbirds. Winters in the southwestern United States and most of Mexico. Greatest abundance in summer is in the Dakotas. This is a state endangered species in Indiana.

Size: 9.5 inches.

Abundance: Common.

Variation: Breeding adults exhibit slightly brighter colors.

Migratory Status: This species is a year-round resident throughout the state.

Presumed range in Indiana

Habitat: Open, treeless pastures and fields that are kept closely grazed or mowed. They like short grasses and avoid overgrown areas. In winter they are often seen in harvested croplands or emerging wheat fields.

Breeding: Nest is on the ground and well hidden beneath overhanging grasses or under the edge of a grass tussock. 3 to 5 eggs.

Natural History: As might be expected of a bird that loves open spaces, the Eastern Meadowlark is least common in forested regions of the state. Even in the heavily wooded regions however, this bird can be found in areas of open habitat. They feed mostly on insects in warmer months, with grasshoppers and crickets being a dietary mainstay in the summer. During winter they will eat seeds and grain. They tend to occur in small flocks during the winter, but pair off and scatter in the breeding season. This species is fond of perching on fence wires and posts. The following species (Western Meadowlark) is nearly identical. Expert birders rely on listening to the bird's songs to make a positive identification.

Size: 9.5 inches.

Abundance: Rare in Indiana.

Variation: Breeding adults exhibit slightly brighter colors.

Migratory Status: This species is a summer resident in northernmost Indiana.

Presumed range in Indiana

Habitat: Open, treeless pastures and fields that are kept closely grazed or mowed. They like short grasses and avoid overgrown areas. In winter they are often seen in harvested croplands or emerging wheat fields.

Breeding: Nest is on the ground. Woven from grass stems and may be open or domed, with or without tunnel-like entrance. Lays 5 or 6 eggs.

Natural History: In appearance (and most other respects) the Western Meadowlark is very similar to the eastern species. Visually, the yellow on the throat of the Western extends farther beneath the lower jaw (malar). One might reasonably wonder how two so similar species can co-exist without interbreeding. The answer is likely in the fact that their songs are decidedly different. Thus breeders respond only to the songs of their own species. Northern Indiana is near the eastern edge of this species range. The bulk of the population resides in the Great Plains region. They also range westward through the Rocky Mountains all the way to the Pacific Ocean. They are regarded as a Species of Special Concern in Indiana.

Class—**Aves** (birds)

Order—**Passeriformes** (songbirds)

Family—**Icturidae** (blackbirds)

Baltimore Oriole *Icturus galbula*	**Orchard Oriole** *Icturus spurius*

Size: 7.5 inches.

Abundance: Common. Most common in northern Indiana.

Migratory Status: A summer resident that begins to return to southern Indiana in late April with migrants arriving through late May in northern Indiana. Winters in Florida, Cuba, Jamaica, and southern Mexico south to northern South America.

Variation: Significant sexual and age-related dimorphism (see photos above). Immature male less vividly colored.

Habitat: Savanna-like habitats are preferred. Pastures with scattered large trees, parks and lawns in urban areas, or farms and ranches in rural areas. During migration may be seen in a variety of habitats.

Breeding: The nest is an easily recognizable "hanging basket" woven from grasses and suspended from a tree limb. 4 to 6 eggs is typical. Favors elm trees for nesting.

Natural History: These handsome orange and black birds are a favorite with backyard birdwatchers. They will come to nectar feeders and fruits such as oranges, and they relish grape jelly. In addition to nectar and fruit they feed heavily on insects. In some areas of their range they have adapted well to human activities. Small town neighborhoods and city parks are among their habitats today. Although they are fond of semi-open habitats and avoid dense forests, they do like the presence of some mature trees in their habitat. Thus, they may decline from areas where intensive agriculture reduces the presence of woodland patches and large trees.

Size: 7 inches.

Abundance: Fairly common statewide.

Migratory Status: Summer resident that breeds throughout the state. Returns in late April through mid-May. Departs from northern portions of breeding range early as late July. Winters from southern Mexico to northern South America.

Variation: Significant sexual and ontogenetic plumage variation. Immature males resemble female (see photos).

Habitat: This species shows a preference for semi-open habitats and narrow strips of woodland bordering rivers and streams. Their name comes from the fact that they are fond of orchards and they will often nest in fruit trees.

Breeding: The nest is a rounded basket woven from grasses and suspended from a forked tree branch. Four eggs is typical, but can be as many as six.

Natural History: Like the larger Baltimore Oriole, Orchard Orioles will eat fruit. They also feed on a wide variety of arthropods gleaned from tree branches and leaves, as well as from weedy fields. Immature males resemble females but have a large black throat patch. These birds are somewhat gregarious and they often occur in flocks on tropical wintering grounds. They are also known to nest in small colonies where ideal habitat exists. Spraying for insects in orchards can be dangerous for these insect and fruit eaters as it can be for other bird species, many of which are highly susceptible to insecticides.

Class—**Aves** (birds)

Order—**Passeriformes** (songbirds)

Family—**Sturnidae** (mynas)	Family—**Passeridae** (weaver finches)

European Starling
Sturnis vulgaris

Breeding adult
Non-breeding adult

Juvenile

House Sparrow
Passer domesticus

Male

Female

Size: 8.75 inches.

Abundance: Very common.

Migratory Status: A non-migratory year-round resident throughout the state.

Variation: Breeding plumage iridescent dark purple, non-breeding has white speckles. Immatures are drab brown.

Presumed range in Indiana

Size: 6.25 inches.

Abundance: Very common.

Migratory Status: Non-migratory, the House Sparrow is year-round resident of Indiana.

Variation: Males have distinctive gray crown with black face mask. Females are a plain drab brown. See photos.

Presumed range in Indiana

Habitat: Urban and suburban areas as well as farms and ranches. Starlings are closely tied to human activity and are rarely seen in true wilderness. By contrast, they can be quite common in large cities and small towns.

Habitat: The House Sparrow's name comes from its affinity for human habitations. These are mostly urban birds and when they do occur in rural areas it is always near farms and homesteads.

Breeding: Nest is made of grass, leaves, etc., stuffed into a cavity. Often uses cracks or holes in man-made structures. Also old woodpecker holes. Clutch size is typically 5 eggs.

Breeding: House Sparrows build bulky nests of grass, feathers, paper strips, etc. placed in hollows or crevices of barns, outbuildings or even occupied homes. 5 to 6 eggs on average.

Natural History: The Starling is one of the most familiar birds in America, but ironically it is a non-native species. All the Starlings in America are descendant from a handful of birds released in New York City in the 1890s. Contrary to popular belief, the Starling is not related to the blackbirds. Instead they belong to the same family as the old world mynas. These birds have enjoyed remarkable success since being introduced to North America and they are now found throughout the continent. They represent a real threat to many of our native species, especially those that nest in cavities. In winter they often join grackles and blackbirds in large mixed flocks that can become messy nuisance in urban and suburban areas. Along with the blackbirds, these birds are sometimes regarded as a threat to humans due to the avian-borne disease Histoplasmosis. In truth, this threat is exaggerated. The statewide population is probably several million birds.

Natural History: A European immigrant, the House Sparrow was released into the United States about 150 years ago. They have spread across the continent and they are now perhaps the most familiar bird species in America. Originally native to Eurasia they followed European immigrants and have effectively colonized much of the world. They roost communally in dense vegetation. Roosting sites are often in yards or foundation plantings next to houses. They are common scavengers around outdoor restaurants and fast food parking lots. They are often considered to be a nuisance bird, but their tame demeanor endears them to many. Despite being extremely common in urban areas, they are quite rare in wilderness. These highly successful birds may nest up to four times in a season. Despite their common name, House "Sparrow," they are not closely related to sparrows. They belong to an old world family known as the Weaver Finches.

Class—**Aves** (birds)

Order—**Passeriformes** (songbirds)

Family—**Emberzidae** (sparrows)

Swamp Sparrow *Melospiza georgiana*	**Song Sparrow** *Melospiza melodia*	**Lincoln's Sparrow** *Melospiza lincolnii*

Size: 5.75 inches.

Abundance: Fairly common.

Variation: Breeding males are richer in color with a reddish crown.

Migratory Status: Year-round resident in northern Indiana, winter resident in southern Indiana.

Presumed range in Indiana

Habitat: Summers in wetlands. Swamps, marshes (including salt marsh in coastal regions) and wet meadows. More diverse habitats may be used in winter, including upland fields.

Breeding: Nest is made of grasses and placed in cattails, grasses or low bush. Three to six eggs, four is average.

Natural History: Secretive and elusive, the Swamp Sparrow is less familiar to Indianans than most of its kin. They will visit feeders during the winter, but they are rarely a commonly seen bird at feeders. These birds are highly dependent upon wetlands for breeding, and they may be negatively impacted by loss of wetlands. At this time however populations appear stable. Grassy fields are also heavily used and can be an important winter refuge. Although they can be quite common in summer habitats and in the bayous of the deep south in winter, they do not flock and are nearly always seen singly. There are three distinct subspecies of Swamp Sparrow recognized by professional ornithologists.

Size: 5.5 inches.

Abundance: Common.

Variation: Many subspecies nationwide with light and dark morphs.

Migratory Status: Year-round resident but numbers may be bolstered in winter by migrants.

Presumed range in Indiana

Habitat: Overgrown fields, dense underbrush, and rank weeds are the preferred habitat of the Song Sparrow throughout their range. They are especially common in edge habitats.

Breeding: Nests are built low to the ground in weeds or shrubs. Four eggs is typical.

Natural History: Both the common and scientific names of the Song Sparrow are references to its distinct and melodic song. Primarily seed eaters, these sparrows migrate in response to heavy snow cover, and they are common at bird feeders throughout the southern United States each winter. Sharp-shinned and Cooper's Hawks are major predators of adults, and the young and eggs are vulnerable to a variety of snake predators. However, they remain a thriving species. There are dozens of subspecies nationwide with light and dark color morphs. Most Indiana specimens resemble the photo above. One of the earliest and most comprehensive studies of bird biology was conducted on this species.

Size: 5.5 inches.

Abundance: Uncommon to rare.

Variation: No significant variation between sexes or juveniles.

Migratory Status: Spring and fall migrant. Possibly seen statewide during migration.

Presumed range in Indiana

Habitat: Summer habitat is boreal regions of Canada and northern Rockies where it occupies damp woodlands with dense brush such as willow. Spruce bogs and wetlands are favored.

Breeding: Nests on the ground amid sedges or at the base of willow in boreal wetlands. Lays 3 to 5 eggs.

Natural History: Lincoln's Sparrows are more common west of the Mississippi and are rather rare in Indiana. In addition it is shy and secretive and tends to stick to heavy cover. Add to this the fact that it is a transient species in the state and sightings are uncommon. During migration they are believed to be fairly widespread across the state. When excited they will raise the feathers on the back of the head giving them a "crested" look. Due to their secretive habits the biology of these sparrows is not well understood. Feeds on insects in summer and seeds in winter. Unlike many sparrows they rarely visit feeders except during periods of harsh winter weather. Very similar to the Song Sparrow, but has finer streaking.

Class—**Aves** (birds)
Order—**Passeriformes** (songbirds)
Family—**Emberzidae** (sparrows)

Chipping Sparrow *Spizella passerina*	**Clay-colored Sparrow** *Spizella pallida*	**Field Sparrow** *Spizella pusilla*

Chipping Sparrow
Spizella passerina

Size: 5.5 inches.

Abundance: Common.

Variation: Females and winter males are sparrow-like in color.

Migratory Status: A summer resident that returns as early as March.

Presumed range in Indiana

Habitat: Edge areas and woods openings. Thrives in human altered habitats including farmsteads, suburban yards and parks.

Breeding: Breeds earlier than most other sparrows. Nests may be complete and eggs can be laid as early as mid-April.

Natural History: Chipping Sparrows move to the deep south in winter. Nesting has been recorded throughout the state but they may be more common as breeding birds in the central and northern parts of the state. They adapt well to the human disturbance of natural habitats and they are undoubtedly more common today than prior to settlement. They can be quite common in areas of intensive agriculture and also in urban/suburban environments. In fact, this is one of the most common sparrows in the state during summer months and will forage in lawns. They can also be a common bird at feeders in early spring. They feed mostly on the seeds of grasses and forbs, and do most of their foraging on the ground. Insects are eaten during the breeding season and are fed to the young.

Clay-colored Sparrow
Spizella pallida

Size: 5.5 inches.

Abundance: Rare in Indiana.

Variation: Non-breeding birds are paler. No sexual dimorphism.

Migratory Status: Spring migrant in the northernmost portion of the state.

Presumed range in Indiana

Habitat: This is an open country species that prefers grasslands. Often uses abandoned fields taken over by weeds, grass, and brush.

Breeding: Typically nest is close to the ground in grassy or brushy environments. 4 eggs is typical. Breeding is well to the north of Indiana.

Natural History: This species may be a newcomer to the Midwest. In Ohio the first observations occurred in the 1940s. The core range for this species is in the Great Plains region. Range expansion eastward into the Great Lakes region apparently began in the 1920s. It is still an uncommon to rare bird in Indiana but it may be increasing in numbers. In its core range in the Great Plains ecosystem this species continues to maintain healthy population numbers in spite of the fact that this is one of the most damaged of all America's natural habitats. It is still one of the more common birds in the northern plains of Canada and North Dakota in summer. Winter range extends south into Texas and Mexico. A drab bird that lacks prominent features. In fall plumage they are difficult to distinguish from the Chipping Sparrow.

Field Sparrow
Spizella pusilla

Size: 5.75 inches.

Abundance: Common.

Variation: Immature birds have dark streaks on the breast.

Migratory Status: Year-round resident in most of the state, but summer only in north.

Presumed range in Indiana

Habitat: Open and semi-open areas with good cover in the form of weeds and taller grasses. Also shrubby, early regenerative woodland areas.

Breeding: Nest is on the ground usually at the base of a clump of grass or in a low bush. Two broods per year is common. Two to five eggs.

Natural History: Another species that has adapted well to man-made changes in natural landscapes, the Field Sparrow is probably more numerous today than in historical times. Unlike many sparrows however, the Field Sparrow is a "country" sparrow that prefers rural regions over towns and suburbs. Although they are seen year-round in southern Indiana, some southerly movement probably occurs in northern populations in winter. Food is mostly grass seeds. Insects are also eaten, especially during the breeding season. Very similar to the American Tree Sparrow, but has all pink bill instead of dark upper mandible. Although still a common species the Field Sparrow has experienced population declines in recent years. Perhaps due to habitat changes in much of its range.

Class—**Aves** (birds)

Order—**Passeriformes** (songbirds)

Family—**Emberzidae** (sparrows)

American Tree Sparrow *Spizelloides arborea*	**Lark Sparrow** *Chondestes grammacus*	**Savannah Sparrow** *Passerculus sandwichensis*

American Tree Sparrow — *Spizelloides arborea*

Size: 6.25 inches.

Abundance: Fairly common in winter.

Variation: Immatures have dusky streaks on the sides and breast.

Migratory Status: A winter resident throughout Indiana. Summers in the far north.

Presumed range in Indiana

Habitat: In winter they use overgrown fields, edge areas and brushy patches with weeds and grasses. Tallgrass Prairies are a favorite refuge. Summer habitat is typically open tundra and taiga.

Breeding: Nest is on the ground. 4 to 6 eggs. These hardy sparrows will nest as far north as the Arctic Circle and well above the tree line.

Natural History: The American Tree Sparrow is a northern species that is only seen in Indiana in winter when heavy snow cover in the northern regions pushes migrating flocks southward. Like most sparrows, seeds are the staple food in winter. Seeds are also eaten in summer months but insects are more important, especially when rearing young. Seeds of a wide variety of grasses and weeds are consumed and this species is regularly seen at bird feeders in northern states. Despite its name this species can be found in summer on treeless, arctic tundra. Winter migrants begin to arrive in the northern US by late October and may reach southernmost Indiana by November. Degree of southerly movement can be dictated by weather conditions.

Lark Sparrow — *Chondestes grammacus*

Size: 6.25 inches.

Abundance: Uncommon in Indiana.

Variation: Immatures have dark streaks on the breast.

Migratory Status: Summer migrant and resident that is a rare breeder in the state.

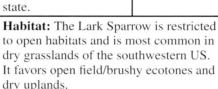
Presumed range in Indiana

Habitat: The Lark Sparrow is restricted to open habitats and is most common in dry grasslands of the southwestern US. It favors open field/brushy ecotones and dry uplands.

Breeding: Nest is usually on the ground but may be in a low bush. 3 to 6 eggs is typical. Known to sometimes use the abandoned nest of another bird.

Natural History: A western species that ranges into Indiana but rather sporadically, mostly occurring in the western part of the state. They have expanded their range in the state since European settlement. Although they are an uncommon breeding bird in Indiana, in their core range west of the Mississippi River they are a common sparrow species. Males are reported to perform a courtship "dance" that resembles that of a turkey's strutting behavior. The Lark Sparrow's facial pattern of vivid black and white stripes with chestnut cheek patch is distinctive. As with most sparrows, seeds are the primary food in winter. During warmer months both seeds and insects are eaten. Grasshoppers are reported to be a major food item in summer.

Savannah Sparrow — *Passerculus sandwichensis*

Size: 5.5 inches.

Abundance: Fairly common.

Variation: Highly variable with as many as 28 subspecies.

Migratory Status: Summer resident in northern Indiana. Winter resident in south.

Presumed range in Indiana

Habitat: Pastures, grasslands, mowed areas, cultivated fields, and vacant lots in urban areas are all used in Indiana. Elsewhere salt marsh, tundra and bogs are also habitats.

Breeding: Nests on the ground beneath overhanging vegetation. 4 to 5 eggs is typical. Nesting in Indiana is mostly in glaciated regions of the state.

Natural History: This is one of the most widespread sparrow species in America. Between breeding range, winter range, and migration routes the Savannah Sparrow may be seen anywhere on the continent. In Indiana they are a summer resident in all but the southern tip of the state, where they can be seen in winter and during migration. They feed on arthropods in summer and seeds in winter. The name comes from the Georgia town of Savannah (where the first specimen was described) rather than from the habitat type. As with many grassland animals the Savannah Sparrow has experienced population declines in areas of intensive agriculture or urbanization. Delaying cutting of hayfields benefits the species by allowing young time to fledge.

Class—**Aves** (birds)
Order—**Passeriformes** (songbirds)
Family—**Emberzidae** (sparrows)

Henslow's Sparrow *Ammodramus henslowii*	Grasshopper Sparrow *Ammodramus savannarum*	Nelson's Sparrow *Ammodramus nelsoni*

Henslow's Sparrow

Size: 5 inches.

Abundance: Uncommon.

Variation: Females and winter males are sparrow-like in color.

Migratory Status: Summer resident that winters in the lower Gulf Coastal Plain.

Presumed range in Indiana

Habitat: Undisturbed, overgrown grassy/weedy fields in open areas. Unmowed hayfields and re-claimed strip mines are used today. Original habitat is Tallgrass Prairie.

Breeding: Nest is on the ground in thick grass and well concealed. 2 to 5 eggs are laid in May. Double-broods are known.

Natural History: Henslow's Sparrow is nowhere a common species and its relative scarcity and secretive nature make it one of the least familiar birds in the state. This is a species in decline throughout its range. Not surprising since the tallgrass prairies that once provided ample nesting habitat are all but gone. Insects, especially grasshoppers and crickets, are important food items in the summer. In winter eats mostly seeds, especially small grass seeds. Snakes are reported to be a major predator on nests, along with a variety of carnivorous mammals. Breeds sparingly across much of Indiana but presumably can be seen throughout most of the state. However it is today usually quite rare and regarded as an endangered species in Indiana.

Grasshopper Sparrow

Size: 5 inches.

Abundance: Uncommon in Indiana.

Variation: No sexual dimorphism and no significant variation.

Migratory Status: Summer resident. Late April to August or September.

Presumed range in Indiana

Habitat: A grassland species, the Grasshopper sparrow likes short and mid-grass prairie. In the eastern regions of its range it uses heavily grazed pastures and hayfields.

Breeding: Nest is on the ground and well hidden beneath overhanging grass. Two broods per summer is usual with 4 to 5 eggs per clutch.

Natural History: In many ways similar to the preceding species, but much more common. Its name is derived from the sound of its song which mimics the buzzing sound made by some types of orthopteran insects. Throughout its range (which includes most of the US east of the Rocky Mountains) it is a rather inconspicuous bird. Though uncommon in the state and unfamiliar to most Indianans, in the high plains region of the north-central US it is commonly seen (and heard). Feeds entirely on the ground. Food is mostly grasshoppers and other insects in summer. In winter eats both insects and seeds, especially tiny grass seeds. Although it has been experiencing a population decline for several years, it is not yet regarded as a threatened species.

Nelson's Sparrow

Size: 5 inches.

Abundance: Rare in Indiana.

Variation: No sexual dimorphism and no significant variation.

Migratory Status: Rare in the state, but possible migrant in most of Indiana.

Presumed range in Indiana

Habitat: Primary habitat is marshes, both fresh (in summer) and brackish and salt marshes in winter. Breeding habitat includes wet meadows. Also may use grassy fields during migration.

Breeding: Nest is a cup-like structure placed amid and supported by upright grass stems. 3 to 5 eggs is typical, with a minimum of 2 and maximum of 6.

Natural History: Nelson's Sparrow winters along the southeastern coastline of the US from the Chesapeake Bay to Texas. Most spend the summer in the Canadian plains or along the southern shore of Hudson Bay. A few will pass through Indiana enroute to and from summer breeding grounds in Canada and winter range along the Gulf Coast. Until recently this species was considered conspecific with the Salt Marsh Sparrow. This species requires large tracts of undisturbed marshland or grassland habitat and both habitats have experienced significant alteration or outright destruction. Additionally, loss of grassland habitat in central Canada and loss of coastal marshes also pose a significant threat to this species. This is one of America's handsomest sparrows.

Class—**Aves** (birds)

Order—**Passeriformes** (songbirds)

Family—**Emberzidae** (sparrows)

Eastern Towhee *Pipilo erythrophthalmus*	Fox Sparrow *Passerella iliaca*	Vesper Sparrow *Pooecetes gramineus*

Size: 8 inches.

Presumed range in Indiana

Abundance: Common.

Variation: Sexually dimorphic. See photos above,

Migratory Status: Year-round in southern Indiana. Summer resident in northern IN.

Habitat: Successional woodlands, overgrown fields/fence rows, edges of stream courses and woodlots where honeysuckle, briers, weeds and saplings are predominate.

Breeding: Nests are low to the ground or even on the ground. Usually 4 eggs. Nesting can occur throughout the state. Nest is usually well hidden.

Natural History: Our largest member of the sparrow family. Sometimes called "Rufous-sided Towhee." Its "tow-wheee" song is a familiar sound beginning as early as March. The widespread range of the Eastern Towhee corresponds closely to the Eastern Temperate Forest ecoregion, but they normally do not occur in dense populations. Most bird feeders in rural areas of the eastern US will have a pair for the winter, but rarely more than two pairs. Spends most of its time on the ground or in low bushes and thickets. Food is mostly seeds in winter and insects in summer. Berries and fruits like crabapple are also consumed when in season. Historical publications suggest this species may be expanding its range farther to north.

Size: 7 inches.

Presumed range in Indiana

Abundance: Uncommon.

Variation: Variable. Photo above is typical for Indiana specimens.

Migratory Status: A winter resident in most of the state. Migrant in NE corner of the state.

Habitat: The Fox Sparrow is a lover of dense cover and thickets. Thick weeds and shrubs bordering woodlands or thickets. A mixture of brier, saplings, weeds, regenerating timberlands, etc.

Breeding: Nests are low to the ground or even on the ground. Breeding is in the boreal forests of Canada and in the northern Rockies. Usually 4 eggs.

Natural History: The Fox Sparrow is widespread across the North American Continent, summering in the far north (Canada, Alaska, and the northern Rockies) and wintering across much of the southern United States. Several distinct subspecies are recognized. The "Red" subspecies (*iliaca*) is the form seen in the eastern US and Indiana specimens will resemble the photo above. They feed on a variety of insects and other arthropods in summer and subsist mainly on seeds in winter. They can be an occasional to regular visitor at bird feeders during winter, especially during periods of snowy weather. Unlike many other sparrows, the Fox Sparrow is never seen in large flocks and it is rare to have more than one or two at a time visiting feeders.

Size: 6.25 inches.

Presumed range in Indiana

Abundance: Fairly common.

Variation: No sexual dimorphism and no significant variation.

Migratory Status: Summer resident. Most common in northern Indiana.

Habitat: This is a bird of open country. Its natural habitats are grasslands and today it also uses agricultural fields. Prefers dry areas and upland fields over wet meadows or marshes.

Breeding: Nest is on the ground in open fields, sometimes concealed by grass tussock. 3 to 5 eggs. May produce two broods per year.

Natural History: The Vesper Sparrow is much more common in the western region of North America, but they are a fairly common breeding bird in the northern portion of Indiana and may breed statewide in suitable habitats. They are declining in the eastern portions of their range which includes much of the Midwest and great lakes region. They winter across the southern US and southward to northern Central America. In some places this species may nest in crop fields. Thus it may be fairly common in agricultural regions of the state. By contrast, it is uncommon, rare, or absent in much of the more heavily wooded regions of the state, although it may occur there in re-claimed strip mine areas or otherwise altered and open habitats.

Class—**Aves** (birds)
Order—**Passeriformes** (songbirds)
Family—**Emberzidae** (sparrows)

White-throated Sparrow *Zonotrichia albicollis*	**White-crowned Sparrow** *Zonotrichia leucophrys*

Size: 6.75 inches.	Presumed range in Indiana	**Size:** 6.25 inches.	Presumed range in Indiana
Abundance: Common in winter and during migration.		**Abundance:** Uncommon winter resident.	
Migratory Status: A winter resident in southern Indiana and seasonal migrant throughout the state. Arrives from northern breeding grounds in November and stays through early to mid-May.		**Migratory Status:** A winter resident throughout most of the state, migrant elswhere. Seen in Indiana from October through early May. Like the preceding species will move with changing weather patterns.	

Variation: Two adult morphs. One has bright white eye stripe, other has tan. Immatures have striped breasts.	**Variation:** First year birds have chestnut and beige head stripe as opposed to black and white (see photos above). Sexes alike.
Habitat: Brushy thickets, fence rows, weedy fields, edges areas, and regenerative woodlands. Both in upland and lowland areas. Can be seen in both rural and urban areas but always in the vicinity of bushes, shrubs, tall weeds, or other cover.	**Habitat:** White-crowned Sparrows may be seen in any area where there are weeds, grasses, or brush in sufficient amount to provide good cover for roosting and escape from predators. Woodland edges and overgrown fence rows are best.
Breeding: Breeds in a broad band across Canada and the northeastern US, as well as northern great lakes states (MI, WI, MN). Nest is on the ground in open areas, forest edges, etc. 4 eggs is typical. As many as 7 recorded.	**Breeding:** Breeds in boreal regions, tundra, and mountain meadows. Nest is in a low bush with about 4 eggs. Breeds very far to the north in northern Canada and Alaska. Will summer well into the Arctic Circle beyond the tree-line.
Natural History: This is one of the state's more common sparrows during winter. In early spring just before flying north to summer breeding grounds, the White-throated Sparrow serenades the fields and woodlands with its distinctive whistling song. As these birds are ground foragers, snow cover is one of the most important conditions that influence migratory patterns. Feeds mostly on insects in summer and switches to seeds in winter. Berries are also heavily consumed when in season. When feeding uses both feet with a backwards thrusting motion to clear away leaf litter. They are well represented at bird feeders throughout the Midwest in winter. A short-distance migrator, this species winters mostly within the southern United States.	**Natural History:** Similar in many respects to the White-throated Sparrow to which it is closely related. But the White-crowned ranges farther west (all the way to the Pacific) and farther north. White-crowned Sparrows produce multiple broods (as many as 4 per season in some western populations). Most will have at least two broods annually. Some summer well into the Arctic Tundra and make annual migrations of over 4,000 miles up and down the continent. Eats insects and seeds in summer, mostly seeds in winter. Forages on the ground near cover. Less common than the White-Throated Sparrow, but still a familiar bird at winter feeders. This is one of the most highly studied songbirds in America.

Class—**Aves** (birds)

Order—**Passeriformes** (songbirds)

Family—**Emberzidae** (sparrows)	Family—**Calcariidae** (longspurs & buntings)	

Dark-eyed Junco
Junco hyemalis

Size: 6 inches.

Abundance: Very common in winter.

Variation: Highly variable. Most birds seen in Indiana are the "Slate-colored" morph shown in top photo.

Migratory Status: Winter resident. Often appears at feeders with the first snowfall.

Presumed range in Indiana

Habitat: Occupies a wide variety of habitats in winter, but is most fond of semi-open areas such as woods openings or edges of woods. Summer habitat is boreal forests.

Breeding: Nest is on the ground, often concealed in a clump of ferns. Four eggs is usual. Compact nest is made of dead leaves and grasses with finer grasses as an inside liner. Nesting occurs well to the north. Some populations may produce two broods in a summer.

Natural History: Juncos are a familiar winter bird at feeders throughout America. They arrive with the colder weather fronts and are often associated with snowstorms. In fact a common nickname in much of America is "Snowbird." Northern migrants arrive in Indiana in late fall. Those that summer in the southern United States do so only at the highest elevations in the Appalachian Mountains (above 3,500 feet). The combined summer, winter, and migratory ranges of the Dark-eyed Junco includes nearly all of the North American continent except Florida.

Snow Bunting
Plectrophenax nivalis

Size: 6 inches.

Abundance: Uncommon.

Variation: Exhibits seasonal plumage variations but only winter plumage is seen in Indiana.

Migratory Status: Winter migrant. Usually seen only in harsh winter weather.

Presumed range in Indiana

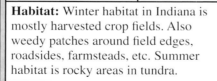

Habitat: Winter habitat in Indiana is mostly harvested crop fields. Also weedy patches around field edges, roadsides, farmsteads, etc. Summer habitat is rocky areas in tundra.

Breeding: One of the most northerly breeding songbirds in the America. Nests within the Arctic Circle. Builds its nest in rock crevices on the arctic tundra. Female sits the eggs and is fed by the male during incubation. Lays 4 to 6 eggs.

Natural History: After summering as far north as the shores of the Arctic Ocean, Snow Buntings will move south in winter as far south as the Great Lakes. Winter range may include the northern half of Indiana. In years of exceptional snowfall or extreme cold they may move as far south as Kentucky. They are obviously very cold hardy birds, but they can be susceptible to winter die-offs if deep snows conceal their food source of seeds and grain. Winter migrants may be seen in mixed flocks with Lapland Longspurs and Horned Larks.

Lapland Longspur
Calcarius lapponicus

Size: 6.25 inches.

Abundance: Fairly common.

Variation: Exhibits seasonal plumage variations but only winter plumage is seen in Indiana.

Migratory Status: A winter migrant and winter resident seen in harsh weather.

Presumed range in Indiana

Habitat: Winter migrants use very open areas with nearly bare ground. Large acreage harvested crop fields are the primary habitat for flocks wintering in the midwestern US.

Breeding: Nests on the ground in a shallow depression on the Arctic Tundra. In places it may be the only nesting songbird. Females begin nesting almost immediately after arriving on the breeding grounds. Eggs (3 to 7) are not laid until early June.

Natural History: This hardy sparrow breeds and summers in Arctic Tundra and is circumpolar in its distribution. It is very common on its breeding grounds where it is sometimes the only songbird present. In winter they move far to the south, but are not very abundant east of the Mississippi River. Birds seen in Indiana are in winter plumage (as above). Lapland Longspur can be seen across most of the Midwest in winter, but they are most common in winter in the central Great Plains region. They often flock with Horned Larks and American Pipits.

Class—**Aves** (birds)
Order—**Passeriformes** (songbirds)
Family—**Cardinalidae** (tanagers and grosbeaks)

Scarlet Tanager *Piranga ludoviciana*	**Summer Tanager** *Piranga rubra*

Size: 6.5 inches.

Abundance: Fairly common in forested areas.

Migratory Status: A summer resident that breeds in Indiana and winters in tropical America. Begins to arrive in mid to late April. Leaves for wintering grounds in September.

Presumed range in Indiana

Variation: Sexual and ontogenetic plumage variations. Juvenile males resemble females for the first year of their lives. See photos above.

Habitat: The summer habitat for the Scarlet Tanager closely coincides with the Eastern Temperate Forest Level I ecoregion. It prefers large tracts of unbroken woodlands.

Breeding: The thin, saucer-like nest of the Scarlet Tanager is placed on the fork of an outer branch. Four eggs is typical. Only one brood is produced.

Natural History: The Scarlet Tanager is one of the most strikingly colored birds in America. Unfortunately, this species dependence upon larger tracts of forested land means that its future is uncertain. Forest fragmentation leads to vulnerability to cowbird nest parasitism. Throughout much of the Midwest, where deforestation and fragmentation of forests has been rampant, this species is in decline. In Indiana it is becoming uncommon except where large tracts of deciduous woodlands remain. Food in summer is mostly insects, including wasps and hornets, a habit that makes them a valuable bird to have around the rural homestead. Add to that their gaudy black and red plumage and you have a bird that all Indianans should strive to protect. Winters from Panama to northwestern South America.

Size: 6.75 inches.

Abundance: Fairly common except in agricultural areas.

Migratory Status: Well named, this bird is seen only during summer. It winters in the tropics. Spring arrival is usually late April to early May. Fall migration in September.

Presumed range in Indiana

Variation: Sexual and ontogenetic dimorphism. See photos above. The mottled yellow-green and bright red of the juvenile male entering its second year can be seen in early spring.

Habitat: Like their Scarlet Tanager cousins, Summer Tanagers are birds of the eastern forests. However, this species is more likely to occupy fragmented forests and edge areas.

Breeding: The rather flimsy nest is on a terminal fork of a branch that is usually low over an opening such as a creek bed. The typical clutch size is 3 to 4.

Natural History: Summer Tanagers feed on a variety of woodland insects and larva, but they also eat some berries and fruits. One of their primary food items however is bees and wasps, a fact that makes them an attractive species to have around the rural homestead. Immature males resemble females their first summer. By the following spring they begin transformation into the bright red plumage of the adult male. During this transformation they are one of the most colorful birds in eastern woodlands (see photos above). Breeding bird surveys in recent years have detected a slight decline in populations of this species. Landscape changes in their wintering grounds may be the reason. They will winter from southern Mexico to northern South America. Like many migratory songbirds they often migrate at night.

Class—**Aves** (birds)

Order—**Passeriformes** (songbirds)

Family—**Cardinalidae** (tanagers and grosbeaks)

Dickcissel *Spiza americana*	**Northern Cardinal** *Cardinalis cardinalis*	**Rose-breasted Grosbeak** *Pheucticus ludovicianus*

Size: 6.25 inches.

Abundance: Uncommon in Indiana.

Variation: Sexually dimorphic. See photos above.

Migratory Status: Summer resident. Winters from Mexico to northern South America.

Presumed range in Indiana

Size: 8.75 inches.

Abundance: Very common.

Variation: Sexually dimorphic. See photos above.

Migratory Status: A year-round resident throughout the state.

Presumed range in Indiana

Size: 8 inches.

Abundance: Fairly common.

Variation: Sexually dimorphic. See photos above.

Migratory Status: A summer resident in northern Indiana. Migrant in south.

Presumed range in Indiana

Habitat: Fallow lands with weeds, saplings, and grasses. Weedy fields in open areas are the preferred habitat. Original range was probably natural prairie regions.

Habitat: From undisturbed natural areas to suburbs, the Northern Cardinal favors edge areas with shrubs and brush. Avoids areas of extensive forests in favor of successional habitats.

Habitat: A forest species primarily, but enjoys edge areas and regenerative woodlands with thick shrubby cover. May be fairly common in suburbs with adequate cover in the form of bushes.

Breeding: Breeds across much of Indiana. Produces only one brood per year. Nest is in a shrub low to ground. 4 eggs usually but may be as many as 6.

Breeding: Nest is usually in a thick shrub or bush. About 4 eggs on average. Most nesting is from mid-April to August. Two broods per year.

Breeding: 3 to 5 eggs are laid in a nest of twigs, grass, and plant fibers. Nesting begins in late May. May rarely produce two broods per year.

Natural History: The bulk of the Dickcissel's summer range is in the central Great Plains. It probably always nested in Indiana's natural praries but today has expanded its range into suitable habitats created by deforestation and subsequent conversion of woodlands to cropland and pasture. Indiana is outside their core breeding range and they are distributed sporadically in the state. But they are also known to wander well outside their core range. Flocks numbering in the thousands have been recorded during migration. Eats seeds almost exclusively during migration and on winter range. During breeding is more omnivorous, consuming insects and seeds. An open country bird, the Dickcissel avoids the more heavily forested regions of the state.

Natural History: Conspicuous and highly recognizable, the Northern Cardinal enjoys the distinction of being the state bird for a total of seven states (including Indiana). They are mainly seed and berry/fruit eaters, but they will eat insects and feed insects to the young. They are common birds at feeders throughout their range, especially during winter, and they are equally abundant in rural and urban regions. In the last century they have expanded their range farther to the north into the Great Lakes region and New England. Today they are seen throughout much of the United States east of the Rockies. The southern extent of their range is northern Central America. More common in southern Indiana. Throughout their range they are often known by the name "Redbird."

Natural History: Many Rose-breasted Grosbeaks seen in Indiana are passage migrants that nest farther to the north. But nesting is widespread in the northern third of the state where they will reside throughout the summer. A few will nest in central Indiana as well. In southern Indiana they merely pass through the state in spring and again in the fall enroute to wintering habitats in Central and South America. Food in summer about 50/50 insects and plant material such as seeds, fruits, flowers, and buds. During migration they are readily attracted to bird feeders where sunflower seeds are a favorite food. Birdwatchers throughout the state enthusiastically await the return of migrant songbirds each spring, and the Rose-breasted Grosbeak is a favorite.

Class—**Aves** (birds)

Order—**Passeriformes** (songbirds)

Family—**Cardinalidae** (tanagers and grosbeaks)		Family—**Fringillidae** (finches)

Blue Grosbeak
Passerina caerulea

Indigo Bunting
Passerina cyanea

Pine Siskin
Spinus pinus

Size: 6 inches.

Presumed range in Indiana

Abundance: Rare in Indiana.

Migratory Status: Summer resident. Winters in Mexico and Central America.

Variation: Sexually dimorphic. Female is chestnut brown.

Size: 5 inches.

Presumed range in Indiana

Abundance: Very common.

Migratory Status: A summer resident that arrives in late April and leaves in early fall.

Variation: Sexually dimorphic. See photos above.

Size: 5 inches.

Presumed range in Indiana

Abundance: Fairly common.

Migratory Status: Winter migrant. Exhibits erratic movement in winter.

Variation: Sexually dimorphic. See photos above.

Habitat: On summer range the Blue Grosbeak enjoys overgrown fields dominated by forbs and saplings. Also uses fencerows, thickets, brambles, etc.

Habitat: Edge areas, fence rows, rural roadsides with substantial brushy/weedy cover, and overgrown fields or early successional woodlands.

Habitat: Pine Siskins prefer coniferous woodlands but in winter they are often seen in mixed or even pure hardwood forests.

Breeding: Nest is a tightly woven cup placed in a low bush or tangle of vines, brush. About 4 eggs. Double brooding is known in the southern part of range.

Breeding: Two broods are common. Lays 2 to 4 eggs in a nest of woven grasses that is usually placed in thick cover only a few feet above the ground.

Breeding: Nest is woven of grasses, twigs, rootlets, etc. and lined with mosses or fur. Three to four eggs is typical. May nest in loose colonies.

Natural History: Although the Blue Grosbeak may be expanding its range farther to the north, it remains a uncommon to rare bird in most of Indiana. It is most common in the southern tip of the state, but recent breeding bird surveys suggest that this species is expanding its range northward and they may soon become more common in northern regions. During summer they feed mostly on crickets, grasshoppers and other insects, but eat mostly seeds in the early spring and fall, and they will often visit bird feeders at these times. Waste grain may also be a food source in fall. The summer range of the Blue Grosbeak stretches from coast to coast across the southern US. The bright blue color of the male is in sharp contrast to the reddish-brown color of the female.

Natural History: Indigo Buntings are common in summer throughout the eastern half of America. Probably more so today than in historical times when forests dominated the state's habitats. The neon blue color of the male makes it one of the most striking of North American birds. These birds are found throughout the eastern United States in summer, generally ranging from the short grass plains eastward to the Atlantic and as far north as southern Canada. They are most common in the southeastern US. Their annual migration may encompass up to 2500 miles and many make the long flight across the Gulf of Mexico. Large flocks appear along the gulf coast in early April. Seeds and berries are the primary food but insects are eaten during the breeding season.

Natural History: The Pine Siskin is a coniferous forest species. Though it is also found in mixed deciduous/ coniferous woodlands and in pure deciduous woods during winter irruptions. It is mostly a bird of the far north and the Rocky Mountains. They sometimes range as far south as the gulf coast in winter. In Indiana they are most common in the northern part of the state, but their erratic movement means they may be common in one area and rare in another. Likewise they may be present in an area one year and absent the next. Feeds on seeds of coniferous trees, grass seeds and weed seeds and will regularly visit feeders in winter and where thistle seeds are favored. Insects are also eaten during breeding. They are often seen in the company of Goldfinches.

Class—**Aves** (birds)

Order—**Passeriformes** (songbirds)

Family—**Fringillidae** (finches)

Goldfinch	Purple Finch	House Finch
Spinus tristis	*Haemorhous purpureus*	*Haemorhous mexicanus*

Goldfinch	Purple Finch	House Finch
Size: 5 inches.	**Size:** 6 inches.	**Size:** 6 inches.
Abundance: Common.	**Abundance:** Fairly common.	**Abundance:** Common.
Migratory Status: Year-round resident.	**Migratory Status:** Winter migrant.	**Migratory Status:** Year-round resident.
Variation: Sexual and seasonal plumage variations. Female resembles winter male.	**Variation:** Significant plumage differences between the sexes. See photos above.	**Variation:** Significant plumage differences between the sexes. See photos above.

Presumed range in Indiana (for all three)

Habitat: Edge areas and successional habitats, fence rows, overgrown fields and floodplains in open and semi-open areas.

Habitat: Summer habitat is moist coniferous forests. In winter they are seen in almost all habitats across the eastern half of the United States.

Habitat: As implied by the name, House Finches are usually associated with human habitation. Found both in cities and rural areas.

Breeding: 4 to 6 uniformly white eggs are laid. Nest is a tightly woven cup of grasses usually wrapped around a triad of upright branches.

Breeding: Nest of twigs, roots and grasses is built in a fork on the outer portion of a branch of a conifer. 3 to 6 eggs per clutch. 2 broods per year.

Breeding: Typical woven nest of grasses is usually placed in dense evergreen shrub, cedar, or conifer tree. Lays 3 to 5 eggs and multiple broods are common.

Natural History: This well-known species is widespread across North America. The transition of the male Goldfinch into its strikingly yellow breeding plumage in spring is a profound example of a condition that is common in many male birds in which they acquire bright colors during the breeding season. The Goldfinch is a common visitor to bird feeders and is especially attracted to thistle seeds. Unlike many other species that eat seeds in winter and insects in summer, the Goldfinch is mainly a seed eater. Weed seeds, grass seeds, and especially seeds from forbs like thistles, sunflowers, and coneflowers are consumed. This species is apparently immune to parasitism by the Brown-headed Cowbird, as young cowbirds cannot develop on a diet that contains no insects.

Natural History: The Purple Finch seems to be a declining species in the eastern United States. Competition with the House Finch may be to blame. Although Purple Finches are seen in Indiana every winter, they may be sporadic in occurrence. Some will move well south in some years; all the way to the gulf coast in years of poor cone production. Seeds are the major food item, including seeds of trees (elm, maples, ash) and seeds of fruits. Buds are also eaten. Insects are also consumed. As with most other seed eaters, the Purple Finch will frequent bird feeders in winter. It may be fairly common at feeders one year, but rare or absent the next. Most likely to be seen at feeders during or following snowstorms. Easily confused with the House Finch, but is larger headed and has a heavier bill.

Natural History: House Finches have extended their range into the eastern United States over the last few decades. Originally native to the southwestern United States, the first House Finches appeared in the Midwest in the 1960s and began to become widespread in Indiana in the '80s. Today they are found throughout the United States including all of Indiana. Primarily a seed eater, these birds can be very common at urban feeders. Weed seeds, fruit, buds and flowers are also reported to be eaten. Birds seen at feeders sometimes exhibit signs of a disease (mycoplasmal conjuctivitis) that causes swelling of the eyes with occasional blindness or death. Similar to and easily confused with the less common Purple Finch, which has a larger head and lacks dark streaking on the belly of the males.

Class—**Aves** (birds)

Order—**Passeriformes** (songbirds)

Family—**Fringillidae** (finches)

Common Redpoll *Acanthis flammea*	Evening Grosbeak *Coccothraustes vespertinus*	Red Crossbill *Loxia curvirostra*

Size: 5 inches.

Presumed range in Indiana

Abundance: Rare in Indiana.

Migratory Status: Winter migrant.

Variation: Shows varying amounts of red. Females are darker. Juveniles have brown streaks.

Habitat: Summer habitat is in the far north where they occupy edge areas of coniferous forests, open subarctic tundra, arctic tundra, and taiga.

Breeding: Nest is on a branch (forest) or in low vegetation (tundra). Lays 5 eggs. May double brood in good years.

Natural History: Circumpolar in distribution (northern hemisphere), this is one of the world's most northerly songbirds and some will stay through the winter in the far north. But many will move south, some as far as northern Indiana. In extreme winters they may range as far south as central or even southern Indiana. Though some Common Redpolls can be seen almost every winter in extreme northwestern Indiana, they only approach being a fairly common bird in years of major eruptions. These eruptions are thought to be associated with poor cone production in boreal forests, which is the major winter food source for this species in boreal regions. In addition to conifer seeds they also eat small seeds produced by other trees and shrubs such as birch, willow, and alder. Grass seeds are also eaten and arthropods are fed to the young.

Size: 8 inches.

Presumed range in Indiana

Abundance: Rare in Indiana.

Migratory Status: Winter migrant.

Variation: Female is gray-brown with yellowish wash. Male is brighter with yellow stripe on forehead.

Habitat: Boreal forests of conifer and mixed conifer/deciduous. Summer habitat includes the forested regions of Canada and the Rocky Mountains.

Breeding: Saucer-like nest of twigs and rootlets is placed high in a tree at or near the trunk. Lays 3 to 4 eggs.

Natural History: The Evening Grosbeak is a northern species. The main food in winter is the seeds of trees like maples, Box Elder, etc. as well as conifer seeds and weed seeds. In a year of exceptionally poor seed production they will migrate southward great distances in a phenomena know to birdwatchers as an "irruption." In irruption years they may rarely be seen as far south as the southern US. During these rare "irruption events" they might be seen anywhere in the state. However, in typical winters northernmost Indiana represents the southern edge of their winter range. In some winters they may not be seen in Indiana at all. Thus sightings of this bird in the state usually elicit excitement from the state's birdwatching community. The map above probably represents an average winter range in Indiana.

Size: 6.5 inches.

Presumed range in Indiana

Abundance: Very rare in Indiana.

Migratory Status: Rare winter migrant.

Variation: Males show a decidedly reddish color. Females are more yellowish. Juveniles are heavily streaked.

Habitat: Red Crossbills use taiga forests in Canada as their summer habitat. Western populations exist in the conifer forests of the Rockies.

Breeding: Nest is made of twigs and lined with lichens, grass, or conifer needles. 3 eggs are usual.

Natural History: The unique scissor-like beak of the crossbills is an adaptation for feeding on the seeds of conifers. The curved, crossed beak is used to pry open cones enough to allow the tongue to scoop out the seed. Seeds of pine, hemlock, spruce and fir are the primary foods, but a variety of other seeds are also eaten and they will visit feeders for sunflower seeds. Their foraging habits are nomadic and small flocks wander through the forests searching for cone-bearing trees. Like the other boreal species on this page they are prone to nomadic "irruptions." During an irruption year they could be seen almost anywhere in the state. In a typical year northern MN, northern WI, and northern MI, represents the southernmost edge of their range in the Midwestern US. In most winters this species will not be seen in Indiana at all.

Class—**Aves** (birds)

Order—**Apodiformes** (swifts & hummingbirds)

Family—**Apodidae** (swifts)

Chimney Swift
Chaetura pelagica

Size: 5.5 inches.

Abundance: Fairly common.

Migratory Status: Summer resident that winters in the Amazon basin.

Variation: No sexual dimorphism. Immatures slightly lighter.

Presumed range in Indiana

Habitat: Mainly seen in open and semi-open country and in urban/suburban areas.

Breeding: Nest is a flimsy cup plastered to the inside of a chimney. 2 to 5 eggs are laid.

Natural History: This is a species that has benefited from human population expansion. Historically, the Chimney Swift nested mainly in hollow trees. These birds require a vertical surface within a sheltered place for nesting. When people began to build houses and large structures like schools, churches, and factories equipped with chimneys, their populations exploded. Today they are perhaps less common than a few decades ago when most dwellings and other buildings had chimneys. Some nesting in natural hollows still occurs. Swifts have long, narrow, pointed wings that allow for extreme maneuverability and these birds feed entirely on the wing. Small flying insects are their prey. During migration they are sometimes seen in large flocks that can contain over 1,000 birds. Today the greatest population densities occur in the vicinity of urban centers.

Family—**Trochylidae** (hummingbirds)

Ruby-throated Hummingbird
Archilochus colubris

Male
Female

Size: 3.75 inches.

Abundance: Common.

Migratory Status: A summer resident that winters mostly in Central America.

Variation: Female lacks ruby throat patch. See photos above.

Presumed range in Indiana

Habitat: Woodlands. Both deciduous and mixed forests are utilized. Edge areas and open fields are used for feeding.

Breeding: Nest is a tiny cup of fine plant fibers and lichens glued together with spider webs. 2 eggs is typical.

Natural History: The tiny hummingbirds are ounce for ounce one of the world's greatest travelers. Many fly across the Gulf of Mexico each year during migration! Considering that they weigh barely more than one-tenth of an ounce that is a remarkable feat of endurance. The range of the Ruby-throated Hummingbird includes all of the Eastern Deciduous Forest Level 1 Ecoregion, as well as portions of the Boreal Forest and Great Plains Ecoregions. Nectar is the major food item for hummingbirds and they show a preference for red, tubular flowers. They possess a highly specialized beak and tongue for reaching nectar deep within flowers. They will also eat some small, flying insects caught on the wing, and are known to pluck tiny invertebrates from foliage or small spiders from their webs. These birds will readily use artificial nectar feeders containing a 1 to 4 mix of sugar water.

Order—**Coraciiformes** (kingfishers)

Family—**Alcedinidae** (kingfisher)

Belted Kingfisher
Megaceryle alcyon

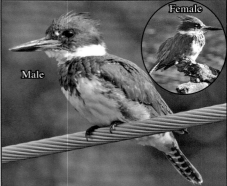
Female
Male

Size: 13 inches.

Abundance: Uncommon.

Migratory Status: Year-round resident. Some may move south in winter.

Variation: Female has a rust-colored band across belly.

Presumed range in Indiana

Habitat: Kingfishers require water to feed and they haunt creeks, rivers, lakes, swamps and farm ponds.

Breeding: Kingfishers nest in burrows they excavate into vertical banks of dirt or sand that are at least 8 feet high.

Natural History: The Belted Kingfisher is one of the most widely distributed birds in North America. In fact they range throughout the continent from Alaska and northern Canada south to Panama. Although widespread (they may be seen in any county throughout the state) they are widely dispersed. They are least common in the intensive agricultural regions. The presence of suitable nesting habitat in the form of vertical earthen cliffs may be a limiting factor in their abundance. Human activities such as digging of quarries and road cuts through hills and mountains may have helped this species in modern times by providing the requisite vertical banks for nest sites. Small fish are the primary food item. They are known for diving headfirst into the water from either a perch or while hovering to catch fish near the surface. They are a shy species that is difficult to approach.

Class—**Aves** (birds)

Order—**Piciformes** (woodpeckers)

Family—**Picidae** (woodpeckers)

Pileated Woodpecker *Dryocopus pileatus*	Northern Flicker *Colaptes auratus*	Red-headed Woodpecker *Melanerpes erythrocephalus*

Size: 16.5 inches.	**Size:** 12.5 inches.	**Size:** 9.25 inches.
Abundance: Uncommon to rare.	**Abundance:** Fairly common.	**Abundance:** Uncommon.
Migratory Status: Year-round resident in forested regions.	**Migratory Status:** Year-round resident but less common in winter.	**Migratory Status:** Year-round in southern IN. Summer in north.
Variation: Male has a red cheek patch and more extensive red on the head.	**Variation:** Male has black "mustache." Two color morphs but only one occurs in Indiana.	**Variation:** No sexual variation. Juveniles have gray-brown heads and brown wings.

Presumed range in Indiana

Presumed range in Indiana

Presumed range in Indiana

Habitat: A forest species, the Pileated Woodpecker prefers mature woodlands. It is also seen in semi-open areas where large tracts of woods occur nearby. Floodplain forests are a favorite habitat.

Habitat: Semi-open areas and open lands with at least a few large trees. Farmlands, older urban neighborhoods and parks are also used. Least common in dense, mature woodlands.

Habitat: Savanna-like habitats with widely spaced, large trees are the preferred habitat of the Red-headed Woodpecker. They seem to show a preference for areas near lakes or rivers.

Breeding: Nest is a hollow cavity excavated into the trunk of a tree (usually a dead tree, but sometimes living). Nests are usually fairly high up. 4 eggs.

Breeding: Nest is usually excavated in a fairly large-diameter dead tree. Also known to use natural hollows. Averages 6 to 8 eggs.

Breeding: Nest hole is usually in a dead tree but it is also fond of using utility poles. 5 eggs is typical and some may produce two broods per summer.

Natural History: By far America's largest woodpecker, Pileated Woodpeckers play an important role in the mature forest ecosystem. Their large nest cavities are utilized as a refuge by many other woodland species including small owls, Wood Ducks, bluebirds and squirrels. In the boreal forests of Canada the Pine Marten is reported to use their holes. Using their powerful, chisel-like beaks to break apart dead snags and logs they also help accelerate decomposition of large dead trees. In addition to mast and fruit such as wild cherries, they eat insects, mainly Carpenter Ants and beetle larva. They occur only in regions where ample forests exist. Successional forest are used but they do need mature trees and especially, large dead trees and logs.

Natural History: In addition to feeding on insects (mainly ants) usually caught on the ground, the Flicker also eats berries and in winter grains (including corn). Two distinct subspecies of Northern Flicker occur in North America. The "Yellow-shafted Flicker" is native to Indiana and the rest of the eastern US. In the Rocky Mountain west the "Red-shafted Flicker" occurs. The two are distinguished by the dominant color on the underneath side of the wing, which is visible only in flight. As with our other large woodpecker (Pileated), the Northern Flicker is regarded as a "keystone" species that is important to other species which use its excavations for shelter and nesting. Thus recent declines in the population of this species is cause for concern.

Natural History: Once regarded as very common, this handsome woodpecker has declined significantly in the last century. It eats large amounts of acorns and other mast, especially in fall and winter, and may move about in fall and winter in search of areas with good mast crops. Insects are regularly eaten in warmer months and some may be caught on the wing, but they also commonly forage on the ground. They may be found throughout the state in summer but populations in the north may migrate south in winter. They seem to be relatively uncommon, and overall this species has experienced a nationwide population decline. The Red-headed Woodpecker was apparently well known to many native Americans, and was a war symbol of the Cherokee.

Class—**Aves** (birds)
Order—**Piciformes** (woodpeckers)
Family—**Picidae** (woodpeckers)

Red-bellied Wood Pecker *Melanerpes carolinus*	**Downy Woodpecker** *Picoides pubescens*	**Hairy Woodpecker** *Picoides pubescens*

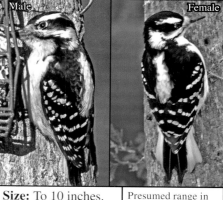

Size: 9.5 inches.

Presumed range in Indiana

Abundance: Common.

Migratory Status: Year-round resident.

Variation: Female has gray crown.

Habitat: A woodland species that inhabits all forest types in the eastern US.

Breeding: Nests in holes excavated by the adults. 4 to 5 eggs are laid in mid-April to early June.

Natural History: Feeds on all types of tree dwelling arthropods as well as seeds, nuts, fruit and berries. Widespread and common throughout the eastern half of the US, generally east of the Rocky Mountains. These woodpeckers are known to take over the nest holes of the endangered Red-cockaded Woodpecker where their ranges overlap in the southern United States. Conversely, the introduced Starling sometimes takes over the nest hole of the Red-bellied Woodpecker. Due to its fairly large size and its tendency to be quite vocal year round, the Red-bellied Woodpecker is a fairly conspicuous bird in both rural and urban area throughout the state. Because both males and females have a significant amount of red on the head they are often misidentified as the much rarer Red-headed Woodpecker. Like other woodpeckers they will come to bird feeders for suet or sunflower seeds.

Size: 6.5 inches.

Presumed range in Indiana

Abundance: Very common.

Migratory Status: Year-round resident.

Variation: Male has red spot on nape.

Habitat: Occupies a wide variety of woodland habitats throughout the state.

Breeding: Nests are usually excavated in a dead limb. Eggs range from 3 to as many as 8. Eggs hatch in 12 days.

Natural History: Ranging across all of North America except the far north and the desert southwest, the Downy is one of the most widespread woodpeckers in America and is the most common woodpecker in Indiana. These appealing little woodpeckers are well known and frequent visitors to bird feeders where they eat suet and seeds. Arthropods are the most important food item making up as much as 75 percent of the diet. Fruit and sap is also eaten. Like other woodpeckers, the Downy's nest holes in dead limbs and trunks may be utilized by a wide array of other species as a home and shelter. Many small cavity nesting birds may use old woodpecker holes, and mice, lizards, snakes, treefrogs, spiders and insects can often be found using their abandoned nests. The Downy Woodpecker is very similar to the Hairy Woodpecker but is smaller and has a thinner beak. It is also much more common.

Size: To 10 inches.

Presumed range in Indiana

Abundance: Fairly common.

Migratory Status: Year-round resident.

Variation: Male has red spot on nape.

Habitat: A forest species that likes woodlands with large, mature trees.

Breeding: Nest hole may be in dead snags or living trees with heart rot. 4 eggs is typical.

Natural History: The range of the Hairy Woodpecker closely coincides with that of the smaller Downy Woodpecker. The two are often confused but the Hairy is a much larger bird and has a heavier, longer bill. Like the Downy, this woodpecker excavates nest holes that may be used by a variety of other species, making it an important species in forest ecosystems. A wide variety of insects and other arthropods are eaten along with seeds and fruits. This species can be seen at feeders throughout the state and although it is less common than its smaller cousin it can often be seen in the company of the smaller Downy Woodpecker. When both are seen together, size differences become more apparent. The Hairy Woodpecker varies somewhat geographically in both size and coloration. Western specimens have fewer white spots on the wings. Specimens shown above are typical for the eastern United States.

Class—**Aves** (birds)

Order—**Piciformes** (woodpeckers)	Order—**Cuculiformes** (cuckoos, anis, & roadrunner)
Family—**Picidae** (woodpeckers)	Family—**Cuculidae** (cuckoos)

Yellow-bellied Sapsucker
Sphyrapicus varius

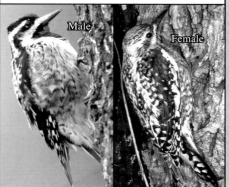

Black-billed Cuckoo
Coccyzus erythropthalmus

Yellow-billed Cuckoo
Coccyzus americanus

Size: 8.5 inches.

Presumed range in Indiana

Abundance: Uncommon.

Variation: Male has red patch on throat.

Migratory Status: Winter resident in southern Indiana. Migrant elsewhere in the state.

Habitat: In winter this woodpecker occupies a wide variety of woodland habitats. Birds that winter in Indiana use deciduous and mixed woodlands.

Breeding: Nest is an excavated hole in dead tree or a living tree with heart rot. Clutch size ranges from 2 to 7 eggs.

Natural History: The Yellow-bellied Sapsucker is unique among Indiana's woodpeckers in that it creates feeding opportunities by drilling small holes into the bark of trees. These holes, called "sap wells" fill with sap which the sapsucker then drinks. Sapsuckers regularly visit the "sap wells" to maintain them and defend them from other sapsuckers. Many other birds species benefit from the sapsuckers activities, especially the Ruby-throated Hummingbird which will also drink sap from the woodpecker holes. The sap also attracts insects which in turn feed many species of insectivorous birds. In addition, the nest holes excavated by the sapsucker may be used by other birds, flying squirrels, etc. Though widespread across Indiana during migration, they are not a common bird anywhere in the state.

Size: 12 inches.

Presumed range in Indiana

Abundance: Uncommon.

Variation: Sexes alike. No variation.

Migratory Status: Migrant in southern Indiana. Summer resident in northern half of the state.

Habitat: Successional areas, thickets, and mature woodlands with some open areas. Shows a preference for being near water (riparian areas, lakes, etc).

Breeding: Breeds sparingly throughout the northern half of Indiana. Clutch size averages 2 to 4 eggs.

Natural History: Although once common, the Black-billed Cuckoo has declined in abundance over the past several decades. Widespread use of pesticides may be to blame. Caterpillars are a primary food and pesticide depleted caterpillar numbers results in a scarce food source for the birds. Ironically, large flocks of these handsome birds once acted as a natural control of caterpillars and historical observers reported seeing flocks of Black-billed Cuckoos descend on a tree full of caterpillars and eat every caterpillar on the tree! Today it is rare to see more than one or two of these birds at a time. Cicadas are another important insect food, and in years of cicada outbreaks cuckoos (and many other birds species) will produce larger clutches and successfully rear more young. Arrives in late April or May after wintering in South America.

Size: 12 inches.

Presumed range in Indiana

Abundance: Fairly common.

Variation: Sexes alike. No variation.

Migratory Status: Summer resident throughout the state. More common than Black-billed Cuckoo.

Habitat: Open woodlands, edge areas, regenerative woodlands near open fields, overgrown fence rows, etc. Uses similar habitats on winter range.

Breeding: Breeds from early June through the summer. Nest is flimsy and placed in thick vegetation. 2 to 4 eggs.

Natural History: The Yellow-billed Cuckoo is one of the latest arriving of Indiana's neotropical migrant songbirds. They often go by the nickname "Raincrow" and folklore states that they call right before a rain. Although much more common than the Black-billed Cuckoo, Yellow-billed Cuckoos are not abundant birds today. Like our other cuckoo, their numbers have diminished significantly in modern times. Caterpillars are an important food and widespread pesticide use is likely the major contributing factor in their decline. These are secretive birds that are heard more often than seen. Their call is quite distinctive and is heard most frequently during the "dog days" of mid to late summer. The young of this species develop rapidly and may leave the nest within 17 days of hatching. Eggs may be laid as much as five days apart.

Class—**Aves** (birds)

Order—**Columbiformes** (doves)

Family—**Columbidae** (doves)

Rock Pigeon *Columba livia*	**Mourning Dove** *Zenaida macroura*	**Eurasian Collared-Dove** *Zenaida decaocto*

Rock Pigeon

Size: 13 inches.

Abundance: Very common.

Migratory Status: Year-round resident.

Variation: Highly variable.

Habitat: Farms and ranches in rural areas, parks and streets in urban environments.

Presumed range in Indiana

Breeding: Nests on man-made ledges and beneath overhangs in cities. Bridges and barns are used in rural areas. Multiple nesting with 2 eggs per clutch.

Natural History: Although the Rock Pigeon is about the same overall length as the Mourning Dove and Collard Dove, the pigeon is a much stockier, heavier bird that weighs over twice as much as the Mourning Dove. Despite the fact that this familiar bird ranges from coast to coast across North America, the Rock Pigeon is not a native species. It was introduced into North America by the earliest European settlers in the 1600s. Pigeons followed the first settlers into the west (including into Indiana), colonizing towns and settlements and living in close proximity to rural farms and livestock. Today they are one of the most familiar urban birds in America and are also common around farms and ranches. Young pigeons known as "Squab" are eaten in many places throughout the world. Rock Pigeons are incredibly variable and can exhibit almost any color or pattern. Also sometimes called "Rock Dove."

Mourning Dove

Size: 12 inches.

Abundance: Very common.

Migratory Status: Year-round resident.

Variation: No variation among adults.

Habitat: Agricultural areas and open lands with short grass or areas of bare ground.

Presumed range in Indiana

Breeding: Builds a flimsy nest of small sticks in sapling or low branch usually from 6 to 15 feet above ground. 2 eggs is usual with multiple broods per year.

Natural History: Although these birds are found year-round in Indiana their numbers swell each fall with migrants from farther to the north. Mourning Doves are regarded as a game species throughout much of the United States, including Indiana. The US Fish & Wildlife Service estimates that as many as 20 million are killed each fall across America during dove season. While that seems an appallingly high number, the Mourning Dove is actually one of the most numerous bird species in America and the total population is estimated at around 350 million birds! Seeds are the chief food item. They will eat everything from the tiniest grass seeds to every type of seed crop produced by man, including corn, wheat, sorghum, millet and sunflower as well as peanuts and soybeans. This abundant species may face competition from the invasive Eurasian Collard Dove, which occupies a similar ecological niche.

Eurasian Collared-Dove

Size: 13 inches.

Abundance: Rare but increasing.

Migratory Status: Year-round resident.

Variation: No variation among adults.

Habitat: Open lands. Agricultural areas and small towns are favored.

Presumed range in Indiana

Breeding: Usually nests in trees or bushes near human habitation. Lays 2 eggs per clutch but can nest several times per year.

Natural History: This bird is a newcomer to the state of Indiana. Originally native to Eurasia, the Collared-Dove has colonized much of the southern United States since its release in the Bahamas in the 1970s. Since then they have rapidly expanded their range north and west. The first record for Indiana was in 1999. They may soon colonize the entire state of Indiana if they have not done so already. In food habits and other aspects of its biology the Collard-Dove is similar to the Mourning Dove. Young Collard-Doves disperse widely and this species continues to increase across North America. Cold weather does not seem to be a limiting factor but food availability may limit range expansion. How far this species will extend its range in North America is still unknown. As with all other members of the Columbidae family, young birds are fed a semi-liquid "crop milk" regurgitated from the adults crop.

Class—**Aves** (birds)

Order—**Galliformes** (chicken-like birds)

Family—**Phasianidae** (grouse)

Ruffed Grouse *Bonasa umbellus*	**Wild Turkey** *Meleagris gallopavo*	**Ring-necked Pheasant** *Phasianus colchicus*

Size: To 19 inches. Presumed range in Indiana	**Size:** To 47 inches. Presumed range in Indiana	**Size:** To 35 inches. Presumed range in Indiana
Abundance: Rare in Indiana.	**Abundance:** Fairly common.	**Abundance:** Uncommon.
Migratory Status: Year-round resident where not extirpated.	**Migratory Status:** Non-migratory year-round resident.	**Migratory Status:** Year-round resident. Not migratory.
Variation: Two color morphs, red and gray. Male has larger "ruff" on neck.	**Variation:** Females are smaller, have less red on head and neck and lack the "beard."	**Variation:** Female smaller and mottled brown. See photos above.
Habitat: Forests. Mainly successional forests, forest clearings, and disturbed woodlands.	**Habitat:** Inhabits all major habitats in the state except for urban areas. Most common in mixture of woods and farms.	**Habitat:** Prefers a mosaic of crop lands interlaced with cover such as wetlands, grassy patches, overgrown fence rows.
Breeding: Nest is on the ground in woodland. Usually placed near the base of a tree, stump or beneath downed tree. 9 to 14 eggs.	**Breeding:** Nests on the ground in thick cover such as thickets, honeysuckle, Multiflora Rose, or tall grasses. Lays up to 14 eggs.	**Breeding:** Nests on the ground in thick cover such as tall grasses, cattails, etc. Lays up to 15 eggs. Rarely, two females will use the same nest.
Natural History: Mainly a bird of the northern forests, the Ruffed Grouse ranges southward in the Appalachian chain as far as northern Georgia. Their range in Indiana today is poorly known, though they once probably occurred statewide. Re-introduction into some areas has had only limited success. They do still occur in some of the forested regions in the southern half of the state and may exist sporadically in their historical range in the northern tier of counties. The name comes from the "ruff" of feathers around the neck which are erected by the males during courtship displays. At this time the male also produces a deep, resonate sound similar to that produced by blowing across the top of a soda bottle. Known as "drumming," the sound carries quite a distance in the spring forest. They were listed as State Endangered by the IDNR in 2020.	**Natural History:** The courtship of the male Wild Turkey includes a "strutting" display that involves spreading the tail feathers, drooping the wings and producing a low frequency "drumming" sound. When attempting to attract females in the spring breeding season males become quite vocal and regularly emit a loud "gobble" that can be heard for a mile. The saga of the disappearance and resurgence of the Wild Turkey in America is one of wildlife management's greatest success stories. In pioneer days turkeys were found throughout Indiana but by the early 1900s they had disappeared from the state. Re-stocking efforts by the Indiana Department of Natural Resources, aided by sportsmen groups like the National Wild Turkey Federation has been highly successful and Wild Turkeys are now found in suitable habitats throughout the state.	**Natural History:** Ring-necked Pheasants are an alien species from Asia that were introduced into America in the late 1800s. The species has thrived in the Great Plains region where adequate natural habitats still exist. It was once a more common bird in northern Indiana, but began to decline as more land was cleared for row crops. Despite conservation efforts recovery to the numbers seen prior to modern agriculture has not occurred. More recent conservation efforts aimed at restoring patches of natural grasslands should help this and many other wildlife species. This is a popular game bird throughout its range in America and sportsmen's organizations such as "Pheasants Forever" are actively involved in raising money for habitat conservation and restoration. The range of this species in the Midwest correlates with glaciated regions.

Class—**Aves** (birds)

Order—**Galliformes**	Order—**Caprimulgiformes**	
Family—**Odontophoridae** (quail)	Family—**Caprimulgidae** (nightjars)	

Northern Bobwhite *Colinus virginianus*	**Common Nighthawk** *Chordeiles minor*	**Whip-poor-will** *Antrostomus vociferus*

Male Female

Size: 10 inches.

Presumed range in Indiana

Abundance: Uncommon.

Variation: Sexually dimorphic. See photos.

Habitat: Small woodlands, edge areas and overgrown fields bordering agricultural land are the favorite habitats.

Migratory Status: Year-round resident.

Breeding: Ground nester. Clutch size averages about 15 eggs but nest failure due to predation is high. Multiple nestings are common.

Natural History: Bobwhite have always been an important game bird in the United States. In recent decades however the species has experienced significant population declines, especially in the northern portions of its range. Some blame a resurgence in predators for the decline. But the real culprit is modern agricultural practices that have eliminated fence rows and created expansive crop fields with no ground cover. This is the main factor contributing to the decline of the Bobwhite. Through fall and winter they will stick together in family groups known as a "covey." In spring adults pair off for breeding with the resultant offspring and their parents producing the next fall's covey. Mortality through the winter is high and survivors from more than one covey will often join together as winter wanes. Quail Unlimited is a conservation organization that works to protect habitat.

Size: 9.5 inches.

Presumed range in Indiana

Abundance: Fairly common.

Variation: Sexes alike. No variation.

Habitat: Open and semi-open areas. Can be common around cities and towns but also in rural areas.

Migratory Status: Summer resident.

Breeding: No nest is constructed and 2 eggs are laid on bare gravel. Many nests are on flat, gravel covered rooftops. Eggs are heavily mottled with gray.

Natural History: Nighthawks often go by the nickname "Bullbat." They can be quite common in urban areas in summer but they are also seen in open and semi-open rural areas. Like our other nightjars the Common Nighthawk feeds on the wing, catching moths and other flying insects. But unlike the others this bird is active both at night and at dawn and dusk, or sometimes on cloudy days. Around towns and cities they chase airborne insects attracted to streetlights at night. This is one of the great travelers of the bird world, wintering in South America. Their summer range includes nearly all of North America south of the Arctic. Nighthawks are usually seen in flight, but they will occasionally be spotted resting atop a fence post in open country or sitting on the ground in gravel areas. They often migrate in large flocks, sometimes numbering over 1,000 birds. They have experienced a precipitous decline in recent years.

Size: 12 inches.

Presumed range in Indiana

Abundance: Uncommon.

Variation: Sexes alike. No variation.

Habitat: Forest edge, power-line cuts through wooded areas and xeric woods.

Migratory Status: Summer resident.

Breeding: Nests on the ground amid leaf litter. No nest is built and the eggs (usually 2) are laid on the ground. Eggs are white with brown speckles.

Natural History: Few animals exhibit a more cryptic color and pattern than this species. When resting on the forest floor during the day they are nearly invisible. This is an uncommon species that is absent from deforested regions of the state. A very similar species, the **Chuck-wills-widow** (*A. carolinensis*)is a rare summer resident in southern Indiana. It is smaller (9.75 inches) and browner than the Whip-poor-will. The two are easily differentiated by their songs, usually described as *whip,prrr-weel* for the Whip-poor-will and as *chuk-wills wee-dow* for the Chuck-will's-widow. Both calls are usually repeated rapidly and at times incessantly. Equipped with a very large mouth for feeding on moths and other large flying insects, both species are nocturnal and catch most of their food in mid-air. Both species have experienced an unexplained decline in populations over the last decade.

Class—**Aves** (birds)

Order—**Strigiformes** (owls)

Family—**Tytonidae** (barn owl)	Family—**Strigidae** (typical owls)	
Barn Owl *Tyto alba*	**Eastern Screech Owl** *Megascops asio*	**Snowy Owl** *Bubo sciandiacus*

Red morph — Gray morph

Male

Barn Owl

Size: 16 inches.

Abundance: Endangered in Indiana.

Migratory Status: Year-round resident.

Breeding: Nested in hollows in trees or in caves historically. Now uses old buildings or barns. Up to 11 eggs.

Presumed range in Indiana

Variation: Very little variation. Females have more buff on breast and sides. Also more buff spotting on breast and belly. Males appear nearly pure white below, but do have a few spots.

Habitat: Prefers open and semi-open habitats. Short grass pastures are a favorite hunting ground. Probably more common around farms and small towns.

Natural History: The Barn Owl is one of the most widespread owl species in the world, being found throughout most of North America south of Canada, all of Central and South America, most of Europe and sub-Saharan Africa, parts of southern Asia and all of Australia. In spite of its wide range they are usually not common anywhere. Small rodents are the primary prey, especially mice and voles. When feeding a large brood of young a pair of Barn Owls may catch over two dozen mice in a single night. Like other owls their hearing is so acute they can catch mice unseen beneath leaves by homing in rustling sounds. Ironically, man's attempts to control rodents with poisoned baits may be in part responsible for the demise of rodent eating species like the Barn Owl.

Eastern Screech Owl

Size: 8.5 inches.

Abundance: Common.

Migratory Status: Year-round resident.

Breeding: Nest is in tree hollows and old woodpecker holes. 4 to 6 eggs are laid and young fledge in June.

Presumed range in Indiana

Variation: Two distinct color morphs occur. Gray phase (inset), is more common in the Appalachian Mountains but both red and gray morphs can occur in Indiana.

Habitat: All types of habitats within the state may be used, including suburban areas and in the vicinity of farms. Favors edge areas, fence rows, etc.

Natural History: The eerie call of the Screech Owl is often described as "haunting and tremulous." Despite being at times vocal birds, these small owls often goes unnoticed. They may even live in suburban yards and small towns, especially if older, large trees with hollow limbs and trunks are present. They feed on insects such as crickets and grasshoppers and on a wide variety of small vertebrate prey including mice, voles and songbirds that are plucked from their roosts at night. These wide-ranging birds are found throughout the eastern United States from the Atlantic to the Rocky Mountains and from southern Canada to Florida and Mexico. Birds in the northern portions of their range can be negatively impacted by severe winters.

Snowy Owl

Size: 24 inches.

Abundance: Very rare in Indiana.

Migratory Status: Winter migrant.

Breeding: Nest is on the ground in open tundra and built on a hummock. Lays 5 to 15 eggs.

Presumed range in Indiana

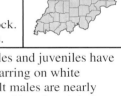

Variation: Females and juveniles have extensive black barring on white background. Adult males are nearly pure white below with reduced dark bars and spots dorsally.

Habitat: Summer habitat is the high Arctic and open tundra. Birds that wander south in winter favor expansive open fields, pastures or airports.

Natural History: A true icon of northern wilderness, the sight of a Snowy Owl in Indiana is often met with excitement. Winter migrants appear fairly regularly in the northernmost portion of the state and in rare winters they can be seen as far south as the Ohio River. Every now and then large numbers of these giant owls appear in winter in the northern United States in a phenomena known as an "irruption." The exact cause of these irruptions are not completely understood, but they may relate to food availability in the far north. One of this bird's primary food items is lemmings. Populations of these rodents vary considerably from year to year in what amounts to a boom-bust cycle. In years of low lemming numbers many owls will move south.

Class—**Aves** (birds)

Order—**Strigiformes** (owls)

Family—**Strigidae** (typical owls)

Barred Owl *Strix varia*	Great Horned Owl *Bubo virginianus*

Fledgling

On nest

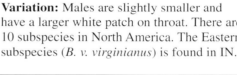

Size: 21 inches.

Abundance: Fairly common.

Variation: No sexual variation. Three subspecies are known in America with a fourth in central Mexico, only one (Northern Barred Owl-*S. v. varia)* occurs in Indiana.

Migratory Status: Year-round resident.

Habitat: Woodlands primarily. Especially in bottomlands, swampy areas, and riparian corridors, but also upland woods.

Presumed range in Indiana

Breeding: Nest is usually in tree cavities but known to nest tree crotches or old hawk nests. Usually 2 (rarely 3 or 4) eggs are laid.

Natural History: The Barred Owl ranges throughout the eastern half of the United States from the eastern edge of the great plains eastward. The eight noted call of the Barred Owl is described as "Hoo-hoo, hoo-hoo, hoo-hoo, hooaahh." In addition the species is capable of a wide array of hoots, screeches and coarse whistles. Small vertebrates are the main prey, especially rodents like voles, mice and flying squirrels. Birds, lizards, small snakes, and amphibians are also eaten. In the eastern United States the range of the Barred Owl closely coincides with that of the Red-shouldered Hawk and the two predators are often regarded as ecological counterparts occupying the same niche at different times. In Indiana this species is probably most common along the major river valleys of the state and in the southern tip of the state. It is least common in open areas where there is intensive agriculture.

Size: 23 inches.

Abundance: Fairly common.

Variation: Males are slightly smaller and have a larger white patch on throat. There are 10 subspecies in North America. The Eastern subspecies (*B. v. virginianus*) is found in IN.

Migratory Status: Year-round resident.

Habitat: Woodlands, semi-open and open habitats are all utilized, but most common in mosaic of upland woods and fields.

Presumed range in Indiana

Breeding: One of the earliest nesting birds in America. Horned Owls may be sitting on eggs by late January. Nest is often an old hawk nest. 2 eggs is usual.

Natural History: This widespread species occurs throughout the Americas from Alaska to southern South America. In the US specimens from the western portions of the country are much paler than those seen in the east. In the eastern United States Red Cedars and other evergreen trees are a favorite roosting site. The Great Horned Owl is the ecological counterpart of the Red-tailed Hawk, hunting much the same prey in the same regions; with the hawk hunting by day and the owl at night. These powerful predators eat a wide variety of small animals. Rabbits are a favorite food item. They are also known to eat larger mammals like muskrats, groundhogs, and even skunks or rarely, domestic cats! They can be a problem at times for those who raise chickens and leave them out in the open at night. But they also consume many rodents. Once regarded as a varmint, they are now federally protected.

Class—**Aves** (birds)
Order—**Strigiformes** (owls)
Family—**Strigidae** (typical owls)

Short-eared Owl *Asio flammeus*	Long-eared Owl *Asio otus*	Northern Saw-whet Owl *Aegolius acadicus*

Size: 15 inches.

Presumed range in Indiana

Abundance: Uncommon to rare.

Variation: Females tend to be slightly darker.

Migratory Status: Mostly a wintertime resident or winter migrant, but some breeding has been recorded.

Habitat: These are open country birds and the primary habitat is prairie, marsh, and tundra. In forested regions they haunt fields, pastures, meadows, etc.

Breeding: Nest is on the ground. A slight depression is scraped out by the owl and lined with grasses. 5 or 6 eggs is typical.

Natural History: In Indiana the Short-eared Owl is most likely to be seen in open regions during winter, but a few have nested in the state. Reclaimed strip mines are used as a refuge in the southern part of the state. The food is mostly small rodents. Voles are the most significant item in their diet. Rodent prey is located mostly by sound while flying low and slow over open, grassy fields. Most hunting is done at night or dusk and dawn, but these owls are more diurnal than most and may hunt during the day. The erectile feathers on the face that form the "ears" are not usually visible unless the owl is agitated or defensive. They appear to be in decline in much of America and are an endangered species in Indiana.

Size: 15 inches.

Presumed range in Indiana

Abundance: Rare in Indiana.

Variation: Female is darker, more rusty facial disk, slightly larger.

Migratory Status: Mostly a winter migrant, or less commonly a winter resident.

Habitat: Prefers open and semi-open woodlands and riparian habitats in open regions. Breeds and summers in boreal regions and mountains.

Breeding: Usually nests in trees in abandoned stick nests built by hawks, crows or other large bird species. 5 or 6 eggs is typical.

Natural History: Although this rare owl could possibly be seen anywhere in the state, most sightings are in the northern portions of the state. They are most likely to be seen in winter, but there are a very few records of breeding in the state. Their name comes from the well-developed feather tufts on the head which are erected when resting. These "ear tufts" are folded against the head and not visible on owls in flight. Long-eared Owls during winter can sometimes be seen in small flocks that roost in close proximity to each other. They show a definite preference for conifers for their daytime roosts. Their food is almost exclusively small mammals, mostly voles and mice of the *Peromyscus* genus.

Size: 8 inches.

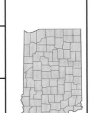
Presumed range in Indiana

Abundance: Uncommon in Indiana.

Variation: Immature has buff belly, dark facial disk, white eyebrow.

Migratory Status: Occurs mainly as a fall and winter migrant but also as a winter resident. Very rare as a breeder.

Habitat: Spruce-fir-pine dominated forests in the north and in the Rocky Mountain west. In the east uses mostly mixed deciduous/conifer forests.

Breeding: Uses old woodpecker holes almost exclusively for nesting. 5 or 6 eggs is typical with a survival rate to fledging of about 50 percent.

Natural History: Small mammals (mice, voles, and shrews) make up the bulk of this little owl's diet. Mice of the genus *Peromyscus* make up as much as three-fourths of the food consumed. Insects are oddly not listed as a major food item, but small songbirds are known to be eaten. Small and secretive, the Saw-whet Owl roosts in thick evergreens and is typically silent except during the breeding season. Thus these birds are difficult to observe in the wild. Within its range in the Rockies and Appalachians, seasonal migration is mostly vertical, with the owls moving to lower elevations in winter. These uncommon owls are probably most common in northern half of the state. But they can occur anywhere in the state in winter.

Class—**Aves** (birds)

Order—**Falconiformes** (raptors)

Family—**Accipitridae** (hawks, eagles, kites)

Red-tailed Hawk—*Buteo jamiacensis*

Typical adult showing red tail

Light morph

Dark morph

Juvenile eating Gray Squirrel

Typical adult

Presumed range in Indiana

Size: 19 to 22 inches.

Abundance: Common throughout the state. Perhaps slightly more common in glaciated regions.

Migratory Status: Year-round resident. Numbers are supplemented in winter with migrants from farther north.

Variation: Highly variable. Can vary from nearly solid dark brown to very pale (almost white). Most adult birds are like the typical adult specimens pictured above. Light and dark morphs are mostly winter migrants in Indiana. Females are about 20 percent larger than males. Juveniles have brownish tails with dark crossbars. Some experts recognize as many as 16 subspecies throughout North America.

Habitat: Found in virtually all habitats within the state. Likes open and semi-open areas and is least common in continuous forest, although they do occur there. Favors a mosaic of woodlands, farmland, fencerows, overgrown fields, etc.

Breeding: In the eastern US the large stick nest is built high in trees. Nest is usually situated in place that is remote from human activities. Lays 2 to 4 eggs. Young fledge at six weeks.

Natural History: This is the most common and widespread large *Buteo* hawk in America. Their range includes all of North America south of the Arctic and much of the Caribbean and Central America. The Red-tailed Hawk is generally regarded as the daytime counterpart of the Great Horned Owl, hunting by day many of the same species in the same habitats utilized by the owl at night. "Red-tails" prey mostly on rodents (mice, voles and ground squirrels). But much larger prey like rabbits may also be taken on occasion. In some areas ground dwelling birds like pheasants and quail are taken, and they have been known to attack large flocks of blackbirds. In summer they also take large snakes such as the Woodland Rat Snake (*Pantherophis*). Large examples of these snakes (which are strong constrictors) have been known to turn the tables and end up killing a hungry hawk. During winter these large hawks sometimes resort to eating carrion and can sometimes be seen feeding on road kills. In Indiana (and in much of the eastern US), the Red-tailed Hawk is often known by the nickname "Chicken Hawk" in the mistaken belief that they prey on chickens. Although they may certainly catch a few chickens occasionally, their main food is rats, mice and other rodents, making them an overall useful species to man. Their habit of perching conspicuously in dead trees, snags and power poles along highways makes them one of the more easily observed of America's hawk species. Historically, the Red-tailed Hawk and other raptors were regarded as varmints and for many decades they were shot on sight by uninformed individuals. By the 1950s many birds of prey were becoming scarce in America. Since the amendment of the migratory bird treaty act in the early 1970s providing federal protection to all of America's raptor species, Red-tailed Hawks have become common once again.

Class—**Aves** (birds)
Order—**Falconiformes** (raptors)
Family—**Accipitridae** (hawks, eagles, kites)

Broad-winged Hawk *Buteo platypterus*	Rough-legged Hawk *Buteo lagopus*	Red-shouldered Hawk *Buteo lineatus*

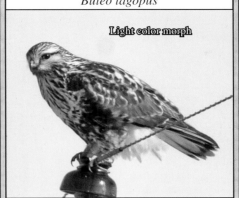
Light color morph

Juvenile | Adult

Broad-winged Hawk

Size: 16 inches.

Abundance: Uncommon in Indiana

Migratory Status: Summer resident.

Variation: First year plumage is mottled brown (similar to juvenile Red-shouldered Hawk on this page).

Presumed range in Indiana

Habitat: Favors large tracts of unbroken deciduous woodlands in upland areas. More common in Indiana in the southern part of the state.

Breeding: Stick nest is in a tree crotch, usually in deep woods. Lays 2 to 3 eggs on average.

Natural History: A decidedly woodland raptor whose breeding range in North America closely mimics the Eastern Temperate Forests Level I ecoregion. This species is more common in unglaciated regions of Indiana as those regions are typically more heavily forested. They may be seen as a migrant throughout the glaciated regions of Indiana but the lack of large tracts of forest in those regions precludes nesting in much of that area. They are less conspicuous than most hawks except during the migration when they band together in large flocks known as "kettles." Extremely large flocks that may contain 200 birds are usually seen during fall migrations. Food includes insects, but consists mostly of small vertebrates like rodents as well as a large amount of reptile and amphibian prey. Small snakes are high on their list of prey species.

Rough-legged Hawk

Size: 21 inches.

Abundance: Uncommon in Indiana.

Migratory Status: Winter migrant.

Variation: Two distinct color morphs, a dark phase and a lighter morph with pale head and shoulders.

Presumed range in Indiana

Habitat: This is a northern species that summers as far north as the Arctic. Favors tundra in summer and farmlands and prairies in winter.

Breeding: Nests well to north in Arctic or subarctic regions of tundra and taiga. Clutch size (3 to 7) is prey dependent.

Natural History: The Rough-legged Hawk is an arctic species that moves south in winter. In Indiana they are most likely to be seen in the northern part of the state. Their migrations are sporadic depending upon weather, snow cover and prey availability, but they can usually be seen every winter in Indiana. They prey primarily on small mammals and lemmings are an important food on the breeding grounds. During years of high lemming populations more eggs will be laid and more young fledged. In winter they take mice, voles, and shrews mostly. Hunts by soaring and hovering over open country. They can face into the wind and remain in a stationary hover for over a minute. While these are fairly large hawks, they have relatively small feet and small beaks, and are thus unable to take the larger prey taken by hawks like the Red-tailed Hawk.

Red-shouldered Hawk

Size: 17 inches.

Abundance: Uncommon in Indiana.

Migratory Status: Year-round resident.

Variation: 4 subspecies. Ours is the eastern race (*B. l. lineatus*). Female is larger. Ontogenetic variation.

Presumed range in Indiana

Habitat: Woodlands of all kinds, but especially likes woods bordering swamps or rivers, or along wooded creek-sides. Less common in uplands.

Breeding: Bulky stick nest is in the fork of a tree about 20 to 40 feet high and often near water. 2 to 4 eggs in April.

Natural History: The Red-shouldered Hawk is the daytime counterpart of the Barred Owl, and the two species often occur in the same territory. These are vocal birds. Their call, described as "kee-ah, kee-ah, kee-ah" is rapidly repeated about a dozen times. They can be fairly tame if unmolested and their raucous calling will not go unnoticed when the nest is nearby. They feed on a wide variety of small vertebrates but mostly eat reptiles, amphibians and rodents. The range of the Red-shouldered Hawk coincides closely with the level 1 ecoregion known as the Eastern Temperate Forest. However, a disjunct population (subspecies *elegans*) is found on the west coast of North America in the Mediterranean California Ecoregion. In Indiana this hawk is most common in portions of the state that are more heavily forested.

Class—**Aves** (birds)

Order—**Falconiformes** (raptors)

Family—**Accipitridae** (hawks, eagles, kites)

Golden Eagle *Aquila chrysaetos*	**Bald Eagle** *Haliaeetus leucophalus*	**Osprey** *Pandion haliaetus*

Size: 30 inches.	Presumed range in Indiana	**Size:** 31 inches.	Presumed range in Indiana	**Size:** 30 inches.	Presumed range in Indiana

Golden Eagle	Bald Eagle	Osprey
Abundance: Very rare in Indiana.	**Abundance:** Uncommon in Indiana.	**Abundance:** Endangered in IN.
Migratory Status: Winter migrant. October to April.	**Migratory Status:** A year-round resident and winter migrant.	**Migratory Status:** Summer resident. Winters in the south.
Variation: Female is about 20 percent larger. Juveniles have white in tail.	**Variation:** May not acquire the characteristic white head and tail until five years of age.	**Variation:** No variation. Females are slightly larger than males.
Habitat: Rugged mountains, deserts, and open plains of the western US and rugged regions of Canadian tundra.	**Habitat:** In Indiana Bald Eagles are associated with large rivers and lakes, especially Lake Michigan.	**Habitat:** Typically seen in the vicinity of large lakes and rivers. Increasing in numbers throughout the Midwest.
Breeding: A large stick nest up to 6 feet across is usually built on the face of a steep cliff. Usually lays 2 eggs.	**Breeding:** Extremely bulky stick nest is re-used and gets larger each year. Usually only 2 eggs per clutch.	**Breeding:** Bulky stick nest is often built on man-made structures like bridges and power line towers. 2 to 4 eggs.

Natural History: Although they are slightly smaller than the Bald Eagle, Golden Eagles are probably the most fearsome hunting bird in America. Ground squirrels and other small mammals make up to bulk of their prey, with larger species like jackrabbits and the young of wild sheep, goats, and Pronghorn also being taken. They are sometimes persecuted by sheep ranchers in western North America, who blame them for killing young lambs in the spring. Indigenous to the entire northern hemisphere, in America the Golden Eagle is found mostly in the west. Like many large raptors they are capable of significant seasonal movements. Although very rare east of the Great Plains, they may sometimes show up almost anywhere in North America, including Indiana, especially during winter months. Mongolian falconers trained them to hunt wolves!

Natural History: One of the great conservation success stories, Bald Eagles were highly endangered just a few decades ago. Stringent protection, banning of the pesticide DDT, and a widespread education campaign has lead to a remarkable recovery. They first began to recover as a breeding species in most of the country in the 1980s following years of strict protection and banning of DDT. Bald Eagles feed largely on fish and carrion but are also capable hunters. Some birds specialize in hunting migratory waterfowl in winter, picking off birds wounded by hunters. Bald Eagles wander widely in the winter and may be seen virtually anywhere in the state, but they are nowhere numerous. Most nesting is around large rivers, lakes or expansive wetlands. Today there are several hundred nesting pairs in Indiana. Adopted as the national emblem of the United States by Congress in 1782.

Natural History: Subsists mainly on fish. Hunting tactics consist of a steep dive that ends with the Osprey plunging feet first into the water, allowing them to catch fish up to three feet below the surface. Most fish caught in fresh water are non-game species, thus they have little to no impact on sport fisheries. Like the Bald Eagle, Osprey populations in the mid-United States plummeted dramatically in the first half of the 20th century. The same types of conservation efforts that restored the Bald Eagle (including re-introduction programs), have brought Osprey numbers back to respectable levels. Once regarded as federally endangered, the Osprey has recovered enough to have recently been de-listed. Most states now boast healthy populations of nesting Ospreys and they continue to increase across the country. In 2020 the IDNR reported over 100 nests in IN.

Class—**Aves** (birds)

Order—**Falconiformes** (raptors)

Family—**Accipitridae** (hawks, eagles, kites)

Northern Goshawk *Accipiter gentilis*	**Sharp-shinned Hawk** *Accipiter striatus*	**Cooper's Hawk** *Accipiter cooperi*

			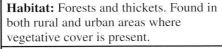		
Size: To 24 inches.	Presumed range in Indiana	**Size:** 9 to 13 inches.	Presumed range in Indiana	**Size:** 14 to 19 inches.	Presumed range in Indiana

Abundance: Very rare in Indiana.

Abundance: Fairly common.

Abundance: Fairly common.

Migratory Status: A rare winter migrant in extreme northern Indiana.

Migratory Status: Winter resident, seasonal migrant and very rare summer resident.

Migratory Status: Year-round resident and some winter residents from northern regions.

Variation: Females are larger. Juveniles are heavily streaked with dark brown.

Variation: Ontogenetic plumage variation. Females can be twice the size of males.

Variation: Ontogenetic plumage variation. Females can be 30 percent larger than males.

Habitat: A bird of coniferous and boreal forests. In winter sometimes uses mixed deciduous/conifer woodlands.

Habitat: Forests and thickets. Found in both rural and urban areas where vegetative cover is present.

Habitat: Woodlands, regenerative areas, and edge habitats are favored. Can also be seen in tree-lined urban yards.

Breeding: Large stick nest can be 3 feet across, usually built in the largest tree in the area. 2 to 4 eggs on average.

Breeding: Conifers are a favored locale for placing the nest. Lays as many as 8 eggs, with 5 to 6 being the average.

Breeding: Stick nest is built high in tree and eggs are laid in April or May. Clutch size averages 4 to 6.

Natural History: This is a bird of wilderness. It inhabits most of Canada and the Rocky Mountains. Their primary food consists of several species of grouse, but they also take smaller birds as well as squirrels, rabbits, and animals as large as the Snowshoe Hare. Known for fearlessness, the Goshawk has been known to attack humans who venture to close to its nest. It is equally courageous on the hunt and will crash headlong into thickets in pursuit of fleeing prey. This characteristic coupled with its speed and large size have made the Goshawk a favorite bird among those who practice the ancient art of Falconry. Although this species is widespread across the northern half of North America, they are an uncommon bird even within their core range. In Indiana they are seen only very rarely in winter in the northernmost section of the state.

Natural History: A relentless hunter of small songbirds, the Sharp-shinned Hawk is sometimes seen raiding backyard bird feeders, and they are known to pluck baby songbirds from nests. These small raptors are capable of rapid, twisting flight while pursuing their small songbird prey through woodlands and thickets. In Indiana they are more common during migration periods when birds that summer farther north move southward. Although some birds may be breeding residents in the state, most nest far to north, some as far north as Alaska and the Yukon Territory. The Sharp-shinned Hawk is a widely distributed species that ranges across all of North America south of the arctic region and southward all the way to southern Central America. These small hawks are easily overlooked since they favor dense thickets and woodland habitats.

Natural History: Feeds almost exclusively on birds and is known to haunt backyard bird feeders. These hawks are a major predator of the Bobwhite, an important game species that is in decline throughout most of its range. Cooper's Hawks are fierce hunters that will fearlessly attack birds as large or larger than themselves, including grouse, waterfowl and domestic chickens. Although quite widespread and fairly common, they are not as observable as the *Buteo* hawks. Cooper's Hawks tend to stay in wooded areas and thickets with heavier cover than their bulkier cousins. These birds are fast fliers and capable of great maneuverability, an adaptation to hunting in forest and thickets. They have adapted well to human activities and they sometimes exist in urban areas, especially in parks and heavily wooded neighborhoods.

Class—**Aves** (birds)

Order—**Falconiformes** (raptors)

Family—**Accipitridae** (hawks, eagles, kites)

Northern Harrier *Circus cyaneus*	**Mississippi Kite** *Ictina mississippiensis*

Size: To 24 inches.

Abundance: Fairly common as a seasonal migrant. Uncommon as a winter resident.

Variation: Male is slate gray. Female is chocolate brown. Juveniles resemble females in color. Immature males have greenish yellow eyes. Juvenile females have brown eyes. As adults both sexes have yellow eyes.

Migratory Status: Mostly a winter migrant and winter resident. At one time this species was also a summer resident and breeder in the northern parts of the state. A few individuals may still summer in northernmost Indiana.

Presumed range in Indiana

Size: 14 inches.

Abundance: Rare in Indiana.

Variation: Juveniles are streaked with brown on the breast.

Migratory Status: A rare summer resident in extreme southwestern IN.

Presumed range in Indiana

Habitat: Open country. Pastures, marshes, agricultural fields, wet prairies and grasslands. In Indiana today it hunts croplands in winter and during migration. It also will use reclaimed strip mine lands.

Habitat: In Indiana the Mississippi Kite mostly frequents the regions along the Ohio and lower Wabash Rivers.

Breeding: This is one of the few hawks that nests on the ground. The nest is usually placed in thick grasses and is built from grasses and weed stems. Lays 4 to 6 eggs with as many as 9 recorded. Historically this species bred in the northern part of the state, but today it is a very rare breeder in Indiana if at all.

Breeding: Builds a stick nest high up in a large tree. Nesting in Indiana is rare but possibly increasing. Lays 2 eggs.

Natural History: The range of the Northern Harrier is holarctic and includes Europe and northern Asia as well as North America. Unlike most diurnal raptors that hunt entirely by sight, the Northern Harrier mimics the technique used by owls and hunts largely by sound. A special "parabola" of feathers surround the face and direct sound waves to the ears. It hunts by flying low to the ground with a slow, buoyant flight that resembles a giant butterfly. Food is mostly small mammals and birds but reptiles and amphibians are also listed as food items. Roosting and nesting on the ground and hunting as much by sound as by sight, the Northern Harrier is unique among America's diurnal raptors. In historical times before the draining of America's marshes, this was a more common species. They are also commonly called "Marsh Hawk." It is an appropriate name since both fresh and salt water marshes are one of this bird's favorite habitats. Many will winter in the salt marshes and coastal prairies of the southeastern United States. While wintering individuals and especially migrants can be fairly common in Indiana, as a breeding bird this is a State Endangered Species in Indiana. In many respects, the Northern Harrier is a daytime counterpart to the Short-eared Owl. Both favor grassland habitats and both feed mostly on small rodents such as deer mice and voles. Both the summer range and the year-round range of the two species in the US are also very similar. Even their hunting technique and methods of flight are very much alike.

Natural History: With their small beaks and feet the Mississippi Kite appears somewhat delicate looking compared to other raptors. In flight they are one of the most graceful. The several species that make up the raptor group known as kites are mainly tropical birds. The Mississippi Kite is the most northerly ranging of the kites, and can be seen as far north as southern Indiana in summer. Long distance migrants, they arrive in Indiana in May and leave for South America by September. These are gregarious birds that may nest communally and in some parts of their range it is not uncommon to see several nests in close proximity or see groups of birds soaring together. They feed mostly on insects caught in flight.

Class—**Aves** (birds)

Order—**Falconiformes** (raptors)

Family—**Falconidae** (falcons)

American Kestrel *Falco sparverius*	**Merlin** *Falco columbarius*	**Peregrine Falcon** *Falco peregrinus*

American Kestrel
Falco sparverius

Size: 10 inches.

Presumed range in Indiana

Abundance: Fairly common.

Variation: Sexually dimorphic. Male has gray wings, female brown.

Migratory Status: A year-round resident. Winter migrants increase the population in winter.

Habitat: Throughout its range the Kestrel is seen in open country. It is least common in forested regions.

Breeding: Usually nests in tree cavities or old woodpecker holes within trees situated in open fields. May also nest in man-made structures. 4 to 5 eggs.

Natural History: While the Kestrel is a fairly common bird in open regions throughout Indiana, there has been some decline in populations in the eastern United States in recent years. Some blame the decline in Kestrels on predation by the Cooper's Hawk. Though they are sometimes called "Sparrow Hawk," these are small falcons. The Kestrel is widespread throughout North and Central America and as many as 17 subspecies are recognized. They are often seen perched on power lines and poles along roadways in rural farmlands throughout the state, but they are uncommon in the heavily forested regions. Insects are the major food in summer (especially grasshoppers). In winter they eat small mammals and rarely, small birds. Hunts both from a perch and by hovering over open fields.

Merlin
Falco columbarius

Size: 11 inches.

Presumed range in Indiana

Abundance: Rare in Indiana.

Variation: Male has blue-gray back, female and immatures brown.

Migratory Status: A rare spring/fall migrant and very rare winter migrant.

Habitat: Habitat is open regions. Most likely to be seen along major river valleys or along the Lake Michigan shore.

Breeding: Breeds far to the north in Canada, Alaska and parts of the north-central Rockies and plains. Uses old crow or hawk nests as well as cliffs.

Natural History: The Merlin is seen in Indiana only during migration (or as an occasional wandering bird almost any time of year). These small falcons are only slightly larger than the Kestrel and they are easily confused with that species. The facial markings of the Merlin are less distinct than the Kestrels. Summering mostly far to the north and wintering along coastlines, their migration routes are mostly in the western United States or to the east along the Atlantic coast. Like most falcons however, these birds are prone to wander widely. Although they may occur almost anywhere in the state they are an uncommon to rare bird in Indiana. Food is mostly small birds, especially shorebirds, but songbirds and Rock Doves are also eaten. They were once known by the nickname "Pigeon Hawk."

Peregrine Falcon
Falco peregrinus

Size: 17 inches.

Presumed range in Indiana

Abundance: Rare.

Variation: Several variants. Specimen above is typical.

Migratory Status: Mainly a migrant. A few are year-round residents.

Habitat: Prefers cliffs in remote wilderness areas but has adapted to living among skyscrapers in many cities.

Breeding: Nests on ledges of cliff faces and on man-made structures like skyscrapers and bridges. Four eggs is typical, sometimes up to six.

Natural History: Falcons are fast flying birds and the Peregrine is among the fastest. Hunts pigeons, waterfowl, grouse, etc. Hunting technique usually involves soaring high above and diving in on birds in flight, or diving towards resting birds and panicking them into flight. Once airborne, no other bird can match the Peregrine's speed. Diving Peregrines may reach speeds approaching 200 mph, making them perhaps the fastest animal on earth. In Indiana this species has been re-introduced after being extirpated as a breeding bird many decades ago. The name "peregrine" means "wanderer," and these birds may be seen almost anywhere in the state, albeit quite rarely. Historically this falcon went by the name "Duck Hawk." An appropriate name since waterfowl are among its favorite prey.

Class—**Aves (birds)**

Order—**Cathartiformes** (vultures)

Family—**Cathartidae**

Turkey Vulture *Cathartes aura*	**Black Vulture** *Coragyps altratus*

Size: 26 inches.

Abundance: Common. Usually more common in summer than in winter.

Variation: Skin on face is pinkish gray on immature birds, bright pink on adult (see photos above). Feathering on the head and neck recede with age.

Migratory Status: Year-round resident in the southern tip of the state. Individuals in the northern portions of the state will move south in winter. Southward movement dependent upon severity of winter weather.

Presumed range in Indiana

Habitat: Seen in all habitats throughout the state. Less common in urban areas and regions of intensive agriculture. Can be common in urban areas around landfills.

Breeding: Nests on cliff faces, caves, in large tree hollows or on the ground in hollow logs. May use old barns or abandoned buildings. Almost always lays two eggs.

Natural History: The absence of feathers on the head and neck of vultures is an adaptation for feeding on carrion. Vultures may stick the head deep inside a rotting carcass and feathers would become matted with filth. The bare skin on the neck and face on the other hand is constantly exposed to the sterilizing effects of sunlight. Turkey Vultures are one of the few birds with a well-developed sense of smell, and food is often located by detecting the odor of rotting flesh. Sight is also important and they are quick to notice a fresh carcass on a roadway. Newly mowed fields and other disturbed areas within their range are closely scanned for small animal victims. Highly social, they roost communally, sometimes with Black Vultures. Water towers, electrical towers and other man-made structures are used as roosts. Throughout their range vultures have benefited from a constant supply of road-killed animals. These vultures are found across the continental United States and southward through Mexico, Central and South America.

Size: 25 inches.

Abundance: Fairly common in summer. Rare or absent in winter.

Variation: Older birds have lighter gray heads with more wrinkles on skin than immatures. Feathering on the head and neck recede with age.

Migratory Status: Primarily a summer resident in southern Indiana. A few may wander north of the area shown on map. May stay year-round in the southern tip of the state if the weather is mild, but most will go south in winter.

Presumed range in Indiana

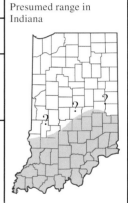

Habitat: Found in a wide variety of habitats within its range. Can be common in urban areas near dumps and landfills. Also may congregate around livestock pens.

Breeding: No nest is built and the two eggs are laid on a bare surface. The nest site may be a hollow log or mouth of a cave or cliff face. Often nests in a derelict building.

Natural History: America's vultures are named for the color of the skin on the face. Turkey Vultures have reddish skin (like a turkey), Black Vulture has dark gray or black facial skin. Black Vultures also have shorter tails and lesser wing span, giving them a much "stubbier" look than the Turkey Vulture. Vultures were once regarded as a threat to livestock by spreading disease. In fact, the powerful digestive juices of the gut of vultures destroys bacteria. Both the Turkey Vulture and the Black Vulture have the unappealing habit of defecating on the legs and feet as a way of disinfecting the feet (which can become quite nasty as the birds feed on rotted carcasses). Black Vultures lack the well-developed sense of smell of Turkey Vultures, but they do have keen eyesight. Although smaller than the Turkey Vulture, they are more aggressive than their larger relatives. Often roosts and soars in the company of Turkey Vultures. The range of the Black Vulture includes all of Mexico, Central and South America, as well as the southeastern US.

Class—**Aves** (birds)

Order—**Ciconiiformes** (wading birds)

Family—**Ardeidae** (herons)

Great Blue Heron	Great Egret	Snowy Egret
Ardea herodias	*Ardea alba*	*Egretta thula*

Size: 47 inches.

Presumed range in Indiana

Abundance: Fairly common.

Migratory Status: Year-round resident in southern Indiana. Summer resident north.

Variation: See Natural History below.

Habitat: Along rivers and streams, swamps, marshes, ponds and wet meadows and floodplains.

Breeding: Nests in colonies. Most nesting in Indiana is in wetland areas. Nest is a platform of sticks in tree or bush above water. 3 to 4 eggs is typical.

Natural History: The largest heron in North America, the Great Blue Heron will eat almost anything it can swallow. Fish and frogs are major foods, but it also eats snakes, salamanders, small mammals and even small turtles. Birds are sometimes eaten, including other, smaller heron species. All food items are swallowed whole. Large prey is killed by stabbing repeatedly with the beak or by bashing against a hard object. Smaller prey is often swallowed alive. Hunts both day and night and reportedly has good night vision. Great Blue Herons are found throughout most of the United States and much of Canada, including in riparian habitats in desert regions. Sexes are alike but juveniles will have streaked breast and neck and are duskier overall than adults. A solid white subspecies is found in parts of southern Florida.

Size: 39 inches.

Presumed range in Indiana

Abundance: Uncommon in Indiana.

Migratory Status: Rare summer resident and uncommon summer migrant.

Variation: Breeders acquire plumes.

Habitat: Along major streams, lakes, swamps and marshes. Also low lying areas subject to flooding.

Breeding: Nesting in Indiana is rare but occurs along the Lake Michigan shore and probably in southwestern IN. Nest is a platform of sticks in tree or bush above water. Lays 3 or 4 eggs.

Natural History: This heron species (along with the Snowy Egret and several other herons) was nearly hunted to extinction during the last half of the 19th century. The long, wispy feathers (known as "plumes") were once used to adorn the hats of fashionable ladies. The plumes are most pronounced during the breeding season. Thus the catastrophic impact of the plume hunters was magnified as hunters killed birds at their nesting colonies. Killing of parent birds doomed nestlings as well. Efforts to save this and other plume bird species lead to some of America's earliest laws to protect wildlife. Today this species is still a symbol of conservation efforts and is the logo of the National Audubon Society. It is also known by the names Common Egret or Great White Egret. As with many other herons, it often nests in colonies.

Size: 24 inches.

Presumed range in Indiana

Abundance: Rare in Indiana.

Migratory Status: Summer migrant, most likely to be seen in southern Indiana.

Variation: Breeders acquire plumes.

Habitat: Along major streams, lakes, swamps and marshes. Also low lying areas subject to flooding.

Breeding: No nesting known in Indiana, but northern nesting has occurred on Lake Erie. Known to nest in colonies with other herons. Nest is made of sticks and twigs. 3 to 5 eggs is average.

Natural History: As with several other heron species, the Snowy Egret during breeding season sports long "plume" feathers on the back. Like other plume bird species the Snowy Egret was nearly wiped out by the feather trade of the late 1800s. Today the species has recovered to healthy numbers but remains under threat due to its dependence upon coastal wetlands. This species feeds on smaller prey such as worms, insects, crustaceans, amphibians and small fish. It is an active feeder that often chases prey through the shallows rather than using the stealth method employed by its larger cousins. It also often feeds by swishing its feet in the mud to disturb benthic organisms. Although they are primarily a southern bird, they may be expanding their range northward and summer migrants might occur anywhere in the state today.

Class—**Aves** (birds)
Order—**Ciconiiformes** (wading birds)
Family—**Ardeidae** (herons)

Little Blue Heron	Cattle Egret	Green Heron
Egretta cearulea	*Bulbulcus ibis*	*Butorides virescens*

Juvenile

Size: 24 inches.

Presumed range in Indiana

Abundance: Rare in Indiana.

Migratory Status: A very rare summer migrant.

Variation: First year birds have white plumage (see inset photo).

Habitat: Wetlands. Probably most likely seen along the lower Wabash River in the southwestern part of the state.

Breeding: Builds a stick nest platform in bushes and low trees in wetlands. Lays 2 to 5 eggs. No nesting in Indiana.

Natural History: Even within the heart of its range along the lower coastal plains of the southeastern US, the Little Blue Heron is generally less common than other heron species. In Indiana it is a rather rare bird. In addition, the dark plumage of adults and its rather secretive nature make it one of the least observable of our herons. Like most herons, it is an opportunistic feeder that eats almost anything it can swallow. Food is mostly frogs, fish, crustaceans and insects. It is a daytime hunter that hunts by stalking slowly through wetland habitats. The transitional plumage of the juvenile Little Blue Heron is unique, and produces for a brief time a white bird with blue splotches. Blue increases throughout the molt ending in a solid blue adult. The range map approximates the range of summer migrants. Range map above represents where it is most likely to occur in state. May wander statewide.

Size: 19 inches.

Presumed range in Indiana

Abundance: Uncommon in Indiana.

Migratory Status: A rare summer migrant and very rare breeder.

Variation: Develops orange on crown and throat during breeding.

Habitat: Unlike other herons, these birds are usually seen in open pastures and fields in association with cattle.

Breeding: Stick nest built in trees or bushes. Nests in large colonies. 3 or 4 eggs is average.

Natural History: The Cattle Egret is one of America's most interesting heron species. Originally native to Africa, Cattle Egrets began an inexplicable range expansion in the early 1800s. They first migrated across the Atlantic to South America and then appeared in North America around 1950. The species continues to expand its range and is today an uncommon summer migrant in much of Indiana. The first specimen was recorded in Indiana in 1964. Their name is derived from their habit of associating with cattle herds in pastures. Before expanding their range out of Africa they associated with herds of Cape Buffalo, Hippopotamus and wild ungulates. They feed mostly on insects that are disturbed by the large grazers they follow through pastures and grasslands. The map above shows the approximate range of summer migrants in Indiana. Nesting has occurred in extreme southwestern Indiana and on Lake Michigan.

Size: 19 inches.

Presumed range in Indiana

Abundance: Fairly common.

Migratory Status: A summer resident that breeds in the state.

Variation: Juvenile birds are browner with a streaked throat.

Habitat: Usually seen in the vicinity of wetlands or rivers and streams. Also common around lakes and small ponds.

Breeding: Usually nests singly rather than in colonies. Nest is a stick platform in a tree fork. Lays 3 to 5 eggs.

Natural History: In many areas the Green Heron often goes by the name "Shy-poke." Also called "Green Backed Heron," This is one of our most familiar herons and its range encompasses all of the eastern United States as well as the west coast. It may be expanding its range northward. It also ranges southward throughout Central America. When flushed it nearly always emits a loud "squawking" alarm call. Feeds mostly in shallow water and often feeds from a perch on a floating log or a limb just above the water's surface. Hunts by stealth and may remain frozen for long periods as it watches and waits for prey. Fish is the primary food item with small frogs probably being the next most common prey. Almost any small animal may be eaten including crayfish, tadpoles, and insects. Amazingly, this species has been reported to catch insects and worms to use as bait for luring in fish.

Class—**Aves** (birds)

Order—**Ciconiiformes** (wading birds)

Family—**Ardeidae** (herons)

Yellow-crowned Night Heron *Nyctanassa violacea*	**Black-crowned Night Heron** *Nycticorax nycticorax*	**Least Bittern** *Ixobrychus exilis*

Yellow-crowned Night Heron

Size: 25 inches.

Abundance: Endangered in Indiana.

Migratory Status: Summer resident.

Variation: Juveniles are heavily streaked with brown and white for the first year.

Presumed range in Indiana

Habitat: Swamps and marshes. Favors heavier cover than many herons.

Breeding: Breeds very sporadically in Indiana in the southern part of the state. Flimsy stick nest is fairly high in tree, usually over water. 3 to 5 eggs.

Natural History: These birds are often active at night, hence the name "night heron." Food is mostly crustaceans. Crabs are important foods in coastal regions, while crayfish are eaten in fresh water areas. A classical ambush predator, the Yellow-crowned Night Heron does most foraging from a stationary position, sitting like a statue and waiting for prey to wander into striking range. They will also stalk slowly and methodically with slow, deliberate movements that are largely undetectable to prey. Diet may be supplemented with fish and invertebrates, but this heron is mainly a crustacean specialist. Has recovered nicely from low numbers decades ago and now seems to be expanding its range farther to the north. Sightings have been recorded across the state but most are seen in the southwestern tip of the state. It is regarded as an endangered species in Indiana.

Black-crowned Night Heron

Size: 25 inches.

Abundance: Endangered in Indiana

Migratory Status: Summer resident.

Variation: Juvenile birds are heavily streaked with brown (see inset).

Presumed range in Indiana

Habitat: Wetlands, river valleys, and in the vicinity of large impoundments.

Breeding: Nests in colonies that are usually situated over swamps or on an island. Colonies may contain hundreds of birds, with 3 or 4 eggs per nest.

Natural History: Although the Black-crowned Night Heron may be locally common near breeding colonies, it is a rarely seen bird in most of Indiana. Surprisingly, this is a widespread species that is found not only in much of the US, but in fact throughout most of the world. They can be found on every continent except Australia and Antarctica. As its name implies this species is often active at night. The food is primarily fish. However, the list of known foods is quite long and includes insects, leeches, earthworms, crustaceans, gastropods, amphibians, snakes, small turtles, small mammals, and even birds! Prefers to feed in shallow water along the margins of weedy ponds, marshes, and swamps. Although most range maps show the entire state of Indiana as being within this species breeding range, breeding in Indiana probably occurs only in a few localities.

Least Bittern

Size: 13 inches.

Abundance: Uncommon to rare.

Migratory Status: A summer resident.

Variation: Male has black cap and black back. See both sexes above.

Presumed range in Indiana

Habitat: Favors marshes with dense growths of tall grasses and sedges.

Breeding: Nest is a well-concealed platform built amid dense growth of cattails or other sedges/grasses. Up to 6 eggs are laid.

Natural History: This smallest of American herons is also a secretive bird that often stays hidden in dense marsh grasses and sedges. When alarmed they point their bill skyward and freeze, mimicking the vertical vegetation of their habitat. These small herons move with ease through thick stands of marsh vegetation. When flushed they fly only a short distance just above the vegetation before dropping back down. They migrate great distances from wintering areas in south Florida and the Caribbean to summer breeding grounds that may be as far north as northern Minnesota. Recorded sightings of migrants in Indiana are almost statewide but breeding is restricted mostly to the northern part of the state. Feeds on small fish, insects, crayfish, and amphibians. This species has declined significantly over the last century. Today they are regarded as an endangered species in Indiana.

Class—**Aves** (birds)		
Order—**Ciconiiformes** (wading birds)	Order—**Gruiformes** (rails & cranes)	
Family—**Ardeidae** (herons)	Family—**Rallidae** (rails)	
American Bittern *Botaurus lentiginosus*	**King Rail** *Rallus elegans*	**Virginia Rail** *Rallus limicola*

Size: 26 inches.

Presumed range in Indiana

Abundance: Endangered in Indiana.

Migratory Status: Both a migrant and a rare summer resident.

Habitat: Large fresh water marshes are used in summer, coastal marshlands in winter.

Variation: None. Sexes alike.

Breeding: Nest is in dense emergent vegetation of the marsh and is well hidden. 3 to 5 eggs is typical. Most breeding is well to the north of Indiana.

Natural History: The biology of this species is not well known. Presumably they may be seen anywhere in Indiana during migration and migrants have been known to use tiny ponds or small pockets of wetlands choked with emergent vegetation like cattails. Few Indianans will ever see one, as they are usually quite secretive. Hunts by stealth and may remain motionless for long periods of time. The eyes of this heron are situated with a downward slant, better facilitating the bird's ability to see into the water. When startled they will throw the head back and point the beak straight up. The streaked brown pattern of the neck and breast is remarkably cryptic amid vertical stalks of marsh grasses and sedges, and an individual in "frozen" posture becomes almost invisible. Like most herons, it is an opportunistic feeder. Eats fish, amphibians, crayfish, small mammals and some insects.

Size: 16 inches.

Presumed range in Indiana

Abundance: Very rare in Indiana.

Migratory Status: Transient migrant and rare summer resident.

Habitat: Marshes. Found mostly along coasts but a few move inland in summer.

Variation: None. Sexes alike.

Breeding: Builds a loosely woven cup from marsh vegetation. Historically breed sporadically in the state, mostly along the Lake Michigan shoreline.

Natural History: While breeding has been recorded in Indiana, the species has declined from its historical breeding range and today this is one of the rarest breeding birds in the state. It is regarded as endangered in Indiana. Rails are well adapted to life in the marsh. They move with ease through thick grasses and rarely fly except when migrating. They can run quite fast through the grass and rarely offer more than a glimpse. They can also swim and dive beneath the surface, using the wings to swim underwater. Despite the fact that rails are listed as a game bird by some state wildlife agencies, almost no one hunts them today, due probably to their scarcity and secretiveness. They feed mostly on aquatic insects and their larva, spiders, and other invertebrates. Some plant material is also eaten. Although they could occur across much of Indiana, they are very rare in the state today and are almost never observed.

Size: 9.5 inches.

Presumed range in Indiana

Abundance: Uncommon.

Migratory Status: Mostly a summer resident. Rare in winter.

Habitat: Primarily a marsh dweller. Migrators visit ponds, swamps, wet meadows.

Variation: None. Sexes alike.

Breeding: Builds a nest platform of aquatic vegetation a few inches above water level. Nest is usually well hidden among vegetation. Lays 8 or 9 eggs.

Natural History: The Virginia Rail is more common than the larger King Rail, both as a migrant and as a breeding bird. Historically, nesting was not uncommon in much of northern Indiana. It probably still breeds in parts of the state and a few have been recorded in winter. Its secretive nature means that it is a species that remains unfamiliar to most Indianans. Formerly, this species was much more common in the state but today very little of the wetland habitats that once occurred in Indiana remain. As a result, this species along with its larger cousin the King Rail are both regarded as endangered species by the Indiana Department of Natural Resources. Two other species of Rail, the **Black Rail** (*Laterallus jamiacensis*) and the **Yellow Rail** (*Coturnicops noveboracensis*) have been observed in the state, but both are so rare and secretive that the chances of seeing either one in Indiana are very low.

Class—**Aves** (birds)
Order—**Gruiformes** (rails & cranes)
Family—**Rallidae** (rails)

American Coot *Fulica americana*	**Common Gallinule** *Gallinula galeata*	**Sora** *Porzana carolina*

American Coot	Common Gallinule	Sora
Size: 15 inches.	**Size:** 14 inches.	**Size:** 9 inches.
Abundance: Fairly common.	**Abundance:** Rare in Indiana.	**Abundance:** Uncommon.
Migratory Status: Year-round in some areas. Winter resident in south. Summer in north.	**Migratory Status:** Rare summer resident. Arrives mid-April. Leaves in September.	**Migratory Status:** Summer resident in northern Indiana. Migrant in south.
Variation: Sexes alike. Juvenile paler gray with yellowish beak.	**Variation:** Sexes alike. Juvenile paler gray without red bill and forehead.	**Variation:** Juvenile lacks black on face and throat. Sexes are alike.

Presumed range in Indiana (for each species)

Habitat: Rivers, lakes, large ponds, marshes and wetlands.

Breeding: Breeds mostly to the north and to the west of Illinois, but does nest sporadically in northern Indiana. Nest is a platform built amid emergent vegetation. About 6 eggs are laid.

Natural History: During migration and in winter American Coots gather in large flocks on open water and behave more like ducks than rails. During the breeding season they act more like rails and live among cattails and reeds in freshwater marshes. But they are not as elusive as the rails and are usually easily observed even in summer. They are considered a game species, but rarely hunted as most waterfowl hunters regard them as a "trash" species. They sometimes go by the nickname "Mud Hen." Although the feet are not webbed as with ducks and geese, their long toes are equipped with lateral lobes which flare out when swimming and create an ample surface for pushing against the water. Thus they are good swimmers. They feed both on land (on grasses) and in the water (aquatic plants, algae, and aquatic invertebrates).

Habitat: Wetlands and lake shores with abundant vegetation.

Breeding: Nest is a platform of vegetation slightly above the water line and usually well concealed. A very rare nester in Indiana. Will lay as many as 10 eggs.

Natural History: Sometimes known as the Common Moorhen, but that name is properly reserved for a very similar bird that lives in Europe. Although these birds may be seen in suitable habitat throughout the state, they are rare in Indiana. Farther south in places like Louisiana and Florida they can be quite common. They feed largely on seeds of aquatic plants but also eat animal matter including most predominately snails and insects. Although similar to the American Coot in size and appearance, the Common Gallinule is rarely seen in the open and prefers to stay close to heavy cover. Additionally, they don't form large flocks as do American Coots. However, they are sometimes quite tame and approachable, especially within the heart of their range in Florida and the lower Coastal Plain. Regarded as a endangered species in Indiana.

Habitat: Primarily a marsh dweller. Favors heavily vegetated wetlands.

Breeding: Builds a nest platform of aquatic vegetation a few inches above water level. Nest is well hidden in dense upright plants. Breeds in northern Indiana. Lays 8 to 11 eggs.

Natural History: The Sora is one of the more observable of America's rails. Still, it is fairly secretive, especially during fall migration. They are usually observable on both breeding and wintering grounds, but catching a glimpse of this species is difficult. They are vocal birds however, and their whinnying call can be heard for a long distance. They feed on a variety of aquatic invertebrates but also eat seeds of aquatic plants, particularly wild rice. Soras have exceptionally long toes, an adaptation that allows for walking across floating vegetation. This is the most widespread rail species in America and its combined breeding, migratory and winter range includes the entire continent south of Alaska and the northernmost Canadian provinces. When disturbed it usually runs into deeper cover and flies reluctantly.

Class—**Aves** (birds)
Order—**Gruiformes** (rails & cranes)
Family—**Gruidae** (cranes)

Sandhill Crane *Grus canadensis*	**Whooping Crane** *Grus americana*

Size: 42 inches.

Abundance: Uncommon in Indiana, but eastern populations are increasing.

Variation: Juveniles have more rusty brown blotches and lack the red crown and white cheek patch of the adults. In the photo above the adult bird is on the left and the juvenile is on the right.

Migratory Status: Seasonal migrant. Frequently pauses during fall migration to rest and feed in portions of northern Indiana. After leaving these "staging areas" they may be seen as a migrant anywhere as they pass through the state.

Presumed range in Indiana

Size: 59 inches.

Abundance: Very Rare.

Variation: Juveniles have rusty blotches and rust-colored heads.

Migratory Status: A rare seasonal migrant. Often travels with Sandhill Cranes.

Presumed range in Indiana

Habitat: Open lands, farm fields, mudflats, marshes and shallow water areas. In migration uses harvested crop fields. Summer habitat is in the far north including wetlands throughout most of Canada as well as into the tundra regions of Canada and Alaska.

Habitat: In migration through Indiana these birds will use expansive open spaces including marshes or harvested agricultural fields.

Breeding: Typically lays 2 eggs on a platform nest built of vegetation. Historically nested in marshes in northwestern Indiana. Today birds that travel through Indiana are nesting in the far north. In addition, there are non-migratory breeding populations in parts of the southern United States.

Breeding: Breeds in shallow marshes. Western population breeds in Woods Buffalo National Park in Canada. Eastern birds nest in Wisconsin.

Natural History: Standing over 3 feet tall, the Sandhill Crane is one of the largest birds seen in America. Populations were seriously depleted by the beginning of the 20th century, but the species has recovered dramatically in the last few decades. The largest populations are seen west of the Mississippi River and number tens of thousands. Eastern populations have been slower to recover but are now reasonably healthy. Several states including nearby Kentucky now treat them as a game species and have regulated hunting seasons. Some conservationists question the wisdom of hunting seasons on this species. Their main concern is the accidental shooting of young Whooping Cranes that superficially resemble Sandhills. These birds also often form into large flocks that when roosting can be vulnerable to natural disasters. As much as 70 percent of the population gathers along a fifty-mile stretch of Platte River Valley in Nebraska in mid-March. A tornado path following the Platte River for a few miles at that time of year could devastate the population.

Natural History: It is possible that this rare species once nested in northern Indiana. At the very least they were likely a regular migrant through the state. The population that migrates through Indiana en route to Florida consists of less than 100 birds. An additional 500 or so birds make up the western population that winters in Texas. While still highly endangered the Whooping Crane is slowly recovering. Few species have enjoyed a more robust effort by humans to salvage them from extinction.

Class—**Aves** (birds)
Order—**Charadriiformes** (shorebirds)
Family—**Charadriidae** (plovers)

Piping Plover *Charadrius melodus*	**Killdeer** *Charadrius vociferus*	**Semipalmated Plover** *Charadrius semipalmatus*

Piping Plover — *Charadrius melodus*

Size: 42 inches.

Presumed range in Indiana

Abundance: Very rare in Indiana.

Migratory Status: Seasonal migrant.

Variation: Seasonal plumage variations. Winter birds are very pale, nearly white.

Habitat: Winter habitat is sandy beaches or pebble beaches. Uses mudflats during migration. Lakeshores or sandbars in rivers in summer.

Breeding: Nest is a scrape on sand or gravel, often near a clump of grass in an elevated place on the beach. 4 eggs. They once bred on the Lake Erie shoreline in Indiana.

Natural History: Summers in the north central Great Plains region and along the northern Atlantic coast. Winters along the coast from the Carolinas to Mexico. This is one of the rarest bird species in Indiana today. The species is both state and federally endangered. Only a handful are seen along the Lake Michigan shoreline annually. Widespread coastal development and near complete utilization of beaches by man has made successful nesting most places very problematic for this species. In recent years conservation efforts which attempt to mitigate human interference may be the only hope for saving the species. Closing of beaches to human activity where nesting occurs along with erecting predator exclusion fences around nests are two conservation actions that are regularly taken.

Killdeer — *Charadrius vociferus*

Size: 10.5 inches.

Presumed range in Indiana

Abundance: Common.

Migratory Status: Year-round resident.

Variation: None. Sexes are alike and there is no seasonal or ontogenetic plumage variations.

Habitat: Open lands. Mudflats, agricultural fields, lake shores, sandbars, heavily grazed pastures and even gravel parking lots.

Breeding: Lays 4 eggs directly on the ground. Nest is often in gravelly or sandy situations in wide-open spaces. Young are very precocial and they will run about within hours of hatching.

Natural History: Although the Killdeer is found state-wide, they are much more common in areas where open habitats are more widespread. This is a species that has likely benefited significantly from human alterations of natural habitats. The creation of open spaces where there was once grassland or forest has resulted in a habitat boom for the Killdeer. They are found all over North America south of the Arctic Circle. They were once hunted for food and their populations suffered a serious decline in the days of "market hunting." They feed on the ground and earthworms are a major food source along with grasshoppers, beetles and snails. A few seeds are also consumed. Baby Killdeer are highly precocious and can walk immediately after hatching. Year round in southern Indiana, migrant in north.

Semipalmated Plover — *Charadrius semipalmatus*

Size: 7.25 inches.

Presumed range in Indiana

Abundance: Uncommon in Indiana.

Migratory Status: Spring/fall migrant.

Variation: See photos above. Both winter and summer plumages may be seen in Indiana.

Habitat: Winter habitat is along coastlines. Summer habitat is open tundra. Migrants favor mudflats, plowed fields and shorelines.

Breeding: Nests on the ground, usually near water. Nesting grounds are in northern Canada and Alaska. 4 eggs. Chicks are precocious and able to feed themselves immediately.

Natural History: Most Semi-palmated Plovers migrate along the coasts of North America, but a few travel overland and they are occasionally seen in Indiana. Most sightings will likely be along the Lake Michigan shoreline as they tend to favor shorelines and other open spaces. They may also be seen in plowed fields in agricultural regions. The food of the Semipalmated Plover is mostly invertebrate animals plucked from the mud. They hunt these "benthic" organisms along the edges of marshes, lakes, seashores, etc. Aquatic food items include insect larva (especially fly larva), polychaete worms, crustaceans and small bivalves. On dry land these plovers will eat spiders, flies, and beetles. Most foraging is done along water's edge or in very shallow water or on exposed mudflats.

Class—**Aves** (birds)
Order—**Charadriiformes** (shorebirds)
Family—**Charadriidae** (plovers)

Black-bellied Plover *Pluvialis squatarola*	**Golden Plover** *Pluvialis dominica*

Size: 11.5 inches.

Presumed range in Indiana

Abundance: Uncommon in Indiana.

Migratory Status: Mostly a spring migrant that will pass through in April and May. Fall migration is more protracted, from September through early November. Many will migrate along America's coastlines, but a number will move through the center of the continent and some will pass through Indiana.

Variation: Seasonal plumage variations (see above). Both plumages may be seen in Indiana, but most birds seen in the state will probably be spring migrants in breeding plumage.

Habitat: Beaches are the preferred winter habitat. Inland migrants will use shorelines, mudflats and plowed fields.

Breeding: Nest is a shallow cup scraped into the Arctic tundra and lined with lichens. 4 eggs are laid.

Natural History: Black-bellied Plovers occur in both the new and old worlds and in fact they are one of the most widespread shorebirds in the world. They occur throughout much of the old world as well as most of the western hemisphere. North American birds winter along both coastlines from just south of Canada to South America, including the Caribbean. Summers are spent within the Arctic Circle of Alaska and Canada. During migration they are seen mostly along America's coastlines and in the great plains region, but some will pass through Indiana. Unlike many shorebirds, the Black-bellied Plover exhibits nocturnal tendencies and will often feed at night. Food items are marine worms and small clams and mussels plucked from the mud at low tide. On the breeding grounds in the far north they will eat insects, small fresh water crustaceans and berries. Climate change may be a threat if tundra nesting habitat undergoes transformation.

Size: 10.5 inches.

Presumed range in Indiana

Abundance: Uncommon in Indiana.

Migratory Status: Spring and fall migrant. Spring migration peaks in late April and early May. Fall migration peaks in September and early October but most fall migrants move southward down the eastern seaboard or even out in the Atlantic. Thus Golden Plovers are more common in Indiana in spring than fall.

Variation: Sexes similar with seasonal plumage variations (see above). Both plumages may be seen in Indiana, but most birds seen in the state will be spring migrants.

Habitat: Beaches are the preferred winter habitat. Inland migrants will use shorelines, mudflats and plowed fields.

Breeding: Nest is a scrape on tundra soil. 4 eggs are laid and young are highly precocial, able to walk immediately.

Natural History: Like the similar Black-bellied Plover, the American Golden Plover is a long distance traveler. It nests in the Arctic and spends its winters in southeastern South America. Its epic migrations sometimes include extensive flights over vast expanses of open ocean. Many migrate through inland regions and they are known for their propensity to appear almost anywhere during migrations. Food items include some plant material (berries, seeds, foliage) as well as a wide variety of invertebrate prey. Like many shorebirds the American Golden Plover was hunted relentlessly during the days of "market hunting" throughout the 1800s. Hundreds of thousands to perhaps millions were killed annually. Today they are still legally hunted in some South American countries. Habitat loss remains an ever present threat and some scientists have expressed concern about potential threats on tundra breeding grounds due to climate change.

Class—**Aves** (birds)

Order—**Charadriiformes** (shorebirds)

Family—**Scolopacidae** (sandpipers)

Sanderling *Calidris alba*	**Pectoral Sandpiper** *Calidris melanotus*	**Dunlin** *Calidris alpina*

Size: 8 inches.

Presumed range in Indiana

Abundance: Uncommon in Indiana.

Migratory Status: Seasonal migrant. Most common in July and August.

Variation: Significant seasonal variation (see photos above).

Habitat: Shorelines. In winter lives on the beach. During migration frequents lake shores and river bars.

Breeding: Nests on arctic tundra on bare ground. Lays 4 eggs.

Natural History: Unlike most members of the sandpiper family, which are more likely to be found on mudflats, the Sanderling is commonly found on seashores. Except during migration or when breeding, these birds inhabit sandy beaches throughout the Americas. Any person who has been to the seashore has probably been amused by watching this species running back and forth in front of the waves. On beaches it feeds by running just in front of oncoming wave and chasing right behind receding wave, picking up tiny marine crustaceans, bivalves, and polychaetes. On the breeding ground it will eat both terrestrial and aquatic invertebrates and insects. Most Sanderlings migrate along the coastlines of America or through the great plains. Some will be seen in Indiana however, especially along the shores of Lake Michigan. Though it may be seen in May, it is most common in Indiana in late summer.

Size: 8.5 inches.

Presumed range in Indiana

Abundance: Fairly common.

Migratory Status: Spring/fall migrant. March through May and July to September.

Variation: Male breeding plumage is darker and more vivid.

Habitat: Migrants use wet meadows, flooded fields, marshes and lake or pond shorelines, as well as mudflats.

Breeding: Nests on the ground in the arctic coastal plain. 4 eggs.

Natural History: Breeding males of this species perform displays in which they erect the feathers of the breast, droop the wings, raise the tail feathers and emit soft "hooting" sounds. They are the only member of the sandpiper family that vocalizes in this manner. They also perform flight displays above the heads of grounded females. These birds are remarkable travelers that breed in the high arctic and winter in the "Pampas" region of southern South America. Some individuals will cross the Arctic Ocean to breed in Siberia, then migrate back to South America, a round-trip journey of over 18,000 miles each year! The food is mostly small mud dwelling invertebrates. In Indiana this species is most likely to be seen during migration in flooded crop fields in agricultural regions or river bottoms and lowlands where receding waters leave mudflats. Climate change may have impacts on arctic nesting habitat.

Size: 8.5 inches.

Presumed range in Indiana

Abundance: Uncommon in Indiana.

Migratory Status: Spring/fall migrant. Seen April/May and September/October.

Variation: Significant seasonal plumage changes (see above).

Habitat: During migration uses flooded agricultural fields, mudflats, and seasonally flooded lowland pastures.

Breeding: Another high arctic breeder. Lays 4 eggs on ground in open tundra.

Natural History: The Dunlin winters along both coasts of North America where it haunts estuaries and inter-tidal regions. In southern Louisiana and gulf coastal Texas it often uses rice fields in winter. Various clams, insects, worms and amphipods are picked from the mud or plucked from vegetation with its moderately long, probing bill. Like other shorebird species it is usually seen in flocks, sometimes numbering in the thousands or even tens of thousands. In the early 1800s market hunters killed these birds in enormous numbers. Using cannon-like shotguns known as "punt guns" that were loaded with bird shot, a single blast could kill scores of shorebirds in a closely packed flock. Today threats include pesticides and other contaminants and loss of wintering habitat. Climate change may produce changes in the Tundra nesting habitat the result of which could be a threat to successful nesting.

Class—**Aves** (birds)

Order—**Charadriiformes** (shorebirds)

Family—**Scolopacidae** (sandpipers)

The "Peep" Sandpipers
Genus—*Calidris* (5 species can occur in Indiana, the 3 most likely seen species pictured below)

Least Sandpiper *Calidris minutilla*	**Semipalmated Sandpiper** *Calidris pusilla*	**White-rumped Sandpiper** *Calidris fuscicolis*

In addition to the other members of the *Calidris* genus seen in this book, there are several other sandpiper species in this genus that can be seen in Indiana. Some of these are quite rare in the state and although technically a part of the state avifauna they may not be seen in some years and thus not pictured above. The three sandpipers shown above are regular visitors to the state during migration. All are remarkably similar in appearance and most lay people will not be able to distinguish between them in the field.

Size: Least Sandpiper 6 inches. Semipalmated Sandpiper 6.25 inches; White-rumped reaches 7.5 inches.

Abundance: The Least Sandpiper and the Semipalmated are the most commonly seen of the "Peep" Sandpipers in Indiana. White-rumped Sandpiper is rare. Two other "peep" sandpiper species, the Baird's Sandpiper, *Calidris bardii* (not shown) and the Western Sandpiper *Calidris mauri* (not shown) are very rare migrants in Indiana.

Migratory Status: All are seasonal migrants that may occur in both spring and fall. Some species are more commonly observed in the fall, others in the spring.

Variation: All five of these "peep" species exhibit seasonal plumage changes. All are comparably paler in winter than in summer.

Presumed combined range of the "peep" Sandpipers in Indiana

Habitat: The name "Mudpiper" would be a more appropriate name for these birds as they favor mudflats and flooded fields over sandy beaches. All can be seen along the coastlines but many migrate through the interior of North America.

Breeding: All "peep" sandpipers nest on the ground in the barren arctic tundra. 4 eggs is typical.

Natural History: These sandpipers are all similar in their natural history and are confusingly alike in appearance. While serious birders and professional ornithologists take pride in being able to correctly identify any species, most casual observers will have to be satisfied with calling all of these homogeneous birds simply "peeps." Food habits and feeding methods are also similar in these sandpipers, with mud dwelling invertebrates making up the bulk of the diet in winter and during migration. Aquatic insect larva and some terrestrial insects are eaten on the breeding grounds. The hordes of mosquitoes for which the arctic tundra is famous in summer make up a high protein smorgasbord for both the adult birds and the newly hatched young. The abundance of this high protein food may be one reason why these small birds travel such huge distances in order to nest and rear their young in the Arctic. All the sandpipers are known for their epic migrations. Some species travel non-stop for a thousand miles or more over open ocean. Flights lasting as long as five days have been reported. Quite a feat of endurance for birds that can weigh as little as 0.75 to 1.5 ounces! Recent population declines have been reported for the Least Sandpiper and the Semipalmated Sandpiper. By contrast, the Western Sandpiper (despite being rare in Indiana) is one of the most abundant shorebirds in America with a total population estimate of 3.5 million birds. It and the Baird's Sandpiper are rare in Indiana due to the fact that their migratory routes are mostly west of the Mississippi River. Likewise is the case with the uncommon White-rumped Sandpiper. Both the Least Sandpiper and the Semipalmated Sandpiper migrate widely across the continent and both can be seen in Indiana every year during migratory seasons.

Class—**Aves** (birds)
Order—**Charadriiformes** (shorebirds)
Family—**Scolopacidae** (sandpipers)

Stilt Sandpiper *Calidris himantopus*	**Upland Sandpiper** *Bartramia longicauda*	**Wilson's Phalarope** *Phalaropus tricolor*

Stilt Sandpiper

Size: 8.5 inches.

Presumed range in Indiana

Abundance: Uncommon in Indiana.

Migratory Status: Migrant. Seen mostly in fall.

Variation: Winter birds are much paler, more grayish. Shown above is summer bird.

Habitat: Ponds, marshes, flooded fields, and lake shorelines. Uses salt marsh and brackish marshes in winter.

Breeding: Nests in lowland areas near the Arctic Ocean. Lays 4 eggs. Both parents incubate eggs for three weeks.

Natural History: The Stilt Sandpiper gets its name from its long legs. The long legs are an adaptation that allow it to feed in deeper water than most other *Calidris* sandpipers. Its body shape and habit of feeding in deeper water rather than on mudflats is unusual for its genus and mimics the yellowlegs sandpipers (genus *Tringa*, next page). The migratory routes for this sandpiper are mainly west of the Mississippi River, but some individuals will pass through Indiana. They nest along the northernmost coast of North America and will spend the winter in the interior of the South American continent. As with many other sandpiper species, the Stilt Sandpiper shows a remarkable fidelity to the nest site. After migrating thousands of miles from South America they often return to the same exact spot on the arctic coastline to lay their eggs. Young are highly precocious.

Upland Sandpiper

Size: 12 inches.

Presumed range in Indiana

Abundance: Rare in Indiana.

Migratory Status: Rare summer resident in northern Indiana.

Variation: No significant variation. Breeding plumages are richer than fall or immature.

Habitat: An obligate of grasslands and prairies. Migrants will use pastures, fields, and airports statewide.

Breeding: Nest is a shallow scrape on the ground lined with grass. 4 eggs. Both sexes incubate for about 4 weeks.

Natural History: The bulk of the Upland Sandpiper's summer range is in the northern Great Plains. A few summer very sparsely east of the Mississippi River into the Midwestern US. Unlike most other members of the sandpiper family, the Upland Sandpiper avoids coastal areas in favor of prairies and grasslands well into the interior of the continent. Historically, these birds were much more numerous. Market hunting in the late 19th century saw countless numbers of dead Upland Sandpipers shipped by rail from their nesting grounds on the northern plains to markets in the east. At the same time they were being hunted mercilessly on their winter habitats in the Pampas of South America. Even more devastating to their populations was the conversion of the native American prairie to cropland. Amazingly, the species survives. But they are now endangered in Indiana.

Wilson's Phalarope

Size: 9.5 inches

Presumed range in Indiana

Abundance: Rare in Indiana.

Migratory Status: Rare summer resident and migrant.

Variation: Sexual, seasonal, and ontogenetic variations. Winter birds are gray.

Habitat: Uses marshes on breeding range, shallow water habitats along lake shores, ponds, etc. in migration.

Breeding: Breeds on inland marshes and wetlands in the west-central US and Canada. Always lays 4 eggs.

Natural History: Phalaropes are known for the unique role reversal of the sexes. In these birds the female is the most vividly colored while the male has drab plumage. Even more unusual, it is the male that incubates the eggs in the nest. These birds are salt lake specialists and during migration they congregate in large flocks around alkaline and highly saline lakes of the interior of North America. The winter habitat is similar saline lakes in the Andes Mountains of South America. Birds seen in Indiana are mostly migrants or rare wanderers, but there is evidence of nesting occurring in the northern parts of the state and they were perhaps historically much more common before the draining of the state's marsh lands. These birds are most likely to be seen in the northernmost portion of the state, and they apparently were once regular nesting birds in extreme northwest IN.

Class—**Aves** (birds)

Order—**Charadriiformes** (shorebirds)

Family—**Scolopacidae** (sandpipers)

Short-billed Dowitcher *Limnodromus griseus*	**Spotted Sandpiper** *Actitis macularia*	**Willet** *Tringa semipalmata*

Size: 11 inches.	**Size:** 7.5 inches.	**Size:** 15 inches.
Abundance: Uncommon, but occasionally appears in large flocks.	**Abundance:** Fairly common in suitable habitats.	**Abundance:** Rare in Indiana. Mostly on Lake Michigan shore.
Migratory Status: Spring/fall migrant. Fall migration starts in July.	**Migratory Status:** Summer resident and seasonal migrant.	**Migratory Status:** Seasonal. April/May and July/August.
Variation: Breeding birds are rich brown. Winter birds uniformly gray with whitish belly (see photos above). Sexes are alike.	**Variation:** Winter birds lack the spots on the breast and are grayer on the back. Most birds seen in Indiana will be in summer plumage.	**Variation:** No sexual dimorphism but does exhibit seasonal plumage variations. Winter plumage is grayer, lacks brown splotches.
Habitat: In inland migrations dowitchers use mudflats and lake shores. Many migrate along the coasts.	**Habitat:** In migration uses edges of ponds, lake shores, stream courses and river bars.	**Habitat:** In migration uses pond banks, mudflats, lake shores, riverbanks, and flooded fields.
Breeding: Breeds in bog and muskeg habitats of northern Canada and Alaska. Lays 4 eggs.	**Breeding:** Nests on the ground in grassy situations. Lays 2 to 4 eggs. Widespread nester in Indiana.	**Breeding:** Lays 4 eggs in nest on the ground. Does not nest in Indiana. Most nesting is on the northern plains.

Presumed range in Indiana

Natural History: Presumably the Short-billed Dowitcher may be seen anywhere in the state in suitable habitat during migratory periods. It is probably more likely to be seen in the northern portions of the state however. This species shows a preference for salt water habitats and is a common migrant along the Atlantic and Gulf Coasts. Migrants headed for the far north will also travel inland across much of the eastern half of the country, including Indiana. The long bill is used to probe the mud for invertebrates and when feeding these birds will repeatedly stab their bills into the mud in a rapid "sewing machine" motion. The nearly identical **Long-billed Dowitcher** *(Limnodromus scolopaceus)* may also be seen in Indiana on rare occasions during migration. The differences between the two species are slight and differentiation is difficult.

Natural History: Unlike most sandpipers that exhibit strong flocking tendencies, the Spotted Sandpiper is always seen singly or in very small groups. This is one of the most widespread sandpipers in America and one of the few that nests in the lower forty-eight. The distinctly spotted breast along with a habit of constantly bobbing up and down makes the Spotted Sandpiper one of the most recognizable members of the Scolapacidae family. Feeds on a wide variety of aquatic and terrestrial invertebrates, especially dipteran (fly) larva. Also eats significant quantities of mayflies, crickets, grasshoppers, caterpillars, beetles, and mollusks, crustaceans and worms. In Indiana this species is fairly common in summer on lake shores and along the major rivers of the state. It can also be seen on mudflats during migration.

Natural History: The Willet is a true "shorebird" that is quite familiar to those who frequent America's seashores. Both coasts of America are home to Willets during the winter, and some will nest in coastal marshes. Others fly into the interior of North America and nest as far north as the central Canadian prairie. It is these migrants that can sometimes be seen in Indiana. Crustaceans, mollusks, insects, small fish and polycheate worms are listed as food items. Feeds both day and night. In the 1800s they were hunted for food and for their eggs which were also eaten, resulting in a significant decrease in populations. Today these are fairly common shorebirds whose population appears stable at an estimate of about a quarter of a million birds. In Indiana the most likely place to see this rare migrant is along lake shorelines.

Class—**Aves** (birds)		
Order—**Charadriiformes** (shorebirds)		
Family—**Scolopacidae** (sandpipers)		

Greater Yellowlegs *Tringa melanoleuca*	**Lesser Yellowlegs** *Tringa flavipes*	**Solitary Sandpiper** *Tringa solitaria*

Size: 14 inches. | **Size:** 10.5 inches. | **Size:** 8.5 inches.

Presumed range in Indiana

Abundance: Greater Yellowlegs is usually the less common of the two, but both species are fairly common during migration.

Migratory Status: Both species are transient spring and fall migrants. Peak spring migration is in late April and early May. A few birds may linger into late May. Fall peak for the Greater Yellowlegs is August/September. Lesser Yellowlegs begins fall migration as early as July.

Variation: Speckled appearance is less prominent on winter adults and juveniles of both species.

Habitat: Both species are seen in a wide variety of wetland habitats during migration, including mudflats, flooded agricultural field and marshes.

Breeding: Greater breeds in northern bogs, Lesser in drier, more upland habitats. Both species nest on the ground and 3 to 4 eggs is the typical clutch size for both.

Natural History: These two related species are frequently seen together. When seen together they are easily recognized by size. When not found in mixed flocks they are best identified by the shape of the bill. Greater's bill is longer and ever so slightly upturned at the tip. The Greater Yellowlegs is the least social of the two, and although it is seen in small flocks it can also be seen singly. Both species were once heavily hunted and during the days of market hunting both species experienced steep population declines. Hunting still occurs in some areas of their migratory range, especially in the Caribbean. Both spend the summer in the boreal regions of Canada and Alaska and winter from the Gulf Coast of the southeastern United States southward into South America. Food items for the Greater include both aquatic and terrestrial invertebrates as well as some small aquatic vertebrates like small frogs or fish. Lesser's food items are mainly invertebrates, both aquatic and terrestrial, but some small fish are also eaten. Both feed mostly by wading in shallows, but the Lesser is a more active feeder, wading rapidly and picking food from both the surface and the water column. It will also feed in this manner in terrestrial habitats such as grassy shorelines or meadow areas. Greater feeds both diurnally and at night, when it employs a sweeping motion of the bill back and forth through the water, apparently catching food by feel. The major threat to both species today is probably loss of habitat, both on wintering grounds in South America (loss of wetlands) and on summer range in North America, logging in boreal forests (Greater), and loss of wetlands in Alaska (lesser). Adult birds begin the return migration to more southerly regions several weeks ahead of the young of the year juveniles, some of which may pass through until early October. In Indiana these birds are generally more commonly observed in the northern portions of the state, but they may be seen statewide in suitable habitat.

Abundance: Fairly common.

Migratory Status: Seasonal migrant. April and May. July to October. Peak fall migration is August.

Variation: More white spots in winter.

Habitat: Pond margins, lake shores and along creeks and rivers.

Breeding: Nests in trees and uses old songbird nests. 3 to 5 eggs, usually 4.

Natural History: As implied by their name, the Solitary Sandpipers are nearly always seen alone during migration. In this respect they differ markedly from most other members of their family. They also differ in their nesting habits, as they are the only North American member of the Scolapacidae family that nests in trees. When feeding it wades in shallows and plucks its food from the surface or beneath the water. Rarely probes the mud with its bill. Food is mostly invertebrates, both aquatic and terrestrial. Insects make up the bulk of the terrestrial foods. They also take aquatic insects and their larva, small crustaceans, snails and some vertebrate prey such as small minnows or tadpoles. Due to their solitary habits and the fact that they breed in trees in remote boreal forests, little is known about their population status, but it appears to be stable. Although this species does not nest in Indiana, some individual birds may linger well into the breeding season.

Class—**Aves** (birds)

Order—**Charadriiformes** (shorebirds)

Family—**Scolopacidae** (sandpipers)

Woodcock *Scolapax minor*	**Wilson's Snipe** *Gallinago delicata*	**Ruddy Turnstone** *Arenaria interpres*

Woodcock
Scolapax minor

Size: 11 inches.

Abundance: Fairly common.

Migratory Status: Summer resident and seasonal migrant.

Variation: No plumage variations. Females are significantly larger.

Presumed range in Indiana

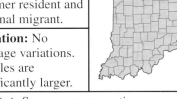

Habitat: Swamps, regenerative woodlands, thickets, and weedy fields in bottomlands or uplands with moist soils.

Breeding: Nest is on the ground and not concealed. Lays 4 eggs as early as late February.

Natural History: The Woodcock is unique among American sandpipers in that it is strictly an inland species. It is also the most common member of its family to breed widely throughout the state. Woodcock are known for their elaborate courtship flights that consist of an upward twisting corkscrew accompanied by a twittering call. The long beak is used to probe moist soils for invertebrates. Among its unique features are a flexible upper bill that aids in extracting the favorite food, earthworms, and eyes which are situated far back on the head, allowing for backward vision while feeding. One of the most remarkably cryptic of the sandpipers, Woodcocks are nearly impossible to detect when motionless on the forest floor. Woodcock are classified as a game bird and hunted in many states.

Wilson's Snipe
Gallinago delicata

Size: 10.5 inches.

Abundance: Fairly common.

Migratory Status: Winter in the south, summer in the north.

Variation: No significant sexual or seasonal plumage differences.

Presumed range in Indiana

Habitat: Mudflats, flooded grassy fields, marshes, river bars, water filled ditches, temporary pools and grassy pond banks.

Breeding: Nesting takes places mostly north of Indiana. But a few nest in the northern part of the state. Lays 4 eggs.

Natural History: As with other members of the sandpiper family, the beak of the Wilson's Snipe contains sensory pits near the tip which helps to locate invertebrate prey hidden in the mud. It also shares the Woodcock's rearward positioned eyes for watching behind and above while feeding. This is another highly camouflaged species that is nearly invisible when immobile. It is one of the most common and widespread members of the sandpiper family that often relies on its cryptic coloration when approached. Sitting quietly until nearly trod upon it will burst from the grass with a twisting, erratic flight while emitting a raspy call. Like the Woodcock the Wilson's Snipe is regarded as a game bird, but few people hunt them. Their populations have been negatively impacted by loss of wetland habitats. Also call "Common" Snipe.

Ruddy Turnstone
Arenaria interpres

Summer

Size: 9.5 inches.

Abundance: Uncommon.

Migratory Status: Seasonal migrant, late spring and early fall.

Variation: Seasonal plumage variations. Breeding plumage shown above.

Presumed range in Indiana

Habitat: Winters on sandy beaches along both coasts. May use lake shores, mudflats, or river banks during inland migrations.

Breeding: Breeds in the arctic tundra and coastlines from Siberia and Alaska across Canada to Greenland.

Natural History: Most Ruddy Turnstones travel up and down America's coastlines during migration, but a few migrate through inland regions of the continent and some of these will frequent the shores of Lake Michigan. This is one of the most northerly ranging birds in America, traveling to the northernmost extreme of the continent to breed each summer. Its name comes from its habit of using its beak to overturn pebbles and stones on beaches in search of small invertebrate prey. It also feeds on ocean carrion found on beaches. On the breeding grounds the primary food source is mosquitoes and other dipeteran insects. The unusual genus (*Arenaria*) contains only 2 species and their position in the phylogeny of the shorebirds is unclear. Migrants may stop for brief periods on bodies of water almost anywhere in state.

Class—**Aves** (birds)

Order—**Charadriiformes** (shorebirds)

Family—**Laridae** (gulls & terns)

Ringed-billed Gull *Larus delawarensis*	**Herring Gull** *Larus argentatus*	**Glaucus Gull** *Larus hyperboreus*

Size: 17.5 inches. **Abundance:** Very common. **Migratory Status:** Mostly a migrant, but may stay year-round on Lake Michigan. **Variation:** Juveniles are brownish gray, have greenish legs and pink bill.	**Size:** 25 inches. **Abundance:** Common. **Migratory Status:** Both a winter resident and a migrant. Can be seen statewide. **Variation:** Younger birds are dark brownish gray with dark eyes.	**Size:** 28 inches. **Abundance:** Rare in Indiana. **Migratory Status:** Winter migrant/resident along Lake Michigan shoreline, **Variation:** Young have pink bill with a black tip and brown tinged plumage.

Presumed range in Indiana

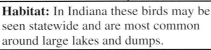

Habitat: Primarily in the vicinity of lakes and rivers, but also in rural crop fields and in urban areas.

Habitat: In Indiana these birds may be seen statewide and are most common around large lakes and dumps.

Habitat: In Indiana look for this gull along the Lake Michigan shoreline on breakwaters and beaches.

Breeding: Nest is usually on the ground on sandbars or rocky beaches. May nest on rooftops in urban areas. Lays 2 to 4 eggs.

Breeding: Nest is on the ground in a bowl-shaped scrape lined with vegetation. Also nest on rooftops in urban areas. 2 or 3 eggs are laid.

Breeding: Nest along the shores of the Arctic Ocean from Alaska in to Newfoundland. Usually lays 3 eggs. Nest may be on a cliff face or flat ground.

Natural History: The Ring-billed Gull is one of the most common and widespread gull species in America. Most population estimates put their number in the millions, and they may be increasing. This is the gull commonly seen around inland lakes in summer and along coastal beaches in winter. They are also seen in urban parking lots or hanging around fast food restaurants ready to swoop in and grab a dropped French fry. They can be common in garbage dumps and may be seen foraging with starlings and other urban birds around dumpsters. These are highly gregarious birds that travel in flocks and nest in colonies. Food is almost anything, from carrion to insects, fish, rodents, earthworms, and human refuse. Probably does not nest in Indiana, but does nest on some of the great lakes.

Natural History: Like the smaller Ring-billed Gull, the Herring Gull is an opportunistic feeder that will eat almost anything, including human garbage. This fact may account in part for their population rebound in recent decades. Like other gull species, they are gregarious and they often nest in large colonies. Only about 50 percent of the young gulls hatched each year reach adulthood, but the species seems to be thriving. Their numbers were drastically reduced during the 1800s but they have recovered completely and may be more numerous now than in historic times. The presence of man-made garbage dumps that serve as a smorgasbord for these birds may explain their recent population expansion. They are widespread in their distribution and are especially common on both of America's coastlines.

Natural History: This is a northern bird that nests and summers within the Arctic Circle. They move south in winter as far as the Great Lakes and the northernmost coasts of the US (New England, Washington and Oregon). Young birds tend to wander widely in winter and they have been recorded as far south as Florida and Gulf Coast. Like many gulls this is an omnivorous species. Food items include marine organisms of all varieties as well as small terrestrial vertebrates. Both a predator and a scavenger and a very opportunistic feeder that will include berries or seaweed in the diet. These are large gulls and they will aggressively steal from other, smaller gulls. They may be forced to move from the Great Lakes to coastal regions when the weather gets cold enough to freeze the lakes.

Class—**Aves** (birds)
Order—**Charadriiformes** (shorebirds)
Family—**Laridae** (gulls & terns)

Laughing Gull	Lesser & Greater Black-backed Gull	Bonapartes Gull
Leucophaeus atricilla	*Larus fuscus & Larus marinus*	*Chroicocephalus philadelphi*

Size: 17 inches.

Presumed range in Indiana

Abundance: Uncommon to rare in Indiana.

Migratory Status: Summer resident along Lake Michigan shorelines.

Variation: In winter the black head is replaced by white with dark smudges.

Size: 23 inches.

Presumed range in Indiana

Abundance: Rare but increasing.

Migratory Status: Winter migrants mostly seen around Lake Michigan.

Variation: Adult plumage not acquired for several years.

Size: 13.5 inches.

Presumed range in Indiana

Abundance: Uncommon in Indiana.

Migratory Status: Spring/fall migrant. Winter migrant along the Ohio River.

Variation: Summer birds have black hood similar to Laughing Gull.

Habitat: These are primarily coastal birds that sometimes wander inland. In Indiana the habitat is Lake Michigan.

Habitat: Typical gull habitats such as beaches, estuaries and coastlines. Congregates around docks and harbors.

Habitat: Frequents large rivers and larger lakes when in Indiana. Summer habitat is wetlands in boreal forests.

Breeding: Nests in colonies along the Atlantic and Gulf Coasts. Nests are built on the ground in salt marshes or on islands. 3 eggs is typical.

Breeding: Lesser is not known to breed in the US at this time. Greater breeds along the northeastern coastline. 3 to 4 eggs are laid. Both parents feed young.

Breeding: The only gull that nests in trees, using conifers bordering remote lakes in Canada and Alaska. Typically lays 3 eggs.

Natural History: Laughing Gulls are primarily birds of the coasts. Although they are commonly seen in a variety of habitats as much as 60 miles inland, they are quite rare in the interior of the continent. They are quite common and familiar along the Atlantic and Gulf coasts. Following breeding, some birds may follow major river systems well into the continent and a few make it into the interior of the country. Likewise some will migrate northward along the Atlantic Coast and some will summer on the Great Lakes. Like many gulls they exhibit seasonal plumage changes as well as age related (ontogenetic) plumage changes. For instance, it takes three years for the Laughing Gull to obtain the characteristic black hood worn in summer plumage. They are known to live to at least 19 years.

Natural History: Both Black-backed Gulls are mainly a coastal species but they will wander widely throughout the eastern half of the US in winter. In Indiana they are most likely to be seen in winter on Lake Michigan. They are more common in the US on the east coast and the Lesser's range includes Eurasia. In a sharp contrast to many bird species in Indiana, the North American population of Black-backed Gulls has been increasing for several decades. In the case of the Lesser Black-backed they began to expand their range out of Europe about a century ago. The first record for this species in Indiana was in 1962. Today they are a rare but regular winter migrant throughout the Great Lakes region. The first Greater Black-backed sighted in Indiana was in 1925. They have been regular since 1974.

Natural History: Many people tend to lump all gull species together and refer to them all as "seagulls." Most species however, including the Bonaparte's Gull, are often inland birds during the breeding season. Like other gulls, many Bonaparte's Gulls will spend the winter along America's coastlines and sometimes far out to sea. Small to moderately large flocks can be seen on inland rivers and lakes throughout Indiana during migration and through early winter. One of America's smallest gulls, they feed mostly on small fish such as shad and shiners, but like other gulls they are highly opportunistic feeders and will eat a wide variety of insects and other invertebrates. Unlike other gull species however, they are not typically seen around towns or dumps. Gathers in large flocks in winter.

Class—**Aves** (birds)

Order—**Charadriiformes** (shorebirds)

Family—**Laridae** (gulls & terns)

Least Tern *Sturnella antillarum*	**Caspian Tern** *Hydroprogne caspia*	**Black Tern** *Chlidonias niger*

Size: 9 inches.

Abundance:
Very rare in Indiana.

Migratory Status:
Mainly a migrant but a few are summer residents in parts of southwest Indiana.

Habitat: Inland birds use river sandbars, lake shores and especially islands.

Presumed range in Indiana

Variation: Juvenile birds are "dusted" with smoky gray on the back and have a black bill. Adults are uniformly pale gray above and have yellow bills.

Breeding: Inland birds nest on sandbars and islands in large rivers. Also uses man-made island habitats in Indiana.

Natural History: During the late 1800s the use of feather plumes to adorn women's hats had evolved to the point where a bird's entire preserved skin (with feathers intact) were often used for decoration. This fashion was popular in both America and Europe. Among the victims of this macabre practice was the Least Tern. Inland populations of the Least Tern also suffered loss of breeding habitat as rivers were dredged and sandbars destroyed to make way for riverboats and barge traffic. The nation's smallest tern was until recently highly endangered. Herculean efforts by conservation organizations (including the Indiana Department of Natural Resources) have resulted in a recent uptick in Least Tern populations.

Size: 21 inches.

Abundance:
Rare in Indiana.

Migratory Status:
Migrant. April/May and again in August/ September. Rarest in summer.

Habitat: Mainly coastal in winter, uses rivers, large lakes and marshes in migration.

Presumed range in Indiana

Variation: In winter birds the black cap becomes mottled with white. Juveniles are similar to winter adults. Sexes are alike.

Breeding: North American populations nest both on coasts and large bodies of water in the interior of the continent. Does not nest in Indiana. 1 to 3 eggs.

Natural History: The world's largest tern and also the most widespread. Found all over the world, the Caspian Tern breeds on every continent except Antarctica. Despite its wide range it is not as common in North America as many other terns. Feeds almost entirely on fish. Feeds by hovering and diving. When diving often submerges completely. Food is mostly fish. This is the only large tern regularly seen inland. They are found along the southern coastlines as well and in winter stay along the coasts. They are also seen inland in winter throughout the Florida peninsula. Although they will nest in some of the great lakes farther to the north, nesting in Indiana is rare. These large terns are known to live up to 26 years.

Size: 9.75 inches.

Abundance:
Uncommon.

Migratory Status:
Seasonal migrant. Spring migration is April. Fall migration is August/September.

Habitat: Summer habitat is shallow marshes, mostly in the western US.

Presumed range in Indiana

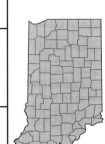

Variation: In winter and in juvenile birds the dramatic black color of the breast and belly is replaced by white. Transitional plumage shown above.

Breeding: Nest is built upon floating vegetation or muskrat platforms. Nests can be vulnerable to flooding. 2 or 3 eggs is typical with a maximum of 4.

Natural History: Winters along coastlines from Central America to northern South America. There is a European subspecies that winters in Africa. Like most terns these birds are highly social and usually seen in flocks. Unlike other terns however they feed heavily on insects, especially in summer. This is the only tern seen in the state that has a dark breast and belly. Although the number of Black Terns today is estimated to be in the hundreds of thousands, this figure is paltry compared to the size of the population that existed before modern agricultural practices destroyed much of their breeding habitat. Once a resident nesting species in the state, today they occur only as a migrant. They are an endangered species in the state.

Class—**Aves** (birds)

Order—**Charadriiformes** (shorebirds)		Order—**Siluiformes** (tropical sea birds)
Family—**Laridae** (gulls & terns)		Family—**Phalacrocoracidae** (cormorants)
Common Tern *Sterna hirundo*	**Forster's Tern** *Sterna forsteri*	**Double-crested Cormorant** *Phalacrocorax auritus*

Common Tern

Size: 13 inches.

Abundance: Uncommon.

Migratory Status: Seasonal migrant statewide. Seen in Indiana from April through August.

Presumed range in Indiana

Habitat: Migrating birds usually associate with major rivers and large lakes. Summers mostly in Canada. Winters along coastlines in South America.

Variation: 1st year juveniles and winter birds have white foreheads and all black bill. White on forehead reduced on 2nd year juvenile in summer colors.

Breeding: Nests mostly in Canada and along the Atlantic coastline. A few nest in Indiana in the vicinity of Lake Michigan. Lays 2 or 3 eggs.

Natural History: The Common Tern is well known to conservationists. They are symbolic of the fight to save many of America's bird species from wanton slaughter. From the early European settlement of North America to the late 1800s, unregulated over-hunting of America's wildlife nearly wiped out many species. Millions of herons, egrets, waterfowl, and shorebirds were killed for food and for the millinery trade. Populations have since recovered, but they are still well below historical numbers. The food of the Common Tern is mostly small fish that are caught by diving from above. Also eats other aquatic organisms including shrimp, insects, worms, squid, etc. Winters as far south as Argentina in South America.

Forster's Tern

Size: 14 inches.

Abundance: Rare in Indiana.

Migratory Status: Seasonal migrant. Spring and fall mostly but also in summer along Lake Michigan.

Presumed range in Indiana

Habitat: May be seen around any large body of water in migration. Marshes are used for nesting. Winter habitat is coastlines or lakes in the deep south.

Variation: In winter has white head with black around the eye. Juveniles have brownish bars on the back. Indiana birds usually look like above.

Breeding: Breeds mostly on inland marshes in the center of the continent. 1 to 4 eggs in nest of matted vegetation. A few may breed on Lake Michigan.

Natural History: In spite of being an uncommon bird in Indiana generally, the Forster's Tern can at times be abundant along the Lake Michigan shoreline. Food is mostly fish but will also eat insects and other aquatic invertebrates. When "fishing" they fly back and forth over water with the bill pointed downward and plunge headlong into the water. They are graceful fliers that sometimes hover when schools of fish are located. The loss of marsh habitat has had a negative impact on some populations. Nests built just above the waterline are subject to flooding. Most nesting occurs in the northern great plains region. Unlike many other terns this species winters along the southern coastlines of the US.

Double-crested Cormorant

Size: 33 inches.

Abundance: Fairly common.

Migratory Status: Season migrant through the state, but some may linger well into winter.

Presumed range in Indiana

Variation: Juveniles are much browner and have whitish throat and breast. Adults are quite dark and have bare orange patch on the face and throat.

Habitat: Lakes, rivers, estuaries, coastlines and swamplands. In Indiana they are most common on larger lakes and rivers.

Breeding: Nests in colonies mostly well to the north of Indiana but breeding range is expanding. Bulky nest of sticks and floating debris. Lays 2 to 4 eggs.

Natural History: Cormorants are rarely seen far from water. They are thoroughly aquatic birds that have webbed feet and frequently submerge and swim underwater in search of fish. Their exclusive diet of fish and their uncanny aquatic abilities have caused these birds to come into conflict with man. Occurring in large flocks, they will concentrate in areas where food is most readily available. Under natural conditions they catch a wide variety of fish species and thus do not impact significantly upon fisheries. However, around fish farms or hatcheries they can become quite a nuisance. In some regions they have become an ecological problem by crowding out other colonial nesting species such as herons and egrets.

Class—**Aves** (birds)

Order—**Pelecaniformes** (pelicans)	Order—**Gaviiformes** (loons)	
Family—**Pelecanidae**	Family—**Gaviidea**	

White Pelican
Pelecanus erythrorhynchos

Size: 62 inches.

Abundance: Uncommon.

Migratory Status: Spring/fall migrant.

Variation: Juvenile birds are duskier and have a dusky gray bill. Breeding adults develop a projection on the bill.

Presumed range in Indiana

Habitat: Restricted to larger lakes and rivers in Indiana. Elsewhere commonly uses large marshlands, natural and man-made lakes, large rivers and coastlines.

Breeding: Nests in colonies in protected areas such as islands on large lakes. Does not nest in Indiana. Lays 2 eggs.

Natural History: The bulk of the White Pelican's migratory path is to the west of Indiana. But wandering flocks may suddenly appear on almost any large body of water in the western half of the state. They have recovered significantly from lows seen during the days of DDT and seem to be expanding their range to the east. Unlike their cousin the Brown Pelican which feeds by plunging into the water, White Pelicans feed in a more placid manner. Flocks of feeding White Pelicans corral fish by swimming in a coordinated group and dipping the head beneath the surface in perfect unison. The appearance of a feeding flock is that of a perfectly choreographed ballet. Competition between baby White Pelicans in the nest is fierce, and the strongest nestling often kills its sibling.

Common Loon
Gavia immer

Size: 62 inches.

Abundance: Uncommon.

Migratory Status: Winter migrant.

Variation: Sexes are alike but exhibits significant seasonal plumage changes. See photos above.

Presumed range in Indiana

Habitat: Highly aquatic. In inland areas the Common Loon lives on lakes. They may also be seen along both of America's coasts in winter.

Breeding: Nests are built on small islands in northern lakes. Usually lays 2 eggs. Chicks often ride on adults back.

Natural History: On lakes and marshes in the far north the call of the Common Loon echoes through the wilderness. The sound is so distinctive and unique that it has inspired many poetic depictions. "Haunting," "ethereal," and "lonely" are words that are often used in conjunction with describing its yodeling cry that can carry for a great distance. They call both day and night on the breeding grounds in the northern half of the continent, but they are rarely heard calling on their winter range. Remarkable swimmers, they dive beneath the surface and propel themselves through the water with their powerful webbed feet. Fish caught in this manner are the main food item. In Indiana the Common Loon is a winter migrant and these migrant birds may be seen statewide on rivers and lakes.

Red-throated Loon
Gavia stellata

Size: 33 inches.

Abundance: Rare in Indiana.

Migratory Status: Winter migrant.

Variation: Exhibits seasonal plumage changes but birds seen in Indiana will be in winter plumage.

Presumed range in Indiana

Habitat: Thoroughly aquatic. In inland areas in summer or on migration they may be seen on lakes and rivers. In winter they use mostly coastlines.

Breeding: Breeds in small ponds in remote tundra. Nest is a large mound of aquatic vegetation. 2 eggs.

Natural History: These birds occur mostly along the coastlines in winter. Migrants are seen on the Great Lakes from fall through spring. Winter migrants can show up on almost any large body of water throughout the state, but they are very rare except on Lake Michigan. In winter plumage they are very similar to the Common Loon but are smaller and have white spots on the back. These are mostly northern birds that summer all the way to the Arctic Ocean. They are circumpolar in distribution and occur throughout Scandinavia. The legs of loons are situated very far back on the body which works well for propelling through water, but makes movement on land very difficult. This species appears to be in decline in North America. No explanation for this decline is known at this time.

Class—**Aves** (birds)

Order—**Podicipediformes** (grebes)

Family—**Podicipedidae**

Red-necked Grebe *Podiceps grisegena*	**Pied-billed Grebe** *Podilymbus podiceps*	**Horned Grebe** *Podiceps auritus*

Red-necked Grebe		Pied-billed Grebe		Horned Grebe	
Size: 18 inches.	Presumed range in Indiana	**Size:** 13 inches.	Presumed range in Indiana	**Size:** 14 inches.	Presumed range in Indiana
Abundance: Rare in Indiana.		**Abundance:** Fairly common.		**Abundance:** Uncommon.	
Migratory Status: Seasonal migrant and rare winter resident.		**Migratory Status:** Summer in northern IN, winter in south.		**Migratory Status:** Spring, fall and winter migrant.	
Variation: Winter plumage is gray and white (summer plumage pictured above).		**Variation:** Winter birds are grayer and lack the prominent dark ring on bill.		**Variation:** Seasonal plumage changes. Winter plumage is usually seen in Indiana.	

Habitat: Summers on shallow lakes, marshes, and bays of large lakes across Canada and Alaska. Winters in marine habitats. Bays, estuaries, and offshore.

Habitat: Completely aquatic, the Pied-billed Grebe uses everything from large lakes to small farm ponds. Also open water areas of swamps and marshes.

Habitat: In Indiana this species uses the larger lakes as well as large marshes with open water. They are not usually seen on small ponds.

Breeding: Nesting is on northern lakes. 4 to 5 eggs is typical (as many as 9).

Breeding: Nests on floating platform among emergent vegetation. 4 to 8 eggs.

Breeding: Nests on floating platform among emergent vegetation. 5 to 7 eggs.

Natural History: By mid-winter most of these grebes are along the coasts. But some will linger in the Great Lakes into winter. In Indiana these birds are mostly restricted to the immediate area of Lake Michigan. But in severe winters when the great lakes freeze over, large numbers may irrupt southward and at these times they may be seen on open water anywhere in the state. They are circumpolar in distribution in the northern hemisphere. Grebes are known for their elaborate courtship displays and "dances." As many as a dozen different postures may be displayed during one of these courtship dances. Pairs often engage in mutually responsive movements that gives the appearance of two highly choreographed dancers. Most feeding is in shallows but they are capable swimmers and divers and they may feed in deep water. Food items include fish, crustaceans and aquatic insects.

Natural History: A night-time migrator, this little grebe evades potential threats by submerging and re-surfacing away from the threat. They sometimes swim with just the head sticking out the water. They feed on a wide variety of small fish and other aquatic vertebrates as well as crustaceans and insects. This is the most widespread and common grebe in North America and they range from coast to coast. They are most common during summer in the "Prairie Pothole" habitats of the west-central US and Canada. In winter they move as far south as Central America. They can be seen all winter across the southern half of the US, but tend to concentrate along the gulf coast in winter. Most breed in more northerly regions of the continent, but there are 'widespread records of Pied-billed Grebes breeding in northern Indiana. These little grebes escape threats by diving and swimming.

Natural History: As is the case with other grebes (and loons), their adaptations for an aquatic lifestyle include the legs being positioned far back on the body. The legs can also be flared outward to a remarkable degree to facilitate underwater swimming maneuvers. As a result of this adaptation, these birds are very clumsy on land and walk with difficulty. Breeding on marshes and lakes in the northernmost portions of the continent, these birds are a transient migrant in Indiana. Breeding birds are handsomely marked with chestnut neck and flanks and golden brown head stripe that flares out to form "horns." The specimen shown above is in winter plumage and is typical of fall migrants. Food is small fish, crustaceans, insects, etc. Most of their breeding range is west and north of Indiana, but they may be seen anywhere in the eastern US during migration and in winter.

Class—**Aves** (birds)
Order—**Anseriformes** (waterfowl)
Family—**Anatidae** (ducks, geese & swans)

Mallard *Anas platyrhynchos*	Black Duck *Anas rubripes*	Northern Pintail *Anas acuta*

Size: 23 inches.

Abundance: Common.

Migratory Status: Year-round resident and seasonal migrant.

Variation: Pronounced sexual plumage variation (see photos above).

Presumed range in Indiana

Size: 23 inches.

Abundance: Uncommon.

Migratory Status: Seasonal migrant and winter resident.

Variation: Sexes are very similar, females have a darker bill than males.

Presumed range in Indiana

Size: To 25 inches.

Abundance: Uncommon in Indiana.

Migratory Status: Seasonal migrant and winter resident.

Variation: Profound sexual dimorphism (see photos above). Male is larger.

Presumed range in Indiana

Habitat: Found in aquatic situations everywhere, from deserts to tundra to southern swamplands, ponds, lakes, etc.

Habitat: Fond of estuaries and coastal marshes. Inland will use other aquatic habitats (lake, marshes, swamps, etc.).

Habitat: Open country. In Indiana uses large flooded bottomland fields and marshes along river valleys.

Breeding: Nests on the ground in close proximity to water. Lays up to 13 eggs and will re-nest if nest is destroyed.

Breeding: For breeding favors coastal marshes or beaver ponds and bogs in boreal forests. Lays up to 14 eggs.

Breeding: Breeds in marshes, potholes and tundra in the northern and western portions of the continent. 3 to 12 eggs.

Natural History: By far the most familiar duck in America. The Mallard has been widely domesticated but it is also the most common wild duck in the United States. Many parks and public lakes around the country have semi-wild populations that are non-migratory. Highly adaptable, this is the most successful duck species in America, perhaps in the world. It is the source of all breeds of domestic duck except the Muscovy and they are thus an important food source for humans. They are also a highly regarded game bird and they are hunted throughout North America. They range throughout the northern half of the globe and their range in the western hemisphere closely coincides with the North American continent. Between wild ducks and semi-tame populations in urban parks, breeding could possibly occur in every county in the state.

Natural History: The Black Duck is very similar to the Mallard in size, shape, and voice, and the two species are known to hybridize. In appearance and other traits however they are quite different. This is one of the few puddle ducks that does not range throughout the continent, being restricted to the eastern half of America. Like many of America's duck species, the Black Duck has been impacted negatively by human related changes to the landscape and environment in America. Drainage of wetlands, urbanization along northeastern coastlines, and deforestation have hit this species harder than most other ducks and the population has declined significantly in the last half-century. Interbreeding with the more adaptable Mallard may also be a threat to this uniquely American Duck. They may be seen throughout the state as a seasonal migrant or winter resident.

Natural History: Northern Pintail populations are in decline. Modern agricultural practices on the great plains of the US and Canada are the greatest threat. They are also highly susceptible to droughts in the prairie regions, which limit breeding habitat. Food is mostly plant material but some aquatic invertebrates are also eaten. On wintering grounds waste grain from farming operations has become an important food source. In recent decades the species has benefited from a number of conservation efforts by state and federal agencies as well as private organizations, most notably Ducks Unlimited, an organization funded by duck hunters. Conservation efforts that have recently benefited the species are reduced hunter harvest and changing agricultural practices in the prairie pothole region. Although they do migrate through Indiana, they are not common.

Class—**Aves** (birds)

Order—**Anseriformes** (waterfowl)

Family—**Anatidae** (ducks, geese & swans)

Gadwall *Mareca strepera*	**American Wigeon** *Mareca americana*	**Green-winged Teal** *Anas crecca*

Gadwall
Mareca strepera

Size: 20 inches.

Presumed range in Indiana

Abundance: Fairly common.

Migratory Status: Winter resident in southern IN, seasonal migrant elsewhere.

Variation: Significant sexual dimorphism (see photos above).

Habitat: Marshes and potholes of the great plains in summer. Uses all aquatic habitats in winter.

Breeding: Nests among thick vegetation near water, often on islands in marshes or lakes. Lays 7 to 12 eggs.

Natural History: Gadwalls breed and summer largely in the great plains region. In winter they are seen all across the southern half of America, with the greatest numbers wintering along the western gulf coast coastal plain. Some will winter in southern Indiana in mild winters. Populations of this duck can fluctuate significantly depending upon water levels in the prairies of Canada and the north-central US. Droughts and poor agricultural practices that eliminate habitat can cause populations to plummet. Conversely, good rainfall and good wildlife conservation practices by farmers have proven to be a real boon to this and many other duck species that depend on the marshes and potholes on the great plains for nesting habitat. Adult Gadwalls feed mostly on plant material. Ducklings rely heavily upon high protein invertebrates for growth and development.

American Wigeon
Mareca americana

Size: 19 inches.

Presumed range in Indiana

Abundance: Fairly common.

Migratory Status: Winter resident in southern IN, seasonal migrant elsewhere.

Variation: Significant sexual variation. See photos above.

Habitat: Winter range includes all types of aquatic habitats in the state (swamps, marshes, lakes, ponds, etc.).

Breeding: Nests near shallow fresh water wetlands and potholes mostly in the North American prairie. 3 to 12 eggs.

Natural History: The American Wigeon also goes by the name "Baldpate," a reference to the white crown of the male. This duck has a very similar old world counterpart, the Eurasian Wigeon, which ranges throughout much of Europe and Asia. American birds feed mostly on plant material, but females when breeding opt for a higher protein diet of invertebrates. One of the more northerly ranging members of the "puddle duck" group, some individuals will summer as far north as the Arctic coastal plain of Alaska. These ducks may be seen in Indiana from September through April, but peak numbers occur in late fall or early spring. Some merely pass through the state during north-south migrations, but some may reside throughout the winter in the southern half of the state. As with other puddle ducks, this species is susceptible to population declines during droughts.

Green-winged Teal
Anas crecca

Size: 14 inches.

Presumed range in Indiana

Abundance: Fairly common.

Migratory Status: Mostly a spring/fall migrant. Rare in winter in SW Indiana.

Variation: Significant sexual variation. See photos above.

Habitat: Migratory habitat includes all types of aquatic habitats in the state (swamps, marshes, lakes, ponds, etc.).

Breeding: Nest is in dense vegetation in wetland habitats of the far north. 6 to 9 eggs are laid as early as May.

Natural History: This is the smallest of America's "puddle ducks," and also one of the more common. They range throughout the northern hemisphere, with a distinct subspecies being found in Eurasia. They are fast and agile fliers and flocks of Green-winged Teal move back and forth across the southern half of the continent all winter in response to weather patterns. Populations of this duck appear stable and may even be increasing. About 90 percent of the population breeds in Canada and Alaska where they favor river deltas and boreal wetlands over the typical "pothole" habitats used by many puddle ducks. Their remote nesting habitats in the far north are largely undisturbed by man, which may account in part for this species' abundance. As with many species, the increasing daylight hours of spring triggers migration and breeding instincts.

Class—**Aves** (birds)
Order—**Anseriformes** (waterfowl)
Family—**Anatidae** (ducks, geese & swans)

Blue-winged Teal *Anas discors*	Shoveler *Spatula clypeata*	Wood Duck *Aix sponsa*

Size: 15.5 inches.	**Size:** 19 inches.	**Size:** 18.5 inches.
Presumed range in Indiana	Presumed range in Indiana	Presumed range in Indiana
Abundance: Fairly common.	**Abundance:** Fairly common.	**Abundance:** Common.
Migratory Status: Summer resident in northern third of Indiana. Migrant elsewhere.	**Migratory Status:** Winter resident in southern IN. Spring/ fall migrant statewide.	**Migratory Status:** Year-round resident. Becomes scarce in north during winter.
Variation: Significant sexual dimorphism (see photos above).	**Variation:** Significant sexual dimorphism (see photos above).	**Variation:** Significant sexual dimorphism (see photos above).
Habitat: Marshes, beaver ponds, bays and other shallow water habitats.	**Habitat:** Prefers shallow habitats. Swamps, marshes, flooded fields, bays.	**Habitat:** Beaver ponds, swamps, flooded woodlands and farm ponds.
Breeding: Nest is concealed in dense vegetation near water but above high water line. Lays 6–12 eggs.	**Breeding:** Breeds in northern and western United States (including Alaska) and in Canada. Averages 10 to 12 eggs.	**Breeding:** Nests in tree hollows and takes readily to artificial nest boxes. Lays about 8 to 12 eggs typically.

Natural History: The food of this species is mostly plant material including algae and aquatic greenery. Many seeds and grains are also eaten, especially in winter when they converge on rice fields and other flooded agricultural areas in America's lower coastal plain. Breeding females will consume large amounts of invertebrates during the breeding season. The Blue-wing Teal is not a cold hardy species and these ducks are early fall migrators. They are also one of the last to migrate back north in the spring. Many will winter as far south as South America, but substantial numbers can be seen along the lower coastal plain of North America all winter. Most breed and spend the summer on the central prairies of the US and Canada. But widespread breeding has been documented in Indiana. Young ducks are typically highly precocial, and babies will leave the nest within hours of hatching.

Natural History: The Shoveler's name is derived from the unique shape of its bill, which is a highly effective sieve for straining tiny organisms from water. They are often observed swimming along with the bill held under water or skimming the surface. Like several of America's duck species, the Shoveler is holarctic in distribution and breeds in Europe and Asia as well as North America. Eurasian birds winter southward to north Africa and the Pacific region. All ground nesting birds are vulnerable to mammalian predators and the Shoveler is no exception. Red Foxes and Mink are significant predators on the nesting females, while skunks are a major threat to the eggs. The nationwide population of these ducks seems to be on the increase, but waterfowl populations tend to be subject to significant annual variations. There are rare records of nesting in Indiana in the northwest corner of the state.

Natural History: Male Wood Ducks are one of the most brilliantly colored birds in America. The bulk of the Wood Duck population in America occurs in the forested eastern half of the country. Populations plummeted during the latter half of the 19th century as America's forests were felled and swamplands drained. Populations began to recover by the 1950s and today the species is thriving. Most state wildlife agencies in America began placing Wood Duck nest boxes in suitable habitat many decades ago. The ducks responded favorably and a very high percentage of babies hatch in the man-made nests annually. Wood Ducks are widely hunted and make up a significant number of ducks killed by hunters each fall. Although they are a small duck, they are considered by many as highly palatable. Along with the Mallard, the Wood Duck is the most common breeding duck in Indiana.

Class—**Aves** (birds)

Order—**Anseriformes** (waterfowl)

Family—**Anatidae** (ducks, geese & swans)

Lesser Scaup *Athya affinis*	**Ring-necked Duck** *Athya collaris*	**Redhead** *Athya americana*

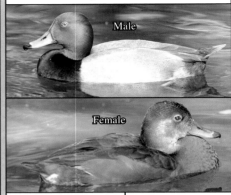

Size: 16.5 inches.	**Size:** 17 inches.	**Size:** 19 inches.
Abundance: Common.	**Abundance:** Uncommon.	**Abundance:** Fairly common.
Migratory Status: Winter resident and spring/fall migrant.	**Migratory Status:** Winter resident and spring/fall migrant.	**Migratory Status:** Winter resident and spring/fall migrant.
Variation: Sexually dimorphic. See photos above.	**Variation:** Sexually dimorphic. See photos above.	**Variation:** Sexually dimorphic. See photos above.

Presumed range in Indiana (for each species)

Habitat: Likes larger bodies of water and deeper water than many other ducks. Regularly uses large lakes and rivers in the state as well as flooded river bottoms.	**Habitat:** Open water habitats including shallow bays and flooded river bottoms. Also uses open marshes and large rivers and lakes, where it tends to use mostly shallow water areas.	**Habitat:** Primarily a marshland species that alternates between prairie potholes and gulf coastal marshes. In migration they will use a variety of wetland habitats, especially the bays of large lakes.
Breeding: 8 to 10 eggs is typical. Nests in west-central US, Canada and in Alaska.	**Breeding:** Nests in subarctic regions of Canada and the northern Rockies in the United States. Lays 6 to 14 eggs.	**Breeding:** Breeds almost entirely in the "prairie pothole" region. Females often lay their eggs in other duck's nests.

Natural History: These ducks are the most widespread and common of the "diving ducks." Diving ducks are capable of diving deeper and prefer deeper waters than the "puddle ducks." They are also more clumsy on land and need a running start on the water to get airborne. They thus favor larger lakes and rivers over small ponds and swamplands. These ducks often gather in large flocks on open water. These large flocks are called "rafts." Rafts of Lesser Scaup are a common sight on large lakes in winter. A slightly larger version of the Lesser Scaup, known as the **Greater Scaup** (*Athya marila*) can also be seen in Indiana in winter. Both species like open water. The Greater Scaup tends to favor coastal areas and salt or brackish marshes, but it does migrate through much of the eastern US.

Natural History: Closely related to and very similar in appearance to the scaups, the Ring-necked Duck should be called the Ring-billed duck. Although there is a brownish ring around the neck of the male, it is only visible when the bird is in the hand. The broad white ring near the tip of the bill and the narrow white ring at the base of the bill are both readily discernible on birds in the field. Unlike its relatives the scaups which will feed on crustaceans, insects, and other aquatic invertebrates, the diet of the Ring-necked Duck is mostly vegetarian. Unlike their similar relatives the Scaups, Ring-necked Ducks favor small lakes, ponds and swamps over large rivers and lakes. Like other North American ducks, their movements in winter are determined by weather. Freeze ups will instigate movement.

Natural History: An entirely North American species, the Redhead is mostly a vegetarian and feeds heavily on tubers and aquatic vegetation. Most Redhead's congregate in winter on the western gulf coast of Louisiana, Texas and northwest Mexico. In fact hundreds of thousands will concentrate in this region each winter. Here they feed mostly on the roots of shoal grass. They will also eat some animal matter, mostly aquatic invertebrates. Redheads are easily decoyed and during the days of the market hunting their populations suffered dramatic declines. Recovery in the last few decades has been significant and in a good year the population may reach a million birds. Most breeding takes place in the northern plains and northern rockies, but some will breed in the interior of Alaska.

Class—**Aves** (birds)		
Order—**Anseriformes** (waterfowl)		
Family—**Anatidae** (ducks, geese & swans)		

Canvasback *Athya valisineria*	**Bufflehead** *Bucephala albeola*	**Common Goldeneye** *Bucephala clangula*

Size: 21 inches.	Presumed range in Indiana	**Size:** 13.5 inches.	Presumed range in Indiana	**Size:** 18.5 inches.	Presumed range in Indiana
Abundance: Uncommon.		**Abundance:** Fairly common.		**Abundance:** Uncommon in IN.	
Migratory Status: Winter resident and spring/fall migrant.		**Migratory Status:** Winter resident and spring/fall migrant.		**Migratory Status:** Seen in Indiana mostly in winter.	
Variation: Pronounced sexual dimorphism. See photos above.		**Variation:** Pronouced sexual dimorphism. See photos above.		**Variation:** Pronounced sexual dimorphism. See photos above.	

Habitat: The primary breeding habitat for this species is known as "Aspen Parkland" habitat, which is found mostly in Canada. Winters mostly in marshes and bays along both coasts.

Habitat: Most winter in salt water habitats on the coast but some overwinter on inland lakes and rivers. In summer they use boreal forests and parklands in Canada.

Habitat: In winter this species uses large lakes and rivers. They are also fairly common in winter in coastal regions. In summer they are a bird of the boreal forests.

Breeding: The large nest is built from grasses and hidden in vegetation. Clutch size averages around 7 or 8.

Breeding: Cavity nester. Nest is often an old woodpecker hole. Clutch size ranges from a few to over a dozen eggs.

Breeding: Cavity nester that will use artificial nest boxes. Some may nest over a mile from water. 7 to 12 eggs.

Natural History: One of the most adept of the diving ducks, Canvasbacks have been known to dive to a depth of 30 feet. Feeds mostly on plant material including roots and rhizomes, but will also eat mud-dwelling invertebrates. This is strictly a North American species and is one of the least common duck species in America. They are vulnerable to droughts, habitat loss (mostly from agriculture) and water pollution that can impact the abundance of aquatic food plants. The Canvasback population is closely monitored by the US Fish and Wildlife Service and in years of low numbers hunting of this species may be banned. Even in years when hunting is allowed, the bag limits are typically very low (1 per day). They are regarded by some as the best table fare among the waterfowl.

Natural History: The smallest of America's diving ducks, the Bufflehead is one of the few duck species that will remain with the same mate year after year. Breeding pairs usually return to the same pond or marsh to breed each year as well. With the exception of some seeds, these ducks are mostly carnivorous, feeding on aquatic insects, crustaceans, and mollusks. Unlike the puddle ducks which often feed on the surface, the Bufflehead finds all its food by diving. Although they are often seen on deep water lakes, they feed in the shallows along the banks or in the backs of bays. Although rarely seen in large flocks, this is one of the few duck species that has actually increased in numbers in the last few decades. They may be seen on large lakes throughout Indiana during most winters.

Natural History: As with other diving ducks the Common Goldeneye is an excellent swimmer that feeds by diving beneath the surface. They propel through the water using only the feet, with the wings held tight against the body. They are mostly carnivorous but they do eat some plant material in the form of tubers and seeds. Aquatic invertebrates are the main food and include (in order of importance) crustaceans, insects, and mollusks. Fish constitute only a small portion of the diet. Male Common Goldeneyes engage in a complex courtship display to attract females or reinforce the pair bond. These ducks are holearctic in distribution, breeding in boreal forests throughout the northern hemisphere. Conservationists have discovered that this species will use artificial nest boxes.

Class—**Aves** (birds)
Order—**Anseriformes** (waterfowl)
Family—**Anatidae** (ducks, geese & swans)

Ruddy Duck *Oxyura jamaicensis*	**Long-tailed Duck** *Clangula hyemalis*	**White-winged Scoter** *Melanita fusca*

Size: 15 inches.

Abundance: Uncommon in Indiana.

Migratory Status: A transient migrant and winter resident.

Variation: Sexually dimorphic. See photos above.

Presumed range in Indiana

Habitat: Marshes, ponds, lakes and to a lesser extent rivers. This is a true "Prairie Pothole" species and nearly 90 percent of nesting occurs in the prairie pothole habitats in the northern plains.

Breeding: Nest is usually built in cattails or other aquatic vegetation. 7 or 8 eggs is average.

Natural History: Ruddy Ducks are primarily western birds that range generally from the Great Plains to the west coast. Winter range includes most of the eastern US and some are regularly seen in Indiana in winter. The larva of aquatic insects of the order Diptera (flies, mosquito, midges) are the primary food of these ducks. Although these are small ducks, their eggs are quite large and are in fact the largest eggs (relative to body size) of any North American duck. Populations of ducks of all species including the Ruddy Duck are today well below historical numbers. But this species seems to be expanding its breeding range eastward into the Great Lakes region. Breeding has been recorded in northeastern Illinois. About 80 percent of the population winters along the coasts.

Size: To 21 inches.

Abundance: Rare in Indiana.

Migratory Status: Winter migrant on Lake Michigan shorelines.

Variation: Males have very long tails and are more strikingly colored.

Presumed range in Indiana

Habitat: Summer habitat is arctic wetlands and seashores and deep water lakes. Winter habitat mostly coastal marine environments, but also large fresh water lakes, especially the Great Lakes.

Breeding: Nests in the arctic region on islands and peninsulas of fresh water lakes or in wetland tundra. 6 to 8 eggs.

Natural History: Also known as "Oldsquaw" these are primarily northern ducks that often wander far south in winter. Although they have been recorded in a variety of localities around the state, they are most likely to be seen around Lake Michigan. Rare individuals may go as far south as the Ohio River. The vast majority spend the winter along the northern Atlantic and north Pacific coasts. These little ducks are great divers, and can dive to depths over 150 feet to reach marine invertebrate foods consisting mostly of benthic crustaceans. Also eats insects and their larva and to a lesser extent fish and fish eggs. This is one of the most northerly breeding ducks in the world and they nest well into the arctic. They often roost in large "rafts" well offshore along coastlines or in large inland lakes.

Size: 21 inches.

Abundance: Rare in Indiana.

Migratory Status: Winter resident and spring/fall migrant.

Variation: Male has white eye spot. Juveniles are brownish.

Presumed range in Indiana

Habitat: They are most common in winter in coastal regions. Some may be seen on the great lakes in winter. In summer they are a bird of the boreal forests.

Breeding: Nests near shallow inland lakes in the far north, often well into the Arctic Circle. 7 to 12 eggs.

Natural History: There are a total of three Scoter species in North America and all three have been seen in Indiana during winter months. They are most likely to be seen on Lake Michigan. But they usually associate with coastal waters and they are often collectively referred to as "Sea Ducks." They will summer inland in the far north of northern Canada and Alaska. Waterfowl of all species are well known for wandering widely and sometimes appearing in areas far from their normal habitats. In addition to the White-winged Scoter shown above two other scoter ducks, the **Black Scoter** (*M. nigra*) and the **Surf Scoter** (*M. perspicillata*) can also be seen in Indiana. All are very dark, nearly black ducks and they are difficult to distinguish, especially when viewed from shore far out on the lake.

Class—**Aves** (birds)
Order—**Anseriformes** (waterfowl)
Family—**Anatidae** (ducks, geese & swans)

Common Merganser *Mergus merganser*	Red-breasted Merganser *Mergus serrator*	Hooded Merganser *Lophodytes cucullatus*

Common Merganser
Mergus merganser

Size: 25 inches.

Presumed range in Indiana

Abundance: Uncommon.

Migratory Status: Winter resident and spring/fall migrant.

Habitat: In winter uses large lakes and rivers. Small creeks are used in summer.

Variation: Exhibits pronounced sexual dimorphism in breeding plumage with males having dark greenish head and white breast. Winter plumages (usually seen in Indiana) are similar in both sexes.

Breeding: Nests in tree cavities or sometimes in root crevices on the ground. 10 or 12 eggs is average.

Natural History: Most Common Mergansers seen in Indiana will be in non-breeding plumage. A bird of northern climates and cold waters, the Common Merganser spends the summer on lakes in the boreal forests of Canada, Alaska and in the cold water streams of the Rocky Mountains. They are also found throughout Eurasia. Fish is the primary food for this species. Their bill is serrated for holding slippery prey and they are excellent divers and underwater swimmers. They are excellent fishermen and can dive to a depth of tens of yards and have been known to stay submerged up to two minutes. They use their bill to probe in mud or gravel for aquatic insects, mollusks, crustaceans and worms.

Red-breasted Merganser
Mergus serrator

Size: 23 inches.

Presumed range in Indiana

Abundance: Fairly common.

Migratory Status: A spring and fall migrant in Indiana.

Habitat: Uses larger lakes and rivers during migration. Boreal wetlands in summer.

Variation: Significant plumage variations between the sexes during the breeding season. Also exhibits seasonal variation with winter males and juveniles resembling females. Winter plumage is very similar to preceding species.

Breeding: Nests on the ground. Nest is well hidden beneath overhanging vegetation or in cavities. 5 to 24 eggs.

Natural History: During winter these birds show a preference for coastal regions where they use estuaries and salt water bays and salt/brackish water marshes. Like its larger relative the Common Merganser, the Red-breasted has a holarctic distribution and is found in Europe and Asia as well as North America. In summer this species ranges even farther north than its larger cousin, being found as far north as the Arctic Ocean and southern Greenland. Food is mostly small fish that are grasped with the serrated bill. Also eats aquatic invertebrates and amphibians. Feeds both in shallow water and in deep water up to at least 25 feet deep. Flocks may feed cooperatively, with all the birds diving together to corral schools of minnows.

Hooded Merganser
Lophodytes cucullatus

Size: 18 inches.

Presumed range in Indiana

Abundance: Fairly common.

Migratory Status: Year-round resident and seasonal migrant.

Habitat: In winter uses swamps, shallow bays of lakes and river floodplains.

Variation: Shows strong sexual dimorphism. Males are strikingly marked, having black heads with white "hood" and black wings and back. Females colors are much more subdued (see above).

Breeding: Cavity nester. Most nesting is to the north, but some nesting occurs in Indiana. Lays 12 eggs maximum.

Natural History: Unlike our other two merganser ducks, both of which are holarctic in distribution, the Hooded Merganser is strictly a North American duck. Another odd distributional trait is the fact that these birds are rare in the great plains region, where many North American duck species are most common. They have a more diverse diet than the larger mergansers, feeding less on fish and more on aquatic invertebrates that are located by means of well developed underwater vision capability. Winter waterfowl surveys indicate that over 50 percent of the population winters in the Mississippi flyway. Many will winter to the south of Indiana, but they can be seen year-round throughout the state. Will use artificial nest boxes.

Class—**Aves** (birds)
Order—**Anseriformes** (waterfowl)
Family—**Anatidae** (ducks, geese & swans)

Snow Goose *Chen caerulescens*	**Canada Goose** *Branta canadensis*	**Greater White-fronted Goose** *Anser albifrons*

Size: 30 inches.	**Size:** 36 to 45 inches.	**Size:** 28 inches.
Abundance: Uncommon.	**Abundance:** Very common.	**Abundance:** Rare in Indiana.
Migratory Status: Winter migrant.	**Migratory Status:** Resident and migrant.	**Migratory Status:** Winter migrant.
Variation: Two distinct color phases occur (see above). Juveniles are gray.	**Variation:** No significant variation. Sexes and juveniles are all alike.	**Variation:** Juveniles lack white on the face and black spots on belly. Sexes are alike.

Presumed range in Indiana

Habitat: During migration through the the eastern US these geese are mostly seen in very large agricultural crop fields. Summer habitat is Arctic Tundra

Habitat: Habitat includes all types of aquatic situations, from urban parks to remote and inaccessible marshes, swamps or beaver ponds.

Habitat: When migrating through Indiana they will use large agricultural fields for feeding and roost on open water or bays in large lakes.

Breeding: Nests only in the high Arctic Tundra of Canada and Alaska.

Breeding: Nests above the water line but near water. 4 to 8 eggs is typical.

Breeding: Breeds in the Arctic Coastal Plain. Average clutch size is 4 or 5.

Natural History: Snow Goose populations have exploded in the last few decades, probably as a result of having so much habitat and food available throughout migration routes and on wintering grounds. The grain fields of Midwestern and southern United States provides more than an adequate food source. Mid-continent populations are expanding their migration routes eastward from their historical range west of the Mississippi River. Today they can be found east of the Mississippi every winter and they are sometimes seen as far east as the Appalachian Plateau. There is also an east coast population that winters the along the Atlantic coast from New Jersey to the Carolinas. Snow Geese often occur in huge flocks numbering thousands of birds. The **Ross's Goose** (*C. rossii*) is a is a smaller version of the Snow Goose that may rarely be seen in the company of regular Snow Geese.

Natural History: This is the most recognized wild goose in America, due in large part to the fact that tame and semi-tame populations are found in parks and on rivers, ponds and lakes in both urban and rural regions. Resident Canada Geese are numerous, but their numbers are swelled dramatically during winter, as birds from farther north visit the state for either a brief stopover or a months long stay. The characteristic "V formation" of Canada Geese in flight is a familiar sight and their musical, honking call is to many a symbol of wild America. They are heavily hunted throughout America both for sport and for food. They are long-lived birds and have been known to survive over forty years. There are several races of Canada Goose and they vary in size. An identical dwarf species of goose called the **Cackling Goose** (*B. hutchinsii*) is the size of a Mallard. It sometimes occurs with flocks of Canada Geese.

Natural History: Although they may migrate throughout the much of state, White-fronted Geese are found in their greatest numbers west of the Mississippi River. While they are holarctic in distribution, they are not as common in North America as the Canada Goose or Snow Goose. Most of the North American populations of these geese use the Mississippi and Central Flyways, but a smaller population occurs in the Pacific Flyway. Oddly, they are rarely seen in the Atlantic Flyway. Mississippi Flyway birds will usually winter along the gulf coast from Louisiana and Texas to northeastern Mexico. During migration small flocks may be seen traveling with larger flocks of Canada or Snow Geese, but they tend to segregate themselves when resting or feeding. Like the Snow Goose, they appear to be expanding their migration routes eastward, and in the last few decades have become a more common visitor to Indiana.

Class—**Aves** (birds)

Order—**Anseriformes** (waterfowl)

Family—**Anatidae** (ducks, geese & swans)

Mute Swan *Cygnus olor*	**Tundra Swan** *Cygnus columbianus*	**Trumpeter Swan** *Cygnus buccinator*

Size: 60 inches.

Abundance: Fairly common.

Migratory Status: Year-round resident.

Habitat: Ponds, lakes, marshes and swamps in both urban and rural areas. Most often seen in urban parks.

Presumed range in Indiana

Variation: Some juveniles are brownish for the first year.

Breeding: Nest is platform of grasses up to 6 feet wide. Near water but above floodplain. About 6 eggs per clutch.

Natural History: The Mute Swan is a Eurasian species that is common in parks, zoos, farms, and private preserves all across America. Many have become feral or semi-feral and the species seems to be increasing in the wild. They may be seen almost anywhere in the state but are most common in northern Indiana. Their impact on native wildlife populations is largely negative, and IDNR regards them as a nuisance animal. Many state wildlife agencies have active removal programs. In some other states they are protected. These large waterfowl are primarily vegetarians, but they will eat small amounts of animal matter. When threatened Mute Swans arch the wings over the back and pull the long neck back between the wings in a display known as "busking." They are graceful and elegant in flight or on the water, but rather clumsy on land due to the fact that the legs are located so far back on the body.

Size: 52 inches.

Abundance: Rare in Indiana.

Migratory Status: Seasonal migrant.

Habitat: Large lakes and large, open agricultural fields are used in migration. In summer found on tundra.

Presumed range in Indiana
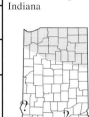

Variation: Juveniles are "dingy" white with orange bill.

Breeding: Breeds on the tundra of the Arctic Coastal Plain. 3 to 5 eggs are laid.

Natural History: Although the Tundra Swan is America's most common native swan species, these large swans are rare in Indiana. Most winter along the Atlantic coast from the Chesapeake Bay south to North Carolina and on the Pacific Coast from Washington to central California. In winter they use coastal estuaries and will fly inland to forage on waste grain in agricultural fields. Young swans stay with the parents throughout the first year until returning to their arctic breeding grounds the following spring. Prior to the passage of the first migratory bird protection legislation in 1918, these birds had become quite rare. Today their numbers have recovered substantially and a few states now allow a limited harvest during waterfowl season. Migratory flights over inland regions may include flocks numbering hundreds of swans, but smaller groups one or two dozen is more common. Most likely to be seen in northern IN.

Size: 60 inches.

Abundance: Very rare in Indiana.

Migratory Status: Year-round resident.

Habitat: Uses wetlands, lakes, etc. In western US found on rivers, lakes and fresh water marshes.

Presumed range in Indiana

Variation: None in adults. Juveniles are grayish.

Breeding: Nest is a hummock in wetland area. May use muskrat house or beaver lodge. 4 to 6 eggs.

Natural History: Trumpeter Swans were eradicated from the eastern United States by European settlers about 200 years ago. They managed to cling to existence in northern and western North America but were highly endangered until recent decades. Today the species has recovered significantly and populations in the western half of North America appear secure. In Indiana they are still quite rare but a few winter in the state and in recent years there has been very rare nesting reported. Although increasing in numbers it still faces an uncertain future. The main threats to the species today are probably loss of habitat, pollution, ingestion of lead sinkers used by fishermen and competition from Mute Swans. Food is mostly plant material, mainly aquatic plants but also some terrestrial plants. Adult birds often show a reddish wash on the head and neck as a result of foraging for tubers in mud that is rich in iron.

CHAPTER 5

THE TURTLES OF INDIANA

TABLE 3

— THE ORDERS AND FAMILIES OF INDIANA TURTLES —

Class—**Chelonia** (turtles)

Order—**Cryptodira** (straight necked turtles)

Family	**Chelydridae** (snapping turtles)
Family	**Kinosternidae** (mud & musk turtles)
Family	**Emydidae** (sliders & box turtles)
Family	**Trionychidae** (softshell turtles)

Class—**Chelonia** (turtles)

Order—**Cryptodira** (straightneck turtles)

Family—**Chelydridae** (snapping turtles)

Common Snapping Turtle	Alligator Snapping Turtle
Chelydra serpentina	*Macrochelys temminckii*

Size: Maximum length 20 inches. Record weight 86 pounds.

Variation: No variation occurs in Indiana specimens. Specimens found on the Florida peninsula differ slightly.

Abundance: Very common.

Habitat: Found in virtually every aquatic environment in the state. Ponds, lakes, rivers, creeks, swamps, and marshes.

Breeding: Eggs are deposited in underground chambers excavated by the female turtle. A typical clutch contains 25 to 50 eggs. Hatchlings are about the size of a quarter.

Presumed range in Indiana

Size: Maximum length 31 inches. Record weight 251 pounds.

Variation: No variation in Indiana. Males attain a larger size than females. All really large specimens are males.

Abundance: Extirpated in Indiana.

Habitat: Large rivers and their impoundments. Also oxbow lakes and small tributaries near their confluence with rivers.

Breeding: Adult females leave the water to lay up to 50 eggs in an underground chamber dug by the turtle. The leathery shelled eggs hatch in three or four months.

Presumed historical range in Indiana

Natural History: These common turtles can be found in any aquatic habitat in the state, including tiny farm ponds or tributaries narrow enough for a person to step across. They even can exist in waters that are heavily polluted with sewage and industrial effluents. They will feed on some plant material but are mainly carnivorous and will eat virtually anything they can swallow. Fish, frogs, tadpoles, small mammals, baby ducks, crayfish, and carrion are all listed as food items. Hatchlings turtles often must travel long distances to find a home in a pond or creek, and adults occasionally embark on long overland treks, presumably in search of a more productive habitat after depleting the food source in a small pond or creek. These long hikes overland usually occur in the spring. The ferociousness of a captured snapping turtle is legendary and their sharp, powerful jaws can inflict a serious wound. When cornered on land they will turn to face an enemy and extend the long neck in a lunging strike that is lightning fast and so energetic that it may cause the entire turtle to move forward several inches. By contrast when under water they almost never bite.

Natural History: Alligator Snapping Turtles are the most completely aquatic of any American fresh water turtle. In fact, they never leave the water except for egg laying excursions by the female. Unlike most aquatic turtles, they do not bask and rarely show more than the tip of the snout when coming up to breath. They spend most of their time "bottom walking" or lying in ambush in the muck or mud. They possess a specialized structure on the tongue that resembles a worm and can be wriggled to effectively lure fish into striking distance. They also eat other turtles, carrion, crayfish and in fact probably any type of animal matter that can be swallowed. Mussels are reportedly an important food item, the hard shell being no match for the powerful jaws of these huge turtles. The longevity of this turtle in the wild is unknown, but some specimens have been in captivity for over 70 years, suggesting a long life-span. These unique turtles have declined significantly throughout their range. The last sighting of a wild turtle in Indiana was in 1991. Although protected as an endangered species, it is probably now an Extirpated Species, meaning that it no longer occurs in the state.

Class—**Chelonia** (turtles)
Order—**Cryptodira** (straightneck turtles)
Family—**Kinosternidae** (mud & musk turtles)

Common Musk Turtle *Sternotherus oderatus*	**Common Mud Turtle** *Kinosternum subrubrum*

Size: Mature adults are about 4 inches in length.

Abundance: Fairly common.

Variation: In some regions females are larger than males. Young are more vividly marked and have knobs on the shell.

Habitat: Primarily a stream dweller, but can be found in a variety of aquatic habitats including swamps, oxbows, lakes, etc. They prefer still or slow moving waters. They reach their highest densities in waters with abundant aquatic vegetation.

Presumed range in Indiana

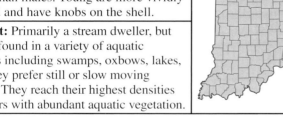

Size: Adults range from 4 to 4.75 inches in length.

Abundance: Rare in Indiana.

Variation: There are 3 subspecies. Indiana specimens are the subspecies *K. s. subrubrum*, (Southeastern Mud Turtle).

Habitat: Found in all aquatic habitats within its range, but prefers shallow water areas with abundant aquatic vegetation. They are turtles of the lower elevations and are most common along river floodplains.

Presumed range in Indiana

Breeding: Female lays 2 to 5 eggs under leaf litter or sometimes merely on top of the ground. Eggs hatch into tiny turtles that are barely an inch in length.

Breeding: Reaches breeding age at about 5 to 7 years old. Breeds in the spring. Females dig a hole and deposit an average of 2 to 4 eggs, sometimes as many as 8.

Natural History: Nocturnal and crepuscular and completely aquatic in habits. Unlike most aquatic turtles in America, the Musk Turtle rarely basks, but when it does it may climb several feet up into branches that overhang the water. When disturbed while basking they will launch themselves clumsily into the safety of the water. Since they seldom leave the water, the carapace is often covered with a thick growth of algae. Their name comes from the presence of musk-producing glands that emit an unpleasant odor when the turtles are handled. This musk also accounts for their other common name "Stinkpot." The Common Musk Turtle is widespread throughout the eastern US, being found from the gulf coast north to the great lakes, but they are absent from most of the higher elevations of the Appalachian Plateau. Although originally ranging statewide, in Indiana they have become rare and possibly extirpated in regions of intensive agriculture. They are an omnivorous species that feeds on a variety of aquatic plant and animal matter. Like many turtle species, the Eastern Musk Turtle is a long-lived species and one captive zoo specimen lived for 55 years.

Natural History: Although this is a very aquatic turtle, they sometimes embark on overland treks, presumably to find new habitats or seek a mate. These aquatic turtles have a double hinged plastron, a characteristic that is rare in North American turtles and shared with the Box Turtles (genus *Terrepene*). Their diet is omnivorous. A variety of aquatic plants are eaten and animal foods include crustaceans, aquatic insects, mollusks, amphibians and carrion. Locates food by "bottom walking" when in water, but may also feed on land near the water's edge. They can remain under water for up to twenty minutes. These small turtles have been known to live up to forty years and perhaps can survive even longer. This species is similar to and often confused with the preceding species (Common Musk Turtle). If the specimen is in hand a positive ID can be made by examining the plastron (bottom shell) of the turtle. In the Mud Turtle there are two "hinges" in the plastron allowing for some movement of the plastron in both the front and the back. In the Musk Turtles only the front of the plastron is hinged. This is a state endangered species in Indiana.

Class—**Chelonia** (turtles)		
Order—**Cryptodira** (straightneck turtles)		
Family—**Emydidae** (water & box turtles)		
Red-eared Slider *Trachemys scripta*	**Spotted Turtle** *Clemmys guttata*	**Painted Turtle** *Chrysemys picta*

Old male

Red-eared Slider

Size: 6 to 8 inches.

Abundance: Very common.

Variation: Males are smaller than females and have longer claws on the front feet. Hatchlings have a yellowish carapace boldly marked with green and black lines or circular patterns.

Presumed range in Indiana

Habitat: Most common in large bodies of water but can be found in any aquatic habitat in the state except for very small streams.

Breeding: Females leave the safety of the water and crawl hundreds of yards to upland areas to deposit their eggs in an underground nest chamber dug with the hind legs. Large females may lay 20 eggs. Younger females lay fewer.

Natural History: Highly aquatic but sometimes seen far from water. Eats a variety of water plants as well as mollusks, minnows, dead fish, aquatic insects, crustaceans, etc. Young are more carnivorous while mature turtles will consume more plants. Old specimens tend to darken with age and very old specimens can be nearly all black (see inset). These are hardy turtles that will emerge from the mud to bask on logs on warm, sunny days throughout the winter. There are 3 subspecies of slider turtles in America, one of which, the **Red-eared Slider** (subspecies *elegans*) is found in Indiana. They have been widely introduced into many regions outside their natural range.

Spotted Turtle

Size: To 4.5 inches

Abundance: Very rare in Indiana.

Variation: Yellow spots are most vivid on young specimens and tend to fade with age. Very old Spotted Turtles may be nearly solid black. Females average slightly larger than males.

Presumed range in Indiana

Habitat: Prefers sluggish waters. Inhabits lakes, marshes, swamps and slow moving rivers. Sometimes found in wet meadows or wet woods.

Breeding: Mating takes place in early spring through early summer with eggs being laid from May to July. Female digs a flask-shaped hole and deposits from 1 to 8 eggs. Two clutches per year is not uncommon.

Natural History: These handsome little turtles range throughout the Atlantic slope of the eastern United States from southern Maine to northern Florida. A disjunct population is found throughout the Great Lakes region, and it is to this population that the Indiana Spotted Turtles belong. The Great Lakes population is in decline and this species is regarded as endangered in Indiana. The Spotted Turtle is both an omnivore and a scavenger. Aquatic grasses and algae make up the vegetarian diet with insects, crustaceans, snails, amphibian larva, and fish listed as other food items. Opportunistic feeding on carrion is also reported. They are shy and docile and rarely attempt to bite when captured.

Painted Turtle

Size: 4 to 6 inches.

Abundance: Very common.

Variation: There are at least three subspecies of this widespread turtle in America. The form seen in Indiana is known as the Midland Painted Turtle (*C. p. marginata*).

Presumed range in Indiana

Habitat: Avoids fast flowing streams in favor of still or slow moving waters. Common in swamps, marshes, ponds and lakes throughout its range.

Breeding: Females lay 10 to 15 eggs within a flask-shaped underground nest chamber dug with the turtles hind legs. Egg laying occurs from late May to early July. Eggs hatch in about 10 weeks. Hatchlings are the size of a quarter.

Natural History: The Painted Turtles are among the most common and widespread of the Emydidae turtles in America. Like other members of their family they spend a great deal of time basking on floating logs and they are quick to slide into the water if approached too closely. These are omnivorous turtles that eat a very wide array of plant and animal foods as well as carrion. They are one of the most widespread turtles in America. These are hardy little turtles that range northward well into Canada. They have been shown to be able to survive temperatures below freezing. Although an aquatic turtle, they may be seen well away from water sources, especially in the spring.

Class—**Chelonia** (turtles)

Order—**Cryptodira** (straightneck turtles)

Family—**Emydidae** (water & box turtles)

Eastern River Cooter *Pseudemys concinna*	**Blanding's Turtle** *Emydoidea blandingii*
	 Old adult

Size: 10 to 12 inches.

Abundance: Fairly common.

Variation: Males are smaller than females and have long, needle-like claws on the front feet. There is no geographic variation in Indiana specimens (see Natural History section below).

Habitat: Primarily a turtle of large rivers and lakes, but they can also be common in swamps and oxbows that are adjacent to larger streams. Range in Indiana is along the major river valleys in the southwestern tip of the state.

Presumed range in Indiana

Breeding: Lays about 20 eggs in an underground chamber dug with the females hind legs. Egg deposition is in late spring or early summer with the eggs hatching in August or September. Babies are slightly larger than a quarter.

Natural History: The largest member of the Emdidae family in the state. They primarily eat aquatic plants, including large quantities of algae. Some animal matter is consumed usually in the form of aquatic invertebrates or fish, especially so with younger turtles that need a higher protein diet. In habits they are strictly diurnal. Like many other aquatic turtles, they spend the winter buried in the mud at the bottom of a body of water. Their metabolic processes slowed significantly by cold temperatures, they absorb oxygen from water through the lining of the cloaca. They may emerge on warm winter days to bask in the sun, usually using floating logs or emergent objects such as rocks or stumps. These are large turtles that are sometimes utilized as food by humans. The phylogeny of the *Pseudemys* genus has undergone repeated revisions in recent years. Today most experts consider all *Pseudemys* found in Indiana to be Eastern River Cooters (*P. c. concinna*). Although they are widespread and fairly common in the eastern US in general, they are an endangered species in Indiana.

Size: Maximum of 11.125 inches.

Abundance: Uncommon in Indiana.

Variation: Amount of irregular spots and lines on carapace is variable. Some individuals have patterns significantly faded or no pattern at all. Newly hatched babies tend to lack spots.

Habitat: The habitat is marshes and wetlands. Especially along the margins of glacial lakes. Also uses wet meadows or to a lesser extend mesic woodlands. Though semi-aquatic, they are commonly seen on land, sometimes far from water.

Presumed range in Indiana

Breeding: 10 to 15 eggs are laid by the female in an underground nest chamber that she digs at night. Only one clutch per year is produced. Females may travel long distances away from wetlands in search of suitable nesting sites.

Natural History: The oldest known wild specimen of Blanding's Turtle was calculated to be 77 years old. Crayfish are reported to be the favorite food item. Among aquatic foods listed are insects, fish, fish eggs, and frogs are along with algae. On land they will eat earthworms, slugs, insect larva, leaves, grasses and berries. It is thought that the Blanding's Turtle is closely related to the more terrestrial Box Turtle. Like the Box Turtle the Blanding's does posses a hinged plastron. Like their cousin the Box Turtle, the greatest threat to adult Blanding's Turtles is the automobile. Adults moving from one wetland area to another are vulnerable when crossing roads. Additionally, their nests are raided by a variety of predators including foxes, Opossums, Raccoons and especially Striped Skunks. This is a vanishing species throughout its range in the great lakes region and it is regarded as endangered in Indiana. The main threat is loss of wetland habitats. As much as 80 percent of the original wetlands in Indiana have been lost, mostly to agriculture.

Class—**Chelonia** (turtles)

Order—**Cryptodira** (straightneck turtles)

Family—**Emydidae** (water & box turtles)

False Map Turtle *Graptemys pseudogeographica*	**Common Map Turtle** *Graptemys geographica*	**Ouachita Map Turtle** *Graptemys ouachitensis*

Female

Male top, female bottom

Size: Maximum of 11 inches.

Presumed range in Indiana

Abundance: Rare in Indiana. Restricted to southwestern Indiana.

Variation: Two very similar subspecies are recognized. Males have longer claws on the front feet. Pattern fades with age.

Size: Males 6.5 inches. Females 11 inches.

Presumed range in Indiana

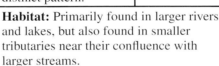

Abundance: Fairly common, but they have declined in some areas.

Variation: In mature adults, females are larger and have larger heads. No subspecies. Young have a more distinct pattern.

Size: Males 5 inches. Females to 10 inches.

Presumed range in Indiana

Abundance: Fairly common in the Wabash watershed.

Variation: Males are smaller and have longer front claws. Young resemble adults but have markings on the plastron.

Habitat: The habitat is mostly in rivers and large creeks with mud bottoms. Abundant basking sites in the form of floating logs or down trees are favored.

Habitat: Primarily found in larger rivers and lakes, but also found in smaller tributaries near their confluence with larger streams.

Habitat: Primarily lives in rivers and river impoundments. They can also be found in the oxbows and swamps associated with major rivers.

Breeding: 10 to 15 eggs are laid by the female in an underground nest chamber that she digs at night. Only one clutch per year is produced.

Breeding: Breeds in early spring and eggs are laid in June. Most egg laying occurs in the morning. The average clutch size is about 10 eggs.

Breeding: Breeds in spring and fall. Eggs are laid in early summer and average about 10 per clutch. May lay two clutches per year.

Natural History: When not feeding or breeding these turtles spend most of their time basking. They are quite wary and will dive into the water at the slightest disturbance. They eat mainly insects but also eat other aquatic invertebrates and will scavenge on dead fish. They eat less plant material than other aquatic turtles. The longevity record for this species is 35 years. With the exception of the three map turtle species shown on this page, this genus of turtles are mostly animals of America's Lower Gulf Coastal Plain. It is here that they reach their greatest diversity and some have very small geographic ranges. The False Map Turtle has two subspecies and specimens from southeastern Indiana appear to be intergrades between the two subspecies.

Natural History: Diurnal and crepuscular in activity. These turtles are fond of basking on logs but are very wary and will disappear into the water if approached. Food items include, crustaceans, fish, insects, and aquatic plants. They also eat mollusks and the thick, crushing surface of the jaws suggests that small mussels may be an important element in the diet. The Common Map Turtle is one of the more widely distributed of the map turtles and can be found from the great lakes southward into Arkansas and Alabama. They also range widely throughout Indiana and they probably occur statewide, although they have not been documented from every county in the state. They have a lifespan in the wild of at least twenty years.

Natural History: Food includes insects, dead fish, aquatic invertebrates, and plant material, especially algae. The carapace (top shell) of this species has a rough, serrated appearance that is more pronounced in younger turtles. They are good climbers and will bask on steep trunks or limbs overhanging water. This turtle's name is derived from the Ouachita River in Arkansas, where the first specimen described to science was found. This species is more widespread to the west of Indiana but occurs along many of the major rivers of the state. The map above is at best an approximation, as the exact range of this species in the state may not be fully known. The Indiana Herp Atlas Online shows recent documentation for only twelve counties in Indiana.

Class—**Chelonia** (turtles)
Order—**Cryptodira** (straightneck turtles)
Family—**Emydidae** (water & box turtles)

Eastern Box Turtle *Terrapene carolina*	**Ornate Box Turtle** *Terrapene ornata*

Female laying eggs

Size: Averages 4 to 6 inches. The record is just under 8 inches.

Abundance: Common in southern Indiana. Uncommon in north.

Presumed range in Indiana

Variation: There are three subspecies of this common land turtle. Only the eastern subspecies occurs in Indiana. It is a highly variable subspecies. In fact, no two specimens look exactly alike (see photos above). The color and pattern on each specimen is as individual as a fingerprint. Sexes can be differentiated by examination of the bottom part of the shell (plastron). Males have a concave plastron and females a flat plastron. In adult turtles, males tend to be slightly larger than females.

Habitat: Occupies a wide variety of habitats from open fields and pastures to deep woods. Can be found in both upland areas and lowlands, but is most common in damp woods, edge areas near creeks and streams, and wooded bottom lands.

Breeding: Breeding takes place in late April and May with egg deposition in late June or early July. Up to 6 eggs may be laid but 2 or 3 is more common. Females may dig the nest by day or night. Young hatch in late fall and some may overwinter in their underground nest chamber before emerging the following spring. Newly hatched baby Box Turtles do not possess the hinged plastron and are thus unable to tightly close themselves within their shell.

Natural History: These familiar turtles often go by the name "Terrapin." They are primarily diurnal and are most active in the morning and the late afternoon. They sometimes burrow into the mud during hot weather, and overwinter by burrowing themselves into loose soil or deep leaf litter. The hibernation burrow is quite shallow, only a few inches deep. Studies have shown that they are tolerant of some freezing, a trait that enables survival of such a shallow hibernator. Still, hibernation is a significant source of mortality among adults. Their diet is omnivorous and they consume berries, fruits and mushrooms as well as a wide variety of insect prey and other invertebrates. Earthworms and snails are a favorite animal food and blackberries and mulberries are among the favorite plant foods. Box Turtles are known for their longevity and reports of their living up to a century are common but difficult to verify. Some researchers report a life span of 80 years, some say over 100, while others say 30 to 40 years is probably the average in the wild. When threatened they will retract the head and feet into the shell which can then close tightly by means of hinges on the front and back of the plastron. The muscles that close the shell are remarkably strong and efforts to pry open the shell of a frightened Box Turtle are futile. They are tough little turtles that can sometimes survive serious injury such as the shell being cracked open by a glancing blow from an automobile tire. Turtles with badly deformed but completely healed shells are sometimes found. In regions where wildfires are common many are seen with shells that are completely scarred by fire. There is some concern among conservationists that commercial collecting of these turtles for foreign markets may be a threat to their long-term survival. Habitat degradation and automobiles are much more imminent threats.

Size: Max 6.5 inches.

Abundance: Rare.

Presumed range in Indiana

Variation: Male has concave platron (females is flat) and red eye. Amount of yellow spotting in head is variable as is the prominence of light markings on the carapace.

Habitat: Prefers more xeric conditions than the Eastern Box Turtle. Inhabits remnant prairie and dry woodlands.

Breeding: Lays up to 6 eggs in mid-summer. Eggs hatch in fall. Baby turtles are tiny replicas of the adult, but lack the ability to close the plastron completely until several inches long. Female may lay twice per summer.

Natural History: This turtle could be regarded as a western, dry-land version of the Eastern Box Turtle. They range throughout the great plains and well into the desert southwest. Indiana populations (and those in nearby Illinois) represent the easternmost extension of the species range in America. They are more carnivorous than their eastern cousins, but they do consume some vegetable matter. Insects, snails, and earthworms are probably the main food items. Some small vertebrate prey may be consumed and they are known to scavenge for carrion as well. There are two subspecies recognized, but only the nominate form is found in Indiana. The other is the Desert Box Turtle which ranges well into the Chihauhau Desert region as far west as southeastern Arizona. For unknown reasons, the Ornate Box Turtle spends more time in hibernation than the Eastern Box Turtle.

Class—**Chelonia** (turtles)

Order—**Cryptodira** (straightneck turtles)

Family—**Trionychidae** (softshell turtles)

Smooth Softshell Turtle *Apalone mutica*	**Spiny Softshell Turtle** *Apalone spinifera*

Underwater

Sunning on streambank

Presumed range in Indiana

Close-up of head showing tubular snout

Presumed range in Indiana

Size: 12 to 14 inches.

Size: Maximum of 18 inches.

Abundance: Uncommon in Indiana.

Abundance: Fairly common.

Variation: No significant species variation in Indiana. There are two other *Apalone* Softshell species found in parts of the southeast. Females attain a much larger size than males.

Variation: No subspecific variation among Indiana specimens, but there are a total of five subspecies in America. Adult females may be twice the size of males.

Habitat: Essentially an inhabitant of streams, both large rivers and small creeks. Flowing water is a requirement for this species, but it is found in large river impoundments.

Habitat: Occurs in both large and small streams and in impoundments. May also be found in farm ponds in some areas. Shows a preference for habitats with sandy substrates.

Breeding: Eggs are laid in excavated chambers on exposed sandbars in late spring or early summer. About a dozen eggs is typical.

Breeding: A dozen or more eggs are laid between May and August (most in June or July). Nests are often on sandbars of creeks or rivers.

Natural History: The Smooth Softshell is found mostly in flowing streams with fine gravel or sand bottoms. They are capable of great speed in the water and will actively forage for fish and other small aquatic animals. They are also ambush predators that burrow into the soft substrate of streams and extend their long necks with blinding speed to grab passing fish. Insects are also an important food item, along with various small aquatic animals and some plant material such as seeds and berries. Because of their permeable skin and requirement of clear streams and rivers these turtles may be under significant threat from water pollution. Damming of major rivers can also impede their natural movements and dispersal. Siltation from agricultural runoff alters preferred stream substrates of sand or fine gravel. All species of softshell turtles have elongated, snorkel-like snouts which they will use to breathe when buried in sand or mud at the water's edge.

Natural History: Crayfish, fish, and insects are the primary food items, but dead fish and other carrion can be an important food item, especially in lakes where fishing is common. Spiny Softshells are active from April to October in Indiana. They hunt both by ambush and by active pursuit. When immobile they can remain under water for several hours. Because of the soft, permeable shells and skin, softshells are more susceptible to dehydration than other turtle species and thus they seldom stray far from water. These turtles are harvested as food in many parts of their range, and much of this harvest is to date unregulated. Some believe this practice may pose a long-term threat to the species. A greater threat is water pollution and the widespread degradation of streams. Like all softshell turtles the Spiny has a long and flexible neck, which makes handling these turtles without being bitten difficult. Wild adults may bite savagely if handled.

CHAPTER 6

THE REPTILES OF INDIANA

TABLE 4

— THE ORDERS AND FAMILIES OF INDIANA REPTILES —

Class—**Reptilia** (reptiles)

Order—**Squamata** (lizards & snakes)
Suborder—**Lacertilia** (lizards)

Family	**Phrynosomatidae** (spiny lizards)
Family	**Teiidae** (whiptail lizards)
Family	**Anguidae** (glass lizards)
Family	**Scincidae** (skinks)

Suborder—**Serpentes** (snakes)

Family	**Colubridae** (harmless egg-laying snakes)
Family	**Dipsadidae** (rear-fanged snakes)
Family	**Natricidae** (harmless live-bearing snakes)
Family	**Xenodontidae** (large rear-fanged snakes)
Family	**Crotalidae** (pit vipers)

THE REPTILES OF
INDIANA

PART 1: LIZARDS

Class—**Reptilia** (reptiles)

Order—**Squamata** (snakes & lizards)

Suborder—**Lacertilia** (lizards)

Family—**Phrynosomatidae**	Family—**Teiidae** (whiptails)	Family—**Anguidae** (glass lizards)
Eastern Fence Lizard *Sceloperus undulatus*	**Racerunner** *Aspidoscelis sexlineata*	**Slender Glass Lizard** *Ophisaurus attenuatus*

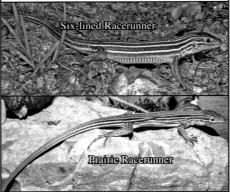

Size: Maximum of 7.25 inches.	**Size:** From 6 to 10 inches.	**Size:** 2 to 3 feet. Record 43 inches.
Abundance: Very common.	**Abundance:** Uncommon.	**Abundance:** Rare in Indiana.
Variation: Males have bright blue patches on each side of the belly. There are no variants in Indiana, but several morphological types in the western US.	**Variation:** Males and subadults are a bit more vividly colored than mature females. Two subspecies occur in Indiana (see photos above).	**Variation:** Males have light and dark speckling. Juveniles resemble females but longitudinal stripes are more vivid on young lizards.

Presumed range in Indiana (Eastern Fence Lizard)

Presumed range in Indiana — Prairie Racerunner / Six-lined Racerunner

Presumed range in Indiana (Slender Glass Lizard)

Habitat: Dry, upland woods. Found in both pure deciduous woods and in pine dominated woodlands.	**Habitat:** Habitat requirements are sandy or gravelly soils in dry upland areas with prolonged exposure to the sun.	**Habitat:** Dry soils with an open canopy seem to be important factors in this lizard's habitat. Woods, fields and edge.
Breeding: Egg layer. Deposits 6 to 15 eggs in rotted logs, stumps, etc. Two clutches per year are common.	**Breeding:** Breeds in April or May. 6 or 8 eggs are laid in an underground nest chamber in sandy soil.	**Breeding:** Females lay a single clutch of eggs in late June or early July. Average clutch size is about 10 eggs.

Natural History: A woodland species, the Eastern Fence Lizard spends much of its time on tree trunks and fallen logs. Its color and pattern perfectly matches the bark of most trees within its range. This is one of the most common lizards in southern Indiana. They are quite arboreal in habits and will regularly climb trees to great heights. Feeds on insects, spiders, etc. Both sexes are often seen perched on rocks, logs, or stumps in wooded areas. Breeding males are especially conspicuous as they attempt to attract females by sitting atop rocks or stumps and methodically raising and lowering their body to show off the bright blue patches on the undersides. The Phrynosomatidae are also called "Spiny Lizards." There are many species in the west, but this is the only member of its family in the eastern US.

Natural History: The Teiidae lizards are a common and diverse family in the southwestern United States, but they are represented in the east by this single species with two subspecies, *A. s. viridis* (Prairie Racerunner) in northern Indiana and *A. s. sexlineatus* (Six-lined Racerunner) in southern Indiana. The Teiidae lizards are famous among biologists because in some species there are no males and reproduction is accomplished by parthenogenesis (the development of unfertilized eggs into embryos). These speedy lizards are aptly named as they can reach a speed of up to 20 mph. They are active at higher temperatures than many reptiles and they will spend the first few minutes of the day basking in the sun to raise their body temperature. At night they retreat to an underground burrow dug into loose soil.

Natural History: These lizards are often confused with snakes due to their lack of limbs. They are easily recognized as lizards however by the presence of ear openings and eyelids. When grasped these lizards will thrash about wildly and break off their tail. The tail is quite long, making up about two-thirds of their total length. The apparent fragility of these lizards and the shiny appearance of their skin has led to the common name "glass lizard." The highly specialized escape mechanism of breaking off the tail is shared with many other lizard species, as is the rare ability to regenerate a new tail. Regenerated tails never attain the original length. Like other Indiana lizards they prey on small invertebrates. In Indiana this species is restricted to the sand prairie regions of northwestern Indiana.

Class—**Reptilia** (reptiles)

Order—**Squamata** (snakes & lizards)

Suborder—**Lacertilia** (lizards)

Family—**Scincidae** (skinks)

Ground Skink *Scincella lateralis*	Five-lined Skink *Plestiodon fasciatus*	Broad-headed Skink *Plestiodon laticeps*
	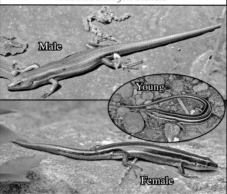 	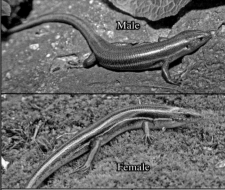 

Size: 3 to 5 inches.

Presumed range in Indiana

Abundance: Fairly common.

Variation: Color may vary from reddish to golden brown or chocolate brown. Color has a metallic quality. Some have small dark flecks on the back.

Habitat: Dry upland woods and pine woodlands. Micro-habitat consists of leaf litter and detritus on the forest floor. Avoids permanent wetlands.

Breeding: Small clutches of 3 to 5 eggs is typical. May lay two clutches per year. Unlike other skinks, the female Ground Skink does not remain with the eggs until hatching.

Natural History: These tiny ground dwellers dive quickly beneath leaf litter when approached and they are easily overlooked. Often, their presence is revealed by the rustling sound made as they forage through the dry leaves. Despite being rarely observed, they can be quite common in many areas. Foods are tiny insects and other small invertebrates living among the leaf litter on the forest floor. They also go by the name "Little Brown Skink." They are widespread throughout the southeastern half of America and are most common in the deep south. In Indiana they are restricted to the Interior Low Plateau Province in southern Indiana. They are the smallest lizard found in Indiana.

Size: 5 to 7 inches.

Presumed range in Indiana

Abundance: Very common.

Variation: Young are brightly colored with distinct pale yellow stripes and blue tails. Females resemble young. Males are brown with reddish cheek patches.

Habitat: Most common in damp woodlands but also found in swamps and in drier upland areas. Patches of sunlit areas for basking is important.

Breeding: Eggs (6 to 12) are laid in May or early June in rotted logs, stumps, sawdust, mulch or other moisture retaining material. Female remains with eggs until hatching.

Natural History: The young of this species are strikingly colored with bright blue tails and they sometimes are mistaken by lay persons as being another species going by the name "Blue-tailed Skink." These common and well-known lizards are fond of sunning on decks, porches, sidewalks and patios of homes in rural areas. They can often be found in suburban environments as well, particularly older neighborhoods with abundant large trees and shrubbery. They feed on a wide variety of insects, spiders and arthropods and they are a useful species in controlling invertebrate pests around the home. Like the male Broad-headed Skink, breeder male Five-lined Skinks develop bright red cheeks.

Size: Max 13 inches.

Presumed range in Indiana

Abundance: Fairly common.

Variation: Young have blue tails and yellow stripes and resemble Five-lined Skinks. Adult females have indistinct lines, males are brown with bright red cheeks.

Habitat: Mesic woodlands, wetland areas and also dry upland woods with moist micro-habitat. Requires some open areas for sunning.

Breeding: Females will vigorously defend their eggs that are usually laid on the ground in a hollowed out depression beneath sheltering log or inside a hollow stump.

Natural History: These very large skinks are quite arboreal and often den in tree hollows many feet above the ground. These arboreal dens are used only during summer and hibernation takes place underground. In much of the southeast they are known as "Scorpion Lizards" and some believe the myth that they are dangerously venomous. Although they will bite if handled, they are totally harmless to humans. This is Indiana's largest lizard species and the largest individuals can barely exceed a foot in length. Insects are the main food but they will also eat small mammals such as baby mice. Breeding males develop bright red, grotesquely swollen cheeks, thus the Broad-headed name.

THE REPTILES OF
INDIANA

PART 2: SNAKES

Class—**Reptilia** (reptiles)

Order—**Squamata** (snakes & lizards)

Suborder—**Serpentes** (snakes)

Family—**Colubridae** (harmless egg-laying snakes)

Eastern Racer *Coluber constrictor*	**Bullsnake** *Pituophis catenifer*

Presumed range in Indiana

Size: Average about 4 feet. Maximum 6 feet.

Abundance: Very common. In fact this is probably the most common large snake species in Indiana.

Variation: Nine subspecies of *Coluber constrictor* are found across North America. Two occur in Indiana, the **Southern Black Racer** (subspecies *priapus*) and the **Blue Racer** (subspecies *foxii*). See photos above. Young racers have a pattern of distinctive saddles (see inset photo).

Habitat: Racers are habitat generalists that may be found in most natural habitats within the state. They favor dry upland woods and overgrown fields. They are most common in ecotone areas.

Breeding: Females lay about a dozen (from 5 to 20) eggs in rotted logs, humus, or frequently in sawdust piles around old sawmills. Eggs are laid in early summer and hatch in about two months. Like most egg layers, the Racer reproduces annually (some live bearing snakes breed only every other year).

Natural History: Racers are alert, active snakes that relentlessly prowl in search of almost any type of animal prey that can be swallowed. They will eat insects, amphibians, lizards, other snakes (including the young of venomous species), nestling birds, eggs, and small mammals. They are also adept at catching fish trapped in drying pools of streams and swamps. Unlike many snake species, the Racer is a diurnal animal and may be active even during the heat of the day in mid-summer. They are apparently intelligent, curious snakes that will follow livestock and other large animals in hopes of capturing insects and other prey that may be disturbed by the larger animals passing. This is probably how they gained the reputation as aggressive snakes that will chase a human. Their name is appropriate as they are probably the fastest snakes in Indiana and one of fastest in America. Quite speedy for a snake, they can reach a blazing 12 to 15 mph. Due to their catholic feeding habits and ability to adapt to a wide variety of habitats, the racers are among the most successful snakes in America. When threatened these snakes can use their speed to literally disappear into thick cover. When hard pressed out in the open they will climb into bushes or shrubs to escape. If captured they will bite vigorously and spray the captor with feces and musk. The Southern Black Racer (subspecies *priapus*) is found in the first few tiers of the southernmost counties in Indiana. The Blue Racer (subspecies *foxii*) ranges throughout the rest of the state. Snakes from the southernmost counties are quite dark, while specimens from the northwestern counties usually exhibit a bluish coloration. In between these two extremes are snakes that may be slate gray, charcoal, or brownish gray in color.

Size: Record 8 feet, 3 inches.

Abundance: Uncommon in Indiana.

Variation: There is no significant variation and young snakes are miniature replicas of the adults.

Habitat: Sand Prairie is the primary habitat for this species in Indiana.

Presumed range in Indiana

Breeding: The eggs are quite large and the baby bullsnakes are over a foot in length at hatching. Clutch size can be up to two dozen but is usually less.

Natural History: Also goes by the name "Gopher Snake," an appropriate name since they are apparently a major predator of the Plains Gopher. Like the Plains Gopher, the range of this species in Indiana probably originally closely coincided with the state's prairie habitats. In addition to gophers and ground squirrels the Bullsnake will eat any type of warm-blooded prey that is small enough to be swallowed, which can include animals the size of tree squirrels and young rabbits. Small rodents probably make up the bulk of its diet but birds and their eggs are also eaten and this species will sometimes climb trees in search of bird nests. When cornered these snakes will hiss loudly and strike repeatedly. They will also rapidly vibrate the tip of the tail and do a pretty good imitation of a rattlesnake. This is the second largest snake in Indiana.

Class—**Reptilia** (reptiles)
Order—**Squamata** (snakes & lizards)
Suborder—**Serpentes** (snakes)
Family—**Colubridae** (harmless egg-laying snakes)

Midland Rat Snake *Pantherophis spiloides*	**Eastern Fox Snake** *Pantherophis vulpinus*

Light morph

Young

Dark morph

Size: Average 5 to 6 feet as adults. Record 8 feet 4 inches.

Abundance: Common. This is probably the second most common large snake in Indiana.

Variation: These snakes exhibit some variation in the dorsal pattern of adults. Most show a blotched pattern on the back, but in some individuals this pattern is obscured by an overall dark coloration. The color between the dorsal blotches also varies. It may be cream or yellowish, brownish, or varying shades of gray. Specimens from the southern tip of the state typically exhibit distinct blotches. Those from farther north may be solid black. Young are light gray with charcoal blotches (see inset photo).

Presumed range in Indiana

Habitat: Found in virtually all habitats within the state, but most common in woodlands. They are least common in areas of intensive agriculture or urbanized areas, but they can persist in urban regions if there is some cover and large trees.

Breeding: An egg layer that breeds in the spring and lays up to twenty (average about a dozen) eggs. Eggs are laid in old woodpecker holes or hollow limbs above ground or on the ground in rotted stumps, beneath logs, or any sheltered place where some form of humus is present to prevent dessication. Breed annually. Eggs are laid in early summer and hatch in late summer or early fall.

Natural History: This is the most arboreal snake species in Indiana and adults spend a great deal of time in trees. They often choose a regular den site in old woodpecker holes or hollows of trees and may be seen sunning with the forepart of the body emerged from a hole. Excellent climbers, they can ascend straight up a tree trunk using only the bark to gain a purchase with their belly scales. They will climb to great heights in search of bird nests. In addition to baby birds and eggs they will also eat rodents, squirrels, and other small mammals up to the size of a rabbit. They are also quite fond of barns and derelict buildings as a habitat. In Indiana these large snakes are well known to rural dwellers and they often go by the nickname "Black Snake." "Chicken Snake" is another common nickname and is a reference to their historical habit of raiding hen houses for eggs and chicks. They are also called "Cowsuckers" in some parts of the state. This name comes from the erroneous belief rural people once had that they would enter barns to suck milk from cows. In fact, they enter barns to hunt rodents. They may also find their way into attics and crawl spaces of homes where they perform a service as a natural rodent control, but this service is frequently not appreciated by the homeowner. This is the longest snake species in Indiana with a record length of 8 feet, 4 inches. Most are fully grown at about 5 to 5.5 feet, but 6 foot individuals are not uncommon.

Size: Max 5 ft 10 in.

Abundance: Fairly common.

Variation: Varying shades of brown. Most are grayish brown with darker brown blotches. Some are reddish brown or yellowish with darker brown blotches.

Habitat: Inhabits woodlands, marshes, and prairies. Most common in ecotones where woodlands meet open fields.

Breeding: Breeding occurs in spring or early summer with egg deposition following fertilization by about a month. Clutch size is about a dozen eggs, though it can be twice that amount.

Natural History: Interestingly, there is population of Eastern Fox Snakes that exists around the western end of Lake Erie in Ohio that is disjunct by many miles from the main population to which Indiana Fox Snakes belong. This probably represents a "relict" population that was cut off from the rest of this snake's contiguous range by habitat changes at some time in the geological/climatological history of the region. In Indiana these snakes are endemic to the northwestern part of the state, mostly in the Central Corn Belt Plains Level III ecoregion. The food of this species is primarily endothermic vertebrates, mostly hatchling birds, bird eggs and small mammal such as mice and voles.

Class—**Reptilia** (reptiles)

Order—**Squamata** (snakes & lizards)

Suborder—**Serpentes** (snakes)

Family—**Colubridae** (harmless egg-laying snakes)

Rough Green Snake *Opheodrys aestivus*	Smooth Green Snake *Opheodrys vernalis*	Southeastern Crowned Snake *Tantilla coronata*

Rough Green Snake		Smooth Green Snake		Southeastern Crowned Snake	
Size: Record 3 feet 11 inches.	Presumed range in Indiana	**Size:** Average 18 inches. Record 31 inches.	Presumed range in Indiana	**Size:** The record length is 13 inches.	Presumed range in Indiana
Abundance: Uncommon.		**Abundance:** Rare.		**Abundance:** Very rare.	
Variation: This species is typically remarkably uniform in appearance. A very rare blue morph can occur with an abnormality omitting yellow pigments.		**Variation:** No variation. Throughout its rather large range across the northern US from New England to the Dakotas this species is uniform in appearance.		**Variation:** There is no variation. Young are miniature replicas of the adults. There are many other species within the genus but none occur in Indiana.	
Habitat: Open fields, pastures, and edges of woods and fields. Often common in wetlands where there are low bushes and shrubs overhanging water. Found in the southern third of Indiana.		**Habitat:** Open fields, pastures, meadows and edges of lakes, ponds or marshes. Generally a snake of open habitats but may be found in open woods. Indiana range is in remnant prairies.		**Habitat:** May be found in a variety of habitats but most common in woodland situations. Micro-habitat is leaf litter and beneath rocks or logs. May also be found within rotted logs or stumps.	
Breeding: 3 to 12 eggs are laid in late spring or early summer. The babies are slender, miniature replicas of the adult.		**Breeding:** Clutch size is relatively small and may be as few as three or four eggs or as high as a dozen.		**Breeding:** From 2 to 5 eggs are laid beneath leaf litter in mid-summer. Hatchlings are only about 3 inches long.	
Natural History: Rough Green Snakes live in dense bushes and shrubs where their bright green color renders them invisible. Arthropods of many varieties are their prey. Food includes spiders, caterpillars, crickets, and grasshoppers to name a few of their favorites. These snakes are sometimes called "grass snakes" in reference to their bright green coloration. There is a widespread belief that they have become extremely rare and endangered. While in much of their range to the south their populations are stable, they are certainly vulnerable to habitat destruction wrought by modern agricultural practices as well as the widespread use of insecticides. In Indiana they are considered to be a species of concern, meaning that they are declining in the state.		**Natural History:** Like the similar Rough Green Snake the Smooth Green Snake often goes by the common name "Grass Snake" or "Green Grass Snake." These small snakes eat a variety of invertebrate prey including slugs, spiders, millipedes, crickets, grasshoppers and caterpillars, to name a few. This diet makes them exceptionally vulnerable to insecticides and widespread applications of chemicals on agricultural fields may pose a serious threat to this handsome little snake. Unlike the larger Rough Green Snake that climbs into bushes and small trees, the Smooth Green Snake tends to stay close to the ground. The Smooth Green snake has smooth scales, the Rough Green has rough (keeled) scales. This is an endangered species in Indiana.		**Natural History:** These are the smallest snakes in America, and the Southeastern Crowned Snake is the smallest snake in Indiana. These tiny serpents are no bigger around than a matchstick. The genus *Tantilla* consists of at least 75 species of very small snakes that range from the southeastern United States to southern South America. They feed on small, soft-bodied invertebrates of all types. Most species in the US live in the southwestern portion of the country and the bulk of the Southeastern Crowned Snakes range is in the southeastern states from Louisiana to the Carolinas. A few examples of this species have been found in Floyd and Clark counties along the Ohio River. Their habitat there is described by Indiana Herp Atlas as "Rocky Glades."	

Class—**Reptilia** (reptiles)	
Order—**Squamata** (snakes & lizards)	
Suborder—**Serpentes** (snakes)	
Family—**Colubridae** (harmless egg-laying snakes)	

Milksnake—*Lampropeltis triangulum*		Common (Black) Kingsnake *Lampropeltis getula*
Eastern Milksnake *L. t. triangulum*	**Red Milksnake** *L. t. syspila*	

Size: The record for the Eastern Milk is 52 inches. Red Milk record is 42 inches.

Presumed range in Indiana

Abundance: Fairly common in Indiana, but both color morphs can be uncommon in some habitats within their range.

Variation: Milk Snakes are one of the most wide-ranging and diverse snake species in America. Experts once recognized as many as 8 subspecies in the US, and several more south of the Mexican border. The two pictures above show typical examples of Indiana's two forms. Some intermediate forms between the Eastern and Red Milk Snakes can be expected to be seen where the populations meet in the state.

Habitat: Like the rat snakes, Milk Snakes often enter barns and outbuilding in search of mice. They can be found in both dry woodlands and in wetland areas. Like many snake species they are most common in ecotone areas such as where a wooded bluff abuts against a bottomland habitat of swamp or marsh. Both subspecies are drawn to fallen logs and dead snags with loose bark as a micro-habitat. Flat stones in rocky areas are often used as a shelter.

Breeding: Milk Snakes are egg layers. Eggs are deposited in rotten logs, stumps, or beneath a flat rock. Six to twenty-one eggs are listed as being recorded from this species.

Natural History: The name comes from the habit these snakes have of entering stock barns in search of mice. Early settlers erroneously thought the snakes were there to suckle from the milk cow (that every pioneer family kept on the farm). These snakes eat many lizards and will also consume other, smaller snakes. Reptile eggs may also be eaten along with amphibians and small mammals like mice. Like the Common Kingsnakes, the Milk Snakes enjoy a resistance to snake venom and baby copperheads, cottonmouths or rattlesnakes may be eaten by large adults. Young snakes feed mostly on skinks. Additionally, eggs and nestlings of ground nesting birds may be a food item on occasion. Both forms of milk snake found in Indiana are primarily nocturnal snakes that usually remain hidden during daylight hours beneath rocks, logs, and other woodland debris. They are thus not as readily observed as many other snakes in the state. A recent evaluation of the Milk Snake complex by herpetologists regards both the above snakes as Eastern Milk Snakes and disregards subspecies status for the Red Milk Snake. Some herpetologists do not accept this new designation and retain the concept of subspecies for this snake. Populations of this snake in much of Indiana are aptly described as "intergrades" and are intermediate in morphology between the two forms.

Size: Average about 4 feet. Max 74 inches.

Presumed range in Indiana

Abundance: Fairly common.

Habitat: Mature woodlands, successional areas, weedy fields and edge habitats in uplands. Also bottom lands, swamp and marsh edges.

Variation: Variable amount of light speckling present. Young snakes always have speckles that fade with age. There are several subspecies of this snake in America. Indiana's subspecies is *nigra* (the **Black Kingsnake**).

Breeding: An annual breeder that lays 8 to 12 eggs in early summer. Eggs are laid inside rotted stumps or logs.

Natural History: All the Common Kingsnake subspecies are best known for their habit of killing and eating other snakes, including venomous species. These powerful constrictors are immune to the venom of pit vipers and will kill and eat any snake that is small enough to be swallowed whole. They also eat rodents, birds, lizards and baby turtles. They are mainly terrestrial in habits but have been found inside of standing dead trees several feet off the ground. They may be active both day and night but are mostly crepuscular and during hotter months tend to become nocturnal. This species is a favorite captive pet of many reptile enthusiasts in America.

150 INDIANA WILDLIFE ENCYCLOPEDIA

Class—**Reptilia** (reptiles)

Order—**Squamata** (snakes & lizards)

Suborder—**Serpentes** (snakes)

Family—**Colubridae** (harmless snakes)	Family—**Dipsadidae** (small rear-fanged snakes)	

Yellow-bellied (Prairie) Kingsnake
Lampropeltis calligaster

Ringneck Snake
Diadophis punctatus

Wormsnake
Carphophis amoenus

Size: Averages about 4 feet. Record 58 inches.

Presumed range in Indiana

Abundance: Fairly common.

Variation: Three subspecies are recognized. Indiana's is the subspecies *calligaster* (**Prairie Kingsnake**). Young snakes are more vividly spotted.

Habitat: Open fields overgrown with weeds, brush and briers, but can also be found in woodlands and woodland edges.

Breeding: Females produce about a dozen eggs that are laid underground. Young snakes are about 9 to 10 inches in length and are vividly spotted.

Natural History: Three subspecies are found in the southern United States but only one of those occurs in Indiana (the **Prairie Kingsnake**, *L. c. calligaster*). This is a subterranean species that is only rarely seen above ground, usually in early spring. It feeds mostly on small mammals which it hunts in their underground burrows. They also eat bird eggs and nestlings, but they are a threat only to those that nest on or near the ground. Despite the fact that this is a fairly common snake within their range in Indiana, they are rarely observed due to their burrowing habits. Young snakes exhibit a dorsal pattern of up to 75 reddish brown saddles. The pattern tends to darken with age (see above). Some may developed dark longitudinal stripes.

Size: Average about 14 inches. Max 2 feet.

Presumed range in Indiana

Abundance: Common.

Variation: A variable species with twelve subspecies nationwide. One in Indiana, the **Northern Ringneck** (subspecies *edwardsi*).

Habitat: A woodland species that lives in rotted logs, stumps, and beneath rocks and leaf litter on the forest floor. Also found in overgrown fields.

Breeding: Lays up to a dozen eggs, usually fewer, in rotted logs or other moisture retaining places. Young are about 5 inches long at hatching.

Natural History: Ringneck snakes are often uncovered by humans beneath boards, stones, leaves, or other debris. The distinctive yellow or cream-colored collar around the neck readily identifies them, and even those unfamiliar with reptiles have no trouble recognizing this species. They feed mostly on soft-bodied insects and other invertebrates. Earthworms are a favorite food. When threatened they will often hold aloft the tightly curled tip of the underside of their bright yellow. This defense mechanism is probably designed to direct an attacker's attention away from the vulnerable head to the less vulnerable tail. Despite having enlarged rear-fangs for inducing mild venom into prey, they are harmless to man.

Size: Average about 8 inches. Max of 11 inches.

Presumed range in Indiana

Abundance: Fairly common.

Variation: Two subspecies but only one in Indiana (*helenae*-Midwest Worm Snake). Indiana specimens are all similar.

Habitat: Found in a variety of habitats, but mostly in woodlands. Its micro-habitat is beneath the leaf litter, rocks, logs, old stumps, etc.

Breeding: From 1 to 12 eggs are laid in late June or July and hatch in 2 or 3 months. Hatchlings are only about 3 inches in length.

Natural History: The specimen shown above is the subspecies *helenae*, the **Midwest Worm Snake**. America's other worm snake subspecies is *ameonus*, **Eastern Worm Snake**. Examination of the head scales using a hand lens is the only sure way to differentiate between the two. A confirmed burrower that lives under leaf litter, logs, rocks and even man-made debris such as old boards, discarded shingles, etc. Feeds almost exclusively on earthworms, but some experts list tiny soft-bodied invertebrates such as insect larva or termites as food. These aptly named snakes do in fact resemble earthworms. Their tiny, conical head and smooth scales help to facilitate burrowing through tiny tunnels created by earthworms or insect larva.

Class—**Reptilia** (reptiles)
Order—**Squamata** (snakes & lizards)
Suborder—**Serpentes** (snakes)
Family—**Natricidae** (harmless live-bearing snakes)

Brown Snake *Storeria dekayi*	**Red-bellied Snake** *Storeria occipitomaculata*	**Smooth Earth Snake** *Virginai valeriae*

Brown Snake		**Red-bellied Snake**		**Smooth Earth Snake**	
Size: Average 12 inches. Record 19 inches.	Presumed range in Indiana	**Size:** 10 to 12 inches. Record 16 inches.	Presumed range in Indiana	**Size:** Usually around 10 inches. Record 15 inches.	Presumed range in Indiana
Abundance: Very common.		**Abundance:** Fairly common.		**Abundance:** Fairly common.	
Variation: None in Indiana. See below.		**Variation:** None in Indiana. See below.		**Variation:** None in Indiana. See below.	
Habitat: Woodlands, grassy fields, and wetlands. Found even in urban areas, especially vacant lots littered with old boards or scrap tin.		**Habitat:** Mostly found in wooded areas, in both lowland and uplands. They can also be found in fields around the edges of woods.		**Habitat:** Smooth Earth Snakes are basically a forest species but they can also be found in open fields near forests and in edge areas.	

Breeding: Gives birth to 5 to 20 young (rarely more, as many as 40). Baby snakes are about 3 inches long with the girth of a toothpick.	**Breeding:** Live-bearer. Litters number from 5 to 15. Newborn babies are only about 3 inches in length and no bigger around than a toothpick.	**Breeding:** These snakes are live bearers that give birth to from 4 to 12 young. The young snakes resemble the adults and measure about three inches.
Natural History: This diminutive snake is often found in vacant lots of large cities and towns, where it hides beneath boards, trash, even small pieces of cardboard. It feeds primarily on earthworms and slugs, but also reportedly eats insects, amphibians eggs, and tiny fishes. Brown Snakes are known to hibernate communally, an odd behavior for a tiny snake that should have no trouble finding adequate crevices in which to spend the colder months. These snakes are sometimes called "Dekay's Snake," in honor of an early American naturalist. These little snakes make interesting pets and will readily eat earthworms in captivity. Formerly several subspecies were recognized by herpetologists. Some still regard these population variants as valid subspecies. Indiana's subspecies would be *wrightorum,* the **Midland Brown Snake.**	**Natural History:** Redbelly Snakes usually remain hidden by day beneath rocks, logs, etc, and emerge at night to hunt insects and small soft-bodied invertebrates such as earthworms, slugs, beetle larva, isopods, etc. These snakes sometimes exhibit a peculiar behavior when threatened. If voiding of feces and musk fails to discourage a handler, they will curl their upper lip in a strange expression of apparent ferocity. It is a purely fallacious display however as their tiny teeth could never penetrate human skin. Although these little snakes are widespread across much of Indiana, they are less common than many other small snake species. They are very similar to the Brown Snake, but are easily identified by their bright red belly. Three subspecies are known. Indiana's is the **Northern Red-bellied Snake,** subspecies *occipitomaculata.*	**Natural History:** The Smooth Earth Snake is a tiny, docile snake that could not manage to bite a human even if they were so inclined, which they are not. They have tiny heads, even for their size, and thus their food consists of very small invertebrates. Insects, snails, and mostly, earthworms. These are secretive little serpents that sometimes emerge to prowl about on the surface after summer rains. Otherwise they are easily overlooked except by herpetologists who know where to find them beneath logs, stones or amid accumulated humus on the forest floor. As with other small snakes that burrow beneath detritus on the floor of woodlands, these little snakes are occasionally turned up by rural residents as they rake mulch from flower beds in the spring. 3 subspecies occur. Indiana's subspecies is *elegans,* the **Western Smooth Earth Snake.**

Class—**Reptilia** (reptiles)

Order—**Squamata** (snakes & lizards)

Suborder—**Serpentes** (snakes)

Family—**Natricidae** (harmless live-bearing snakes)

Kirtland's Snake *Clonophis kirtlandii*	Plainbelly (Copperbelly) Water Snake *Nerodia erythrogaster*	Diamondback Water Snake *Nerodia rhombifer*

Kirtland's Snake

Size: Record length is 24 inches.

Abundance: Uncommon.

Variation: There is very little variation and no subspecies. Dorsal color may vary from brown to grayish or reddish brown.

Presumed range in Indiana

Breeding: Live-bearer. Litters may be as small as 3 or 4 or as many as 10 or 15. Young are born in late summer to early fall,

Habitat: Usually associates with moist environments both in woodlands and fields. Prime habitat for this species appears to be low-lying moist meadows and marsh edges. Habitat seems to be tied to the presence of crayfish burrows.

Natural History: The Kirtland's Snake is an enigmatic species. It is found in several widely dispersed areas in the Midwest and populations are apparently highly fragmented. This is usually the sign of a species in decline and indeed the Kirtland's Snake does appear to be disappearing. It is an endangered species in Indiana. It apparently is at least as common in urban areas as it is in more natural habitats within its range. Earthworms and slugs are listed as its primary prey. When threatened these snakes will flatten the body to such an extreme as to create a ribbon-like appearance to the snake's body.

Plainbelly (Copperbelly) Water Snake

Size: Record length 45 inches.

Abundance: Fairly common to rare.

Variation: There are 3 subspecies nationwide. The Indiana subspecies is *Nerodia erythrogaster neglecta*, the **Copperbelly Water Snake**.

Presumed range in Indiana

Breeding: Large females will produce litters numbering over forty babies. Young are born in late summer or fall. Baby snakes are distinctly blotched.

Habitat: Although this snake is primarily aquatic, it is less tied to water than most water snakes and they will often wander far from permanent water. They may be found in creeks, lakes, ponds, swamps and marshes

Natural History: These snakes feed primarily on aquatic and semi-aquatic vertebrates such as frogs, toads, salamanders and fish. They are active both day and night in the spring but are more nocturnal or crepuscular during hot weather. Like many other water snakes, they are fierce fighters if caught and will bite and smear the attacker with foul smelling feces and a pungent musk. These snakes can be fairly common in the lowlands of the lower Wabash and Ohio River valleys in southwestern Indiana and in the Muskatatuck lowlands in the southeastern portion of the state. The population in extreme northeastern Indiana however is highly endangered.

Diamondback Water Snake

Size: Average 4 feet. Record 64 inches.

Abundance: Uncommon in Indiana.

Variation: The dorsal pattern is more evident on young snakes and freshly molted specimens. Females grow larger than males.

Presumed range in Indiana

Breeding: Produces very large litters of up to 30 or 40 babies in late summer. Babies are 8 to 10 inches long. Beaver lodges can be favored birthing sites.

Habitat: Diamondback Water Snakes frequent most aquatic habitats within their range except for small ponds and smaller streams. They show a definite preference for large swamps and marshes, lakes and reservoirs.

Natural History: The water snakes have a reputation among herpetologists for their pugnacious attitudes and none is more deserving of that reputation than the Diamondback Water Snake. When captured they will thrash wildly and bite savagely and repeatedly. The bite, though harmless, can be painful and may bleed profusely due to an anti-coagulant property in the saliva. These snakes attain an impressive size and can be very heavy bodied. A large female may have a girth the size of a man's wrist. Like all water snakes they are mainly nocturnal during hot summer months. In the early spring they can be very obvious as they bask in the open.

Class—**Reptilia** (reptiles)		
Order—**Squamata** (snakes & lizards)		
Suborder—**Serpentes** (snakes)		
Family—**Natricidae** (harmless live-bearing snakes)		

Common Watersnake—*Nerodia sipedon*		Queen Snake
Northern Watersnake *N. s. sipedon*	**Midland Water Snake** *N. s. pleuralis*	**Queen Snake** *Regina septemvittata*

Size: Average about 3.5 feet. Record 59 inches (Midland Water Snake).

Presumed range in Indiana

Size: Average 2 feet. Maximum 3 feet.

Presumed range in Indiana

Abundance: Both subspecies are very common within their respective ranges.

Abundance: Generally uncommon.

Habitat: These snakes are aquatic animals but they do sometimes wander away from water in search of a mate or as a result of natural dispersal. They are very fond of small farm ponds or small streams as habitat, but they can also be found in large lakes and in swamps and marshes.

Habitat: Creeks with flat stones are a favorite habitat. They will also occupy lakes or large streams.

Breeding: Females may mate with several males in the spring. Birthing occurs in late summer to early fall. Live born young can number two or three dozen, but the largest females may produce even more. Younger females may have as few as 6 or 8.

Breeding: Live-bearers that will produce up to a dozen young per litter.

Variation: There are four subspecies nationwide and two can be found in Indiana (see both above). Both vary somewhat in color, ranging from brown, tan, reddish brown, or gray-brown. They will typically exhibit a pattern of darker bands across the back that contrasts with the lighter color between the bands. In the Northern Water Snake the light spaces between the bands are much narrower than in the Midland Water Snake.

Variation: There are no subspecies of the Queen snake and there is very little variation among specimens. Even the young snakes are remarkably similar and are miniature replicas of the adult with more pronounced dorsal stripes.

Natural History: Northern/Midland Water Snakes adapt well to man-made environments like large lake impoundments where they can thrive in the rip-rap of dams and levees. Frogs and fish are the two favorite food items for these snakes. Around man-made impoundments they can become very numerous near boat docks and fishing areas where they scavenge on dead or dying fish and fish heads left behind by fishermen. Like most other water snake species, they are fond of basking in the sun atop debris and limbs overhanging water. As with other water snakes they are commonly confused with the venomous Cottonmouth, even in areas of the state where the Cottonmouth does not occur (see Cottonmouth range map). Their dorsal pattern of dark brownish bands on a lighter brown background also causes them to be mistaken for another venomous species, the Copperhead. But Copperheads are terrestrial snakes that only rarely enter water. Thus Indiana snakes seen in the water are almost invariably not Copperheads, but water snakes. The Northern Water Snake is found generally in the northern half of the state and the Midland Water Snake in the southern half. In the middle of the state where the two populations meet specimens are often intermediate in appearance between the two subspecies. These individuals are referred to by herpetologists as "intergrades."

Natural History: The Queen Snake is a specialized feeder that preys almost exclusively on recently molted, soft-bodied crayfish. In one study, over 95 percent of stomach contents examined contained crayfish (Branson & Baker 1974). As a result their distribution is limited to areas where this common crustacean is abundant. Shallow creeks with flat stones that serve as a hiding place for crayfish are their preferred habitat. They are often found hiding beneath flat stones in creeks. They seem to be more common in areas with limestone substrates. Like other water snakes they may be seen basking from limbs and branches overhanging water.

Class—**Reptilia** (reptiles)		
Order—**Squamata** (snakes & lizards)		
Suborder—**Serpentes** (snakes)		
Family—**Natricidae** (harmless live-bearing snakes)		

Western (Orange-striped) Ribbon Snake *Thamnophis proximus*	**Eastern Ribbon Snake** *Thamnophis sauritus*	**Butler's Garter Snake** *Thamnophis butleri*

Size: 20 to 30 inches. Record 39 inches.

Abundance: Rare. Special concern species.

Breeding: Live bearing. Gives birth to between 10 and 20 young. Births usually occur in August.

Presumed range in Indiana

Habitat: Lives near semi-aquatic habitats, i.e. wet meadows, swamps, marshes, and edges of streams and lakes. Also brushy fields in sandy areas.

Variation: The color of the stripes can vary from greenish to bluish, yellow, or orange. In Indiana specimens the mid-dorsal stripe is invariably orange.

Natural History: There are 4 subspecies in the US but only *T. p. proximus*, the **Orange-striped Ribbon Snake** occurs in Indiana. Frogs, toads, fish and lizards are listed as some of this snake's prey. During certain times of the year tadpoles and the recently transformed young of frogs and toads are a primary food item. During periods of drought these snakes will gorge on small fishes trapped in drying pools. Insects and earthworms are also important in the diet. The range of the Western Ribbon Snake lies mostly west of the Mississippi River and this snake is found in Indiana primarily in the northwestern portion of the state. Ribbon Snakes are extremely elongated, slender-bodied snakes and they have exceptionally long tails, much longer than what is seen on the similar garter snakes.

Size: 18 to 28 inches. Record 38 inches.

Abundance: Uncommon.

Breeding: 10 to 20 young is typical. Birthing occurs in late summer following breeding in the early spring.

Presumed range in Indiana

Habitat: Occupies aquatic and semi-aquatic habitats from swamps and marshes to streams, stream edges and mesic bottomland woodlands.

Variation: A total of 3 subspecies are found in the eastern United States. Two subspecies range into Indiana (see Natural History section below).

Natural History: The **Northern Ribbon Snake** (subspecies *septentrionalis*) is found in Indiana in the northern portion of the state, while the **Common Ribbon Snake** (subspecies *sauritus*) ranges across much of southern Indiana. They are alert snakes that hunt by both smell and with their excellent eyesight that is attuned to quick movements of fleeing prey. They often climb into low bushes. Food items include insects, frogs, and minnows, crayfish and tadpoles. Although these snakes are nearly always found near water, they tend to live near the edges of wetlands rather than within them. In many ways the ribbon snakes occupy a niche that is halfway between an aquatic and a terrestrial species. Common Kingsnakes are one of their major predators, along with many other carnivorous vertebrates.

Size: 15 to 20 inches. Record 29 inches.

Abundance: Very rare in Indiana.

Breeding: Several males may attend a female in estrous. Young are born alive after as much as 4.5 months.

Presumed range in Indiana

Habitat: Shows a preference for moist or wet conditions. Often seen in the water. Haunts the edges of lakes and ranges throughout marsh and meadow.

Variation: The color of the light vertebral stripe may vary somewhat from yellowish to greenish yellow or orange. Young resemble adults.

Natural History: Butler's Garter Snake has a noticeably smaller head than Indiana's other two garter snake species. It is also an overall much smaller species than the other two. Butler's Garter Snake is an endemic to the Great Lakes region. In Indiana these snakes are native to the northeastern portion of the state where their original range probably once included nearly one-third of the state. Today they are a vanishing species that is regarded as endangered in Indiana. Their greatest threat is loss of habitat to urban development and agriculture. The remaining populations in the state are now fragmented and isolated, which is never a good situation for the continued survival of a species. Surprisingly some have been found in urban parks. The food of this snake is reported to be almost entirely earthworms.

Class—**Reptilia** (reptiles)

Order—**Squamata** (snakes & lizards)

Suborder—**Serpentes** (snakes)

Family—**Natricidae** (harmless live-bearing snakes)

Common Garter Snake *Thamnophis sirtalis*	**Plains Garter Snake** *Thamnophis radix*

Size: 2 to 3 feet. Record 54 inches.

Abundance: Very common. In many areas one of our most common snakes.

Breeding: Live-bearer that gives birth to enormous litters of up to 60 babies. Tiny babies are about 6 inches long with the girth of a matchstick.

Habitat: These snakes are habitat generalists. They occur in fields, woodlands, uplands and lowlands. They are most common in ecotone areas.

Size: Record 43 inches.

Abundance: Uncommon in Indiana.

Breeding: Live-born young can number over two dozen, but usually fewer.

Habitat: Prairies historically. Today uses vacant lots, fields, pastures and meadows,

Presumed range in Indiana

Variation: This species may exhibit significant variation. There are two basic pattern morphs, striped and checkered. The color of the longitudinal stripes may vary from cream to bright yellow or greenish yellow. In addition there are seven subspecies of this ubiquitous snake in the US with two subspecies occurring in Indiana. The **Eastern Garter Snake** (*T. s. sirtalis*) ranges across more than 90 percnet of the state but is replaced in the vicinity of Lake Michigan by the **Chicago Garter Snake** (*T. s. semifasciatus*). The differences between the two subspecies found in Indiana is very slight. In Chicago Garter Snakes the lateral stripe is interrupted on the neck by black bars, otherwise the two are very similar.

Presumed range in Indiana

Variation: Some experts recognize two subspecies, *T. r. radix*, the **Eastern Plains Garter Snake**, ranging from Indiana across Illinois and into eastern Iowa; and a western subspecies, *T. r. haydeni*, the **Plains Garter Snake**, found throughout the rest of the range in the Great Plains region. The differences between the two are very slight and today most experts consider them to be conspecific. Populations in the western plains of the US are thriving but some eastern populations have declined.

Natural History: Garter snakes are non-specialized feeders that will eat insects, earthworms, frogs, toads, salamanders, fish and rarely small mammals such as baby mice or voles. Their name is derived from their resemblance to the old fashioned "garters" that were used to hold up men's socks. The name has been widely familiarized to "Garden Snake" in many places. Still an appropriate name, as they are often seen in rural gardens. They are one of the most well-known snake species in America. Even people who are unfamiliar with snakes typically recognize the Garter Snake as a harmless and useful species. This is a ubiquitous snake species that may be found in both wilderness or urban regions. They are most common in successional areas and edge habitats. If captured these snakes will expel feces and vile smelling musk in an attempt to make themselves as unpalatable as possible to a potential predator. They may bite also, and larger snakes can break the skin causing small lacerations or punctures, but the overall effect of their bite is not a significant injury and there is little chance of infection from the bite.

Natural History: A prairie species whose range extends eastward from the Great Plains into historical prairie regions of Illinois and northern Indiana. Very widespread across the Great Plains region from Oklahoma to the prairie provinces of Canada. This species is well adapted to the cold environments of the northern plains and they are among northern Indiana's earliest snakes to emerge in the spring. Prey species are typical of the Garter Snake/Ribbon Snake clan (i.e. frogs, toads, insects, slugs and earthworms).

Class—**Reptilia** (reptiles)
Order—**Squamata** (snakes & lizards)
Suborder—**Serpentes** (snakes)
Family—**Xenodontidae** (large rear-fanged snakes)

Eastern Hognose Snake
Heterodon platirhinos

Playing dead

Spotted morph

Size: Averages about 2.5 feet. Maximum 45 inches.

Abundance: Generally uncommon in Indiana. It may be fairly common however in regions of dry, sandy, uplands.

Habitat: Hognose Snakes are most common in habitats with sandy soils which facilitate easy burrowing. They tend to be more common in sandy creek bottoms and river valleys or sandy upland prairies. But they can be found in upland woods and fields with less friable soils. The presence of healthy populations of toads may be the most important factor in determining the distribution and abundance of this species. Although they are widespread in Indiana they are only locally abundant and are absent from some areas of their range in the state.

Breeding: Hognose snake breed in early spring and lay up to two dozen eggs. Nests are probably in an underground chamber in sandy soil. Young snakes are about 8 inches in length and always have a spotted pattern. Babies are grayish brown with well defined dark gray or black blotches (see inset photo above).

Variation: Highly variable (see photos). Individuals range from solid black to uniform olive green. Others may be variously spotted or blotched with dark saddles on a yellowish or orange background. Often one color morph will be dominant in a given area. The young always exhibit a spotted pattern.

Natural History: The Eastern Hognose Snake is famous for the elaborate performance it puts on when threatened. First, they will spread the neck like a cobra (hence the nickname "Spreading Adder"), and with the mouth wide open they will strike repeatedly. They always intentionally miss with the strike and never bite even when picked up and handled. The initial "cobra display" is always accompanied by loud hissing. When their complicated bluff fails to deter the threat they will roll onto their backs, stick out their tongue and give a convincing impression of being dead. They do have one behavioral trait that betrays their antics however. If rolled onto their belly while they are feigning death they will immediately flip over onto their backs once again! Their primary food is frogs and toads. They possess enlarged teeth in the back of the upper jaw that are used to puncture the bodies of toads that have gulped air and inflated themselves in an attempt to become too large to be swallowed. The saliva of these snakes is mildly toxic, but is not considered to be a threat to humans. The food is almost entirely toads and frogs, making them one of the more specialized feeders among Indiana snakes. Salamanders are reported to have been found in the stomachs of a few individuals as well. Mice are also sometimes listed as prey items. Anecdotal evidence suggests they may be declining. Their habit of feeding on toads and frogs almost exclusively may make them vulnerable to insecticides, as frog and toads are primarily insect eaters and poisoning through secondary ingestion is a possibility.

Presumed range in Indiana

Class—**Reptilia** (reptiles)
Order—**Squamata** (snakes & lizards)
Suborder—**Serpentes** (snakes)
Family—**Crotalidae** (pit vipers)

Eastern Copperhead *Agkistrodon controtrix*	**Northern Cottonmouth** *Agkistrodon piscivorous*

Size: Average 2.5 to 3 feet. Record 58 inches. Males are larger than females and any over 3 feet are invariably males.

Presumed range in Indiana

Size: Average 3 to 4 feet. Record 50 inches.

Presumed range in Indiana

Abundance: Can be fairly common in suitable habitat, especially in rugged wooded uplands with rock outcroppings.

Abundance: Likely extirpated in Indiana.

Habitat: Copperheads are primarily woodland animals, but they do use overgrown fields and thickets where rodent prey is abundant. Edge areas and small woodland openings choked with briers, saplings, and weeds are prime habitat. They will inhabit both upland and lowland regions, but avoid permanently wet areas such as swamps and marshes. Steep, wooded bluffs with rock outcroppings adjoining overgrown fields are prime habitat.

Habitat: A highly aquatic species, the cottonmouth inhabits mostly swamps and marshes, but they can be found in creeks, lakes, or ponds.

Variation: Indiana specimens can be quite variable in color but always exhibit the same pattern of dark bands on a lighter background. The background color is some shade of brown, tan, orange or grayish with darker brown or gray-brown hourglass shaped crossbands across the back. The specimen above is fairly typical. Until recently their were five subspecies of copperheads in the US. Two subspecies occurred in the eastern US. The **Southern Copperhead** (subspecies *contortrix*) and **Northern Copperhead** (subspecies *mokasen*). Indiana snakes were considered to be the northern subspecies. In addition, there were 3 other subspecies found farther to the west. Today there are no more subspecies but instead two distinct species (**Eastern** and **Western Copperhead**). Thus all copperheads in Indiana are today regarded as **Eastern Copperheads.** Baby copperheads are identical to the adults but have a bright yellow tail tip that is wriggled to lure prey.

Variation: Adults vary from uniform brown to nearly black. Freshly molted specimens often show a pattern of dark bands on an olive or grayish background. Specimens from muddy waters may be stained brown or reddish by silt in the water. Shedding the skin reveals the true color. Young have a strongly banded pattern and resemble their cousin the Copperhead. Like the Copperhead young Cottonmouths have a bright yellow tail tip used to lure prey.

Breeding: Breeds in spring or in the fall. From 4 to 12 young are born in late August through September. The resources required to produce a litter by a live-bearing are considerable and can be quite stressful on the female. Thus many copperheads likely produce litters only every other year.

Breeding: Produces 3 to 12 babies in late August or early September. Unlike the copperhead, female cottonmouths may reproduce annually.

Natural History: Like most pit vipers copperheads are primarily nocturnal, especially during hotter months. In early spring and fall they may be seen abroad during the day. Young snakes eat some invertebrates and small vertebrates such as young frogs, lizards and small snakes. Larger snakes prey on small mammals (mice and voles), and the young of ground nesting birds. Insects are also taken, especially cicadas and during years when the Periodic Cicada emerges by the millions they will stuff themselves with these high protein, high fat insects. In areas of undisturbed habitat these can be common snakes but they are secretive and discreet. Because they are the most common venomous snake in the eastern US, they account for more snakebites than any other venomous snake. Fortunately, their venom is not highly toxic and deaths from copperhead bites are extremely rare.

Natural History: The name "Cottonmouth" is derived from the habit these snakes have of gaping open the mouth when threatened. The inside of the mouth is white, hence the name. Cottonmouths attain a large size and have powerful venom that is capable of killing a human. Frogs, fish, salamanders and small mammals are the main prey. These snakes were always rare in Indiana and apparently no longer occur.

Class—**Reptilia** (reptiles)
Order—**Squamata** (snakes & lizards)
Suborder—**Serpentes** (snakes)
Family—**Crotalidae** (pit vipers)

Timber Rattlesnake *Crotalus horridus*	**Eastern Massassauga** *Sistrurus catenatus*

Size: Average about 4 feet. Record length 6 feet 2 inches. Few Indiana specimens will exceed 5 feet.

Abundance: Uncommon to rare in Indiana. Regarded as a Endangered Species by Indiana Department of Natural Resources.

Variation: Timber Rattlesnakes can be highly variable. Yellow and brown "light morphs," along with very dark (nearly black) morphs occur in some regions of their range in the Appalachians. A southern form from the coastal plain of the southern United States was once regarded as a distinct subspecies known as the "Canebrake" Rattlesnake. Indiana specimens will usually resemble the photos above.

Presumed range in Indiana

Habitat: As their name implies Timber Rattlesnakes are forest animals. Within their woodland habitats they are most common in upland areas with rocky outcrops and talus slopes. They inhabit both mature forests and second growth woodlands, as well as forest edges. In some areas they may occur in bottomland woods as well, but usually only when the lowland areas are in proximity to ridges and uplands.

Breeding: Timber Rattlesnakes typically breed in August and the females delay implantation of embryos until the following spring. The young snakes are then born in late summer or early fall, about a year after breeding. Females will produce young only every other year. Average litter is 6 to 12.

Natural History: This is one of the largest rattlesnake species in America and their bite is quite capable of killing a human. Fortunately they are peace loving animals that only strike as a last resort. Timber Rattlesnake populations are declining in many areas of their range, including in Indiana and they are now regarded as an Endangered Species in the state of Indiana. Though they are still present in healthy numbers in some areas of the Appalachians and the southern United States, they are less numerous than in earlier times and are now rare or extirpated from much of their former range. Today they are absent from many areas of their former range in Indiana. As a result, the Indiana Department of Natural Resources now protects them against exploitation and wanton slaughter. These large snakes feed mostly on mammals, with squirrels and chipmunks being a favorite food. They are known to lie in ambush beside fallen logs that are frequently traveled by ground foraging chipmunks and squirrels. Almost any type of small mammal can be food and many types of mice and voles are eaten. Nestlings of ground dwelling birds can also be prey. Mice are probably the main food for the young and even a newborn Timber Rattlesnake is large enough to swallow a young mouse. This can be a dangerously venomous snake, but the threat they pose to the average outdoorsman is negligible.

Size: Record 39.5 inches.

Abundance: Very rare in Indiana.

Variation: Varies from very dark (nearly black) to light, smoky gray. In some regions ground color may be brownish, tan, or reddish.

Presumed range in Indiana

Habitat: Wetlands primarily. Inhabits swamps, marshes, wooded floodplains. Historically probably ranged across much of glaciated Indiana but has been extirpated from most areas in the state.

Breeding: Young are born in late July, August or September. 5 or 6 babies is common but can be as many as 14. Babies are 8 to 10 inches in length.

Natural History: The name Massasauga comes from the Chippewa Indian name for a marshy area at the mouth of a river. Which is one of this snake's primary natural habitats. During summer months they may leave the sanctity of the swamp or marsh and venture into nearby fields or uplands. Food items include rodents, amphibians, birds, crayfish and insects. In some regions they are known to hibernate in crayfish burrows. Today this is one of the rarest rattlesnakes in America and their remaining populations are highly fragmented and isolated from one another. They are regarded as an Endangered Species in Indiana.

CHAPTER 7

THE AMPHIBIANS OF INDIANA

TABLE 5

—THE ORDERS AND FAMILIES OF INDIANA AMPHIBIANS —

Class—**Amphibia** (amphibians)

Order—**Anura** (frogs & toads)

Family	**Ranidae** (true frogs)
Family	**Hylidae** (treefrogs)
Family	**Bufonidae** (true toads)
Family	**Scaphiopodidae** (spadefoots)

Order—**Caudata** (salamanders)

Family	**Ambystomatidae** (mole salamanders)
Family	**Plethodontidae** (lungless salamanders)
Family	**Salamandridae** (newts)
Family	**Proteida** (mudpuppies)
Family	**Sirenidae** (sirens)
Family	**Cryptobranchidae** (hellbenders)

THE AMPHIBIANS
OF INDIANA

PART 1: FROGS & TOADS

Class—**Amphibia** (amphibians)

Order—**Anura** (frogs & toads)

Family—**Ranidae** (true frogs)

Bullfrog *Lithobates catesbeianus*	**Green Frog** *Lithobates clamitans*

Green morph — Brown morph

Size: Record 8 inches (snout to vent length). Averages 4 to 5 inches.

Abundance: Very common. Has declined somewhat in areas of intensive row crop agriculture, possibly due to the draining of the many small farm stock ponds that once dotted the landscape across much of rural Indiana.

Variation: Dorsal color varies from green to brown. Ventral color varies from nearly white with grayish mottling to pale gray with heavy, charcoal gray mottling. Breeding males have a bright yellow throat. Males also have a larger tympanum (ear membrane) than females and grow to a larger size.

Presumed range in Indiana

Size: Record 4.5 inches (snout to vent).

Abundance: Very common. Perhaps the most common frog in Indiana.

Variation: No variation in Indiana. Formally two subspecies recognized (see below).

Presumed range in Indiana

Habitat: Found in virtually every aquatic habitat type within the state, from small ponds and large lakes to streams. Also common in wetlands such as marsh and swamp.

Habitat: Found virtually every aquatic habitat in Indiana, including ephemeral pools.

Breeding: Breeding and egg laying occurs from late spring through mid-summer. Several thousand eggs (as many as 10,000) can be laid and two clutches per year is not uncommon. The eggs are encased in a mass of a clear jelly-like substance. Always breeds in permanent water since tadpole development is very prolonged. Tadpole metamorphosis in the Bullfrog does not occur until the following summer or in northern populations metamorphosis may not occur until the third year.

Breeding: Breeds May to August. As with other frogs, eggs are fertilized externally by the male who clasps onto the female's back and deposits sperm onto the eggs as they are extruded by the female. Lays up to 4,000 eggs.

Natural History: These are the largest frogs in Indiana (and in fact in the US). Their hind legs are considered to be a delicacy by many. They are regarded as a game animal and are hunted for food during the annual "frog season." In some places they are raised commercially for food and for research or teaching laboratories. They may venture far from water and will travel from pond to pond during rainy weather. The ability to traverse long distances on rainy nights allows them to colonize newly constructed ponds and lakes. Insects are important food items for young frogs and are also eaten by adults. Crayfish are another important food item. The list of animals known to be consumed by these voracious predators includes almost any animal small enough to be swallowed, including other frogs. There is even a record of a large Bullfrog eating a baby rattlesnake! The original range of the Bullfrog was the eastern half of America. But they have been widely introduced across the continent and even into many foreign countries. Introduced populations of Bullfrogs have become a threat to other frog species in some areas, especially in the desert southwest where small pockets of wetland habitats can be over run by Bullfrogs. The original frog residents are often endemic species with limited distributions. The much smaller native frogs become food for the larger Bullfrog and are rapidly decimated. The bellowing call of the Bullfrog will carry for long distances and is a familiar nocturnal sound in summer in rural regions of Indiana.

Natural History: A drive through a wetland on a rainy night in late summer when the tadpoles of *Rana clamitans* are emerging onto land will reveal astounding numbers of small frogs crossing the roadway as they disperse into new territories. Adult frogs feed on insects primarily but other arthropods including small crayfish are frequently eaten. Minnows and other small aquatic vertebrates are also potential prey. These frogs are easily confused with the much larger Bullfrog, but are distinguished by the presence of a fold of skin (known as a dorso-lateral fold) that runs along each side of the back. A southern form with a bronze snout was once regarded as a subspecies known as the "Bronze Frog." Today they are considered conspecific.

Class—**Amphibia** (amphibians)
Order—**Anura** (frogs & toads)
Family—**Ranidae** (true frogs)

Wood Frog *Lithobates sylvatica*	Northern Leopard Frog *Lithobates pipiens*	Southern Leopard Frog *Lithobates sphenocephalus*

Size: About 3 inches. Record 3.25 inches.	Presumed range in Indiana	**Size:** 3 to 4 inches. Record 4.375 inches.	Presumed range in Indiana	**Size:** Average 3 inches. Record 5 inches.	Presumed range in Indiana
Abundance: Fairly common.		**Abundance:** Fairly common.		**Abundance:** Common.	
Variation: There is single, wide ranging species of Wood Frog found across the entire northern half of the continent. Varies from light tan to dark brown.		**Variation:** The color of the skin between the dark spots varies from greenish to brown or tan. Always has a spot on the snout. No subspecies.		**Variation:** Individuals dorsal colors vary from bright green to light tan. Very similar to the preceding species but without a spot on the snout.	

Habitat: This is a forest species that is most common in forested areas. It prefers mesic woods near streams. Also rocky hillsides and bottomlands.	**Habitat:** Wet meadows, vegetated fields, wetlands, and stream edges. This species will wander extensively into grassy fields in bottomlands.	**Habitat:** Found in virtually all aquatic habitats within its range. Like the Northern Leopard Frog they often wander in to grassy fields far from water.
Breeding: Breeds in winter. This is one of the earliest breeding frogs and they may breed as early as February in southern IN. Eggs are laid in ephemeral pools and small fishless bodies of water.	**Breeding:** Breeding occurs in the early spring in ponds, marshes and swamps. Females will lay 2 to 5 thousand eggs. Tadpoles grow from less than an inch to nearly 4 inches before transforming.	**Breeding:** Breeds mostly in April and May. Breeding localities are ponds, ditches, marshes, and swamps. Lays up to 5,000 eggs in several clumps. Young frogs emerge in mid-summer.
Natural History: Despite the fact that this is the most widespread frog species in America, there is but a single species that shows little variation. Wood frogs from Canada and Alaska are identical to those found northern Alabama or northern Georgia. This is the most cold tolerant frog species in Indiana and it ranges farther to the north than any of its kin. They can be frozen solid and recover without harm when thawed. Food is a variety of small invertebrates. Like many frogs, Wood Frogs migrate overland during periods of heavy rainfall. They can be commonly seen on roadways at night during the breeding season. They sometimes shift habitat seasonally and may move into drier upland areas in the fall.	**Natural History:** Insects and spiders are the mainstay of this frog's diet. It is not uncommon for these frogs to be seen far from water during the summer months. But they return to ponds and wetlands in the late fall to hibernate in the mud underwater. These are familiar animals to anyone who has dissected frogs in a biology class. For several years their numbers in the wild experienced an unexplained decline. In many regions specimens were being found with deformities to limbs. Some possible causes include chemical pollutants, acid rain, a pathogenic fungus that attacks frogs, or a combination of these and other, as yet unknown, factors. In Indiana there is evidence this decline has begun to reverse.	**Natural History:** Leopard frogs are frequently found some distance from permanent water sources in meadows and overgrown fields. They can even be seen in rural lawns on occasion, especially in late summer. Southern Leopard Frogs can be told from their northern cousin by the lack of a dark spot on the snout. They are easily discerned from the Pickerel Frog by their round rather than squarish spots; while the Northern Crayfish Frog is much stouter with a more rounded snout. In the Plains Leopard Frog the dorso-lateral fold is interrupted at the groin. Wide variety of insects, spiders and other invertebrates are eaten. Like most frogs, they spend the winter in the mud at the bottom of a pond, creek, or other permanent water.

Class—**Amphibia** (amphibians)

Order—**Anura** (frogs & toads)

Family—**Ranidae** (true frogs)

Plains Leopard Frog *Lithobates blairi*	**Pickerel Frog** *Lithobates palustris*	**Crayfish Frog** *Lithobates areolatus*

Plains Leopard Frog		Pickerel Frog		Crayfish Frog	
Size: To 3.75 inches. Record 4.375 inches.	Presumed range in Indiana 	**Size:** Average about 3 inches.	Presumed range in Indiana 	**Size:** Average 3 to 4 in. Record 4.5 inches.	Presumed historical range in Indiana 
Abundance: Very rare in Indiana.		**Abundance:** Uncommon.		**Abundance:** Rare in Indiana.	
Variation: Ground color (skin color between the spots) varies from tan to brown or greenish. There are no subspecies.		**Variation:** Ground color (skin color between the spots) varies from tan to brown. There are no subspecies of this frog.		**Variation:** There are two subspecies, but only *L. a. areolatus*, the **Northern Crayfish Frog**, occurs in Indiana.	

Habitat: Mainly a prairie species. In Indiana occupies lowlands, river valleys, and remnant prairie near water.	**Habitat:** Prefers spring-fed streams and clear, cool waters in woodland areas. May also occur in fields near streams.	**Habitat:** Floodplains, bottomland fields, and other low-lying areas with mesic substrates supporting crayfish.
Breeding: Breeding is in March and April. Lays up to 6,500 eggs. Tadpoles transform into froglets by mid to late summer.	**Breeding:** Breeds in ponds, ditches or permanent streams. Lays 2,000 to 4,000 eggs. Tadpoles transform in about three months.	**Breeding:** An early breeder. Most breeding apparently occurs during periods of heavy rainfall in March. Up to 7,000 eggs may be laid.
Natural History: The bulk of this frog's range is far to the west and north in the Great Plains region. There it can be a common species. It was perhaps once more common in Indiana before the state's prairies went under the plow. Loss of many small ponds that once dotted the landscape in the days of subsistence farming has also probably impacted this and other frog species. Todays large crop fields can be deserted of wildlife, especially amphibians. In places it shares its range with the more common Southern Leopard Frog and hybrids between the two species are known. Food is mostly insects and other invertebrates. In Kansas this species has been reported to sometimes emerge from hibernation during warm spells in mid-winter. This frog's range in Indiana coincides with the region of the state that historically was prairie.	**Natural History:** Pickerel Frogs are distinguished from Leopard Frogs by their square rather than round spots. These frogs secrete a toxin from the skin that protects them from many predators and is strong enough to kill other frogs kept with them in a small container. Among the predators that are able to eat them however is another frog species, the Bullfrog. Pickerel Frogs show a preference for clean water and an intolerance for pollution. In this respect the Pickerel Frog may be an indicator species that can provide an early warning regarding environmental threats like water pollution. Sadly for those who appreciate nature, populations of this frog, (and in fact frogs in general) may be declining in the state. In Indiana pickeral frogs are most common in regions with limestone substrates and karst topography.	**Natural History:** This frog's name is derived from their habit of utilizing crayfish burrows as a home. They are quite secretive and are rarely observed except during the breeding season when they will travel overland in search of suitable breeding ponds or pools in wetland areas. Crayfish, other amphibians, small reptiles, and of course insects are food items. This frog is a species in sharp decline. Modern agricultural practices such as tiling of wetland meadows to remove water and thus enable row cropping, along with the filling of small isolated ponds is possibly the cause of this decline. Remaining populations appear to be fragmented and isolated from each other, which is never a good thing for the survival of a species. The range map above indicates the presumed historical range. It is today absent from much of this area.

Class—**Amphibia** (amphibians)

Order—**Anura** (frogs & toads)

Family—**Hylidae** (treefrogs)

Blanchard's Cricket Frog *Acris blanchardi*	**Spring Peeper** *Pseudacris crucifer*	**Midland/Boreal Chorus Frogs** *Pseudacris triseriata/Pseudacris maculat*
		 Midland Chorus Frog / Boreal Chorus Frog

Size: Tiny, usually less than 1 inch.	Presumed range in Indiana 	**Size:** About 1 inch. Record 1.5 inches.	Presumed range in Indiana 	**Size:** 0.75 to 1.25 inches. Average about 1 inch.	Presumed range in Indiana  Boreal Chorus Frog / Upland Chorus Frog
Abundance: Very common to uncommon.		**Abundance:** Common, especially in wetlands.		**Abundance:** Very common.	
Variation: Varies from brown to reddish brown or tan. May also be green. Many will have markings on the back that may be greenish or brownish.		**Variation:** Ground color varies. Usually tan or brown. Sometimes grayish or reddish. Always has a darker "X" shaped marking on the back.		**Variation:** Two nearly identical species occur in Indiana. The best way to distinguish between the two in Indiana is to refer to the range map.	

Habitat: Shorelines of ponds, along creeks, temporary pools, marshes, swamps, wet meadows and uplands.	**Habitat:** Woodlands and thickets, usually near water. Most common in lowlands (swamps, marshes, etc).	**Habitat:** Low wet fields, bottomland woods, swamps, marshes, ponds or bogs. May use temporary pools.
Breeding: Breeds from spring through late summer. Up to 400 eggs are laid in small clusters of 10 to 15 per cluster. Tadpoles and froglets are tiny.	**Breeding:** Spring Peepers begin breeding activity as early as late winter and continue into early spring. Several hundred eggs are laid in shallow water.	**Breeding:** Very early breeders that may begin breeding as early as February. Breeding is in ephemeral pools in flooded fields, roadside ditches, etc.
Natural History: These tiny frogs are most commonly seen along the receding shorelines of ponds and lakes in late summer or early fall. When startled by a passing human they will often jump into the water and then immediately swim back to shore. This may be an "out of the frying pan into the fire" behavior intended to keep them from the jaws of hungry fish. They are often seen far from water in fields and woodlands, but are always more common in wetland habitats and permanently damp areas. Their name comes from their call which resembles that of a cricket, but is more accurately described as sounding like two small stones being rapidly clicked together. This is one of the most common frog species in southern Indiana, but they have become less common in northern Indiana.	**Natural History:** Another diminutive frog that is heard more often than seen. The name comes from the sound made when breeding frogs are calling. The call is a rapidly repeated "peep, peep, peep." Despite being members of the treefrog family they live mostly on the ground. The species name "crucifer" is Latin for "cross bearer" and refers to the x-shaped mark that is always present on this frog's back. These little frogs, along with their cousins the Chorus Frogs, are a true harbinger of spring throughout much of the eastern United States. They may breed in the same flooded field pools with Chorus Frogs or even in the same pool. They are widely distributed throughout the Eastern Temperate Forest Level I Ecoregion and probably occur in every county in Indiana where suitable habitat still exists.	**Natural History:** Breeding may be interrupted several times by cold snaps and freezing weather. The name comes from their "chorus" of breeding calls that carries over quite a long distance. Standing water in flooded bottomlands and shallow, water-filled depressions in croplands are favorite breeding sites for this frog. Though amazingly common during the brief breeding season, most of the rest of the year they seem to disappear. There are several different species of Chorus Frogs in America. Two nearly identical species range into Indiana and their collective ranges include the entire state. The distinction as different species is questioned by some experts who regard them as a single species with different subspecies. The species designation is supported by DNA analysis, but is controversial.

Class—**Amphibia** (amphibians)
Order—**Anura** (frogs & toads)
Family—**Hylidae** (treefrogs)

Gray Treefrog complex	**Green Treefrog**
Hyla chrysoscelis & Hyla versicolor	*Hyla cinerea*

Gray phases

Green phase

Size: Averages about 2 inches. Maximum of just under 2.5 inches.

Presumed range in Indiana

Abundance: Fairly common to common.

Variation: There are actually two identical species in the Gray Treefrog complex. They can only be reliably differentiated by the sound of their call or by laboratory examination of the number of cell chromosomes. The two species are known as the Cope's Gray Treefrog (*Hyla chrysoscelis*), and the Gray Treefrog (*Hyla versicolor*). Both species have the ability to change color from gray to green. Additionally, the shade of gray can range from a dark sooty gray to a light smoky gray (see photos above).

Habitat: Habitat is chiefly woodlands. These treefrogs are more adapted to dry uplands than most members of their genus and they can be found far from water in dry upland woods.

Breeding: Breeds from late spring through summer in small bodies of water ranging from small ponds to roadside ditches. Rapid tadpole development means they can breed successfully in ephemeral pools. Up to 2,000 eggs are laid. Where their ranges overlap interbreeding is probably prohibited by their different calls.

Natural History: These highly arboreal treefrogs are rarely seen on the ground and they often climb high into treetops to forage for insects. They are mainly nocturnal but they may be active by day on cloudy or rainy days or in cooler weather. They shelter by day in small hollows in tree trunks or limbs and have been known to take up residence in small bird nest boxes such as a wren box or bluebird box. They will also live in the rain gutters of house roofs. They can sometimes be seen sitting in the opening of their hiding place with the head and front feet exposed. They possess remarkable camouflage abilities and the gray, lichen-like pattern of their skin will perfectly match the bark of the tree they occupy. They can produce a natural anti-freeze in the blood which allows them to hibernate in tree hollows above the ground, or in leaf litter on the forest floor. Most members of the genus *Hyla* are southern animals, but these frogs range far into the northern states and even into parts of southern Canada. Food items are small insects and arthropods. Differentiating between these two species is very difficult. Those with a "good ear" can tell the difference between their calls. Other researchers must resort to a laboratory analysis of chromosomes. Cope's Gray Treefrog has the typical diploid set of chromosomes (2 chromosomes) while the Gray Treefrog is tetraploid (4 chromosomes) in its chromosome count. In Indiana the Cope's Gray Treefrog is found mostly in the northern half of the state while the Gray Treefrog occupies the southern half. There appears to be some overlap in the range in the middle part of the state. Toxic secretions can cause a burning sensation to sensitive skin if they are handled.

Size: Record 2.5 inches.

Presumed range in Indiana

Abundance: Rare.

Variation: Varies in the amount of yellow spots on the back. May have several or none at all. In cold weather color will turn to dark brown.

Habitat: Green Treefrogs are lowland animals that are found in swamps and marshes mostly.

Breeding: Breeds in early to mid-summer. Lays up to 1,500 eggs in shallow waters of swamps or marshes. Multiple clutches may be produced in a summer.

Natural History: Similar to green phase of the Gray Treefrog, but has smooth skin and usually a yellow stripe on the side. One of this frog's favorite daytime perches are the stems of cattails and sedges where its deep green color renders it almost invisible. Its primary prey consists of caterpillars, spiders, grasshoppers, and other insects. Green Treefrogs are primarily nocturnal in habits but they are sometimes seen during the day, especially during rainy weather. As with most other treefrogs of the genus *Hyla* this is a mainly southern species. It appears this species has recently extended its range northward into southwestern Indiana into the lowlands of the lower Ohio and lower Wabash River valleys. Some speculate that it may be moving northward in response to a warming climate.

Class—**Amphibia** (amphibians)

Order—**Anura** (frogs & toads)

Family—**Bufonidae** (toads)		Family—**Scaphiopodidae** (spadefoots)

American Toad
Anaxyrus americanus

Dwarf American Toad

Fowler's Toad
Anaxyrus fowleri

Eastern Spadefoot
Scaphiopus holbrookii

Size: To 6.125 inches.

Abundance: Common.

Habitat: Uses a wide variety of habitats from woodlands and fields to urban lawns and gardens.

Variation: There are two subspecies and both occur in Indiana.

Presumed range in Indiana

American Toad

Dwarf American Toad

Size: To 3.75 inches.

Abundance: Common.

Habitat: Uses a wide variety of habitats from woodlands and fields to urban lawns and gardens.

Variation: Variable. Dark brown, reddish brown, tan, or grayish.

Presumed range in Indiana

Size: 2 to 3 inches.

Abundance: Uncommon in Indiana.

Habitat: The main habitat requirement is loose, sandy soil that facilitates easy burrowing.

Variation: Color varies from brown or olive to gray or black.

Presumed range in Indiana

Breeding: Breeds as early as March. Eggs are laid in long strings of clear gelatinous material. Breeds in small ponds, water filled ditches, or temporary pools in seasonally flooded lowlands.

Breeding: Breeding is in May in shallow ponds, flooded ditches, creeks, inundated fields (including crop fields), creeks, etc. From 5,000 to 10,000 eggs are laid.

Breeding: Breeds explosively during periods of heavy rainfall from late spring throughout the summer. Up to 5,000 eggs hatch within a few days. Spadefoot tadpoles transform rapidly.

Natural History: American Toads eat a wide variety of insects and other small arthropods. They are adept burrowers and like other toads possess hardened spade-like structures on the hind feet that are used for digging. These toads can be told from the similar and sympatrically occurring Fowler's Toad by their larger warts and the fact that the dark spots on the back never have more than two warts per spot. The similar Fowler's Toad may have up to six warts per dark spot. Although they are sometimes active by day, these toads are primarily nocturnal in habits. When attacked by a predator they will inflate their bodies by gulping air. This tactic may work if the predator is an animal like a snake that must swallow its food whole. A small subspecies (*charlesmithi*), the **Dwarf American Toad**, replaces the American Toad in southern Indiana (see map above).

Natural History: The natural history of the Fowler's Toad is similar to that of the American Toad. Fowler's Toads breed later in the spring and young toadlets do not emerge from the tadpole stage until late summer. Like many toads (and many treefrogs) the Fowler's Toad secretes a toxic substance from the skin when threatened. While this toxin can cause irritation to sensitive areas and membranes, the old wives tale that toads cause warts is a fallacy. Food is insects and other small invertebrates and toads are recognized by many for the valuable role they play in controlling destructive insect pests around the yard and in the garden. Savvy gardeners encourage toads by placing shallow water dishes in the garden. Many predators avoid toads due to their toxic secretions. The common Eastern Garter Snake along with the Eastern Hognose Snake are two of the major predators of toads.

Natural History: The name "Spadefoot" come from a sickle-shaped horny structure on the hind feet that is used for digging into the ground. They spend much of their lives in burrows only a few inches deep and emerge only on rainy nights. During dry weather they may spend weeks in the burrow without feeding. They secrete a toxic substance which is highly irritant to mucus membranes, thus making these anurans unpalatable to many potential predators. Touching the face or other sensitive skin after handling a Spadefoot will result in an uncomfortable burning sensation. Although widespread and quite common farther to the south, in Indiana the Spadefoot is sporadically distributed and may be absent from some areas shown on the range map above. Spadefoots are known for the rapid transition of tadpoles into baby spadefoots. Metamorphosis can occur in two weeks.

THE AMPHIBIANS
OF INDIANA

PART 2: SALAMANDERS

Class—**Amphibia** (amphibians)

Order—**Caudata** (salamanders)

Family—**Ambystomatidae** (mole salamanders)

Tiger Salamander *Ambystoma tigrinum*	**Spotted Salamander** *Ambystoma maculatum*	**Streamside Salamander** *Ambystoma barbouri*

Tiger Salamander

Size: Average about 8 inches. Maximum 14.

Abundance: Fairly common.

Variation: Light markings can appear as irregular spots, blotches, or stripes. The color of light pigments may be yellow, orange, or greenish.

Presumed range in Indiana

Habitat: Woodlands and fields, in both upland an lowland areas. Apparently absent from mountainous regions or areas of extremely hilly terrain.

Breeding: Breeds in small bodies of water like stock ponds, vernal pools and "borrow pits." Breeding occurs in mid-winter a few hundred to several thousand eggs produced by the female. Males meet females in breeding ponds and fertilize the eggs as they are laid. Eggs are encased in a ball of jelly-like material and hatch in about a month.

Natural History: The large size of the Tiger Salamander allows it to feed on much larger prey than most salamander species. Although invertebrates such as earthworms and insect larva are the major foods, small vertebrates may also eaten and captive specimens will eat baby mice. Despite their large size, Tiger Salamanders are rarely seen except during the late winter breeding season when they make their nocturnal overland treks to breeding ponds. At this time they can sometimes be seen on rural roadways on stormy, rain soaked nights.

Spotted Salamander

Size: Average 6 inches. Maximum 9 inches.

Abundance: Common where found in Indiana.

Variation: The spots on the Spotted Salamander may be yellow or orange. The number of spots varies widely. On rare individuals spots may be absent.

Presumed range in Indiana

Habitat: Primarily woodland areas, but also found in overgrown fields and edges bordering agricultural lands. Found in both lowland and upland habitats.

Breeding: Breeds during periods of heavy rainfall in late winter. Eggs are deposited in large gelatinous masses in ponds or wetland pools. Larva transform in two to four months. Like all other amphibians, eggs are fertilized externally. The males clasp onto the female and release sperm onto the eggs as they are lain, rather like a fish.

Natural History: Primarily subterranean in habits. Lives in underground burrows and beneath rocks, logs, or leaf litter on the forest floor. During periods of hot dry weather retreats deeper underground or stays in the vicinity perennially wet areas. Feeds on a wide variety of insects and invertebrates as well as a few small vertebrates. This is one of the most common members of the "mole salamander" group. In the late winter breeding season they are easily observed on rural roads at night during rainy weather, as they make the migration to breeding ponds.

Streamside Salamander

Size: Average 4 to 5 inches. Max 6.5 inches.

Abundance: Common within range.

Variation: Varies in color from uniform dark gray to light or blue gray. Amount of silver or whitish flecking also varies and may be absent.

Presumed range in Indiana

Habitat: Found mostly in upland woods within close proximity to streams. Occurs less commonly in forested creek bottoms and river valleys.

Breeding: Breeds in limestone bottomed streams in late fall to early winter. This is the only *Ambystoma* salamander that breeds strictly in streams. It also lays fewer eggs than others and its eggs are deposited singly rather than in large clumps. Eggs are attached to the underneath side of a flat rock, typically in a limestone stream.

Natural History: In most respects other than breeding habits the natural history of the Streamside Salamander is similar to that of the very similar looking Smallmouth Salamander. The two species are very difficult to distinguish based on appearance alone and until a few decades ago they were regarded as being members of the same species. The two are best differentiated by range. Soft bodied invertebrates are probably the main food item for the adults and the larva are known to eat small crustaceans (isopods, etc.) as well as worms and other benthic organisms.

Class—**Amphibia** (amphibians)

Order—**Caudata** (salamanders)

Family—**Ambystomatidae** (mole salamanders)

Small-mouthed Salamander *Ambystoma texanum*	**Blue-spotted Salamander** *Ambystoma laterale*	**Jefferson Salamander** *Ambystoma jeffersonianum*

Size: 4 to 5 inches as an adult.

Presumed range in Indiana

Abundance: Fairly common.

Variation: Varies in color from uniform dark gray to blue-gray with varying amounts of silver or light gray flecking Some have no light flecking at all.

Habitat: Found in a variety of habitats from woodlands to grassy meadows. Most common in lowlands and stream bottoms but also in upland areas.

Breeding: Breeds in late winter or very early spring. May lay up to several hundred eggs in large clumps. Ponds, wetland pools or flooded roadside ditches may be used for egg deposition. Larva transform into adults in about 6 to 8 weeks, sooner in warmer weather.

Natural History: Like other members of its genus the Smallmouth Salamander spends most of its time in underground burrows or beneath rocks, logs, or leaf litter. They will emerge on rainy nights to forage above ground. Feeds on a wide variety of soft-bodied invertebrate prey such as earthworms, slugs, and grubs. The Smallmouth Salamander is very similar in appearance to the Streamside Salamander and the best clue to identification of the two species is to refer to their respective range maps. Morphologically this species is indistinguishable from the Streamside Salamander. They differ in reproductive biology and DNA.

Size: 4 to 5 inches average. Record 6.25.

Presumed range in Indiana

Abundance: Fairly common within range.

Variation: Considerable variation in the amount of blue spotting present. Hybrid "unisexual" forms can be confusingly similar (see below).

Habitat: Another forest species. May also be found in wet meadows and swamps. Favors areas with loamy soils. Often in the vicinity of water.

Breeding: Breeds in early spring. Courtship activity involves the male grasping the female from above and rubbing the nose across her body. The male then deposits sperm packets which are picked up by the female's cloaca. Hybridizes with other *Ambystoma*.

Natural History: Hybridization with the Jefferson's Salamander regularly occurs. All hybrids have triploid chromosomes and all are females, hence the term "Unisexual Salamander." Hybrids were once regarded as distinct species. Those with more chromosomes from the Blue-spotted were known as "Tremblay's Salamander." Hybrid individuals with more chromosomes from the Jefferon's were called "Silvery Salamander." Food is small insects and other invertebrates such as worms, sow bugs, snails, spiders, etc. The Blue-spotted is a boreal salamander that ranges well to the north in eastern Canada. It is the most northerly ranging of the *Ambystoma*.

Size: Up to 8 inches. Average 4.5 inches.

Presumed range in Indiana

Abundance: Fairly common.

Variation: There is some variation in the amount of light blue specks on the sides. Older adults tend to lose their specks and become darker.

Habitat: An upland forest species mostly. They may also occur in bottomland forests that adjoin or are nearby to wooded uplands.

Breeding: Breeding occurs in late winter or early spring, with eggs being deposited in woodland ponds. As with all *Ambystoma* salamanders, the eggs hatch into larva that spend up to a year as thoroughly aquatic, gilled salamanders before transforming into adults.

Natural History: Like all terrestrial salamanders in Indiana, this is mainly a fossorial species. They will surface at night or on rainy, heavily overcast days with dim light and forage on the forest floor. They regularly hybridize with the Blue-spotted Salamander in regions where their ranges overlap. Hybrids have tripoid chromosomes are always females. These hybrids are known as "Unisexual Salamanders." Many of the drab-colored salamanders in central Indiana are these "Unisexual" salamanders. Smallmouthed and Streamside Salamanders also are similar and identification is difficult in many areas of Indiana where these species overlap.

Class—**Amphibia** (amphibians)

Order—**Caudata** (salamanders)

Family—**Ambystomatidae** (mole salamanders)

Mole Salamander *Ambystoma talpoideum*	**Marbled Salamander** *Ambystoma opacum*	

Marbled Salamander Male

Marbled Salamander Female

Size: Adult to 4 inches. Record nearly 5 inches.

Presumed range in Indiana

Size: 3 to 4 inches. Record 5.25 inches.

Presumed range in Indiana

Abundance: Rare in Indiana.

Abundance: Fairly common.

Variation: Some are uniformly dark gray. Others have a significant amount of light gray flecking on the sides.

Variation: Sexually dimorphic. Light colors are grayish or silver in the female and whiter in the male. Females are a bit larger.

Unisexual Salamanders
Ambystoma species (no photo)

Size: Maximum size probably 8 inches.

Presumed range in Indiana

Abundance: Fairly common in Indiana.

Variation: Varies depending upon hybridization selection. Often shows intermediate characters of two or more parent species.

Habitat: Swamps, marshes and bottomland woods prone to seasonal flooding. Less commonly in upland woods.

Habitat: Most fond of bottomlands (especially during breeding) but also common in upland woods.

Breeding: Breeding occurs in late fall or early winter and overland treks to breeding areas are made. Eggs are laid in the waters of swamps and marshes. After a few months the gill breathing larva develop into air breathing adults.

Breeding: Breeds in the fall during rainy weather. Overland migration is common. Eggs are laid on land under rocks, logs, etc. in low lying areas subject to flooding. Hatching is delayed until eggs are flooded by fall rains.

Breeding: The all female Unisexual Salamanders can reproduce parthenogenically or breed with males of up to four other species, producing an array of morphological characters. Eggs are laid in temporary forested wetlands.

Natural History: This decidedly fossorial salamander is the namesake of the "mole salamander" family. This species is rarely seen above ground except during the breeding season when they will emerge on rainy nights and travel to areas of breeding congregations. They can sometimes be turned up beneath logs or other objects in low, perennially moist areas. These salamanders have a stout bodied appearance and a large head which distinguishes them from the similarly colored Small-mouthed Salamander and Streamside Salamander. When captured they will sometimes assume a defensive posture that consists of raising the body off the ground while lowering the head. In Indiana this species is only found in Posey County.

Natural History: This is one of the few salamanders to exhibit sexual dimorphism. The light markings are wider and whiter on the male and narrower and more silver or grayish on the female. Like other members of the "mole salamander" family, Marbled Salamanders are fossorial in habits. In fact, this species may be even more secretive than many of its kin. Thus, though they are fairly common they are not readily observed. They can reportedly produce a noxious secretion from the tail which may help to ward off some predators. Adults probably feed on most any small animal they can swallow, mostly invertebrates. Larva have been known to eat the eggs of small frogs and have also been known to be cannibalistic.

Natural History: The Unisexual Salamanders of the Great Lakes states have thrown a curve ball to herpetologists who study amphibians. This population of salamanders are all female and have arisen from the hybridization of several species of *Ambystoma* salamanders. Among the species known to be contributing genetic material to this population are the Blue-spotted Salamander, Jefferson's Salamander, Smallmouth Salamander and Tiger Salamander. Hybrid individuals containing DNA from two, three, or four species are known. In years past at least two forms of these hybrids were considered to be typical species that went by the names Tremblay's Salamander and Silvery Salamander.

Class—**Amphibia** (amphibians)

Order—**Caudata** (salamanders)

Family—**Plethodontidae** (lungless salamanders)

Northern Zigzag Salamander *Plethodon dorsalis*	**Eastern Redback Salamander** *Plethodon cinereus*	**Northern Slimy Salamander** *Plethodon glutinosus*
		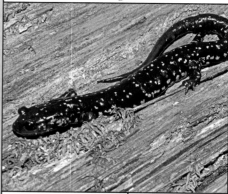

Northern Zigzag Salamander

Size: Average 3 to 4 inches.

Presumed range in Indiana

Abundance: Fairly common.

Variation: Varies in ground color and in the intensity of the zigzag stripe. Some are uniformly gray above and lack the dorsal stripe.

Habitat: This is a forest species (mesic woodlands) and it is most common in regions with a limestone substrate.

Breeding: Lays only a few eggs (as few as 4 or 5). Eggs are deposited into an underground nest chamber.

Natural History: The name "Zigzag" Salamander comes from the reddish stripe often present on the back of this salamander, which has an irregular zigzag pattern. In the similar Red-backed Salamander the dorsal stripe (when present) is smooth edged. In specimens lacking the dorsal stripe the Zigzag will have orange around the "armpits." These are terrestrial salamanders that spend much of their life beneath leaf litter, logs, or other cover on the forest floor. They do emerge at night and forage for small invertebrate prey. They also capture worms and tiny insects beneath the leaf litter. Like all members of the *Plethodon* genus of salamanders, young salamanders hatch fully formed. The eggs develop directly into tiny salamanders and bypass the larval stage that is common in many amphibians. Inhabits hilly, forested regions.

Eastern Redback Salamander

Size: 3 to 4 inches. Maximum 5 inches.

Presumed range in Indiana

Abundance: Very common in Indiana.

Variation: Considerable variation in the dorsal pattern. Some Redback Salamanders are not red on the back at all, but uniformly gray.

Habitat: Chiefly woodlands. This is another terrestrial but retiring species that hides beneath leaf litter, logs, etc.

Breeding: Female lays about 10 eggs on land and guards them until they hatch. Babies hatch fully formed.

Natural History: Most of this salamander's range is to the north and east of Indiana as far north as the Canadian provinces of Quebec, Nova Scotia, and New Brunswick. In the heart of its range this is not only the most common salamander species, but one of the most common vertebrate species. It is widespread in Indiana and probably the state's most common salamander species. They are very similar to the Zigzag Salamanders and can be very difficult to differentiate where their respective ranges overlap. Close examination with the specimen in hand is about the only way to make a positive ID. The similar Northern Zigzag Salamander has orange coloration around the "armpit" of the front legs and the dorsal stripe when present is smooth edged. Like other small terrestrial salamanders its food is tiny invertebrates.

Northern Slimy Salamander

Size: Adults are 5 to 7 inches in length.

Presumed range in Indiana

Abundance: Common within range.

Variation: Ground color is consistently black or very dark gray. Varies in amount of light flecking. Flecks are white, silver or gold.

Habitat: Another woodland species. More common in upland woods and hillsides than in bottomlands.

Breeding: 12 to 15 eggs seems to be the average. As with other *Plethodon* Salamanders, young hatch fully formed.

Natural History: The name is derived from the fact that slimy salamanders exude a thick, sticky mucus from the skin when handled. This material is difficult to wash off and once dried becomes black and crusty. Herpetologists capturing slimy salamanders sometimes wear the residue of salamander mucus on their hands for days before it finally wears off. The food of these woodland species is undoubtedly a wide variety of soft bodied insects, insect larva, annelids, small crustaceans and other tiny invertebrate life found among the leaf litter on the forest floor. Until the advent of DNA technology there was only one ubiquitous species of Slimy Salamander that ranged across most of the eastern United States. There are now over a dozen remarkably similar species. Only one (Northern Slimy Salamander) occurs in Indiana.

Class—**Amphibia** (amphibians)

Order—**Caudata** (salamanders)

Family—**Plethodontidae** (lungless salamanders)

Northern Ravine Salamander *Plethodon electromorphus*	**Southern Two-lined Salamander** *Eurycea cirrigera*	**Cave Salamander** *Eurycea lucifuga*

Northern Ravine Salamander

Size: About 4 inches. Maximum 5.75 inches.

Presumed range in Indiana

Abundance: Fairly common within their limited range.

Variation: The color of the metallic-like flecking can vary from silverish to gold, or may be absent on some. Body color dark gray to black.

Habitat: As its name implies this species prefers the steep slopes of deep, forested ravines in rugged terrain.

Breeding: As with other *Plethodon* salamanders there is no larval stage and the young develop fully in the egg and hatch into miniatures resembling adults.

Natural History: This is a recently described "new" species that was previously regarded as conspecific with nearly identical the Southern Ravine Salamander. The two can only reliably be differentiated by the highly technical laboratory process of electrophoresis of their DNA (hence the species name "electromorphus"). Some herpetologists argue against overriding morphological characters as a species designation, while others point out that DNA analysis provides a clearer picture of phylogeny (the evolutionary history) of populations. Like many other small amphibians they disappear underground during hot, dry weather. They re-emerge during rains or in cooler seasons. They are most active in the spring and fall and may be active in winter.

Southern Two-lined Salamander

Size: Maximum 4 inches, average 2 to 3 inches.

Presumed range in Indiana

Abundance: Common in suitable habitat within its range.

Variation: Ground color varies slightly from bright yellow to dingy brownish. Dorsal stripes can be obscure on dark specimen.

Habitat: Streams, wetlands and seeps. Mostly a lowland animal but also in mesic upland environments near creeks.

Breeding: Several dozen eggs are attached to the underside of rocks in brooks. Eggs hatch into aquatic larva that transform in one or two years.

Natural History: The members of this genus (*Eurycea*) are often called "Brook Salamanders," in reference to their propensity to inhabit small, clear streams. Other habitats are also utilized and the Southern Two-lined Salamander is often found in swamps or bottomland woodlands in the vicinity of seeps. Springs and seeps that emerge from ridges and upland areas that border bottomlands and swamps are good places to find this small and secretive salamander. Brook Salamanders differ from their family relatives the "Woodland Salamanders" (genus *Plethodon*) in that their affinity to aquatic stream habitats persists as adults. They are also different in another important respect. Brook Salamanders must undergo an aquatic larval stage in their life cycle.

Cave Salamander

Size: Record 7.125 inches.

Presumed range in Indiana

Abundance: Fairly common but rarely observed.

Variation: Varies somewhat in the amount of dark spots on the dorsum. Body color varies from bright red to reddish brown or orange.

Habitat: Although frequently found in caves, this salamander also lives in upland woods beneath rocks, logs, etc.

Breeding: Several dozen eggs are attached to the underneath side of rocks underwater in springs or waterways both inside and outside of caves.

Natural History: The distribution of this species is generally regions with predominantly limestone substrates and karst topography. Thus in Indiana they are absent from many areas of the state. Adults of this species have prehensile tails and they are good climbers. They are sometimes seen clinging to the walls inside caves. Despite their name these salamanders are not true troglodytes (cave dwellers). They inhabit mostly the twilight zone of caves as well as more typical terrestrial habitats in mesic upland woods. Here they can be found beneath rocks, logs, etc. and they can also be common near springs and seeps in upland areas. Like other salamanders on this page, the tail may break off if grasped. Lost tails can be regenerated, but are rarely as long as the original.

Class—**Amphibia** (amphibians)
Order—**Caudata** (salamanders)
Family—**Plethodontidae** (lungless salamanders)

Long-tailed Salamander *Eurycea longicauda*	Four-toed Salamander *Hemidactylum scutatum*	Northern Dusky Salamander *Desmognathus fuscus*

Long-tailed Salamander
Eurycea longicauda

Size: Record length 7.75 inches.

Abundance: Fairly common.

Variation: Body color varies from yellow to shades of orange. Amount of dark mottling along the back is variable.

Presumed range in Indiana

Habitat: Spring runs, small clear creeks, in the vicinity of seeps, and near cave openings. Also under logs and flat rocks in mesic woodlands

Breeding: Eggs are lain in late winter or early spring in some areas. In Indiana breeding occurs in the fall (Indiana Herp Atlas). Eggs are deposited in streams and springs or in caves. Larva metamorphose in about a year.

Natural History: These salamanders can often be found beneath rocks within small clear streams. They also live in mesic woodland environments, usually in the vicinity of a permanent stream. Here they may be found hiding beneath or within rotted logs or stumps. On rainy nights they can be encountered on roads as they roam around in search of tiny invertebrate prey. Although they can reach an impressive length of over 7 inches, they are a slim bodied animal and over half their length is tail. The two subspecies are the Eastern Long-tailed Salamander (*longicauda*) (found in Indiana) and the Dark-sided Salamander (*melanopleura*), of the Ozark Plateau. Autotomy (breaking off of the tail) is a common defense mechanism.

Four-toed Salamander
Hemidactylum scutatum

Size: 3 to 4 inches. Record nearly 5 inches.

Abundance: Fairly common.

Variation: Some are uniformly dark gray. Others have a significant amount of light gray flecking on the sides.

Presumed range in Indiana

Habitat: Wetlands and mesic woodlands. Aquatic situations where mosses and sedges are present seem to be the favorite habitat in Indiana.

Breeding: Breeding occurs in late fall or early winter and overland treks to breeding areas are made. Eggs are laid on damp plants above the waters of marshes and bogs. The hatchlings drop into water and begin development.

Natural History: The name comes from the fact that they have only four toes on the hind foot (other terrestrial salamanders have five). There is also an obvious constriction at the base of the tail that is unique to this species. It is at this constricted location that the tail will be broken off as a defensive maneuver. The most readily identifiable characteristic of this species is its white belly with black spots. No other salamander is similarly colored and patterned. This salamander has a greater geographic range than any other in America. It is found from Nova Scotia, Canada to the gulf coast and west to Minnesota and Arkansas. But like many amphibians this species is threatened by habitat destruction.

Northern Dusky Salamander
Desmognathus fuscus

Size: Average about 3.5 inches. Max 5 inches.

Abundance: Fairly common.

Variation: Color varies from gray through many shades of brown. Yellowish spots on the dorsum may merge into stripe.

Presumed range in Indiana

Habitat: Springs, seeps, and spring fed brooks in wooded areas. Beneath rocks, detritus or in the muck of forest streams.

Breeding: Eggs are laid under rocks in the vicinity of streams. The eggs (average 15 to 30) are laid in clusters of individual eggs that are not contained in a gelatinous mass like the mole salamanders.

Natural History: The Spotted Dusky and its kin are salamanders that are often well known to rural folk in the southern US. Many a youngster has amused themselves on a hot summer day by rolling stones and logs in streams to try and catch these slippery and quick moving salamanders. They are often collected for fish bait in many areas within their range and sometimes go by the name "Spring Lizards." Other members of the genus are frequently sold in bait stores in the Appalachian region. Although this practice probably has no significant impact on this common species, accidental "by catch" of some rarer species may have an negative impact on those less common salamanders.

Class—**Amphibia** (amphibians)

Order—**Caudata** (salamanders)

Family—**Salamandridae** (newts)

Eastern Newt
Notophthalmus viridescens

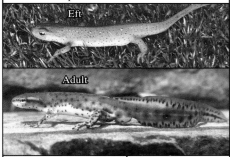

Size: Adults 5 inches. Efts 3 inches.

Presumed range in Indiana

Abundance: Fairly common.

Habitat: Adults are found in ponds, swamps, or other permanent water. Eft stage is a terrestrial animal of woodlands.

Variation: Two subspecies occur, the **Red-spotted Newt** (subspecies *viridescens*), and the **Central Newt** (subspecies *louisianensis*). Indiana populations are mostly Red-spotted Newts.

Breeding: Breeds in spring. Males deposit packages of sperm which are taken up by the female into the cloaca where fertilization occurs internally before eggs are then laid. Hatchlings metamorph into efts in 4 to 5 months. Efts transform into adults in 2 or 3 years.

Natural History: Newts are unique among salamanders in having an extra stage in their life cycle. Following hatching the young spend the summer as aquatic gill breathing larva then undergo a transformation to an air breathing semi-adult that lives on land for up to three years. Newts in this terrestrial stage are call "Efts." After 1 to 3 years the eft returns to the water and undergoes another metmorphosis into a totally aquatic adult. After returning to the water the coarse skin of the eft becomes smooth and the round tail flattens vertically to become fin-like. Their life span can be up to 15 years. Newts produce a neurotoxin in their skin that protects them from many predators.

Family-**Sirenidae** (sirens)

Lesser Siren
Siren intermedia

Presumed range in Indiana

Size: Average 12 to 16 inches. Can reach a maximum length of up to 20 inches.

Abundance: Uncommon in Indiana. More common farther to south in the lower coastal plain where swamps are common.

Variation: No variation in Indiana. There are two subspecies.

Habitat: Wetlands. Swamps, marshes, oxbows, sloughs, slow moving streams and low lying areas along stream courses.

Breeding: Lays several hundred eggs in a nest hollowed out in the mud. Probably breeds in late winter or early spring.

Natural History: A completely aquatic salamander that breathes through external gills that are easily visible just in front of the forelimbs. Known food items include insects, crustaceans, mollusks, and worms, as well as some plant material such as algea. Capable of surviving drought periods by secreting slime which hardens into a cocoon-like structure, creating a sealed chamber in the mud. Like many wetland species the Lesser Siren has been negatively impacted by the conversion of wetlands to agricultural land. Sirens have elongated bodies with very small front legs and lack hind limbs completely. This is one of the few salamanders that is capable of vocalization. They are reported to communicate with each other using clicking sounds and when captured they sometimes emit a yelping sound. They are often confused with eels, but eels are a fish and have internal gills.

Family—**Proteidae** (waterdogs)

Mudpuppy—*Necturus maculosus*

Presumed range in Indiana

Size: Average 8 to 13 inches. Record 19.125 inches.

Abundance: Can be fairly common in some localities.

Variation: Adults and young are similar but young often have a dark dorsal stripe.

Habitat: Utilizes most larger streams and rivers in the state, as well as lakes (including Lake Michigan). Prefers clean waters but can persist in turbid waters.

Breeding: Breeding and egg laying occurs in the fall. Female Mudpuppys hollow out a nest beneath a sunken log or rock where they will lay from a few score to over a hundred eggs. The eggs attach to the underside of a rock or log.

Natural History: Mudpuppys have extensive external gills that resemble downy feathers. Some think the gills are reminiscent of the ears of a dog, thus the name "Mudpuppy." These are totally aquatic salamanders that never lose the gills of the larva. This condition of permanent larval characteristics is known scientifically as "neotony" and is a phenomena that is not rare in salamanders of several species. Mudpuppys prey on fish eggs, insects, mollusks small crustaceans and annelids. The female remains with eggs during incubation. As a totally aquatic animal Mudpuppys may be threatened by water quality issues. The gills of the Mudpuppy are the only known host to the larva of the Salamander Mussel (*Simpsonaias ambigua*).

Class—**Amphibia** (amphibians)
Order—**Caudata** (salamanders)
Family—**Cryptobranchidae** (giant salamanders)
Eastern Hellbender *Cryptobranchus alleghaniensis*

Size: Up to 30 inches in length and very heavy bodied.

Abundance: Very rare in Indiana. Populations throughout its range are in decline.

Variation: Some variation in ground color. Reddish, brown, tan, or chocolate. A very similar but distinct species occurs in the Ozarks region.

Habitat: Clear pure streams. Once found throughout the Appalachians and much of the Interior Plateau. Populations now restricted to remote, unpolluted streams. Large flat rocks are used as a refuge. Historically this species was found in tributaries of most of the larger river systems in the southern region of the state. Today they are regarded as extirpated from all but a few tributaries of the Blue River.

Breeding: Fertilization is external and eggs are laid in a nest guarded by the male. Lays over 400 eggs.

Presumed range in Indiana

Natural History: These huge, totally aquatic salamanders have deep folds and wrinkles in the skin. They have very large, dorso-ventrally flattened heads and laterally flattened, fin-like tails. They are completely aquatic and feed on crustaceans, minnows, and invertebrates with crayfish reported as a primary prey. They require clean, unpolluted flowing waters and they are in decline throughout their range due to stream degradation, siltation, impoundments of free flowing streams, and chemical pollutants. There are two species of Hellbender in America. The other species is native to the Ozark Plateau. Sadly, many streams throughout Indiana (and America) lack their original water quality and can no longer support these bizarre and interesting creatures. Today the Hellbender is a highly endangered animal in Indiana and experts fear it may soon disappear from the state. This is one of America's largest salamander species but it is dwarfed by its larger relative from Japan. The Pacific Giant Salamander is the world's largest salamander species. It is native to pristine streams in the mountains of Japan and it can reach 5 feet in length.

CHAPTER 8

THE RIVERS & STREAMS OF INDIANA

As a preface to the next chapter (Chapter 9, The Fishes of Indiana), this short chapter is intended to provide a brief introduction into the waterways of Indiana, which are home to the state's fish species. Many people are surprised to learn that the state of Indiana boasts over 36,000 miles of rivers and streams within its borders. Much of the southwestern border of Indiana is defined by the Wabash River and the state's entire southern border is marked by the Ohio River. In additon, another aquatic ecosystem, Lake Michigan, defines a portion of the state's northwestern border.

With so many miles of waterways, it is not surprising that Indiana is also home to over 200 fish species. The number of native fish species that can be found in Indiana waters numbers 178 (plus 24 introduced species), making the fishes the second most diverse group of vertebrates in the state.

Figure 10 below shows how the state of Indiana is laced with waterways.

With the exception of the most northerly regions of the state most of Indiana is within the Mississippi River

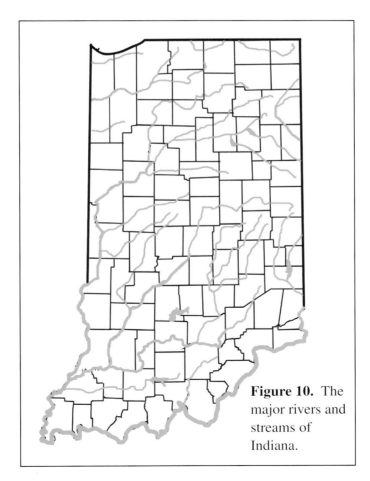

Figure 10. The major rivers and streams of Indiana.

Level I Watershed. Figure 11 below shows how much of the North American Continent is contained within this enormous watershed. The St. Lawrence River Level I Watershed is shown in green. The Great Lakes are contained within the St. Lawrence River Level I watershed, and the northernmost portions of the state of Indiana lie within this Level I Watershed.

Figure 12 below shows how the Mississippi River and St. Lawrence River Level I Watersheds are divided into smaller Level II Watersheds. Three of these Level II watersheds affect Indiana. Most of the state is in the Ohio River Level II watershed. The other two Level II watersheds of Indiana are the St. Lawrence and the Mississippi Level II watershed, the latter of which encompasses only a small area in northwestern Indiana.

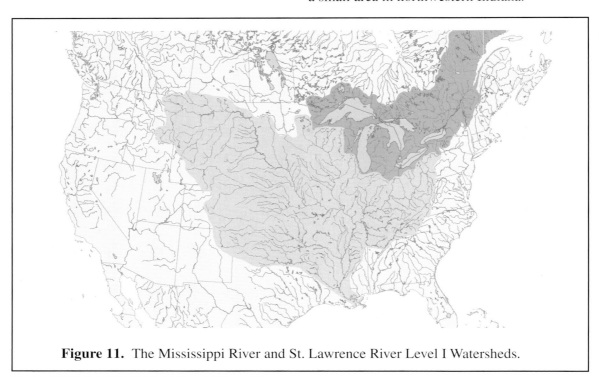

Figure 11. The Mississippi River and St. Lawrence River Level I Watersheds.

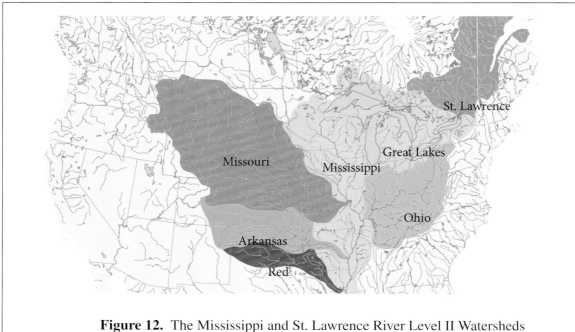

Figure 12. The Mississippi and St. Lawrence River Level II Watersheds
The two maps shown above are derived from maps created by the Commission for Environmental Cooperation.

Figure 13 below shows the same Level II Watersheds depicted in Figure 12, and the Indiana streams which make up those watersheds. On this map the Mississippi River Level II Watereshed is in gray and Ohio River Level II Watershed is in Orange. The green represents the Great Lakes Level II Watershed. All three Level II watersheds depicted in Figure 13 naturally consist of increasingly smaller tributaries, each of which constitutes its own drainage area. The next level of watershed designation after Level II of course is Level III. Figure 14 on the following page shows those Level III Watersheds. The red line on the map designates the division between the state's Level II Watersheds (Mississippi, Great Lakes, and Ohio).

Figure 13. The Level II Watersheds of Indiana.

The watershed divisions illustrated in the series of maps shown in this chapter are useful to natural scientists in many ways. For the purposes of this book, an appreciation of these drainage basins (or watersheds) can provide insight into the distribution of Indiana's fish species. More importantly, conservation organizations can monitor these various watersheds for pollution and other factors that may impact upon the health of fish populations contained within them. Figure 13 on the previous page shows the Level IV watersheds of the state. Even these relatively small watersheds shown below can be divided into subsequently smaller and

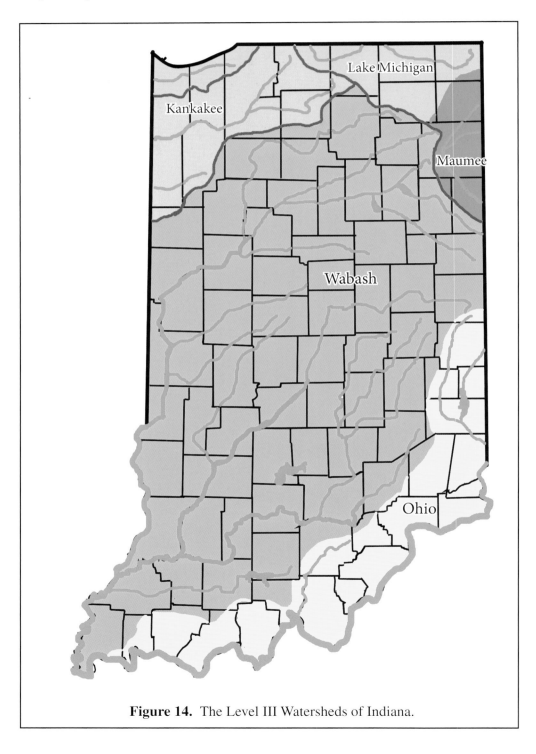

Figure 14. The Level III Watersheds of Indiana.

smaller designations, with each smaller watershed providing a more concise view of the local ecosystem represented by that smaller designation.

Although the state of Indiana still boasts an abundance of fish species, a few species no longer exist in the state. At least 10 species of fishes native to Indiana are now extirpated. A total of 21 more are now regarded as endangered, threatened, or are species of concern. For each of these

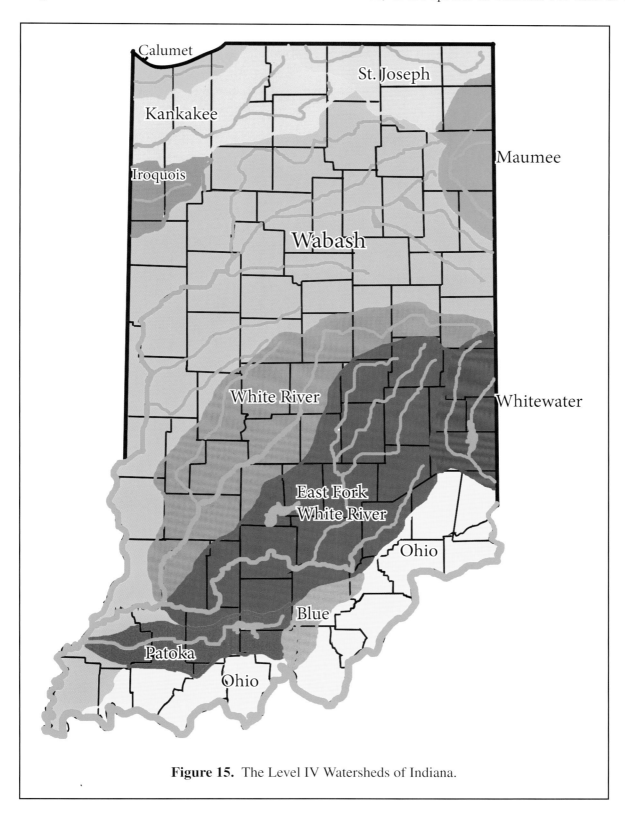

Figure 15. The Level IV Watersheds of Indiana.

there is cause for concern regarding their continued survival in Indiana waters.

Like all other habitat types within the eastern United States, the waterways of Indiana have been highly altered by man. There are a number of major impoundments on larger river systems. Countless smaller dams have inundate portions of many small creeks. Direct pollution from industry and urbanization is an important source of stream degradation in the state. But of equal importance is indirect contamination from agriculture. Agricultural related pollution and stream degradation can come in the form of chemical runoff from herbicides, pesticides, and chemical fertilizers. Also important is the destruction of vegetated buffer zones by farmers needing to maximize the production area of their land. Erosion and siltation from row cropping operations impact nearly every stream in the state. To a lesser extent, livestock operations statewide can also have negative impacts as cattle destroy creek banks and stir up silt from stream bottoms. Large "factory farms" that produce prodigious amounts of animal manure have in recent decades become one of the worst water pollution offenders in the state.

Add to these problems the presence of nearly 7 million people and you have a significant threat to Indiana's fresh water ecosystems. All Indianans use prodigious amounts of water and collectively produce many tons of sewage and waste water, some of which in rural areas may wind up entering the state's waterways.

One environmental organization recently reported that the rivers and streams of Indiana are the most polluted of any state in the US. Many rivers and streams no longer support the high diversity of fish and other aquatic species that once were abundant within their banks and the future for many of the state's fish species is uncertain. If we regard this fact as a warning sign relating to the health of our aquatic ecosystems, and surely they are just that, then all Indianans should be acutely concerned about the future of the state's waterways.

We often hear reasonable people argue against stringent protections of our environment. But few things are more important than these protections. Humans can survive for a maximum of four minutes without air and maximum of four days without water. It follows then that our paramount priorities should be to insure that we all always have clean air to breathe and pure water to drink!

The series of maps shown on the previous pages gives a good representation of how smaller streams and their watersheds are integrated into larger streams and larger watersheds. What also becomes apparent from these maps is that when it comes to water, everything (and everyone) downstream is affected by the quality of the water and the overall environmental health of the waters upstream. The environmental quality of that tiny creek in your backyard or on your farm affects not only the life of organisms living within that stream, but also organisms within the larger streams into which it flows. And ultimately, the wildlife living in Louisiana's coastal marshes, the fishes living in the depths of the Gulf of Mexico, and the magnificent coral ecosystems of the great reefs of the Caribbean.

The range maps shown for the fish species in the next chapter represent the *presumed range* of the species based on currently available data. These maps *may not be an exact representation* of the species distribution in Indiana.

CHAPTER 9

THE FISHES OF INDIANA

TABLE 6

— THE ORDERS AND FAMILIES OF INDIANA FISHES —

Class—**Actinopterygii** (ray-finned fishes)

Order—**Perciformes** (typical fishes)

Family	**Centrarchidae** (sunfishes)
Family	**Elassomatidae** (pygmy sunfishes)
Family	**Scianidae** (drums)
Family	**Moronidae** (true basses)
Family	**Gobidae** (gobies)
Family	**Percidae** (perches & darters)

Order—**Salmoniformes**

Family	**Salmonidae** (salmonids)

Order—**Osmeriformes**

Family	**Osmeridae** (smelts)

Order—**Esociformes** (pikes & mudminnows)

Family	Esocidae (pikes)
Family	Umbridea (mudminnows)

Order—**Gadiformes**

Family	**Gadidae** (codfish)

Order—**Acipenseriformes** (primitive fishes)

Family	**Acipenseridae** (sturgeons)
Family	**Polyodontidae** (paddlefish)

Order—**Percopsiformes** (pirate perch & cavefish)

Family	**Percopsidae** (trout perch)
Family	**Aphredoderidae** (pirate perch)
Family	**Amblyopsidae** (cavefishes)

Order—**Lepisosteiformes** (gar)

Family	**Lepisosteidae** (gars)

Order—**Amiiformes** (bowfin)

Family	**Amiidae** (bowfin)

Order—**Osteoglossiformes** (bonytongues)

Family	**Hiodontidae** (mooneyes)

Order—**Anguilliformes** (eels)

Family	**Anguillidae** (freshwater eels)

Order—**Atheriniformes**

Family	**Atherinidae** (silversides)

Order—**Gasterosteiformes** (mostly small marine fishes)

Family	**Gasterosteidae** (sticklebacks)

Order—**Clupeiformes** (sardines, herrings, & shads)

Family	**Clupeidae** (herring & shad)

Order—**Cyprinodontiformes** (topminnows & livebearers)

Family	**Fundulidae** (topminnows)
Family	**Poeciliidae** (livebearers)

Order—**Cypriniformes** (minnows & suckers)

Family	**Catastomidae** (suckers)
Family	**Cyprinidae** (minnows)

Order—**Siluriformes** (catfishes)

Family	**Ictaluridae** (american catfishes)

Order—**Scorpaeniformes**

Family	**Cottidae** (sculpins)

Class—**Actinopterygii** (bony fishes)

Order—**Perciformes** (typical fishes)

Family—**Centrarchidae** (sunfishes)

Largemouth Bass *Micropterus salmoides*	**Smallmouth Bass** *Micropterus dolomieui*	**Spotted Bass** *Micropterus punctulatus*

Size: May reach 38 inches and 22 pounds. The record size for Indiana is 14 pounds, 12 ounces.

Abundance: Very common in all Level II watersheds.

Natural History: This is probably America's most popular fresh water game fish, pursued by anglers throughout the country. Indeed an entire sporting industry has evolved around the pursuit of this fish. Found in virtually any body of water in the state, including streams and small farm ponds.

Size: Maximum of up to 11 pounds. Indiana record size of 7 pounds, 4 ounces was caught in 1992.

Abundance: Common. Most common in northern half of state.

Natural History: Prefers clearer, cooler, more highly oxygenated waters than the Largemouth Bass. Crayfish are a preferred prey, especially for stream dwelling Smallmouth Bass. Like its cousin the Largemouth Bass, this is an important game species. It is renowned for its tenacious fighting abilities.

Size: Maximum of 8 pounds. Average adult is about 3 to 4 pounds. Indiana record size is 5 pounds, 5 ounces.

Abundance: Fairly common. Absent from northernmost regions.

Natural History: Intermediate between the two previous species in both the size of the mouth and in its habitat preferences. Primarily a fish of flowing waters but can tolerate warmer conditions than the Smallmouth. Avoids the still waters favored by the Largemouth. Tongue feels rough to the touch.

Bluegill *Lepomis macrochirus*	**Longear Sunfish** *Lepomis megalotis*	**Warmouth** *Lepomis gulosus*

Male

Size: Record of 4 pounds, 12 ounces. Indiana record is 3 pounds, 4 ounces caught in 1972 from a farm pond.

Abundance: Very common.

Natural History: The Bluegill is America's best known sunfish. This is the first fish caught on hook and line by many a young angler. It is an important game fish throughout the state. They are regularly stocked in new impoundments and are found in virtually every significant body of water in the state.

Size: World record size is 1 pound, 12 ounces. No records are available for this species in Indiana. Most are about 6 inches in length.

Abundance: Common.

Natural History: Breeding males are one of the most brilliantly colored of the sunfishes. Clear streams with gravelly or sandy substrates are habitat. Two very similar species in Indiana. The **Northern Sunfish** (*L. peltastes*) is found on map in dark gray, while the Longear range is the light gray areas.

Size: Record of 2 pounds, 7 ounces. Indiana record is 1 pound, 7 ounces. Most are about 6 to 7 inches as adults.

Abundance: Uncommon in Indiana.

Natural History: A fish of lowland creeks and swamps, the Warmouth is most common in the southern United States. Although it occurs in Indiana it is sporadically distributed and may be absent from many areas. It prefers waters with thick growths of aquatic plants. Teeth are present on the tongue.

Class—**Actinopterygii** (bony fishes)

Order—**Perciformes** (typical fishes)

Family—**Centrarchidae** (sunfishes)

Redear Sunfish *Lepomis microlophus*	**Pumpkinseed** *Lepomis gibbosus*	**Green Sunfish** *Lepomis cyanellus*

Size: Record 4 pounds, 13 ounces. Indiana record is 3 pounds and 10 ounces. Averages about 8 to 10 inches.

Abundance: Introduced into much of the state but is uncommon.

Natural History: These fish also go by the name "Shellcracker," a reference to their habit of eating small freshwater mollusks such as clams and snails. The natural distribution of this fish was originally the southeastern United States. Today it has been widely introduced throughout much of the eastern US.

Size: The maximum length for this species is 16 inches. There are no angling records available for Indiana.

Abundance: Fairly common in northern Indiana.

Natural History: Found mainly in the northern United States and along the eastern seaboard. Inhabits still or slow moving waters. Snails and bivalves are a major food source. The Pumpkinseed is similar to the Redear Sunfish in both habits and appearance and is the northern counterpart of that species.

Size: Maximum recorded size is 2 pounds, 2 ounces and 12 inches in length. Indiana record 1 pound, 10 ounces.

Abundance: Common. Found statewide in all watersheds.

Natural History: This is a fairly common fish throughout the state. It may be found in ponds and lakes but its natural habitat is quite pools of slow moving streams. It is known to hybridize readily with other *Lepomis* sunfishes, especially the Bluegill. Tolerates warm, low oxygen waters.

Orange-spotted Sunfish *Lepomis humilis*	**Bantam Sunfish** *Lepomis symmetricus*	**Redspotted Sunfish** *Lepomis miniatus*

Size: Average adult size is only 2 to 3 inches. Maximum reported length is about 4 inches. No records available for this species in Indiana.

Abundance: Fairly common.

Natural History: Inhabits creeks and rivers where it favors quiet water pools with cover in the form of brush. When it occurs in lakes and impoundments it is found in shallow bays. Nests in gravel. Eats mainly small aquatic insect larva and small crustaceans. Female is much less colorful than the male.

Size: Due to the rarity of this species in the state, no size data is available for Indiana. Maximum size elsewhere is 3.75 inches.

Abundance: Very rare. Possibly extirpated.

Natural History: Swamps with clean, clear water and ample aquatic vegetation are the favored habitats. The smallest of Indiana's *Lepomis* sunfishes. In Indiana the Bantam Sunfish once inhabited swamps and backwaters of the lower Wabash River. Listed as state endangered and possibly extirpated.

Size: Can reach a maximum of about 6.5 inches but most are about half that size. There is no data available for Indiana size.

Abundance: Uncommon in Indiana.

Natural History: Primarily a southern species that in the deep south often goes by the name "Stumpknocker," which is a reference to its preferred habitat in waters containing cypress trees, stumps and logs. Southwestern Indiana and southern Illinois represent the northernmost extension of range of this species.

Class—**Actinopterygii** (bony fishes)

Order—**Perciformes** (typical fishes)

Family—**Centrarchidae** (sunfishes)

Rock Bass *Ambloplites rupestris*	**Flier** *Centrachus macropterus*	**White Croppie** *Pomoxis annularus*

Rock Bass

Size: Record size 3 pounds. Largest recorded specimen from Indiana is a 3 pound specimen caught in 1969.

Abundance: Common in northern Indiana.

Natural History: Also known as the "Goggle Eye," the Rock Bass is a fish of clear, cool waters. They are primarily a stream fish that is found in clear streams with good water quality mostly in the northern portion of the state. The natural distribution is from the Great Lakes region south into northern Alabama.

Flier

Size: Averages about 5 inches. Maximum of about 8 inches. 3 pounds, 0.5 ounce is the record for Indiana. No record date given.

Abundance: Uncommon.

Natural History: The Flier is a lowland species that is usually found in natural lakes, oxbows, swamps, or sluggish streams. Most often occurs in waters with mud bottom. In Indiana this species is most common in the swamps and backwaters of the lower Wabash and lower Ohio River valleys.

White Croppie

Size: Maximum size about 5 pounds, 3 ounces. No size record for Indiana but Illinois angling record is 4 pounds, 7 ounces.

Abundance: Common in all watersheds.

Natural History: The White Croppie is more tolerant of turbid water conditions than the Black Croppie, though both are often found in the same waters. White Croppie is usually much lighter. Positive ID can be made by counting the stiff spines on the dorsal fin. White Croppie has only 6, Black has 7 or 8.

Black Croppie
Pomoxis nigromaculatus

Family—**Elassomatidae** (pygmy sunfishes)

Banded Pygmy Sunfish
Elassoma zonatum

Family—**Sciaenidae** (drums)

Freshwater Drum
Aplodinotus grunniens

Size: Maximum size about 5 pounds and 19 inches in length. No Indiana records.

Abundance: Statewide but generally less common than the White Croppie.

Natural History: The Black Croppie likes clearer waters than the White Croppie, though they may occur together. Black Croppie are native to the Atlantic slope but have been widely introduced across the eastern US. Usually shows more black pigment than white. Has 7 or 8 stiff spines on dorsal fin.

Size: Maximum 1.75 inches.

Abundance: Very rare in Indiana. Swamps and backwaters of lower Wabash River drainage.

Natural History: These tiny fishes are unknown to most Indianans. They are southern species that can be quite common in the swamps and bayous of the deep south. Like many southern animals and fishes they range northward in the Mississippi and Ohio river valleys as far as the Wabash.

Size: Record size 54 pounds.

Abundance: Common. Found in all watersheds. Most common in larger streams and lakes.

Natural History: This is the only member of the drum family that lives in fresh water. Most are salt water fishes and several are important food and sport fishes. By contrast the Freshwater Drum is not highly regarded by sport anglers. When hooked however they are strong and tenacious fighters.

Class—**Actinopterygii** (bony fishes)

Order—**Perciformes** (typical fishes)

Family—**Moronidae** (true basses)

Yellow Bass *Morone mississippiensis*	**White Bass** *Morone chrysops*	**Striped Bass** *Morone saxatilis*

Yellow Bass

Size: The world record of 2 pounds, 15 ounces was an Indiana fish.

Abundance: Uncommon in Indiana. Found mostly in the Wabash River watershed. Also around Lake Michigan,

Natural History: A clear water fish, the Yellow Bass avoids muddy rivers and streams in favor of lakes, oxbows, and other still waters. Natural lakes with abundant vegetation are its main habitat but it has adapted well to man-made lakes.

White Bass

Size: Indiana record 4 pounds, 3 ounces. Record 5 pounds, 9 ounces.

Abundance: Common. Widespread in most of the major rivers in the state. Also in lakes and impoundments.

Natural History: These important game fish are famous for forcing schools of bait fish to the surface then attacking them in a feeding frenzy. Leaping bait fish indicate the presence of feeding bass. Savvy fishermen look for these eruptions of bait fish known as "jumps."

Striped Bass

Size: World record 78.5 pounds. Indiana record 39 pounds.

Abundance: Although widely introduced into impoundments the Striped Bass is generally uncommon in Indiana.

Natural History: Striped Bass are anadromous fish that live in salt water but spawn in fresh water rivers. Now widely stocked in lakes by wildlife agencies, they have adapted to a fresh water existence. Hybrid Striped/White Bass are known as "Rockfish."

Family—**Moronidae** (true basses)

Family—**Gobiidae** (gobies)

Family—**Percidae** (perch & darters)

White Perch *Morone americana*	**Round Goby** *Neogobius melanostomus)*	**Eastern Sand Darter/Western Sand Darter** *Ammocrypta pellucida/Ammocrypta clara*

White Perch

Size: Maximum size attained is about 22 inches and 3 pounds. No size records available for Indiana.

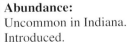

Abundance: Uncommon in Indiana. Introduced.

Natural History: The White Perch is native to streams and brackish waters east of the Appalachian Plateau. They have been introduced into Indiana in the immediate vicinity of Lake Michigan. They are important game fishes within their native range on the Atlantic slope but are an exotic species in Indiana.

Round Goby

Size: Small. Averages about 5 or 6 inches but can reach a maximum length of 10 inches.

Abundance: They are quite common in Lake Michigan.

Natural History: The gobies are exotic invasive species native to Eurasia that appeared in the Great Lakes sometime around 1990. As is often the case with exotic species, these fish have not been good for the great lakes. Though relatively small, they are voracious predators of fish eggs and fry.

Eastern Sand Darter/Western Sand Darter

Size: The Eastern Sand Darter can reach a maximum of 3.25 inches. Western Sand Darter 2.75 inches.

Abundance: Western is rare. Eastern is uncommon.

Natural History: The nearly identical Sand Darters are associated with sandy substrates of medium to large streams. When not swimming about in search of food or a mate they stay buried in the sand except for the top of head. Their translucent-colored bodies render them effectively invisible.

Class—**Actinopterygii** (bony fishes)
Order—**Perciformes** (typical fishes)
Family—**Percidae** (perch & darters)

Yellow Perch *Perca flavescens*	**Walleye** *Sander vitreus*	**Sauger** *Sander canadensis*

Size: World record 4 pounds, 3 ounces. Indiana record 2 pounds and 8 ounces. Averages less than a pound.

Abundance: Most common in northern Indiana.

Natural History: Native to the northern and eastern United States, Yellow Perch have recently expanded their range into more southerly regions. They are a popular pan fish in the north. In Indiana they are found in both man-made and natural lakes and are common in Lake Michigan.

Size: World record is 25 pounds. Average is 2 to 4 pounds. Indiana record is 14 pounds, 4 ounces.

Abundance: Fairly common in large rivers and lakes.

Natural History: Walleye live in larger rivers, impoundments, and natural lakes where deep water provides the cool temperatures these fish require. They are regarded as one of the most palatable of the game fishes. Found statewide in large rivers and lakes. Most common in northern Indiana and Lake Michigan.

Size: World record 8 pounds, 12 ounces. Average about a pound. Indiana record is 6 pounds, 1 ounce.

Abundance: Fairly common in large rivers and lakes.

Natural History: Found throughout the Midwest and northward to Canada, the Sauger is a smaller relative of the Walleye that is more adapted to turbid waters. Hybridization between the Walleye and the Sauger results in a fish known as the "Saugeye," which can attain a much larger size than the Sauger.

The True Darters—genus *Etheostoma*—17 species in Indiana (12 shown on next 2 pages)

Natural History of the *Etheostoma* darters: With at least 148 species distributed across North America, this genus boasts more species than any other genus of fresh water fish in the US. Among them are some of America's rarest fish and some of our most common. In coloration they range from a cryptic mottled brown to remarkably colorful. In many species the breeding males rival the most colorful of tropical aquarium fishes. Most species are strongly sexually dimorphic, with the females being more subdued in color and sometimes outright drab. The stunning breeding color of the male is temporary and replaced by a much more faded appearance through the rest of the year following spring breeding. The females of these fishes are often so similar that even expert ichthyologists can have difficulty identifying them. New species have been recently described and there are most likely new species yet to be discovered. Unlike most fishes, they lack air bladders for flotation and they are mostly bottom dwellers that hug the sand and gravel bottoms of flowing streams. When startled they will move in quick, short dashes, hence the common name "darter." Indiana boasts 15 extant species of *Etheostoma* (plus two extirpated species). Collectively their habitats include probably every drainage within the state and they are found in waterways ranging from swamps to large rivers to small creeks. A few species have a very restrictive distribution, being confined to a single drainage. Darters feed on a wide variety of small invertebrate prey. Copepods and other small crustaceans, mosquito larva and other small aquatic insects (both larval and adult). In fact almost any invertebrate small enough to swallow may become prey. In recent years darters have become a favorite species of many aquarists in America. Their wonderful colors and wide variety of species make them an appealing group of fishes to observe and study in an aquarium. In recent years the keeping of native fresh water fish species has grown into a significant hobby. In fact today there is an organization of individuals who keep and study native fishes in home aquariums. The North American Native Fish Association is a national organization with a newsletter and regularly scheduled conventions and field/collecting trips. Many darter species require pristine water conditions and these fish can be a barometer to help determine the quality of waterways. Like "the canary in the coal mine" they are often the first fishes to suffer from the effects of water pollution, siltation, and other forms of stream degradation. Many species are regarded as endangered, threatened or are considered species of concern. Indiana has one endangered and one regarded as a species of concern. In addition to the species shown on the next two pages there are 5 more species that occur in the state. Those species are the **Variagate Darter** (*E. variatum*), **Least Darter** (*E. microperca*), **Tippicanoe Darter** (*E. tippicanoe*), **Spotted Darter** (*E. maculatum*), **Bluntnose Darter** (*E. chlorosoma*).

Class—**Actinopterygii** (bony fishes)

Order—**Perciformes** (typical fishes)

Family—**Percidae** (perch & darters)

Rainbow Darter *Etheostoma caerulum*	**Slough Darter** *Etheostoma gracile*	**Fantail Darter** *Etheostoma flabellare*

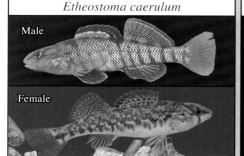
Male
Female

Male
Female

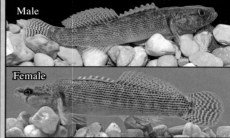
Male
Female

Size: Up to 3 inches. Most are about 2.5.

Abundance: Still fairly common in some streams, but may be extirpated in others, especially in intensive agriculture areas.

Size: Very small. Maximum of 2.25 inches.

Abundance: Mainly a southern fish but ranges northward into Indiana as far north as the Lower Wabash River watershed.

Size: Maximum total length is 3.25 inches.

Abundance: Fairly common. Found nearly statewide in flowing creeks and small to medium size rivers with rocky riffles.

Greenside Darter *Etheostoma blennoides*	**Banded Darter** *Etheostoma zonale*	**Harlequin Darter** *Etheostoma histrio*

Size: Maximum total length is 6.75 inches.

Abundance: Fairly common. Widespread in the state but absent from the northwestern corner and the southwestern corner.

Size: Maximum total length is 3 inches.

Abundance: Two widely separated populations in Indiana. Fairly common within creeks and small rivers within its range.

Size: Maximum total length about 3 inches.

Abundance: Uncommon but less rare than previously believed. Recently removed from Indiana's endangered species list.

Johnny Darter *Etheostoma nigrum*	**Spottail Darter** *Etheostoma squamiceps*	**Mud Darter** *Etheostoma asprigne*

Size: Small. Maximum of up to 2.75 inches.

Abundance: Common and widespread. One of the most common darters in the US and maybe most common darter in Indiana.

Size: Maximum total length is 3.25 inches.

Abundance: Rare in Indiana. Occurs in the state only in the lower Wabash and lower Ohio Rivers in extreme southeastern Indiana.

Size: Maximum total length is 2.75 inches.

Abundance: Uncommon in Indiana. Seems to be restricted to the main channel of the Wabash River. Apparently avoids the tributaries.

Class—**Actinopterygii** (bony fishes)

Order—**Perciformes** (typical fishes)

Family—**Percidae** (perch & darters)

Iowa Darter	**Bluebreast Darter**	**Orangethroat Darter**
Etheostoma exile	*Etheostoma camurum*	*Etheostoma spectabile*

Male

Female

Size: Max 0.75 inches.

Abundance: A northern species whose range extends southward into parts of northern Indiana.

Size: Max 2.25 inches.

Abundance: Uncommon in Indiana and apparently occurring in several disjunct populations around the state.

Size: Up to 2.75 inches.

Abundance: Fairly common and wide-spread. Absent from northernmost and southwestern Indiana.

Genus *Percina*—Logperch Darters (7 species in Indiana, 4 shown below)

Logperch—*Percina caprodes*

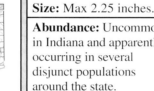

Size: Averages 3 to 5 inches with a maximum of about 7 inches.

Abundance: Fairly common. Probably occurs in suitable habitats in all Level IV watersheds in Indiana. Not all streams contain suitable habitat.

Blackside Darter—*Percina maculata*

Size: 2 to 3 inches typically. Maximum length 4.5 inches.

Abundance: Fairly common. Probably occurs in suitable habitat in every Level IV watershed in the state. Not all streams will have suitable habitat.

Dusky Darter—*Percina sciera*

Size: Averages 3 to 4 inches with a maximum of 5 inches.

Abundance: Uncommon in Indiana. Found mostly in the streams of the Wabash River Level III watershed.

Gilt Darter—*Percina evides*

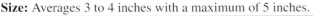

Size: Averages over 3 inches. Maximum 3.75 inches.

Abundance: Uncommon and endangered in Indiana. Possibly has experienced declines in recent decades.

Natural History of the *Percina* darters: The darters of the genus *Percina* were originally represented by a total of 9 species in Indiana. Today 2 species have been extirpated, leaving 7 extant species in the state. Only the Blackside Darter and the Logperch can be regarded as fairly common fish in Indiana. There as many as 40 *Percina* species in the US and collectively they range throughout much of the eastern United States east of the Rocky Mountains. Most are found east of the Great Plains. The infamous Snail Darter, which was the subject of a great environmental controversy that arose over the construction of the Tellico Dam in Tennesse several decades ago, is a member of this genus. Most *Percina* tend to inhabit the larger creeks (or even rivers), but some can be found in small (even tiny) creeks. The three species occurring in Indiana that are not shown above are the **Channel Darter** (*P. copelandi*), **Slenderhead Darter** (*P. phoxocephali*) and the **River Darter** (*P. shumardi*).

Class—**Actinopterygii** (bony fishes)

Order—**Esociformes** (pikes & mudminnows)

Family—**Esocidae** (pikes)

Grass Pickeral *Esox americanus*	**Northern Pike** *Esox lucius*

Size: Average 8 to 10 inches. Maximum length 14 inches.

Abundance: Fairly common. Statewide but only in clear waters with abundant aquatic vegetation.

Natural History: Inhabits natural lakes, swamps and streams. In smaller creeks it usually is found in quiet pools. This fish likes clear waters and avoids muddy streams. This is the smallest of the pike family and thus feeds on smaller fish and invertebrate prey.

Size: World record size of 62.5 pounds is from Europe.

Abundance: Uncommon. A northern species that is found only in the northernmost counties in Indiana.

Natural History: A fish of clear waters with abundant aquatic vegetation. Like all members of the pike family it is a highly carnivorous ambush predator with a very large mouth. The jaws are equipped with rows of sharp, barracuda-like teeth.

Muskellunge
Esox masquinongy

Family—**Umbridae** (mudminnows)

Central Mudminnow
Umbra limi

Size: Record size 70 pounds. Indiana record 42 pounds, 8 ounces.

Abundance: Uncommon to rare in Indiana except in Lake Michigan. Several lakes in the state are stocked.

Natural History: Known as the "Muskie" by fishermen, this largest of the pikes is a prized game fish and one of the most difficult to catch. They live in both man-made lakes and clear water rivers where they favor the deep pools containing boulders, logs, etc. Hybrids with the Northern Pike are known as "Tiger Muskie."

Size: Maximum length of 5.25 inches. Average about 2 to 3 inches.

Abundance: Fairly common. Apparently absent from some major waterways in the state.

Natural History: The Central Mudminnow is the only Indiana representative of a very small family of fishes found in both North America and in Europe. They live in swamps and still waters of oxbows or slow flowing lowland creeks. Prefers areas with mucky bottom and can tolerate waters with low oxygen.

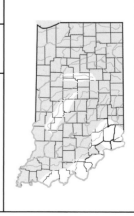

Class—**Actinopterygii** (bony fishes)

Order—**Salmoniformes** (salmonids)

Family—**Salmonidae** (trouts & salmons)

Brown Trout *Salmo trutta*	Lake Trout *Salvelinus namaycush*	Brook Trout *Salvelinus fontanalis*

Size: World record 40 pounds, 4 ounces. Indiana record is 29 pounds, 5 ounces.

Abundance: Fairly common in Lake Michigan. Stocked in some streams in the state.

Natural History: Like the Rainbow Trout this species has been introduced into Indiana where cool, clear waters allow for its survival. It is now found in Lake Michigan and has been stocked into many northern Indiana watersheds. The species is native to Europe but today is widespread in the northern and western states and in Canada.

Size: Indiana record is 37 pounds, 8 ounces. Maximum length is 4 feet.

Abundance: Uncommon but has seen an increase from historic lows a few decades ago.

Natural History: A northern species that reaches its southern limits in the great lakes region. Historically they were more common but they have suffered from parasitism by the Sea Lamprey and from degradation of water quality. These are fish of deep, cold waters and they are usually found well offshore in Lake Michigan.

Size: Indiana record is 3 pounds, 15 ounces. World record 14.5 pounds.

Abundance: Extreme northern Indiana. Native to Lake Michigan and stocked in streams.

Natural History: The Brook Trout is the only trout native to the eastern United States. This fish requires cooler water temperatures than our other trouts and is less tolerant of changes in stream conditions. It is not native to any streams in Indiana, but is native to Lake Michigan and today is stocked by Indiana Division of Fish & Wildlife.

Rainbow Trout *Onchorhynchus mykiss*	Chinook Salmon *Onchorhynchus tshawytscha*	Coho Salmon *Onchorhynchus kisutch*

Size: World record is 42 pounds, 2 ounces. Indiana record is 18 pounds, 8 ounces.

Abundance: Fairly common in Lake Michigan. Stocked irregularly around the state.

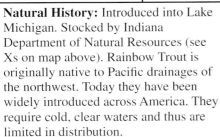

Natural History: Introduced into Lake Michigan. Stocked by Indiana Department of Natural Resources (see Xs on map above). Rainbow Trout is originally native to Pacific drainages of the northwest. Today they have been widely introduced across America. They require cold, clear waters and thus are limited in distribution.

Size: The Indiana record is 37 pounds. World record of 97 pounds, 4 ounces was from Alaska.

Abundance: Lake Michigan populations are declining due to invasive species.

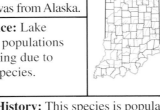

Natural History: This species is popular game fish and it is stocked annually in Lake Michigan by state wildlife agencies. Like most American Salmon they are naturally anadromous fishes of the Pacific northwest. They are an introduced species that has adapted to life in the great lakes but populations are vulnerable to imbalance from invasives.

Size: World record is 33 pounds, 7 ounces. Indiana record is 20 pounds, 12 ounces.

Abundance: Fairly common in Lake Michigan. Threatened by exotic invasive species.

Natural History: Another anadromous species native to the Pacific. Has been stocked in the great lakes since the 1970s. The sport fishery for this and other non-native salmon in the great lakes is maintained by continuous re-stocking state wildlife agencies. These fish often go by the name "Silver Salmon."

Class—**Actinopterygii** (bony fishes)

Order—**Salmoniformes** (salmonids)

Family—**Salmonidae** (trouts & salmons)

Pink Salmon *Onchorhynchus gorbuscha*	**Cisco** *Coregonus artedii*	**Lake Whitefish** *Coregonus clupeaformis*

Size: Record is 14.5 pounds. Indiana record is 2 pounds, 12 ounces.

Abundance: Uncommon in Indiana. In Indiana this fish is restricted to Lake Michigan.

Natural History: An anadromous species native to the Pacific northwest of America. Great Lakes populations have now adapted to a fresh water existence. Spawning occurs in the lower reaches of some eastern great lakes drainages. Spawning fish develop a hump on the back and are called often called "Humpback Salmon."

Size: Indiana record is 3 pounds, 12 ounces. Can grow to 20 inches.

Abundance: Now rare. Occurs in Indiana only in Lake Michigan drainages. Invasive species are a threat.

Natural History: These fish were once so common that a single fisherman might catch over a hundred in days fishing on the Great Lakes. They are now an endangered species in Indiana. A northern fish that reaches the southernmost limits of its range in northern Indiana. Cisco sometimes go by the name "Lake Herring."

Size: Indiana record is 9 pounds, 4 ounces. World record 14 pounds.

Abundance: Has declined significantly from historical numbers due to ecosystem imbalance caused by exotic species

Natural History: A northern species that reaches its southern distribution limits in the great lakes. Inhabits deep, cold waters with high dissolved oxygen content. In summer this species retreats to depths of more than 200 feet. Although not rare, they are much less common than in historical times before the impact of human activities.

Order—**Salmoniformes** (salmonids)	Order—**Osmeriformes**	Order—**Gadiformes**
Family—**Salmonidae** (trouts & salmons)	Family—**Osmeridae** (smelts)	Family—**Gadidae** (cods)
Bloater *Coregonus hoyi*	**Rainbow Smelt** *Osmerus mordax*	**Burbot** *Lota lota*

Size: Averages 8 to 12 inches with a maximum length of 16 inches.

Abundance: Only in Lake Michigan. Endemic to the great lakes.

Natural History: Lives at great depths in Lake Michigan. The name comes from the fact that fish pulled from the depths are "bloated" by the expansion of air in the air bladder. As with many great lakes endemics the Bloater is threatened by ecological imbalance.

Size: Adults average 8 to 10 inches with a maximum of 14 inches.

Abundance: In Indiana found only in Lake Michigan and its immediate tributaries.

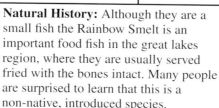

Natural History: Although they are a small fish the Rainbow Smelt is an important food fish in the great lakes region, where they are usually served fried with the bones intact. Many people are surprised to learn that this is a non-native, introduced species.

Size: Record size 18.5 pounds. Indiana record 11 pounds, 7 ounces.

Abundance: Generally uncommon and absent from many watersheds in Indiana.

Natural History: A relative of the salt water cod, haddock, and pollock, all of which are important food fishes. The Burbot is the single fresh water species of the entire order. They are cold water fish that inhabit large rivers. They are usually confined to deep waters.

Class—**Actinopterygii** (bony fishes)

Order—**Acipenseriformes** (primitive fishes)

Family—**Acipenseridae** (sturgeons)

Shovelnose Sturgeon	**Lake Sturgeon**
Scaphirynchus platorynchus	*Acipenser fulvescens*

Family—**Polydontidae** (paddlefish)

Paddlefish
Polyodon spathula

Size: Maximum of 43 inches. Indiana record 14 pounds, 8 ounces.

Abundance: The most common sturgeon in Indiana, but still an uncommon fish. Some populations are endangered.

Natural History: Lives in the deep channels of the Mississippi, Ohio, Missouri, Tennessee, Arkansas and Red Rivers and their major tributaries. Occurs in the Wabash and Ohio rivers in Indiana, and possibly the lower portions of some of those rivers larger tributaries. The Shovelnose Sturgeon is a fish of flowing water rivers and unlike many sturgeon species they do not occur naturally in lakes.

Size: Record 310 pounds. Maximum length 8 feet.

Abundance: Rare. An Endangered Species in Indiana and is under consideration for listing as federally endangered.

Natural History: Now highly endangered, the Lake Sturgeon inhabits the deep channels of the large rivers draining the middle of America. Range includes the Mississippi (except near the mouth), the Missouri, the Ohio, the Cumberland, the Arkansas and the Tennessee rivers as well as the Great Lakes. Lives for up to 150 years. Large females will lay up to 3 million eggs. Females attain a greater size than males.

Size: Can reach at least 180 pounds and over 7 feet.

Abundance: Once common in larger rivers the Paddlefish has declined significantly in many areas of its range, including Indiana.

Natural History: Paddlefish often go by the name "Spoonbill Catfish," but in fact they are not related to the catfishes. They are a member of a very small, primitive order of fishes that contains only two species (the other is a giant found in China that can reach lengths of over 20 feet). Paddlefish have skeletons that are mostly cartilage. Lives in larger rivers with turbid waters. Flesh and roe is edible and is commercially valuable.

Order—**Percopsiformes**

Family—**Percopsidae** (trout-perches)

Trout Perch
Percopsis omiscomaycus

Family—**Aphredodidae** (pirate perches)

Pirate Perch
Aphredoderus sayanus

Family—**Amblyopsidae** (cavefishes)

Hoosier Cavefish
Amblyopsis hoosieri

Size: Maximum of 7.75 inches.

Natural History: This is a species of high latitudes that approaches the southernmost limits of its range in southern Indiana. Found over sand or gravel.

Size: Maximum of 5.5 inches.

Natural History: Likes clear warm backwaters. All of the fishes on this page are unique in having the urogenital pore positioned in the throat region.

Size: 2 to 3 inches as an adult.

Natural History: Found only in a few cave system streams in southern Indiana. Endangered. Like most troglodytic organisms lacks pigmentation and is completely blind.

Class—**Actinopterygii** (bony fishes)	
Order—**Lepisosteiformes** (gar)	
Family—**Lepisosteidae**	

Longnose Gar *Lepisosteus osseus*	**Shortnose Gar** *Lepisosteus platostomus*

Size: Record 50 pounds (6 feet in length). Indiana record 22 pounds, 5 ounces.

Size: Maximum of about 5 pounds and 33 inches. Indiana record 2 pounds, 5 ounces.

Abundance: Fairly common and probably the most common gar in Indiana.

Abundance: Generally less common than the Long-nosed Gar, but can be fairly numerous in certain areas.

Natural History: America's most widespread gar species, the Longnose Gar can be found in both large and medium-sized rivers as well as large creeks. Also common in natural lakes and oxbows and in man-made impoundments. Females average larger than males and can live over 20 years. Highly piscivorous, its elongated snout is an adaptation for feeding on fish, mostly shad and other forage fishes.

Natural History: An inhabitant of quiet pools and floodplains of rivers and large creeks. Also found in swamps and oxbows and can tolerate waters with high turbidity. During periods of severe drought can survive for days in the mud of drying pools. Like all gars its swim bladder is highly vascularized and it can function like a lung. In addition to fish it also eats insects and crayfish.

Spotted Gar *Lepisosteus oculatus*	**Alligator Gar** *Atractosteus spatula*

Size: Indiana record 6 pounds. Maximum length about 3.5 feet.

Size: Can reach 10 feet and 300 pounds. No size records are available for Indiana.

Abundance: Uncommon in Indiana.

Abundance: Very rare in Indiana. Possibly extirpated.

Natural History: Habitat is swamps, sloughs, oxbows, natural lakes and slow moving creeks. In Indiana they are most common in the southwestern tip of the state. They may also found in parts of northern Indiana. This gar prefers clearer waters with less siltation than the similar Shortnose Gar. Heavily vegetated waters are preferred. It is best differentiated from the Shortnose Gar by the presence of dark spots on the snout. Food is mostly fishes but all gar are predators and they may consume a variety of prey.

Natural History: Alligator Gar once ranged well up the Ohio River and its major tributaries well into southern Indiana and all the way to southwestern Ohio. Today this is a rare fish in the northern portions of its range and was possibly extirpated in Indiana for many decades. Recent efforts to restore the species by wildlife agencies in nearby states may have resulted in the return of this fish to Indiana waters. Adult Alligator Gars are highly predaceous and known to eat small mammals and birds as well as fish and even carrion.

Class—**Actinopterygii** (bony fishes)

Order—**Amiiformes**	Order—**Osteoglossiformes** (bony tongues)	
Family—**Amiidae** (bowfin)	Family—**Hidontidae** (mooneyes)	

Bowfin
Amia calva

Size: Maximum of 21.5 pounds.

Abundance: Uncommon and irregularly distributed in Indiana. Perhaps most common in lowland swamps in southwestern Indiana.

Natural History: This is the only surviving species of an ancient family of primitive fishes that dates back to the age of the dinosaurs. Found in swamps and oxbow lakes. They sometimes go by the nickname "Grinnel." These fish are capable of gulping air into the swim bladder to breathe and burrowing into the mud to survive during droughts.

Mooneye
Hiodon tergisus

Size: Maximum 17 inches and 2.5 pounds.

Abundance: Has declined significantly in Indiana waters. Probably as a result of siltation. This fish likes clear, flowing waters.

Natural History: The Mooneye is one of only two species in the family Hiodontidae, a family which is endemic to North America. Their appearance is very similar to their distant relatives the shads and herrings. They live in large rivers and lakes with hard substrates and feed on a wide variety of invertebrate and small vertebrate prey.

Goldeye
Hiodon alasoides

Size: Reaches 20 inches and 3 pounds.

Abundance: Uncommon in Indiana. Has probably declined from historical numbers in the state. Tolerates turbidity better than Mooneye.

Natural History: Similar to the Mooneye but found in rivers with higher turbidity. Unlike the Mooneye, this species does not thrive in impoundments, but does exist in natural lakes and backwaters of large rivers. It is sometimes smoked as a food fish. They often migrate large distances up and down river systems.

Order—**Anguilliformes** (eels)	Order—**Atheriniformes**	Order—**Gasterosteiformes**
Family—**Anguillidae**	Family—**Atherinopsidae** (silversides)	Family—**Gasterosteidae** (sticklebacks)

American Eel
Anguilla rostrata

Size: Averages about 20 inches. Maximum 4 feet.

Abundance: Rare and in decline. Dams hinder migration and are one of the major reasons for decline.

Natural History: Eels have one of the most remarkable life cycles of any fish. After hatching far out in the Atlantic Ocean tiny larva migrate to the coast and swim hundreds of miles upstream in inland rivers. After up to 15 years adults return to the sea to spawn and die. The round trip journey may cover thousands of miles.

Brook Silverside
Labidesthes sicculus

Size: Ranges from 2.5 to 4 inches in length.

Abundance: Fairly common in clear warm waters with little current. Has probably declined in silt laden streams.

Natural History: Silversides travel in large schools near the surface of lakes and rivers and are important prey for larger fish species, including many game fish. They are also preyed upon by wading birds, Kingfishers, and merganser ducks as well as turtles and water snakes. Meanwhile tiny insects and zooplankton are its primary food.

Brook Stickleback
Culaea inconstans

Size: Brook Stickleback can reach 3.5 inches.

Abundance: The Brook Stickleback is probably the most common. The Threespine Stickleback is introduced.

Natural History: There are 3 stickleback species in Indiana and all are northern fishes. The **Ninespine Stickleback** (*C. pungitiuss*) and the **Threespine Stickleback** (*C. aculeatus*) are found in Lake Michigan and the immediate vicinity. The presumed range of the Brook Stickleback (*C. inconstans*) is shown above.

Class—**Actinopterygii** (bony fishes)

Order—**Clupieformes** (sardines, herrings, shad)

Family—**Clupiedae** (shad & herring)

Threadfin Shad *Dorosoma petenense*	**Gizzard Shad** *Dorosoma cepedianum*

Size: Threadfin Shad is the smallest member of this family with a maximum of about 9 inches.

Size: The Gizzard Shad can reach 3.5 pounds and over 20 inches in length.

Abundance: Can be fairly common within its limited range in the state. Probably most common in the Ohio River.

Abundance: Widespread and common in larger streams throughout the state. Also in natural lakes and impoundments.

Natural History: Threadfin Shad are filter feeding fishes occurring in large schools and they are a major food for many important game fishes in America. They are southern fish and not very tolerant of cold temperatures and severe winter cold fronts can cause major die-offs. Thus their range in Indiana is limited to the southernmost portion of the state. They are sometimes netted and used as bait and are reported to be especially good for catching large catfish.

Natural History: Gizzard Shad are another plankton feeder that filters tiny organisms from the water through specialized gill rakers. These fish occur in major rivers and their large impoundments throughout the eastern United States, including all the larger rivers in Indiana. Like the smaller Threadfin Shad they are an important forage species for many popular game fishes. They are also used as bait for large catfishes, usually as cut bait (i.e. cut in several pieces).

Skipjack Herring *Alosa chrysochloris*	**Alewife** *Alosa pseudoharengus*

Size: Skipjack Herring can get to 3.75 pounds (Indiana record is 2.5 pounds).

Size: The Alewife can reach 15 inches, although most are about 10 inches in length as adults.

Abundance: Uncommon. Restricted mostly to larger rivers and their impoundments.

Abundance: Uncommon in Indiana. Restricted to the waters of Lake Michigan.

Natural History: The Skipjack Herring is originally a species that lived in saltwater and returned to freshwaters to spawn. This condition is known as being an "anadromous" species. In Indiana they are now mostly landlocked due to the presence of dams on most major rivers. Although they are sometimes caught by fishermen they are not regarded as good table fare.

Natural History: Like the Skipjack Herring, Alewife are also anadromous fishes by nature. But they have been introduced into the Great Lakes where they have adapted to a year-round life in freshwater. They are regarded as an invasive species that is capable of out-competing native filter feeders such as the Rainbow Smelt and they are likely responsible for the decline of that species in the great lakes.

Class—**Actinopterygii** (bony fishes)

Order—**Cyprinidontiformes** (topminnows & livebearers)

Family—**Fundulidae** (topminnows)

Banded Killifish *Fundulus diaphanus*	Blackstripe Topminnow *Fundulus notatus*	Starhead Topminnow *Fundulus dispar*

Banded Killifish
Fundulus diaphanus

Size: A large *Fundulus* that can reach a maximum length of 5 inches. Most are smaller.

Abundance: Uncommon. Restricted to northwestern Indiana.

Natural History: Inhabits quite backwaters and pools within the great lakes region and along the Atlantic slope the eastern US. There are two subspecies. The Western Banded Killifish (subspecies *menona*) inhabits Indiana waters. It is primarily a northern fish.

Blackstripe Topminnow
Fundulus notatus

Size: Can reach a maximum length of 3.75 inches. Most are smaller.

Abundance: Widespread and common in most of Indiana.

Natural History: The topminnows get their name from the fact that they are always seen right at the water's surface. They have a white spot on the top of the head that is easily visible. They feed on both aquatic insects and tiny terrestrial insects that fall or fly onto the water.

Starhead Topminnow
Fundulus dispar

Size: Can reach a maximum length of 3 inches. Most are smaller.

Abundance: Unknown in Indiana. Generally uncommon elsewhere.

Natural History: There is little information available on this species in Indiana but populations are disjunct and there is evidence of a decline in some northern states. Habitat is still waters and pools in streams. Favors waters with aquatic vegetation.

Northern Studfish
Fundulus catenatus

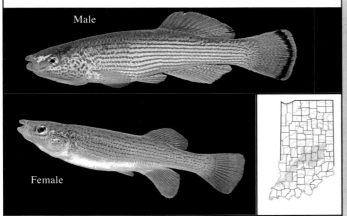

Size: The largest member of the topminnow family in Indiana. Large adults may be as much as 7 inches in length.

Abundance: Uncommon in Indiana generally but may be abundant in streams retaining suitable habitat.

Natural History: This range of this species is poorly known and the map above may not be accurate. There is evidence that it may be extirpated in some drainages while it may have been introduced and established into others. It appears most common in the upper east fork of the White River watershed (Thomerson et.al., 1989). Northern Studfish require clear waters and favor rocky, gravelly or sandy substrates. Excessive siltation (which is often common in Indiana streams) can lead to the extirpation of local populations.

Family—**Poeciliidae** (livebearers)

Western Mosquitofish—*Gambusia affinis*

Size: Females can reach 2.5 inches, males are much smaller, reaching only 1.25 inches.

Abundance: Uncommon in Indiana. Restricted to the extreme southwestern tip of the state.

Natural History: True to their name, these tiny fish eat large numbers of mosquito larva. They are thus an important controller of these nuisance insects. Ironically, attempts to control mosquitoes with chemical pesticides can negatively impact populations of Mosquitofish. Uniquely among Indiana fishes, female *Gambusia* do not lay eggs but instead give birth to fully formed young. They live in the shallows of swamps and backwaters, where they will forage in water less than an inch deep. They are a close relative of the aquarium Guppy.

Class—**Actinopterygii** (bony fishes)
Order—**Cypriniformes** (minnows & suckers
Family—**Catastomidae** (suckers)

Quillback *Carpiodes cyprinus*	Highfin Carpsucker *Carpiodes velifer*	River Carpsucker *Carpiodes carpio*

Size: Maximum about 2 feet and 12 pounds. No size records available for Indiana specimens.

Abundance: Fairly common and widespread in the larger streams in the state.

Natural History: Food is benthic invertebrates sucked from the substrate. Occurs both in rivers and impoundments where it favors areas with gravel or sand substrates. May be less tolerant of turbid conditions than its larger cousin the River Carpsucker. Like the River Carpsucker this is a commercial food fish.

Size: Maximum length about 15 inches and maximum weight about 2 pounds. No size records for Indiana.

Abundance: Uncommon. Requires clear, flowing waters with gravel or sand substrate.

Natural History: This is the smallest of the Carpsuckers and is therefore not highly valued by commercial fishermen. This species inhabits medium to large rivers and favors clearer waters with some gravel substrates. Highfin Carpsuckers are less common than our other two species. Siltation and lake impoundments may be to blame.

Size: Maximum length 25 inches. Record weight 10 pounds. No size records are available for Indiana.

Abundance: Uncommon. Found mostly in the main channels of the Wabash and Ohio.

Natural History: Found in the larger rivers and their reservoirs. Most common in the Ohio and Wabash Rivers and also in the lower reaches of those rivers major tributaries. Food is tiny invertebrates sucked from mud of the bottom of a river or lake. Known to live at least 10 years. Valued as a commercial food fish.

Smallmouth Buffalo *Ictiobus bubalus*	Largemouth Buffalo *Ictiobus cyprinellus*	Black Buffalo *Ictiobus niger*

Size: Maximum probably about 30 pounds. No size data for Indiana.

Abundance: Common in larger rivers. Uncommon in smaller streams.

Natural History: A river fish that also thrives in lakes and impoundments. Less likely to be found in turbid water than the Largemouth Buffalo and also is more fond of waters with some current. Feeds on bottom dwelling invertebrates and plants. Like other *Ictiobus* (buffalo fishes), a commercially valuable fish.

Size: Can reach a maximum of 80 pounds. No size data is available for Indiana.

Abundance: Fairly common and widespread. Introduced into Lake Michigan.

Natural History: Largemouth Buffalo are important commercial food fishes. Found in large rivers and their backwaters and in impoundments and is more accepting of silt laden waters than others of its genus. Breeds during spring in flooded fields and backwaters. Dams restrict movement.

Size: To at least 30 pounds, probably more. No size data available for Indiana.

Abundance: Probably the least common of Indiana's 3 species of *Ictiobus* suckers.

Natural History: Least common of the Buffalo fishes and regarded as a species of concern in places. Morphologically somewhat intermediate between the two previous species. In habits, feeding, etc., most similar to the Smallmouth Buffalo. Found in large and medium-size rivers.

Class—**Actinopterygii** (bony fishes)

Order—**Cypriniformes** (minnows & suckers

Family—**Catastomidae** (suckers)

Longnose Sucker	White Sucker	Blue Sucker
Catastomus catastomus	*Catastomus commersonii*	*Cycleptus elongatus*

Size: Maximum length is thought to be about 25 inches. No data is available for Indiana.

Abundance: Rare in Indiana. Found in Indiana only in Lake Michigan waters.

Natural History: The Longnose Sucker is mainly a fish of the far north and the bulk of the population occurs in Canada. It does occur in the Great Lakes. This fish favors cool streams and lakes with gravel substrates. Its range includes most of Canada and all of Alaska as far north as the Arctic where it appears to be secure.

Size: Maximum of 25 inches and about 7 pounds. No records are available for Indiana.

Abundance: Common. Occurs in streams statewide as well as in Lake Michigan.

Natural History: Name comes from the white belly of the breeding male. They inhabit a wide variety of small rivers and creeks as well as natural and man-made lakes. A bottom feeder that eats mostly benthic insects. Although bony, their flesh is quite palatable and they are sought for food and sport in some regions.

Size: Can probably reach 20 pounds. Current world record is 18 pounds, 14 ounces.

Abundance: Uncommon in Indiana. Found only in the Ohio and Wabash rivers.

Natural History: A unique member of the sucker family, the Blue Sucker is the only species of its genus. Although its range includes all of the Mississippi, Ohio, Missouri, and western gulf coastal rivers, this is today a rare fish throughout most of its range. It prefers fast flowing channels over hard bottom. Dams and siltation impact it negatively.

Northern Hogsucker	Spotted Sucker	Chubsuckers
Hypentelium nigricans	*Minytrema melanops*	*Erimyzon claviformes* & *Erimyzon sucetta*

Size: Up to about 2 feet in length. No size records available for this species in Indiana.

Abundance: Fairly common in clear streams with good current and high quality waters with no siltation.

Natural History: This species is found mostly in large, clear creeks with rocky or gravel substrates. In some regions it is also common in large rivers. This is a bottom dweller that hugs the substrate and sucks small aquatic invertebrates from sand, gravel or silt. They are very cryptically patterned.

Size: Maximum of about 18 inches. Most are about a foot in length.

Abundance: Widespread but not a particularly common species anywhere within its range.

Natural History: Lives in pools and slow moving waters of large and small rivers, as well as larger creeks. Moves into smaller creeks in spring to spawn over gravel or rocks. Feeds on small aquatic invertebrates. Although fairly widespread, this is not a common fish and it may be decreasing.

Size: Both species grow to about 15 inches, although most are about half that length.

Abundance: Creek Chubsucker is common. Lake Chubsucker is restricted to northernmost counties.

Natural History: There are two nearly identical chubsucker species in Indiana. The map above shows the range of the Creek Chubsucker (*claviformes*). The Lake Chubsucker is found in Lake Michigan and northernmost Indiana. It has 11 or 12 dorsal fin rays as opposed to 9 or 10 in the Creek Chubsucker.

Class—**Actinopterygii** (bony fishes)

Order—**Cypriniformes** (minnows & suckers)

Family—**Catastomatidae** (suckers)

Redhorse Suckers—genus *Moxostoma* (7 species in Indiana, 5 shown)

Golden Redhorse *Moxostoma erythrurum*	Black Redhorse *Moxostoma duquesnii*	Shorthead Redhorse *Moxostoma macrolepidotum*

Size: Maximum of about 26 inches and 4.5 pounds.

Abundance: Widespread and perhaps the most common redhorse sucker in Indiana, but has declined significantly in some areas.

Size: Record size 26 inches and 7 pounds. No data for Indiana.

Abundance: Little data available. Requires unpolluted streams with ample current. Probably not very common today.

Size: Can reach 19 inches and just over 3 pounds.

Abundance: Fairly common but less so than the Golden Redhorse. Favors larger rivers and tends to avoid small streams.

River Redhorse—*Moxostoma carinatum*	**Silver Redhorse**—*Moxostoma anisurum*

Size: The largest of the redhorse suckers Reaches at least 29 inches and 10.5 pounds. No size data is available for Indiana.

Abundance: There is little data available regarding the abundance of this species in Indiana and the range map shown to the right may not be an accurate depiction of this fish's range in the state.

Size: Official record 25 inches and 8.25 pounds. Unconfirmed reports of 10 pounds. No size data is available for Indiana.

Abundance: Restricted to large and medium-size rivers. Vulnerable to pollution and siltation and has probably declined in the state in recent decades. Probably an uncommon species today.

Natural History: The Redhorse Suckers are the most diverse group within the sucker family, with 20 species found in North America. The genus ranges across much of the eastern United States and there are 7 species that range into Indiana. All are similar in appearance and can be difficult to properly identify. Collectively, they range throughout the entire state and nearly every major drainage has at least one species. Their flesh is described as good but bony, and they are sometimes pursued by anglers both for food and sport. In some regions of their range there are "gigging seasons" for these species, and they are hunted at night with lights and gigs from specialized boats. This practice is fairly common in the clear rivers of the Ozark Plateau in Missouri. Some anglers will use bow-fishing techniques for these species as well. Although they will persist in reservoirs they always spawn in small to medium sized streams with gravel substrates. These are stream fishes that are typically found in clear waters. Pictured above are 5 of Indiana's *Moxostoma* species. The other two species (not shown) are the **Greater Redhorse** (*M. valenciennesi*), a rare and endangered species found in Indiana only in the St. Joseph River Watershed; and the **Smallmouth Redhorse** (*M. breviceps*) found in streams in the southern tip of Indiana and in the Ohio River. It is very similar to the Shorthead Redhorse shown above. Redhorse are often mistaken for Carp. Unlike the Carp, which is a non-native species from the old world that can live in waters of poor quality, the redhorse suckers require unpolluted waters. In this manner their presence is an indicator of the overall health of a stream. The biology and taxonomy of this group of similar species is a puzzle that is still being put together by ichthyologists and the information on these species contained here may not be entirely accurate.

Class—**Actinopterygii** (bony fishes)

Order—**Cypriniformes** (minnows & suckers)

Family—**Cyprinidae** (minnows)

Grass Carp
Ctenopharyngodon idella

Size: 4 feet and 100 pounds (in Asia).

Abundance: Uncommon but likely widely distributed in the state. Introduced into ponds and lakes to control aquatic plants.

Natural History: Inhabits pools and backwaters of large rivers and both man-made and natural lakes. Introduced into the United States from Asia to control aquatic plant growth in commercial minnow ponds. As with most alien species, the Grass Carp probably does more harm than good to the environments where it has become established.

Silver Carp
Hypophthalmichthys molitrix

Size: Can reach 60 pounds.

Abundance: Currently restricted to the major rivers but spreading rapidly. May be more widespread than shown on map.

Natural History: Native to China, the Silver Carp has become established in the larger rivers of the eastern United States. These fish consume tiny zooplankton and algae that are filtered from the flowing water of large river channels. Originally imported into Arkansas along with the Bighead Carp to control algae blooms in fish ponds.

Bighead Carp
Hypophthalmichthys nobilis

Size: Up to 3 feet and 90 pounds.

Abundance: Currently restricted to the major rivers but spreading rapidly. Highly invasive, may soon invade Lake Michigan.

Natural History: Like the previous species this fish is native to China. Now widespread in the major rivers of the eastern US, this is a filter feeder that inhabits the flowing waters of large river channels. Though both species of *Hypophthalmichthys* were intentionally introduced, they are now regarded as environmentally harmful aliens.

Common Carp
Cyprinus carpio

Size: Angling record is 55 pounds. Indiana record is 43 pounds.

Abundance: Common and widespread. In fact this is one of the most widespread fish species in America.

Natural History: Many people are surprised to learn that the Common Carp is an invasive species in America. Native to Eurasia, they were first brought to the US in the early 1800s. They are now widespread and common in most aquatic habitats in America. A benthic feeder that "roots" like a hog in muddy bottoms and increases water turbidity.

Goldfish
Carassius auratus

Size: Maximum 20 inches and up to 5 pounds.

Abundance: Uncommon but widely distributed. Released bait fish can be found almost anywhere.

Natural History: Native to Asia, the Goldfish is now widely established across most of North America. The gaudy colors commonly seen in fish ponds and pet stores rarely survive in wild populations. Found in most rivers and lakes and can survive in tiny ponds. More tolerant of pollution and siltation than many native species.

Golden Shiner
Notemigonus crysoleucas

Size: Maximum size 14.5 inches. Most are about 8 inches as adult.

Abundance: Common and widespread. A bait minnow that is now one of the most widely distributed minnows.

Natural History: This minnow is well known among fishermen and is sold as a bait fish in many regions of the US. In their natural habitat they are fish of still water pools of streams and backwaters of rivers. They will also thrive in impoundments and small farm ponds. Millions are raised commercially each year to be sold in bait stores.

Class—**Actinopterygii** (bony fishes)
Order—**Cypriniformes** (minnows & suckers)
Family—**Cyprinidae** (minnows)

Creek Chub	**Lake Chub**	**Central Stoneroller**
Semotilis atromaculatus	*Couesius plumbeus*	*Campastoma anomalum*

Size:. Maximum length 12 inches.

Abundance: Very common. Probably every stream in Indiana capable of supporting fish life will have a population of Creek Chubs.

Natural History: One of the most widespread and common creek fishes in America. Like many minnows, breeding males develop tubercles on the head and snout, leading to the common nickname "Hornyhead." In the days when most Americans lived on the farm, fishing in small creeks for Creek Chubs was commonplace entertainment for youngsters.

Size: Can reach a length of up to 9 inches.

Abundance: Fairly common within its core range. In Indiana it occurs only in Lake Michigan and possibly in its feeder streams.

Natural History: Lake Chubs are northern fishes. They are common across Canada from the east coast to British Columbia and the Yukon. They also occur in Montana and Wyoming in the western United States. Lake Michigan represents the southernmost extension of their range in the eastern United States.

Size: Maximum of about 11 inches.

Abundance: A very common species that likely occurs in almost every unpolluted stream within its range.

Natural History: The name "Stoneroller" comes from their habit of aggressively bottom feeding in gravelly stream beds, moving small stones in the process. They tend to occur in large schools as they "graze" algae and micro-organisms from the surface of rocks, gravel, sand, logs, etc. Lives in small to medium size creeks.

Southern Redbelly Dace	**Redside Dace**	**Gravel Chub** & **Streamlined Chub**
Chrosomas erythrogaster	*Clinostomus elongatus*	*Erimystax x-punctatus* & *Erimystax dissmilis*

Size: Maximum of 4.5 inches. Most are about 3 to 4 inches.

Abundance: Status in Indiana uncertain. This species is highly vulnerable to stream degradation.

Natural History: Can be found in very small streams only a few feet across. Requires clean, unpolluted waters with moderate to fast current and abundant riffles and pools. Often very common in small streams in forested regions, especially those that are fed by springs or seeps. This species is an indicator of good water quality. Breeding males are one of America's most colorful minnows.

Size: Can reach a maximum length of 4.5 inches.

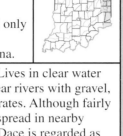

Abundance: Very rare in Indiana. State endangered. Found only in a few streams in southwestern Indiana.

Natural History: Lives in clear water creeks or small, clear rivers with gravel, sand, or rock substrates. Although fairly common and widespread in nearby Ohio, the Redside Dace is regarded as an endangered species in Indiana. Throughout its range this species seems to be in decline. Impoundments, siltation, pollution and urbanization are factors impacting its habitat.

Size: Can reach a maximum length of 4.5 inches.

Abundance: Both are rather uncommon species in Indiana. Gravel Chub may be the most common.

Natural History: These small minnows live in small and medium size rivers. They favor flowing water over gravel bottoms. In addition to the Gravel Chub the nearly identical Streamlined Chub can also be found in Indiana. The range of the two species overlap and Xs on the map above show where the Streamline Chub occurs. Gray area represents Gravel Chub.

Class—**Actinopterygii** (bony fishes)
Order—**Cypriniformes** (minnows & suckers)
Family—**Cyprinidae** (minnows)

River Chub *Nocomis bigutatus*	**Hornyhead Chub** *Nocomis micropogon*	**Pugnose Minnow** *Opsopoeodus emiliae*

Size:. River Chub can reach 13 inches.

Abundance: No information on the current abundance of this species in Indiana but overall IUCN lists it as "Least Concern."

Natural History: Inhabits medium to large rivers in areas of swift currents. Like the many other chubs breeding males have grossly enlarged heads with horny tubercles. During the breeding season the males head also turns purplish or pink. Males gather pebbles with their mouths and stack them to create large spawning mounds that may be several inches high.

Size: Maximum length about 10 inches.

Abundance: Listed as "Apparently Secure" in Indiana by the website NatureServe.org. Probably has declined from pre-settlement.

Natural History:. Large adults are quite carnivorous and feed on small crayfish, snails, and aquatic insects. They will readily take worms on hook and line and many young fishermen learned their trade by catching river chubs from nearby rivers and streams. All species of *Nocomis* develop tubercles on the snout and head that are especially apparent on the males, thus the common name.

Size: Maximum of about 2.5 inches.

Abundance: Although widespread this minnow has declined in many areas of its range. Its abundance in Indiana is not known.

Natural History: This tiny minnow is widespread across the southeast from South Carolina to eastern Texas. It also ranges northward up the Mississippi and Ohio drainages as far as the southern Great Lakes. Habitat is backwaters and pools of low gradient streams having some aquatic vegetation. Also found in swamps and natural lakes with abundant plant life.

Suckermouth Minnow *Phenacobius mirabilis*	**Blacknose Dace** *Rhinichthyes atratulus*	**Longnose Dace** *Rhinichthyes cataractae*

Size: Reaches a maximum length of 4.5 inches.

Abundance: Common. Found nearly statewide but absent from most of northern Indiana. A prairie species mainly.

Natural History: This minnow is a habitat non-specialist that occurs in both small creeks and large rivers. It is tolerant of a wide variety of conditions from clear flowing waters to still waters with some turbidity. The common name "Suckermouth" is derived from the sub-terminal position of the mouth which is typical of the sucker family.

Size: Reaches a maximum length about 4 inches.

Abundance: Fairly common throughout Indiana, but only in clear, fast flowing, gravelly streams.

Natural History: Found in springs and in small (sometimes tiny) spring-fed creeks. Its intolerance for siltation and warm water limits its distribution in the state and it may have declined from some areas due to degradation of water quality. Breeding males developed a bright red stripe along the side. Spawns in gravelly, rapid flowing water.

Size: Reaches a maximum length of 6.5 inches.

Abundance: The Lake Michigan population is common, stream populations are rare in Indiana.

Natural History: This is a widespread fish across the northern portions of North America. In fact it is the most widespread minnow in North America. The inland, stream form is the typical widespread form, but it is quite rare in Indiana. The population found in Lake Michigan is a much paler colored fish than the stream population.

Class—**Actinopterygii** (bony fishes)
Order—**Cypriniformes** (minnows & suckers)
Family—**Cyprinidae** (minnows)
Fathead Minnows—genus *Pimephales* (3 species in Indiana)

Bluntnose Minnow	Bullhead Minnow	Fathead Minnow
Pimephales notatus	*Pimephales vigilax*	*Pimephales promelas*

Size: Maximum length is 4 inches for these small minnows. Males are larger than females.

Abundance: The Bluntnose minnow is the most widespread *Pimaphales* minnow in the state, found in all watersheds. It also probably the most common of the three species in Indiana. The Bullhead Minnow can be found in the main channel of the Wabash and the East and West Forks of the White River. The Fathead Minnow is fairly widespread across the state but appears to be less common than the Bluntnose Minnow. Both the Fathead and the Bluntnose can also be found in Lake Michigan.

Natural History: These are very common minnows that may be found in rivers, creeks, reservoirs, and even ponds occasionally. They are tough little fishes that can survive warm, low oxygen waters and waters with high turbidity. Breeding males of all three species have very dark, nearly black heads and tubercles on the snout. Their resilience, rapid reproductive capacity, and ease in rearing in captivity has led to the Bluntnose Minnow and the Fathead Minnow being widely used as bait minnows, where they are often sold under the nickname "Tuffy." A reddish colored strain of the Fathead Minnow known as "Rosy Red" has also been bred for sale in bait stores. Because of their prolific use for bait, these minnows have become widely established across the United States and Canada and they are today perhaps the most common fish species in North America. These minnows are mostly bottom feeders that eat a variety of tiny invertebrates as well as algae.

Macrhybopis Chubs—genus *Macrhybopsis* (2 species in Indiana shown below)		Hybopsis Minnows—genus *Hybobpsis*
Shoal Chub	Silver Chub	Bigeye Chub
Macrhybopsis hyostoma	*Macrhybopsis storeiana*	*Hybopsis amblops*

Size: Silver Chub is by far the largest of the two species. It can reach 9 inches. Shoal Chub is much smaller and grows to only about 3 inches.

Silver Chub

Abundance: Both species have been documented from the main channel of the Wabash Rivers and the lower portions of the White River and its East Fork. Both species also probably occur in the Ohio River throughout its entire length in Indiana. The number of records for these two species suggest they are fairly common.

Natural History: This genus inhabits rivers and does not tolerate the still waters generally associated with dams. The map above shows the combined ranges of both of the state's *Machrybopsis* fishes. The ranges of the two are nearly identical, which is a little unusual. For two such similar fishes to occur sympatrically without interbreeding is an oddity. The Silver Chub is usually found in deep waters of slow moving rivers. In streams it prefers pools with sandy substrate and it can also be found in Lake Michigan. The Shoal Chubs favored habitat is in fast flowing waters over sandy areas. It can be found in small, medium and large rivers.

Shoal Chub

Size: Can reach a maximum length of 4 inches.

Abundance: Widespread in Indiana and probably fairly common except in the southeast and north.

Natural History: A fish of small rivers and large creeks. In decline over much of its range, probably due to dams and siltation. A similar species, the **Pallid Shiner** (*H. amnis*), also occurs in Indiana. The latter is an extremely rare and endangered species in the state. The Pallid Shiner historically occurred in Kankakee, lower Wabash and lower Ohio Level III watersheds of Indiana. It may now be extirpated in some areas.

Class—**Actinopterygii** (bony fishes)

Order—**Cypriniformes** (minnows & suckers)

Family—**Cyprinidae** (minnows)

| **Redfin Shiner** *Lythrurus umbratilis* | **Scarlet Shiner** *Lythrurus fasciolaris* |

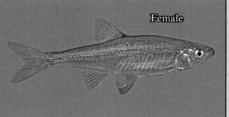

Size: Redfin Shiner grows to a maximum length of 3.5 inches.

Abundance: Common. Found in all Level IV watersheds in the state. This species may be increasing in population. Some minnow species that require clear waters are disappearing from streams impacted by siltation from excessive runoff from both agricultural operations and urbanization. The Redfin Shiner, able to tolerate turbid waters and lower water quality is filling the niche left open by the disappearance of more sensitive species.

Natural History: Redfin Shiner is a stream fish that occurs in small to medium size creeks. Their reproduction habits are noteworthy due to the fact that they often spawn in the nests of other fish species, often using the nest of one of the sunfishes. Food is small aquatic insect larva such as mayfly and midge nymphs supplemented by filamentous algae. Habitats include a wide variety of streams from still water oxbows to faster flowing creeks. Redfin Shiners tolerate both clear and turbid conditions. Longevity for individuals of this genus is short, and most will not survive beyond 3 years.

Size: Up to 4 inches.

Abundance: Uncommon in Indiana with a limited distribution in the state. But listed by natureserve.org as apparently secure in Indiana.

Natural History: Uses the nests of other species for spawning. Preferred habitat is gravel bottom creeks and small rivers where it inhabits riffles and small pools with some current. Will move into riffle areas to spawn and may migrate some distance to suitable spawning areas.

| **Ribbon Shiner** *Lythrurus fumeus* | **Mississippi Silvery Minnow** *Hybognathus nuchalis* | **Cypress Minnow** *Hybognathus hayi* |

Size: Maximum length is 2.5 inches.

Abundance: Uncommon and listed by natureserve.org as vulnerable in Indiana. Not listed as threatened or endangered by IDNR.

Natural History: The Ribbon Shiner is mostly a lowland species of the lower Gulf Coastal Plain that ranges north into much of southwestern Indiana. It inhabits creeks and small rivers over mud or sandy substrates. Lives in streams with little current that are characteristic of lowland regions.

Size: Maximum of 7 inches.

Abundance: This is a wide-ranging minnow species that is generally quite common. It is less common in Indiana than in other regions.

Natural History: Inhabits large creeks and small, medium and large rivers. Low gradient streams with little current are habitat. Often found near the confluence of larger streams with their smaller tributaries. Food is mainly benthic organisms. Little research has been done on this species.

Size: Maximum about 4.5 inches.

Abundance: Uncommon to rare in Indiana. Conservation ranking of S2 by natureserve.org means that it is regarded as imperiled in Indiana.

Natural History: This is a lowland species that is found in low gradient streams, backwaters and swamps. It is primarily a southern species whose range barely enters into Indiana in the southwestern tip of the state. Although common in its core range in the central gulf coastal plain, it is rare in Indiana.

Class—**Actinopterygii** (bony fishes)

Order—**Cypriniformes** (minnows & suckers)

Family—**Cyprinidae** (minnows)

Red Shiner *Cyprinella lutrensis*	**Spotfin Shiner** *Cyprinella spiloptera*	**Steelcolor Shiner** *Cyprinella whipplei*

Size: Can reach a maximum of 3.5 inches.

Abundance: Fairly common. Range in Indiana is limited but in some areas it may be one of the most common minnow species.

Natural History: The Red Shiner ranges throughout the Mississippi Valley and westward through the Great Plains. Within this core range it is often the most common minnow species. Its range barely enters Indiana in the northwestern part of the state. Habitat includes all stream types except for large rivers. Feeds on a variety of tiny aquatic invertebrates.

Size: Spotfin Shiner reaches 4.75 inches.

Abundance: Widespread in Indiana and found in every Level IV watershed in the state, including Lake Michigan.

Natural History: A wide variety of fresh water habitats from creeks to large rivers and also lakes and sloughs. It prefers clear waters. Food is mainly aquatic insects but some plant material is recorded in its diet. The name is derived from the fact that there are small black spots on the rear of the dorsal fin, which distinguishes it from other similar minnow species.

Size: Steelcolor Shiner reaches 5.5 inches.

Abundance: Common and widespread across the southern three-fourths of the state. Apparently absent from the upper White River.

Natural History: This species is very similar to the Spotfin Shiner and for most lay people the two are indistinguishable. Ichthyologists differentiate the two by certain characters such as the number of rays in the anal fin and scalation. Lives in creeks and small rivers. Usually in flowing water. Not usually found in mud bottom streams. Feeds mainly on small aquatic insect life.

Striped Shiner *Luxilus chrysocephalus*	**Common Shiner** *Luxilus cornutus*	**Rudd** *Scardinius erythropthalmus*

Size: Can reach 7.25 inches.

Abundance: Ranges across middle America from the Appalachians to the Great Plains. An abundant species in Indiana.

Natural History: The Striped Shiner lives in streams ranging from small creeks to medium-size rivers. It can also be found in Lake Michigan. Favors clear waters but can tolerate moderate turbidity. Food is mostly small insects.

Size: Maximum of 7.25 inches.

Abundance: Fairly common. A northern species that ranges southward into northern Indiana. Less common than the Striped Shiner.

Natural History: Lives in pools in creeks and small rivers. Likes clear, cool waters with significant current. Can also be found in lakes including Lake Michigan. Feeds on aquatic insects and their larva.

Size: Maximum of 19 inches.

Abundance: Rare in Indiana. Introduced into Lake Michigan and has perhaps become established in streams that flow into the lake.

Natural History: The Rudd is native to Europe and Asia. Like many alien species its presence is problematic. Little is known about its ecological impact, but it has been known to hybridize with the native Golden Shiner.

Class—**Actinopterygii** (bony fishes)
Order—**Cypriniformes** (minnows & suckers)
Family—**Cyprinidae** (minnows)
True Minnows—genus *Notropis*—18 species in Indiana (15 shown below and on next page)

Emerald Shiner
Notropis atherinoides

Size: Maximum length about 5 inches.

Abundance: Presumably occurs statewide. One of the few *Notropis* minnows found in the Great Lakes, including in Lake Michigan.

River Shiner
Notropis blennius

Size: Can reach a total length of 5 inches.

Abundance: Common in the major rivers of the state, i.e., Wabash and Ohio. Also lower White River (east and west forks).

Sand Shiner
Notropis stramineus

Size: Maximum length about 3.5 inches.

Abundance: Can be fairly common in streams with sandy bottoms. Has probably declined in much of Indiana.

Silverjaw Minnow
Notropis buccata

Size: Maximum total length is 3.75 inches.

Abundance: Very Common. Found in every watershed in the state but absent, however, from Lake Michigan.

Ghost Shiner
Notropis buchanani

Size: Usually under 2 inches. To 2.5 inches

Abundance: Uncommon to rare in Indiana. It has a conservation rank of vulnerable in Indiana, but it can be common farther west.

Ironcolor Shiner
Notropis chalybaeus

Size: Maximum total length is 2.5 inches.

Abundance: Uncommon in Indiana. Has probably declined from historical numbers due to siltation and pollution.

Mimic Shiner
Notropis volucellus

Size: To 3 inches.

Abundance: Probably common. Likely occurs in every watershed throughout the state. Conservation rank is apparently secure.

Bigeye Shiner
Notropis boops

Size: To 5 inches.

Abundance: Rank of "apparently secure" by NatureServe.org. Status in IN is unknown,but has declined in parts of its range in both OH and IL.

Spottail Shiner
Notropis hudsonius

Size: To 5.75 inches.

Abundance: A northern species barely ranges into Indiana. Common elsewhere and probably fairly common within its limited range in Indiana.

Class—**Actinopterygii** (bony fishes)
Order—**Cypriniformes** (minnows & suckers)
Family—**Cyprinidae** (minnows)

Pugnose Shiner
Notropis anogenus

Size: Maximum length about 5 inches.

Abundance: Rare. This species is apparently in decline in much of its range. It is regarded as a species of concern in Indiana

Blackchin Shiner
Notropis heterodon

Size: Can reach 2.75 inches.

Abundance: No data is available on abundance from Indiana DNR. Regarded as S2 (Imperiled) by NatureServe.org.

Blacknose Shiner
Notropis heterolepis

Size: Can reach a maximum of 2.75 inches.

Abundance: No data is available on abundance from Indiana DNR. Regarded as S3 (Vulnerable) by NatureServe.org.

Channel Shiner
Notropis wickliffi

Size: Maximum length about 5 inches.

Abundance: No data is available on abundance from Indiana DNR but it is probably fairly common within its range in Indiana.

Rosyface Shiner
Notropis rubellus

Size: Can reach a maximum of 3.5 inches.

Abundance: No data is available on abundance from Indiana DNR but it is probably fairly common within its range in Indiana.

Silver Shiner
Notropis photogenis

Size: Maximum of 19 inches.

Abundance: No data is available from Indiana DNR but it is probably fairly common. Conservation rank is S4 (apparently secure).

Natural History: In the sense that most people think of minnows as being tiny fishes, these are the "true minnows." Members of this genus are among the smallest of Indiana fishes. Several *Notropis* are quite diminutive with a maximum length of only about 2.5 inches. The largest species will barely exceed 5.5 inches. *Notropis* is largest genus of minnows in North America with as many as 83 species across the continent. In fact, this is the second largest generic group of fishes in North America, surpassed only by the darters of the *Etheostoma* genus (family Percidae). The exact status some species included in this genus is problematic and taxonomic changes occur frequently within the group, with occasional species being re-assigned to another genus and some being added from other genera. New species are occasionally described as a segment of a population is determined to constitute a genetically isolated and differentiated sub-population. The distribution of the *Notropis* genus is generally east of the Rocky Mountain Continental Divide, and most species occur within the Gulf of Mexico Drainage Basin. There were at least 19 species native to Indiana but one species, the Popeye Shiner (*N. ariommus*) has been extirpated. Two more are regarded as species of concern and several more are in decline in the state due to water quality issues. There are three species so rarely encountered in the state that they are not shown here. They are the **Silverband Shiner** (*N. shumardi*), the **Bigmouth Shiner** (*N. dorsalis*), and the **Weed Shiner** (*N. texanus*). Collectively, the Shiner Minnows are found in virtually all aquatic habitats within the state and their combined ranges encompass all of Indiana. The breeding males of many *Notropis* species can be colorful. While most species don't acquire significant color on the body they may acquire yellow, orange or red color in the fins of nuptial males. At least one species, the Emerald Shiner (*N. atherinoides*) is widely used as a bait minnow.

Class—**Actinopterygii** (bony fishes)

Order—**Siluiformes** (catfishes)

Family—**Ictaluridae** (american catfishes)

Yellow Bullhead *Ameiurus natalis*	**Black Bullhead** *Ameiurus melas*	**Brown Bullhead** *Ameiurus nebulosus*

Yellow Bullhead
Ameiurus natalis

Size: Maximum of 19 inches. The world record of 6 pounds, 10 ounces was caught in Missouri.

Abundance: Very common. Probably the most common catfish in Indiana.

Natural History: Widespread, common and easily caught on hook and line the Yellow Bullhead is a familiar fish to many Americans. They are often known by the nickname "Mudcat." Ranges across all of Indiana. Can be told from other bullheads by its yellow chin barbels.

Black Bullhead
Ameiurus melas

Size: Maximum length of 24 inches and record weight of 8 pounds. No records available for Indiana.

Abundance: Common and widespread but probably less common than Yellow Bullhead.

Natural History: Black Bullheads are mainly nocturnal fishes that do not feed during the day. They live in still water pools in streams or in natural lakes and man-made impoundments. They can be distinguished from the Yellow Bullhead by their dark chin barbels. Brown Bullhead has darker caudal fin (see photos).

Brown Bullhead
Ameiurus nebulosus

Size: Maximum of 21 inches. The state record of 7 pounds is also a new world record for this species.

Abundance: Probably the least common of the three bullhead species in Indiana.

Natural History: As with other bullheads, the parent fish stay with the eggs until hatching and the newly hatched young swim in schools near the surface with the mother bullhead in attendance. Found in ponds, lakes, sloughs, creeks and small rivers. Bullheads tolerate turbid waters better than most fishes.

White Catfish *Ameiurus catus*	**Blue Catfish** *Ictalurus furcatus*	**Channel Catfish** *Ictalurus punctatus*

White Catfish
Ameiurus catus

Size: Maximum length 2 feet. Indiana record is 9 pounds, 12 ounces.

Abundance: Rare in Indiana. Recorded from only a few locations in the state.

Natural History: A fish of the Atlantic slope introduced into Indiana. Despite its name it is not white. The typical color is bluish gray above with a darker head. It does have white chin barbels and a white (or pale yellow) belly.

Blue Catfish
Ictalurus furcatus

Size: Maximum size 150 pounds and 5 feet. Indiana record is 104 pounds.

Abundance: Fairly common in deep channels of larger rivers in southern Indiana.

Natural History: This is America's largest catfish and old (unverified) reports of specimens in excess of 300 pounds exist. This is an important game fish and also important commercially. Most common in the larger rivers and their impoundments.

Channel Catfish
Ictalurus punctatus

Size: Maximum of about 65 pounds. Indiana record is 37 pounds, 8 ounces.

Abundance: Common and widespread. Indiana's most common large catfish.

Natural History: A popular game species. Grown commercially as a food fish on fish farms in the south and sold in groceries and restaurants. Specimens in clear water are uniformly dark (as in photo above). Individuals from turbid waters are light gray with black spots.

Class—**Actinopterygii** (bony fishes)

Order—**Siluiformes** (catfishes)

Family—**Ictaluridae** (american catfishes)

Flathead Catfish *Plylodictus olivaris*	**Size:** Maximum of about 100 pounds. Indiana record is 79 pounds, 8 ounces.	
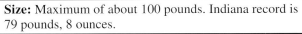	**Abundance:** Fairly common but less common than the Channel Catfish.	
	Natural History: Second in size only to the Blue Catfish. Found mostly in rivers and in impoundments of larger rivers. Adults are mainly nocturnal and will spend the day hiding under submerged rocks or logs or in undercut banks.	

Genus—*Noturus* (madtoms)

Stonecat *Noturus flavus*	**Brindled Madtom** *Noturus miurus*

Tadpole Madtom *Noturus gyrinus*	**Freckled Madtom** *Noturus nocturnus*
 	  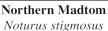
Mountain Madtom *Noturus eleutherus*	**Northern Madtom** *Noturus stigmosus*
 	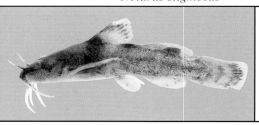 

Size: These are small catfishes. The largest example of the genus is the Stonecat (*N. flavus*) which can reach a length of 12 inches. Most are much smaller. The maximum recorded length for each of Indiana's madtom other species is as follows: Brindled Madtom and Northern Madtom, 5.25 inches; Tadpole Madtom, 5 inches; Freckled Madtom, just under 6 inches; and Mountain Madtom, 5 inches.

Natural History: There are 26 species total in this genus. 6 occur in Indiana. All Madtoms are secretive and nocturnal, and are thus relatively unknown to the general public. Most Madtom species occur in the eastern portion of America, but a few species range well into the Great Plains and the Stonecat can be found as far west as Wyoming and Montana. Like other American catfishes the Madtoms have spiny dorsal and pectoral fins that produce a mild venom. A puncture from one of these spines can result in a significant amount of pain and swelling, but it is not life threatening. Like all catfishes, madtoms have a fleshy fin between the dorsal fin and the tail known as an "adipose fin." In the most madtoms this fin connects to the caudal (tail) fin, a character that immediately separates madtoms from the rest of the catfish family. These are predaceous fish that feed on a wide variety of aquatic life consisting of both invertebrates and very small fishes. They feed and are active mostly at night, and spend the days hidden beneath overhanging root wads or burrowed into detritus of deep pools. Most madtoms are stream fishes that inhabit creeks and small to medium sized rivers. The Mountain Madtom, Stonecat and Northern Madtom can also be found in large rivers.

Class—**Actinopterygii** (bony fishes)

Order—**Scorpaeniformes** (scorpion fish)

Family—**Cottidae** (sculpins)

Banded Sculpin *Cottus carolinae*	**Mottled Sculpin** *Cottus bairdi*

Size: May rarely reach 7 inches. Most adults are about 4 to 5 inches in length.

Abundance: In Indiana the Banded Sculpin is restricted to the southern tip of the state. This is a fish of small to medium size creeks with clear, flowing waters. It is usually associated with spring-fed streams that are unaffected by siltation or excessive runoff, an aquatic habitat that is limited in Indiana.

Size: Can reach a maximum of 6 inches in length.

Abundance: Although generally uncommon, the Mottled Sculpin can be a fairly common fish in suitable habitat of clear, cool streams and in Lake Michigan. It is the most widespread and probably the most common sculpin species in the state and populations appear to be secure.

Natural History: Most of the 250 plus members of this order of fish (Scorpaeniformes) are cold water marine species. About 30 species inhabit freshwater streams in America. Most are found in the western United States and in the northern portions of the continent. The two species shown here are among the few that range east of the Mississippi and south of the Great Lakes. The Banded Sculpin is a stream fish that favors fast flowing water and riffle areas of very small to large streams. A substrate of rock or gravel is a habitat requirement for this species.

Natural History: Typically a fish of upland streams and spring-fed runs where they inhabit the fast flowing regions with gravel or rocky substrates. Also found in Lake Michigan. Requires cold waters. All Sculpins have large mouths that enable them to take larger prey than would be suspected for such a small fish. They are highly cryptic and their color and pattern always matches the substrate of their stream. They are thus nearly impossible to see when motionless on the gravel of stream beds. Of the two sculpin species shown, this is the most common in Indiana.

In addition to the two species shown on this page, there are 2 other sculpin species that inhabit Indiana in the waters of Lake Michigan. Those species are the **Slimy Sculpin** (*C. cognatus*); and the **Deepwater Sculpin** (*Moxocephalus thomposonii*). Both these fishes are northern species found mostly in Canada. Their Indiana range is restricted to Lake Michigan and they are rarely observed by Indianan residents.

REFERENCES

Chapters 1 and 2

Print

Bailey, Robert G. 2009. *Ecosystem Geography, From Ecoregions to Sites.* Springer Science & Business Media, New York, NY.

Hunt, Charles B. 1974. *Natural Regions of the United States and Canada.* W.H. Freeman and Company, San Francisco, CA.

Ricketts, Taylor H., Eric Dinerstein, David M. Olson, and Col. J. Loucks, et al. 1999. *Terrestrial Ecoregions of North America.* World Wildlife Fund and Island Press. Washington, DC.

Internet

US Environmental Protection Agency/Ecoregions of North America—www.epa.gov/wed/pages/ecoregions.htm

The Encyclopedia of Earth—www.eoearth.org

USGS—www.usgs/science/geology/regions

Commission for Environmental Cooperation—www.cec.org

Indiana Division of Forestry/Indiana's Old Growth Forests—www.in.gov/dnr/forestry/files/indianaoldgrowthforests.pdf

Mammal References

Print

Barbour, Roger W. and Wayne Davis, 1974. *Mammals of Kentucky.* University Press of Kentucky. Lexington, KY.

Bowers, Nora, Rick Bowers and Ken Kaufman. 2004. *Mammals of North America.* Houghton Mifflin Company. NY, NY.

Cudmore, Wynn W. and John O. Whitaker Jr. The Distribution of the Smokey Shrew (*Sorex fumeus*) and the Pygmy Shrew (*Microsorex hoyi*) in Indiana with notes on the distribution of other shrews. Proc. Indiana Academy of Science pp. 462–469.

Hoffmeister, Donald F. 2002. *Mammals of Illinois.* University of Illinois Press. Urbana and Chicago, IL.

Johnson, Scott. 1988. *Status and Distribution of the Franklin's Ground Squirrel.* Wildlife Management and Research Notes, Indiana Department of Natural Resources.

Kays, Roland W. and Don. E. Wilson. 2009. *Mammals of North America.* Princeton University Press. Princeton, NJ.

Quin, Vanessa S., Chia-Chun Tsai and Patrick A. Zollner. 2010. *Distribution of the Plains Pocket Gopher (Geomys bursarius) in the Grassland Physiographic Regions of Indiana.* Proceedings of the Indiana Academy of Science 119 (1).

Walker, E.P. 1983. *Walker's Mammals of the World.* The Johns Hopkins University Press. Baltimore, MD.

Whitaker, John O. and Russell E. Munford. 2009. *Mammals of Indiana.* Indiana University Press.

Whitaker, John O. Jr. and W. J. Hamilton Jr. 1998. *Mammals of the Eastern United States.* Cornell University Press. Ithaca, NY.

Wilson, Don E. and Sue Ruff. 1999. *North American Mammals.* Smithsonian Institution.

Ford, Steven D. Range, Distribution and Habitat of the Western Harvest Mouse Reithrodontomys megalotis in Indiana. *The American Midland Naturalist,* Vol. 98, No. 2, 1977. pp 422–432.

Internet

Illinois Department of Natural Resources—www.dnr.illinois/gov

Indiana Department of Natural Resources—www.in.gov/dnr

Illinois Natural History Survey—www.inhs.illinois.edu

Kentucky Department of Fish and Wildlife Resources—www.kdfwr.state.ky.us

Kentucky Bat Working Group—www.biology.eku.edu/bats

International Union of Concerned Naturalists—www.iucnredlist.org

Nature Serve Explorer—www.natureserve.org

Ohio Department of Natural Resources—www.wildlife.ohiodnr.gov

Purdue Extension—www.extension.purdue.edu

Smithsonian National Museum of Natural History—www.mnh.si.edu

Mammalian Species, American Society of Mammologists species accounts—www.science.smith.edu

Encyclopedia of Life—www.eol.org

Bird References

Print

Clark, William S. and Brian K. Wheeler. 1987. *A Field Guide to Hawks-North America.* Peterson Field Guides, Houghton Mifflin Co. Boston, MA.

Dunn, John L., Kimball Garret, Thomas Shultz, and Cindy House. *A Field Guide to Warblers of North America.* Peterson Field Guides, Houghton Mifflin Co. Boston, MA.

Farrand, John, Jr. 1998. *An Audubon Handbook, Eastern Birds.* McGraw Hill Book Co. New York, NY.

Floyd, Ted. 2008. *Smithsonian Field Guide to the Birds of North America.* Harper Collins Publishers. New York, NY.

Harlan, Robert N., Joseph W. Hammond, David C. Dister, Bernard F. Master, and Bill Whan. 2008. *Annotated Checklist of the Birds of Ohio.* Ohio Birds Records Committee, North Bend, OH.

Kaufman, Ken. 2000. *The Birds of North America.* Houghton Mifflin Co., New York, NY.

Mengel, Robert M. 1965. *The Birds of Kentucky.* American Ornithologist's Union Monogram, no. 3. The Allen Press, Lawrence, KS.

Mumford, Russell E. and Charles E. Keller. 1984. *The Birds of Indiana.* Indiana University Press. Bloomington, IN.

Palmer-Ball, Brainard. 1996. *The Kentucky Breeding Bird Atlas.* The University Press of Kentucky, Lexington, KY.

Johnsgard, Paul A. 1988. *North American Owls, Biology and Natural History.* Smithsonian Institution Press, Washington, DC.

Vanner, Michael. 2003. *The Encyclopedia of North American Birds.* Parragon Publishing, Bath, UK.

Internet

Audubon Guide to North American Birds—www.audubon.org

Brock's Birds of Indiana—www.ulib.iupuidigital.org

Cornell University Lab of Ornithology-Birds of North America Online—http://birds.bna.cornell.edu.bna/species.

Ebird—www.ebird.org

Encyclopedia of Life—www.eol.org

Environment Canada—www.ec.gc.ca

Indiana Audubon Society—www.indianaaudubon.org

Indiana Department of Natural Resources—www.in.gov/dnr

Illinois Department of Natural Resources—www.dnr.illinois.gov

Illinois Ornithological Society—www.illinoisbirds.org

McGill Bird Observatory—www.migrationresearch.org

NatureServe Explorer—www.natureserve.org

Ohio Ornithological Society—www.ohiobirds.org

Waterfowl Hunting Management in North America—www.flyways.us

Turtle References

Print

Buhlmann, Kurt. Tracey Tuberville, and Whit Gibbons. 2008. *Turtles of the Southeast.* The University of Georgia Press, Athens, GA.

Collins, Joseph T. and Travis W. Taggart. 2009. *Standard Common and Scientific Names for North American Amphibians, Turtles, Reptiles & Crocodilians.* The Center for North American Herpetology, Hays, KS.

Conant Roger, and Joseph T. Collins. 1998. *Reptiles and Amphibians of Eastern/Central North America.* Houghton Mifflin Co., Boston–New York.

Ernst, Carl H., Jeffrey E. Lovich, and Roger W. Barbour. 1994. *Turtles of the United States and Canada.* Smithsonian Institution Press, Washington and London.

Niemiller, Matthew L., R. Graham Reynolds, and Brian T. Miller. 2013. *The Reptiles of Tennessee.* The University of Tennessee Press, Knoxville, TN.

Trauth, Stanley E., Henry W. Robison, and Michael V. Plummer. 2004. *The Amphibians and Reptiles of Arkansas.* The University of Arkansas Press, Fayetteville, AR.

Internet

Encyclopedia of Life—www.eol.org

Illinois Department of Natural Resources—www.dnr.illinois.gov

Illinois Natural History Survey—www.inhs.illinois.edu

Indiana Herp Atlas—www.inherpatlas.com

Indiana Department of Natural Resources—www.IN.gov

Kentucky Department of Fish & Wildlife Resources—www.kdfwr.state.ky.us

NatureServe Explorer—www.natureserve.org

Reptile References

Print

Collins, Joseph T. and Travis W. Taggart. 2009. *Standard Common and Scientific Names for North American Amphibians, Turtles, Reptiles & Crocodilians.* The Center for North American Herpetology, Hays, KS.

Conant Roger, and Joseph T. Collins. 1998. *Reptiles and Amphibians of Eastern/Central North America.* Houghton Mifflin Co., Boston–New York.

Meade, Les. 2005. *Kentucky Snakes. Their Identification, Variation, and Distribution.* Kentucky State Nature Preserves Commission.

Minton, S. A. Jr. 2001. *Amphibians and Reptiles of Indiana.* Indiana Academy of Sciences, Indianapolis, Indiana.

Trauth, Stanley E., Henry W. Robison, and Michael V. Plummer. 2004. *The Amphibians and Reptiles of Arkansas.* The University of Arkansas Press, Fayetteville, AR.

Powell, Robert, Roger Conant and Joseph T. Collins. 2016. *Reptiles and Amphibians of Eastern/Central North America.* Houghton Mifflin Co., Boston–New York.

Niemiller, Matthew L., R. Graham Reynolds, and Brian T. Miller. 2013. *The Reptiles of Tennessee.* The University of Tennessee Press, Knoxville, TN.

Shupe, Scott. 2005. *US Guide to Venomous Snakes and Their Mimics.* Skyhorse Publishing, New York, NY.

Trauth, Stanley E., Henry W. Robison, and Michael V. Plummer. 2004. *The Amphibians and Reptiles of Arkansas.* The University of Arkansas Press, Fayetteville, AR.

Internet

Encyclopedia of Life—www.eol.org

Illinois Department of Natural Resources—www.dnr.illinois.gov

Illinois Natural History Survey—www.inhs.illinois.edu

Indiana Herp Atlas—www.inherpatlas.com

Indiana Department of Natural Resources—www.IN.gov

Kentucky Department of Fish & Wildlife Resources—www.kdfwr.state.ky.us

The Center for North American Herpetology—www.naherpetology.org

NatureServe Explorer—www.natureserve.org

Amphibian References

Print

Collins, Joseph T. and Travis W. Taggart. 2009. *Standard Common and Scientific Names for North American Amphibians, Turtles, Reptiles & Crocodilians.* The Center for North American Herpetology, Hays, KS.

Conant, Roger, and Joseph T. Collins. 1998. *Reptiles and Amphibians of Eastern/Central North America.* Houghton Mifflin Co., Boston–New York.

Niemiller, Matthew L. and R. Graham Reynolds. 2011. *The Amphibians of Tennessee.* University of Tennessee Press, Knoxville, TN.

Trauth, Stanley E., Henry W. Robison, and Michael V. Plummer. 2004. *The Amphibians and Reptiles of Arkansas.* The University of Arkansas Press, Fayetteville, AR.

Powell, Robert, Roger Conant and Joseph T. Collins. 2016. *Reptiles and Amphibians of Eastern/Central North America.* Houghton Mifflin Co., Boston–New York.

Trauth, Stanley E., Henry W. Robison, and Michael V. Plummer. 2004. *The Amphibians and Reptiles of Arkansas.* The University of Arkansas Press, Fayetteville, AR.

Dodd, C. Kenneth. 2013. *Frogs of the United States and Canada.* Johns Hopkins University Press, Baltimore, MD.

Internet

AmphibiaWeb—amphibiaweb.org

Berkley Mapper—berkleymapper.berkley.edu

Illinois Department of Natural Resources—www.dnr.illinois.gov

Illinois Natural History Survey—www.inhs.illinois.edu

Indiana Herp Atlas—www.inherpatlas.com

Indiana Department of Natural Resources—www.IN.gov

International Union of Concerned Naturalists—www.iucnredlist.org

Kentucky Department of Fish & Wildlife Resources—www.kdfwr.state.ky.us

NatureServe Explorer—www.natureserve.org

OhioAmphibians.com

The Center for North American Herpetology—www.naherpetology.org

Fish References

Print

Clay, William M. 1974. *The Fishes of Kentucky.* Kentucky Department of Fish & Wildlife Resources, Frankfort, KY.

Eddy, Samuel. 1969. *How to Know the Fresh Water Fishes.* Wm. C. Brown Company Publishers, Dubuque, IA.

Etnier, David A. and Wayne C. Starnes. 1993. *The Fishes of Tennessee.* The University of Tennessee Press, Knoxville, TN.

Fisher, Brant E. 2008. *Current Status and Distribution of Indiana's Seven Endangered Darter Species (Percidae).* Proceedings of Indiana Academy of Science, 117 (2): 167–192.

Goldstein, Robert J. with Rodney Harper and Richard Edwards. 2000. *American Aquarium Fishes.* Texas A&M University Press, College Station, TX.

Lyons, J., D. Marshall, S. Marcquenski, T. Larson, & J. Unmuth. Conserving the Starhead Minnow, *Fundulus dispar* in Wisconsin. *American Currents* (Spring 2021) *20–26.*

Miller, Rudolph J. 2004. *The Fishes of Oklahoma.* The University of Oklahoma Press, Norman, OK.

Page, Lawrence M. and Brooks M. Burr. 2011. *Peterson Field Guide to Freshwater Fishes of North America North of Mexico.* Houghton Mifflin Harcourt, Boston–New York.

Pflieger, William L. 1975. *The Fishes of Missouri.* Missouri Department of Conservation, Springfield, MO.

Burr, Brooks M. & Melvin L. Warren, Jr. 1986. *A Distributional Atlas of Kentucky Fishes.* Kentucky Nature Preserves Commission.

Smith, Philip W. 2002. *The Fishes of Illinois.* University of Illinois Press. Urban and Chicago, IL.

Thomerson, J. & L. Smith. 1989. Distribution and Conservation Status of the Northern Studfish *Fundulus catenatus* in Indiana. *Southeastern Fisheries Council Proceedings* Vol. 1, Number 20.

Internet

FishBase—www.fishbase.org

FishMap.org

Illinois Department of Natural Resources—www.dnr.illinois.gov

Illinois Natural History Survey—www.inhs.illinois.edu

Indiana Division of Fish & Wildlife—in.gov/fish&wildlife/

North American Native Fish Association—www.nanfa.org

National Fish Habitat Action Plan—www.fishhabitat.org

NatureServe Explorer—www.natureserve.org

USGS Fact Sheets—www.search.usgs.gov

Kentucky Department of Fish & Wildlife Resources—www.kdfwr.state.ky.us

Encyclopedia of Life—www.eol.org

Land Big Fish—www.landbigfish.com

GLOSSARY

Aestivate/Aestivation	Dormant state of inactivity usually brought on by hot, dry conditions. The opposite of hibernation, which is a wintertime dormancy.
Amphipod	A Crustacean of the order Amphipoda. Includes the freshwater shrimps.
Anadromous	Ascending into freshwater rivers to spawn.
Annelid/Annalida	A class of invertebrate organisms commonly known as worms.
Anuran	A member of the amphibian order Anura (the frogs & toads).
Arboreal	Pertaining to trees.
Arthropod	A member of the invertebrate phylum Arthropoda.
Aspen Parkland	An open or semi-open area (usually grassland) that is intermingled with groves of Aspen.
Barbel	A long "whisker-like" appendage originating near the mouth of fishes, often sensory.
Barrens	Open areas within normally forested or brushy habitats.
Benthic	Pertaining to the bottom of a stream or lake.
Bivalve	An organism of the phylum Molluska (mollusks) or Branchiopoda having a shell consisting of two halves.
Boreal	Northern.
Borrow Pit	Shallow ditches and ponds created by road construction when earth is "borrowed" from a nearby area to build up road beds.
Buteo	A hawk belonging to the genus Buteo. Also known as the "Broad-winged Hawks."
Cache	The act of storing or hiding food for future use.
Carapace	The top half of the shell of a turtle.
Carnivore	A meat eater.
Caudal	Pertaining to the tail.
Chromosome	Long strand of proteins and DNA found within the nucleus of a cell.
Circumpolar	Literally, around the poles. Usually used in reference to the geographic range of an organism, that is found throughout the northern hemisphere.
Cloaca	A common opening for reproductive and excretory functions in an organism. Typical for all animals except mammals.
Congeneric	Belonging to the same genus.
Conspecific	Belonging to the same species.
Contiguous	In contact with or adjoining.
Copepod	A group of tiny crustaceans belonging to the suborder Copepoda. Many are microscopic and aquatic and are important food for tiny fishes and other small aquatic organisms.
CRP	Conservation Reserve Program.
Crustacean	A member of the class Crustacea. A class of Arthropod organisms that includes the crayfish, lobsters, crabs, shrimps, barnacles, copepods, and water fleas.

Cryptic	Pertaining to concealment.
Diploid	Having the normal set of two chromosomes.
Dipteran	An insect of the order Diptera. Includes flies, mosquitoes, gnats and midges.
Disjunct	Not attached to or not adjoining.
Dessicate/Dessication	Dry out.
Diurnal	Pertaining to day. Being active by day.
DNR	Department of Natural Resources.
Dorsal	The top or back of an organism.
Dorso-lateral Fold	A fold of skin that runs along both sides of the back on certain frog species.
Dorso-ventral	The region between the side and the belly of an organism, or along the lower side adjacent to the belly.
Echolocate/Echolocation	The use of sound waves to navigate or move about. As in bats.
Ecoregion	A large unit of land or water containing a geographically distinct assemblage of species, natural communities, and environmental conditions.
Ecotone	The region where one or more habitats converge.
Embryo	A young animal that is developing from a fertilized egg. Embryonic stage ends at birth or hatching.
Endemic	Native to a particular area.
Endotherm/Endothermic	An organism that regulates its body temperature internally. Warm-blooded.
Ephemeral	Fleeting. Temporary.
Extirpated	No longer found within a given area.
Extant	Still present. Opposite of extirpated.
Fecund/Fecundity	Capable of producing abundant offspring.
Fin rays	The bony structures that support the membranes of a fish's fin.
Fossorial	Burrowing or living in underground burrows.
Gastropod	A class of the animal phylum Molluska. Includes snails, slugs, conchs, etc.
Herbaceous	A type of flowering plant which does not develop woody tissue.
Holarctic	The circumpolar region that includes North America, Europe, and Asia.
Homogeneous	Of the same kind.
IDNR	Indiana Department of Natural Resources.
Insectivorus	Insect eating.
Invertivorous	Feeding on invertebrates.
Intergrade	An organism which possesses morphological characteristics that are intermediate between two distinctly different forms.
Irruptive	The sudden movement of animals from one portion of their range to another, often very distant portion of their range. As in when Snowy Owls occasionally move down from the Arctic region into the southern half of North America.
Isopod	An order of Crustaceans that includes the familiar pillbugs.
Karst	A landscape underlain by limestone which has been eroded by water chemically reacting with the the stone to produce acids which over time dissolves the rock and create caves, sinkholes, and fissures in the rock.
Keeled Scales	The presence of a small ridge down the middle of the dorsal scales on snakes.
Lentic	Non-flowing bodies of water, lakes, swamps, ponds, etc.
Lepidoptera/Lepidopteran	Butterflies and moths.
Mandible	The lower jaw of an animal or the bill of a bird.

Marine	Pertaining to living in a salt water environment.
Market Hunting	The practice of hunting and killing of wildlife for sale as food items. Market hunting was widely practiced in America from the early days of European colonization until around early 1900s.
Mast	Seeds produced by plants in a deciduous forest. Usually means the cumulative production of acorns, nuts, berries, seeds, etc., which are widely utilized by wildlife as food.
Melanistic	A predominance of the dark pigment known as melanin. The opposite of Albinistic.
Mesic	Damp or moist.
Metabolic/Metabolism	The sum of the chemical activity that occurs within a living organism. Usually relates to the digestion of food and utilization of food compounds within the body.
Metamorphose	Change of the body. Usually refers to the change from an immature stage to a more mature stage (as in a tadpole to a frog).
Metamorphosis	Abrupt physical change of body form.
Millinery Trade	The sale of bird feathers.
Monotypic Species	A species with no subspecies.
Molt	The shedding of and renewal (replacement) of skin, hair, or feathers.
Moraine	Large mass of earth, sand, gravels, and rock bulldozed by glacial movement. Moraines usually accumulate along the sides and in the front of glaciers.
Morphology	The study of the body form, shape, and structure of organisms, including colors or patterns.
Muskeg	A Sphagnum bog occurring in the boreal (northern) regions of North America.
Neotropical	Pertaining to the tropical regions of the western hemisphere.
Nuptial	Pertaining to breeding.
Obligate	In biology means occurring within a restricted environment.
Omnivore	Eats both plant and animal matter.
Ontogenetic	Related to the development or age of an organism.
Opercle flap	The bony structure on the side of a fish's head that covers the gills. Also sometimes called gill cover.
Organism	A living thing.
Orthopteran	A member of the insect order Orthoptera. Includes such well-known insects as crickets and grasshoppers.
Ossification	The formation of bone.
Palearctic	The geographic region that includes Europe and northern Asia.
Parthenogenesis	The development of an ovum (egg) without fertilization.
Passage Migrant	Refers to birds that merely migrate through an area without staying any appreciable amount of time.
Pectoral	Pertain to or located in the chest area.
Pelage	Fur.
Pelvic	Pertaing to or located in the region of the pelvis (hips).
Phylogeny	The evolutionary relationships and/or evolutionary history of organisms.
Physiography	Refers to the natural features of a landscape, i.e. mountains, rivers, plains, etc.
Piscivorous	Fish eating.
Plastron	The ventral (bottom) portion of a turtle's shell.

Plumage	The feathers of a bird.
Polychaete worms	Annelid worms (Phylum Annelida) belonging to the class Polychaeta. Mostly marine but some are fresh water.
Polygamous	Mating with more than one individual.
Precocious	Having adult (or highly developed) characteristics in the young.
Precocial	Being highly precocious.
Predaceous	Feeding on other animals, being a predator.
Puddle Duck	Ducks belonging to the genus *Anas*.
Prehensile	Grasping. As in a prehensile tail that is able to wrap around and grasp a tree limb.
Regenerative	Refers to the ability to repair or replace damaged or destroyed tissues or structures.
Riparian	Pertaining to the bank of a stream or river.
Sexual Dimorphism	Morphological differences between the sexes.
Snout to vent length	A measurement consisting of the distance between the tip of the snout and the cloaca. Typically used as a measurement to describe the length of frogs and toads, but sometimes applied to fishes and other vertebrates.
Species of Concern	A species or subspecies which might become threatened under continued or increased stress.
Species of Special Interest	A species that occurs periodically and is capable of breeding in the state.
Successional woodlands/areas	Landscape areas (usually woodlands) that are undergoing change from an early stage of development to an older stage. As in woodlands regenerating following logging operations.
Sympatric/Sympatrically	A condition where more than one species occurs in the same or overlapping area or habitat.
Tactile	Refers to the sense of touch or feel.
Taiga	A type of forest occurring in the far north. Usually dominated by dwarfed spruces.
Tetraploid	Possessing four chromosomes.
Topography	The configuration of the land surface. Literally, "the lay of the land."
Troglodyte	Cave dwelling. Usually refers to organisms that live in caves.
Turbid	Water that is opaque due to the high amount of suspended silt particles.
Tympanum	The circular ear structure on the side of the head of frogs and toads.
USF&WS	Acronym for the United States Fish & Wildlife Service.
Ventral	Pertaining to the belly or bottom side of an organism.
Vernal	Pertaining to spring. Also frequently used to describe temporary ponds and pools that hold water only during the wet season.
Vestigial	A rudimentary structure. Usually a remnant, degenerative structure that was once (in the evolutionary history of the organism) a fully functioning structure.
Xeric	Dry.
Zygote	A fertilized egg that has not yet begun to divide.

INDEX

PHOTO CREDITS

John R. MacGregor

Least Weasel, Allegheny Woodrat, Masked Shrew, Hoary Bat, Eastern Red Bat, Northern Bat, Gray Bat, Silver-haired Bat, Slender Glass Lizard, Eastern Redback Salamander, Four-toed Salamander, Hellbender, Southern Bog Lemming, Meadow Jumping Mouse.

Matthew R. Thomas

Eastern Sand Darter, Harlequin Darter, Mud Darter, Goldeye, Threadfin Shad, Skipjack Herring, Starhead Minnow, Quillback; River Redhorse, Pugnose Minnow, Bullhead Minnow, Shoal Chub, Silver Chub, Mississippi Silvery Minnow, Mimic Shiner, Rosyface Shiner, Silver Shiner, Stonecat, Tadpole Madtom, Northern Madtom.

David Speiser www.lilibirds.com

Yellow-bellied Flycatcher, Alder Flycatcher, Sedge Wren, Mourning Warbler, Connecticut Warbler, Snow Bunting, Long-tailed Duck (male).

Don Martin Bird Photograpy

Willow Flycatcher, Ruby-crowned Kinglet (male), Clay-colored Sparrow, Henslow's Sparrow.

Konrad Schmidt

Iowa Darter (male), Iowa Darter (female), Rainbow Smelt, Trout Perch, Silver Redhorse, River Shiner, Ghost Shiner, Spottail Shiner, Blackchin Shiner, Blacknose Shiner, Brook Silverside, Channel Shiner, Freckled Madtom, Bloater, Mooneye, Pink Salmon, Chinook Salmon, White Perch.

Brian Zimmerman

Brook Stickleback, Banded Killifish, Highfin Carpsucker, Pugnose Shiner.

James Kiser

Northern Short-tailed Shrew, Evening Bat, Bluebreast Darter.

T. Travis Brown

Franklin's Ground Squirrel, Mottled Sculpin.

Phil Myers

Meadow Vole, Smoky Shrew

Margaret Novak

Rudd

Dave Neely
Ribbon Shiner, Cypress Minnow
Michael Jeffords
Plains Pocket Gopher

Wayne T. Helfrich
Star-nosed Mole

Tom Murray
Northern Goshawk

Nathan Peterson
Western Harvest Mouse

Brant Fisher, Indiana Department of Natural Resources
Hoosier Cavefish

* All other photographs by Scott Shupe.

ABOUT THE AUTHOR

Photo by Sophia Osho

Naturalist Scott Shupe began his professional career in 1971 at the famed Ross Allen Reptile Institute and Venom Laboratory in Silver Springs, Florida, where he served as a lecturer and curator and extracted venom from captive snakes in that facility's venom laboratory. He later performed similar duties at the St. Augustine Alligator Farm in St. Augustine, Florida, and in the 1980s engaged in a contract to train raptors and perform the Birds of Prey Show at Reptile Gardens in Rapid City, South Dakota.

During his eclectic career as a freelance naturalist he has hosted a nature-oriented television series for the Outdoor Channel, produced a life-science instructional video series marketed to public schools nationwide, served as director of a private zoo/nature center in his home state of Kentucky, and founded a school assemblies company that provided wildlife education programs to schools in over 30 states; as well as contracting interpretive naturalist services with state parks, US Forest Service, and US Army Corps of Engineers facilities. He has enjoyed a longtime personal and professional relationship with the Kentucky Reptile Zoo and Venom Laboratory in Slade, Kentucky, where he formally served as Outreach Ambassador for Educational Programming.

He has twice been recognized by the US Fish & Wildlife Service for his contribution to conservation efforts, been named naturalist of the year by the Kentucky Society of Natural History, and was awarded the Environmental Stewardship Award by the Kentucky Environmental Quality Commission. In 1996 he was awarded the Jesse Stuart Media Award by the Kentucky School Library Association for his educational life science video products and won that award a second time in 2018 for the book *Kentucky Wildlife Encyclopedia.*

Since his semi-retirement in 2018 he has focused on eco-travel, wildlife photography, and writing natural history reference books for the lay public. Among his most recent naturalist endeavors are consulting for the Birds of Prey Program at Reptile Gardens in Rapid City, South Dakota, completing a term as Onsite Naturalist at the Desert Tortoise Research Natural Area in California's Mojave Desert, and serving as Naturalist Instructor for the Road Scholar program leading groups into Yosemite, Kings Canyon, and Sequoia National Parks.

The *Indiana Wildlife Encyclopedia* is the sixth book in a series of state-by-state wildlife encyclopedias produced for Skyhorse Publishing.

Contact Scott Shupe at kscottshupe@gmail.com.